S0-AGZ-117

PARENTING ASSESSMENTS IN CHILD WELFARE CASES

A Practical Guide

Recommendations of child protection workers to remove children from a home environment they perceive to be unsafe have frequently been challenged, legally and otherwise, and have raised scepticism about the criteria used in advising such a drastic measure. *Parenting Assessments in Child Welfare Cases* seeks to clarify these procedures, offering a model that facilitates comprehensive assessments and useful and viable recommendations that benefit children.

Terry Pezzot-Pearce and John Pearce guide practitioners through the steps of assessment, from negotiating the initial referral through data collection and report writing to court testimony. They also alert assessors to practice issues they are likely to encounter as they approach these complex evaluations. Specific sections of the book address areas of concern to people who seek or use these assessments, such as when to make a referral and how to determine if the completed assessment is appropriate. This thorough, up-to-date guide will be essential reading for social workers, psychologists, members of the legal profession, family therapists, and others concerned with child welfare practice.

TERRY D. PEZZOT-PEARCE is a child clinical psychologist in independent practice in Calgary.

JOHN PEARCE is a staff psychologist at the Alberta Children's Hospital and an adjunct associate professor with the Program in Clinical Psychology at the University of Calgary.

PARENTING ASSESSMENTS IN CHILD WELFARE CASES

A Practical Guide

Terry D. Pezzot-Pearce

John Pearce

UNIVERSITY OF TORONTO PRESS
Toronto Buffalo London

Toronto Buffalo London
Printed in Canada

ISBN 0-8020-8702-7 (cloth)
ISBN 0-8020-8654-3 (paper)

Printed on acid-free paper

National Library of Canada Cataloguing in Publication

Pezzot-Pearce, Terry D.
Parenting assessments in child welfare cases : a practical guide/
Terry D. Pezzot-Pearce and John Pearce.

Includes bibliographical references and index.
ISBN 0-8020-8702-7 (bound).
ISBN 0-8020-8654-3 (pbk.)

1. Parenting – Evaluation. 2. Child welfare. 3. Family assessment. I. Pearce, John W. II. Title.

HQ755.8.P49 2004 362.82 C2004-900618-5

University of Toronto Press acknowledges the financial assistance to its publishing program of the Canada Council for the Arts and the Ontario Arts Council.

University of Toronto Press acknowledges the financial support for its publishing activities of the Government of Canada through the Book Publishing Industry Development Program (BPIDP).

To our parents
Robert and Victoria
Victor and Claire

Contents

Foreword

Imagine yourself at your desk about to prepare or maybe review a parenting assessment report involving a child who may be at risk. What you need more than anything is to have at your fingertips an authoritative 'how to' book to guide the way. Child welfare professionals, be they clinicians, child welfare workers, social workers, professors, lawyers, or judges, have waited too long for a book like *Parenting Assessments in Child Welfare Cases: A Practical Guide,* a manual written by first-rate psychologist-clinicians with insight that only years of first-hand experience can bring.

I am one of the fortunate ones to have worked in the area of child welfare with Dr Terry Pezzot-Pearce and Dr John Pearce in my days as a lawyer in Calgary. Their compassion, high ethical standards, and long-time commitment to helping children make it most appropriate that they should write this definitive book.

We all know the importance of child protection. In a case dealing with a parent's right to legal representation in child welfare proceedings, none other than former Chief Justice of Canada Antonio Lamer said, 'Besides the obvious distress arising from the loss of companionship of the child, direct state interference with the parent-child relationship, through a procedure in which the relationship is subject to state inspection and review, is a gross intrusion into a private and intimate sphere' (*New Brunswick (Minister of Health and Community Services) v. G (J)* [1999] 3 S.C.R. 46). This 'gross intrusion,' in the form of child welfare proceedings, creates tension related to the potential severance of the child/parent relationship and the state's obligation to protect children at risk. Assessing that risk can be a complex and momentous task: it demands child welfare professionals plan carefully, practise competently, and communicate effectively. This text guides you through all three steps.

The authors describe how to systematically plan and deliver parenting assessments that get results and, in turn, benefit children. This comprehensive guide covers everything that drives successful assessments, from the basic concepts to the smallest details. Drawing on their years of experience as clinicians, teachers, and expert witnesses, the authors provide a practical guide stressing thoroughness and the integration of data when preparing assessments. A pro forma approach will not do. The assessment must be relevant and personalized to the particular parent and child. To help you, the authors deliver a practical and functional model that really works. I know. I have seen it in action.

As you become familiar with the model, you will learn in the first seven chapters how to develop and deliver a high-calibre assessment addressing important child and parenting factors. As a potential expert, giving your opinion in meetings or in court, you will find the last five chapters steer you towards enhancing your role as a practitioner and integral player in the child welfare and justice system.

The first word that comes to mind in describing this book is 'relevance.' Readers will ask: 'Would a clinician use this book?' 'Would this be a good book to teach students?' 'What would this book tell lawyers and judges that they did not already know?' Given the authors' professional standards, it is not surprising to discover that this work adeptly provides assessors and other child welfare professionals with what they should be looking for in conducting parenting assessments. The authors speak to us on the important subjects of identifying issues, integrating data, and practising cautiously and ethically in the contemporary world of child welfare.

It is clear from this book that Dr Terry Pezzot-Pearce and Dr John Pearce care deeply about children, if caring about children means concern for the child/parent relationship. This book is, among other things, an essential treatise on the science and art of parenting assessments. Back to my starting image of you at your desk: I cannot imagine you not being within arm's reach of this text.

The Honourable Justice Bryan E. Mahoney
The Court of Queen's Bench
Calgary, Alberta
Victoria Day, 2004

Acknowledgments

We wish to thank the many people who have helped and supported us while we were writing this book. Virgil Duff expressed keen interest in our manuscript, expertly guiding us through the publishing process with the University of Toronto Press. Virgil and his staff have been helpful and delightful, especially Lauren Freeman and Anne Laughlin. We particularly appreciated Terry Teskey, who exercised such expertise as our copy-editor. Also, we are grateful to Dr. Sally During and Dr. Pat Petrie in Calgary, who carefully read and incisively critiqued an earlier version of the manuscript, and to Elizabeth Bell, who prepared the index with great diligence.

Although we will not name them all, we must acknowledge the many professionals in our community with whom we have worked regarding these difficult cases. These people include numerous dedicated and caring child welfare workers and supervisors, skilled and knowledgeable foster parents, thoughtful and energetic clinicians and child care staff, and humane and questioning lawyers and judges. These professionals have provided considerable stimulation to our thinking and practice.

We have hidden the identities of all children and families mentioned in the book. Some of the clinical material is a compilation of cases. Although we cannot divulge the identities of these families, it has been a privilege to serve them and many others over the years. Thay have taught us to focus on areas of both strength and difficulty as we work towards finding interventions and solutions that are truly in the best interests of children.

Finally, we have been fortunate to have good friends. Doug and Diane Lindbloom, Jane Matheson, David Westelmajer, Karen Walsh,

Don Schwartz, Elva Jolly, Pat Petrie, and Mary Ross continue to offer their support and humour, enriching our lives. We are grateful to our parents, Bob and Victoria Pezzot and Claire and Vic Pearce, for the years of sensitive parenting they gave us. While Claire and Vic are no longer with us, Bob and Victoria continue to provide their sustaining love, as do Susan and John Kennedy, our sister and brother-in-law. We want to thank our children, Clarissa, Tim, and Kathleen, for their love and the lessons we learn from them about the challenging but delightful task of parenting.

PARENTING ASSESSMENTS IN CHILD WELFARE CASES

A Practical Guide

1 Why a Book about Parenting Assessment?

CASE 1: Jill, a ten-year-old girl, was referred for a psychological evaluation of school and relationship difficulties by her social worker from a Children's Aid Society. She had been apprehended from her mother's home nine months earlier during a drinking party. At the same time, two female half-siblings, aged eighteen and thirty months, were removed from the mother's home and placed with Jill in an experienced foster home. By the time Jill was first seen one month later, her worker had requested assessments of her siblings and evaluations of the children's parents. These included Jill's mother, Jackie, and father, Matt, who were divorced, as well as the younger children's father, Harry. Within the space of six weeks, a referral of one child for a routine psychological assessment had expanded to a full parenting assessment of three children and three parents. The situation was complicated by the fact that Matt worked at a job that made it difficult for him to attend appointments. Harry was reportedly a violent man who was incarcerated awaiting trial for assault and drug charges. Jackie's telephone was often disconnected and she could not be easily reached.

During the initial appointment, Matt alleged Harry had sexually abused Jill and Jill alleged Harry had physically assaulted her mother and youngest sister, Karen. Jackie denied all these allegations but acknowledged Jill's sexual assault by a stranger some years earlier. Jackie denied any current life problems and believed she had resolved a childhood history of abuse and neglect through several years of therapy. She demanded the children be returned to her immediately as she thought she provided a secure, safe, and stimulating environment. She detested the ongoing supervision of access required by the Children's Aid Society. Foster parents were appalled by her lack of attention to the children during visits. Given the children's developmental delays and behavioural difficulties, authorities speculated that they had been exposed to serious neglect and abuse.

As this case example demonstrates, parenting assessments may be one of the most challenging tasks we as clinicians undertake in our daily practices. They are also often one of the clinical activities for which we receive the least training, preparation, and ongoing guidance. Professional associations may provide guidelines for conducting parenting assessments in different contexts. For example, the American Psychological Association has two sets of guidelines: *Guidelines for Psychological Evaluations in Child Protection Matters* (1999) and *Guidelines for Child Custody Evaluations in Divorce Proceedings* (1994). However, few courses in parenting assessment are offered in graduate or continuing education programs. Skills are usually acquired in a piecemeal fashion, and assessors learn the 'how to's' by trial and error and through informal discussions with colleagues. We generally assume that if we can complete good psychological, psychiatric, or social work assessments of individuals or families, then we are capable of undertaking parenting assessments. Unfortunately, this is not always the case. These evaluations tend to be complex, and the resulting reports and recommendations are often used in the courts, which subject them to stringent cross-examination and analysis that can identify many potentially serious practice errors and induce significant anxiety in the reporting professionals.

The major goal of this book is to present a model that facilitates comprehensive assessments and useful and viable recommendations that benefit children. The primary question in every parenting assessment is, 'Can *this parent* meet the needs of *this particular child?*' Every clinician normally brings specific theoretical or practice orientations to clinical work and to the process of evaluating parenting. These theoretical orientations, which include psychodynamic, behavioural, family systems, or other models, are helpful in understanding clients and their behaviour. Clinicians need not jettison these theoretical orientations in parenting assessments. However, we suggest that clinicians employ an additional model of factors that influence parenting behaviour in order to structure assessments and integrate data. With a focus on the interaction of factors, this model does not rely on a sole variable or a specific set of dynamics to explain parenting behaviour. It thus makes assessment and prediction of good and poor parenting more challenging, but is likely more representative of the complexity and richness of people's lives.

A second goal of this book is to walk assessors through the practical steps of conducting parenting assessments. These range from negotiating the initial referral to collecting and integrating data, writing the report, and testifying in court. This way of organizing the assessment process can do much to make it more manageable and less stressful for all involved parties, as well as helping to develop recommendations that are truly in the best interests of children. These practical steps can be used in situations where a single assessor is undertaking the parenting assessment, or they can be adapted to situations where two or more assessors work as a team to evaluate parenting.

Another goal of this book is to identify potential errors in parenting assessments so assessors can take steps to avoid them. Some assessors begin parenting assessments without adequate preparation and awareness of relevant issues. For instance, many clinicians have had the experience, when working with a client to improve parenting, of the client's children being apprehended by child welfare authorities. Clinicians might be tempted to offer an opinion about the return of the children to the parents' care. However, it would be inappropriate to offer such an impromptu opinion without undertaking a detailed assessment of the parents' capacity to care for their children. Similarly in other cases, a client might say, 'I'm so worried that my child is being abused by my ex-spouse. Would you mind seeing my child to see if she should move back to my home?' Being helpful, some might agree to see the child and, given the reports of the client, might make such a recommendation. This action could be foolhardy because the recommendations would not be based on an evaluation of both parents. Additionally, in both of these examples clinicians might be subject to what are likely valid malpractice complaints to their professional associations. Or again, clinicians in educational psychology or some other child welfare field might be tempted to do parenting assessments because of their considerable experience with children and parents. But the focus in parenting assessments is quite different than in these other areas; without additional training and supervision, clinicians might be practicing beyond the limits of their competence.

During actual assessments, many other choice points exist that can result in erroneous conclusions or serious practice and ethical violations. These will be identified in discussion and in the 'Practice Alerts' that occur throughout the text. While the inclusion of such practice alerts may seem alarmist, they are critical considerations in these assessments. Kirkland and Kirkland (2001) state that the area of child custody evaluations is potentially one of the most dangerous and risky endeavours that psychologists can undertake, given the high level of stress, threat of litigation, risk of board complaints, and even the possibility of personal harm. After obtaining information about complaints from thirty-four boards of the Association of State and Provincial Psychology Boards (ASPPB), they found a high number of complaints but a trend to few findings of probable cause for discipline. Regardless, the threshold for complaints appears to be low, and as Kirkland and Kirkland indicate, practitioners who work in the area of child custody evaluation should expect to encounter a formal board complaint. Indeed, the associate registrar of the College of Alberta Social Workers indicates that many Alberta social work practitioners have ceased undertaking these assessments due to the risks inherent in this practice area (A. MacDonald, personal communication, 2 June 2003). Relatedly, the registrar of the College of Alberta Psychologists says that complaints arising from parenting assessments occur in regard to both custody/access and child welfare cases, but with greater frequency in the custody/access context (A. Kinkaide, personal communication, June 2003). Some practitioners feel that practice in this area is much like walking in a minefield.

Of course, one might ask, 'Do we really need yet another assessment book?' A number of texts already focus on parenting assessments following the separation and divorce of parents, that is, on the assessments of clients who are involved in custody/access litigation. They centre on children's reactions to parental separation and divorce and offer recommendations for workable custody and access arrangements. However, many other parenting assessments in child welfare cases involve parents who are abusive or neglectful. Many children are already seriously and negatively affected by the poor care they have received, making them more difficult to parent. Questions arise regarding the potential of these parents to learn to care adequately for their children, including their ability to meet the specialized needs of children who present with a wide array of emotional and behavioural problems. Kuehnle, Coulter, and Firestone (2000) indicate that few practice manuals or professional books specifically address parenting assessments in the context of child welfare concerns. One book in this area was published in Britain several years ago (Reder & Lucey, 1995), but no subsequent volumes have been published. Yet books dealing with custody/access assessments may not be entirely applicable to child welfare cases, given the former's focus on developing a workable parenting plan in separating families where no abuse or neglect exists. There is a gap between the concerns of these two areas, and this book is meant to address that need. While it focuses on child welfare cases, it may also be useful to professionals involved in custody/access cases, given its review of factors that affect parenting, its description of steps in parenting assessments, and its identification of potential practice errors. Portions of this book may also be useful to child welfare workers and supervisors, lawyers, and judges who rely upon assessments to make decisions about the needs of children and whether they are being met. Chapter 12 will in this respect be of particular interest, as it reviews criteria to evaluate the quality and utility of parenting assessments.

Chapter 2 begins by outlining some preliminary contextual, legal, and personal issues for clinicians to consider prior to initiating child welfare evaluations. These apply to parenting assessors regardless of whether they are seasoned practitioners or novices and whatever their professional background and training. Practitioners, whether they are clinical psychologists, social workers, psychiatrists, or some other type of counsellor, need to keep the same points in mind as they begin a parenting assessment. Chapter 2 concludes by describing a multifactorial model that is particularly useful in parenting assessments even though practitioners may use varied procedures for data collection. Chapter 3 reviews the needs of children who are developing normally. Chapters 4 and 5 describe conditions and situations that require specialized parenting practices in response to the multiple problems that children in the child welfare system exhibit. Chapter 5 also reviews specific events in the lives of children that pose particular challenges to parents, such as maltreatment, divorce, and adoption. Chapter 6 examines parental factors that increase the risk of poor parenting, and Chapter 7 considers contextual social conditions that may attenuate the risk of poor parenting. The remainder of the book describes the practical steps in parenting assessments. All chapters include case examples that illustrate issues and practice dilemmas. Checklists and sample reports follow in the appendices.

Overall, this book encourages clinicians to critically examine the approaches they use in parenting assessments. They will learn to systematically plan assessments in order to gather and integrate data and consequently make reasonable and workable recommendations, as well as present findings in a coherent and useful written format. Given that the information and recommendations of many parenting assessments are used in courts, assessors will learn how to prepare their reports and themselves to enter this arena. Many clinicians are unfamiliar with the legal process and experience considerable anxiety at the thought of testifying in court. They may feel much more comfortable in doing so if they have completed a systematic and comprehensive parenting assessment and carefully prepared themselves for testimony. Finally, with careful planning and practice, assessors should learn to enjoy this challenging and fascinating area of clinical work. Parenting assessments present an opportunity for clinicians to thoroughly assess individuals and families, and to integrate data from diverse sources to arrive at a comprehensive understanding of the situation. Clinicians often experience a strong sense of accomplishment and efficacy when they have completed evaluations that result in recommendations that truly improve the situations of their young clients.

2 Preliminary Considerations

Fundamental Questions in Parenting Assessments

Before clinicians begin an investigation, it is important that they understand the purpose of parenting assessments. Although referrals may be derived from several sources, the basic purpose remains essentially the same: assessments evaluate the capacities of parents to provide ongoing good care to their children. The fundamental question in any parenting assessment is the same: 'Can *this parent* meet the needs of *this particular child?*' When parents live together, their capacity to jointly meet the needs of children must be considered; in other circumstances, as where they are separated or divorced, parents' capacities are compared. Furthermore, children's needs are idiosyncratic; each child in a family has different needs and abilities, and we cannot assume that parents can care for all of their children equally well. For instance, parents might do extremely well with a complacent and adaptable child but encounter real difficulty with one who is demanding and irritable. They might employ practices that verge on abuse to gain the child's compliance, or interpret the child's obstinacy as deliberate rather than a function of inborn temperamental qualities.

In parenting assessments the needs of children must always be placed ahead of the needs and wishes of parents. In clinical and legal practice, the basic guideline of 'the best interests of the child' is routinely used to make decisions regarding children (Folberg, 1991). However, detailed information regarding how to do this is seldom available. People are complex, and the behaviour of individuals and families is determined by the interaction of multiple variables. There is no simple reason why some parents are able to meet the needs of their children while others cannot. Additionally, our measurement strategies are imprecise. Personality, motivation, and other 'people' factors cannot be measured exactly and must be inferred from behaviour, client reports, or psychological test responses. This brings considerable subjectivity to the decision-making process. Nor do we know precisely how various child and parent characteristics interact to generate adequate parenting, and we tend not to have specific legal or clinical guidelines to inform our assessments. There are no ready and easy approaches, although some cases are easier than others. For example, it is relatively easy to recommend that children not be returned to parents who have raped them. It is more difficult to arrive at recommendations in a case where parents provide adequate physical care but fail to ensure safety by allowing young children to roam the neighbourhood. However, we do have research-based knowledge that allows us to identify risk factors for poor parenting and other factors that enhance parenting. We also have information about children's development and the impact of events such as abuse, neglect, divorce, and adoption. We review all of these factors in subsequent chapters, but do not offer a comprehensive and detailed review of the myriad of studies that support various findings. Instead, we provide some basic references that will direct readers to information regarding the more robust findings. These can serve as jumping-off points to a more sophisticated review of the literature.

Contexts of Parenting Assessments

Cases from the Child Welfare System

As noted in Chapter 1, most parenting assessments are undertaken in child welfare cases where child protection issues have been raised and agency personnel have conducted an initial risk assessment; parenting assessments are initiated after these initial risk assessments. Sometimes children are removed from their homes, while in other cases they remain at home and various support services are provided to the family. Usually agency workers who have been involved with a family request parenting assessments to help in long-term planning. At other times, parents and their legal counsel arrange for independent parenting assessments when litigation is pending and parents are trying to have their children, who are in temporary care of child welfare authorities, returned to them.

Although child welfare parenting assessments address the fundamental question, 'Can this parent meet the needs of this particular child?,' they frequently focus on *'minimal parenting capacity'* rather than optimal capacity. Budd and Holdsworth (1996) indicate that an accepted definition of 'minimal capacity' is lacking and caution assessors to be particularly careful to not invoke 'middle-class' expectations when evaluating marginal parents. Essentially, assessors must try to predict whether parents can provide 'good enough' parenting so children can be safe and develop in a healthy manner if they remain in parental custody. When assessors cannot offer such a conclusion, they may recommend a temporary or even permanent termination of parental rights, as well as commenting upon the nature of parent contact and type of alternate living arrangements children require.

Parenting assessments in child welfare cases are challenging. For example, often clients are threatened by the assessment and do not want to attend sessions, particularly if they are ordered to come by the court. Evaluators must use all of their clinical skills to engage such clients. It may be difficult and frustrating to engage a family that has had long-standing and negative interactions with child welfare. Given their own childhood histories, parents might mistrust anyone associated with child welfare agencies, especially a clinician who might recommend permanent removal of their children. However, unless some cooperation is obtained, these assessments will tend to be superficial and probably invalid.

Related to parenting assessments of biological parents in child welfare cases are assessments of other caregivers who foster or adopt children from the child welfare system. Although some foster placements and adoptions, particularly of newborns, are undertaken privately, most foster and adopted children are or were under the guardianship of child welfare agencies. Many older children have problematic or even tragic histories as well as numerous problems, but even newborns may have significant problems if they are born with multiple handicaps or medical problems (Pearce & Pezzot-Pearce, 2001). Consequently, children placed in foster care or adoption often have specific needs and require specialized and responsive parenting.

Many people regard evaluations in foster and adoption cases as less serious than parenting assessments in other contexts. Usually these assessments are briefer and are based primarily on social information. They often do not involve formal psychological or psychiatric examinations. Even the common name 'home studies' seems less formal than the term 'parenting assessments.' Perhaps these assessments are viewed less seriously because they are concerned with potential placement of children rather than their removal from parental care. People might also assume that because foster and adoptive parents want to care for children and have taken the trouble to proceed through the application process, they must have better-than-average parenting skills. This may very well be the case in many circumstances. Some foster and adoption applicants are seasoned parents who understand children implicitly and know how to respond appropriately, based upon both experience and intuition. However, some have never parented or have parented relatively problem-free children, and others may have limited sensitivity and poor parenting skills. A few have inappropriate motivations for wanting to parent. For example, they may want to replace a dead child without appropriately grieving their loss, or they may want to use this type of parenting experience to deny their infertility.

While home studies may suffice for relatively undamaged or healthy children, more comprehensive parenting assessments are necessary when difficult children are being placed in homes, for placement decisions can have a long-standing and profound impact on children and other family members. Already-compromised children from the child welfare system can be helped significantly if they are placed in appropriate foster or adopted homes that meet their needs. Conversely, they can be further damaged if homes are inappropriate, resulting in placement breakdowns, repeated moves, and sometimes even additional abuse. Foster and adopted families themselves, while they may benefit tremendously and derive considerable satisfaction from the experience of caring for these children, can also be traumatized. Some foster and adopted children may, for example, sexually abuse other children in the home, torture animals, or steal from parents or the community. Such a high level of tension and conflict is engendered that families request that children be removed from their care. This results in highly distressed and discouraged parents and children whose expectations that the world is an unloving and uncaring place are reinforced.

In most cases, assessments are undertaken prior to matching a child with a family. Applicants may never have parented before, and assessors cannot ask practical questions about their knowledge and understanding of a specific child. Consequently, assessors must have a good working knowledge of the kinds of issues children might present in the home, allowing them to present case scenarios as part of the assessment process. For example, an assessor has to be aware of the problems presented by international adoptees who were institutionalized if this is the type of child applicants wish to adopt. The same applies to requests for children born with drug- and alcohol-related birth defects, children who have been severely abused and neglected, and youngsters who are older and have experienced multiple placements.

Potential parents must convey some understanding of the possible challenges that lie ahead and be able to anticipate their emotional and behavioural responses. This understanding is critical, even if parents have parented other children successfully. Additionally, children must be evaluated prior to placement, and parents may merit further assessment once children are matched with them. Several professionals may undertake these comprehensive parenting assessments, generally over a longer time period than is typically the case in the child welfare context that we first described. Clear and open communication among these professionals is critical to optimize chances of successful placements.

Custody/Access Cases

Although not a specific focus in this book, another common context for parenting assessments occurs in custody/access cases. While some clinicians avoid these assessments at almost any cost because of their often intensely adversarial legal nature, other practitioners find them fascinating and challenging. Such assessments are requested when parents and lawyers have been unable to resolve custody and access issues following parental separation. Judges, lawyers, and sometimes parents themselves initiate referrals. Assessments may be called for in the traditional litigation context or in the newly evolving field of collaborative law. In the latter, both parents and lawyers agree to avoid litigation and work collaboratively towards settlement of issues (Mucalov, 2001; Tessler, 2001). In either situation, clinicians may be asked to undertake an assessment of parenting capacity and children's needs in order to make recommendations regarding legal custody, daily decision-making authority, and living arrangements. On occasion, legal custody has already been decided and access arrangements are the only issue under consideration. Financial support arrangements usually do not fall within the purview of parenting assessments.

Clinicians should note that the level of animosity in these litigation cases is frequently high, as they derive from the small portion of parents who cannot agree about arrangements for their children. 'High-conflict' is a descriptor often applied to these seemingly intractable cases, although an agreed-upon definition has yet to be developed (Flory, Dunn, Berg-Weger, & Milstead, 2001). Doolittle and Deutsch (1999) indicate that in cases where parents continue to litigate and cannot resolve their post-divorce situation in the first two years after separation, children are more likely to be negatively impacted by their family situation. Furthermore, parents are likely to remain intensely engaged with each other on an emotional level: they hotly contest numerous issues, and clinicians must be prepared to function within such a highly charged context, taking care not to inflame the situation further. Clinicians must also be ready to cope with their own feelings towards some parents. They may find themselves becoming frustrated with parents who personally function at relatively high levels but whose acrimony towards former spouses compromises their ability to recognize and respond to their children's needs. Parents may interfere with the relationships between children and the other parent, model inappropriate ways to resolve conflict that also may expose children to potential emotional and/or physical harm, be violent to their former spouse, and allege child neglect and physical or sexual abuse by the other parent (Flory et al., 2001). Behaviours such as allegations of child neglect and abuse may necessitate involvement of child welfare authorities in these cases, while police are likely to become involved if violence occurs.

Although this context for assessments tends to be highly charged and legally adversarial, the fundamental question that must be addressed is, as always, 'Can this parent meet the needs of this particular child?' However, in this situation the abilities and capacities of one parent are compared to those of the other to determine which parent can optimally meet the children's needs. As Schutz, Dixon, Lindenberger, and Ruther (1989) discuss, 'goodness of fit' between the children's needs and the parents' functional abilities is a particularly useful concept in these cases. This emphasizes the interactional nature of parent-child relationships. For example, the parenting style or functional parenting abilities of one parent may be ideal for one child but not for another. A parent who is organized and methodical may do well with a child who requires external structure, but the same parent may do poorly with a child who is independent and self-motivated. The latter child may struggle against the parent and resent rigid rules and routines. A somewhat more flexible parent might be a better fit for this child.

It is important to realize that courts will not often change de facto post-separation custody arrangements unless good cause or evidence of changed circumstance exists. Hence, assessments must be thorough and clearly identify why one parent is more likely to meet the individualized needs of the children if a change in custody is being contemplated. Although the situation is rare, assessors may recommend parental rights of one or both parents be terminated if they cannot provide even minimal and safe care, then possibly necessitating involvement of alternate caregivers and child welfare personnel.

Common Problems in Parenting Assessments

Before we discuss other considerations in parenting assessments, it is instructive to consider problems that commonly occur in parenting assessments. Perhaps the most glaring and significant problem is that many assessors undertake these assessments without the appropriate training and the broad range of theoretical knowledge and clinical experience necessary to do a competent job. Assessors must first have the capacity to work with children and understand the ways in which their thinking and needs differ from adults'. In other words, assessors must have a developmental orientation and the knowledge to recognize the impact of developmental variations and life events on children. Assessors also must have the capacity to work with adults and understand their development, as well as a broad range of issues that can affect them as individuals and parents. For example, assessors need to have some understanding of such issues as relationships, addictions, family violence, and the impact of parents' own histories of abuse and victimization. Assessors should be familiar with various treatment modalities for children and parents because they may need to make recommendations about intervention. Finally, assessors should have some expertise in various assessment strategies and have some familiarity with diagnostic nomenclature. Although formal diagnoses are not always necessary in parenting assessments, assessors often review previous reports and contact many other mental health professionals as part of the assessment process. Familiarity with diagnostic nomenclature is useful when we review these reports of others and either validate or argue against their conclusions.

Many assessors do not understand the complexity of parenting assessments. They focus on one or two factors as the critical issues in determining parenting competency, when in fact a broad range of risk and compensatory factors exists and must be examined and carefully weighed. For example, some may focus almost exclusively on whatever analysis is currently in vogue, such as attachment theory. Others may focus on religion, culture, or childhood maltreatment as major etiological factors of parenting behaviour. Such narrow-band investigations result in scanty data collection and limited or inappropriate conclusions.

The types of data sources employed in parenting assessments can be problematic. As in any assessment process, consistent multiple data sources add significantly to the validity of observations and conclusions. Unfortunately, not all assessors recognize this and instead rely primarily on one data source. For instance, the exclusive use of parent interviews may not provide accurate information. Parents have many reasons to inaccurately portray events in their lives or their families to convey more favourable impressions. Without checking references, undertaking psychological assessments, or doing home observations, assessors may accept the face validity of these verbal reports, resulting in invalid conclusions or even harmful recommendations. Similarly, other assessors rely exclusively on psychological testing, possibly using test manual interpretations as factual findings without realizing manuals only offer possible interpretations. Clearly, conclusions are more valid when the data that emerge from testing converge with other observations and data. Assessors introduce another source of error where they use several data sources but fail to integrate the information.

Another common problem in parenting assessments is the paucity of planning and thought some assessors invest in the process. In these situations, data collection and interviews occur haphazardly. Sometimes whole areas of inquiry are omitted, documentation is lost, comments by clients are not followed up, and one participant is more thoroughly assessed than another. This creates disorder and even bias, and the process feels arbitrary and out of control for both families and assessors. Clients react poorly to such unprofessional treatment, and assessors can disregard information. Often the gaps in data are not discovered until later, perhaps during the process of data interpretation and report writing or, even more traumatically for clinicians, during court testimony.

Reports are sometimes poorly written and are often incomprehensible, even to other mental health professionals. Excessive jargon confuses readers and detracts from the clarity of the reports' findings and conclusions. Other reports are too long and minutely record every bit of information collected during the assessment; there is little integration and consolidation of the data, with this task seemingly being left to the reader. Still others are so cursory that recommendations seem to appear out of the blue, with the reader questioning how so many hours could be invested in collecting so little information.

This list of pitfalls is not an exhaustive one, but it is instructive to us as assessors. Much of this book is directed towards helping assessors recognize and avoid such difficulties in their own assessments.

Personal Considerations

Clinicians may wish to ask themselves certain questions before they undertake parenting assessments. These personal considerations are important because parenting assessments can be stressful. The questions below may help practitioners prepare themselves for this task, particularly practitioners new to this area of clinical practice.

1. *Do I have the specialized training and knowledge base to competently undertake these assessments?*
   Of all of the personal issues that potential assessors must consider, this is the most critical. Appropriate training in parenting assessments is necessary if this has not been a component of clinical training. Of course, theoretical knowledge is usually obtained through formal academic training. This is supplemented with additional courses, readings, and workshops. Clinical experience can be gained in several ways. Perhaps one of the best is to find a mentor or supervisor who is a seasoned assessor and will provide training and supervision on an individual basis. Such persons can introduce one to the issues by closely supervising several of one's first parenting assessments to ensure that appropriate information is gathered and appropriately integrated. They also can suggest salient readings and help one to recognize and analyse various practice dilemmas. Additionally, they can critique the report and help prepare the novice assessor for court testimony. A combination of formal course work and direct hands-on supervision is critical in preparing for practice in this area. The time and money required for courses, workshops, and direct supervision are worthwhile investments, as they can alleviate much of the trepidation novice assessors experience.

2. *Am I comfortable working in the legal arena with cases that are often highly contentious and adversarial?*
   This is another important question, as mental health professionals are often not familiar with legal work. Many training programs do not expose trainees to legal issues, and some practitioners may work clinically for years without ever testifying in the courtroom. In order to function well in this arena, clinicians must understand the legal system and the role of an expert witness. Since clinicians offer opinions to the court, their work and opinions are examined in minute detail. This can feel threatening, especially if the questions come from rather hostile legal counsel and other mental health professionals whose job it is to criticize reports. Supervisors or mentors should be willing to review issues and dilemmas and to invite students to court when testifying regarding their own assessments, so as to expose students to the workings and protocol of a courtroom. Additionally, it is sometimes helpful to have a competent family law practitioner review one's reports to identify possible problems. Attorneys and supervisors can also help prepare one for the first court experience by reviewing court procedures and identifying questions that are likely to be asked in examination and cross-examination.

3. *Am I comfortable making definite recommendations that may displease clients?*
   In their daily clinical practice, many mental health practitioners work co-operatively with clients towards mutually developed treatment goals. Clinicians support clients' progress and try to maintain helpful working relationships with them. In parenting assessments, the situation is different. Clinicians must objectively and fairly assess a situation without the intent to maintain ongoing supportive and therapeutic relationships. Moreover, assessors often make recommendations that displease clients, such as recommending that, in child welfare cases all parental rights to children be terminated, or that foster or adoption applicants not be approved. In custody/access cases, at least one parent usually disagrees with the recommendations. Indeed, parents may threaten the professional with legal action or even physical harm. This aspect of making recommendations that clients dislike can be stressful: not all clinicians are able to do this.

4. *Do I have the time to do parenting assessments and am I sufficiently organized to complete them within a reasonable period?*
Clinicians maintain a mix of clients, ranging from those with whom they have just become involved to those with whom they have had considerable contact. This permits work to be modulated so clinicians are not overwhelmed by seeing many new clients at once. Parenting assessments change this pacing. At a minimum, two clients (a child and his or her parent) require individual and joint assessment sessions. However, most families have more than two people. Sometimes when new spouses are involved, the number of people who require assessment can increase to five or six, thereby increasing the amount of clinical time and effort required to complete the evaluation. Furthermore, once data are collected, assessors must integrate the information and write reports. Given the number of people and complexity of the issues, these reports can be lengthy and require considerable preparation time. If clinicians have busy practices, they must ensure time is set aside to complete these tasks in a relatively short time frame. For example, an average assessment may require twenty to fifty hours over a two to three-month period.

If clinicians cannot set aside the necessary time, assessments may stretch for many months. Such a situation is unfair to all concerned. Not only do families experience stress during the assessment and while waiting for the recommendations, but circumstances and children's needs may change. This is particularly so for very young children, who grow and develop rapidly. For example, circumstances may change for a one-year-old child in foster care when an assessment takes eight months to complete. Not only would the toddler have different needs for parenting than when he or she was placed in care, but a separation of over eight months might significantly affect the child's attachment relationships with biological parents, making it more difficult for the family to successfully reunite.

Additionally, the data and information collected can be voluminous. It is common for a parenting assessment file concerning several family members to quickly become several inches thick. Clinicians must manage this type of data collection and find ways to organize and integrate it. This is particularly important if court testimony is required. Specific information may need to be tagged for ready reference.

5. *Will the money I receive for doing parenting assessments compensate for the time and stress involved?*
   This is a salient question, particularly for clinicians who undertake parenting assessments in child welfare, foster, and adoption situations. Some provincial and state jurisdictions may compensate professionals at a rate that is not commensurate with the sophisticated skills necessary for these parenting assessments. However, the trade-off is exposure to interesting and complicated cases that truly challenge the clinician. In contrast, parenting assessments in custody/access cases often are lucrative, but the clinician is immersed in a tense and adversarial situation where parents sometimes lose sight of the interests and needs of their children. Clinicians clearly must consider their answer to this question prior to undertaking parenting assessments.

6. *Do I wish to specialize in parenting assessments with child welfare cases?*
   This question does not lend itself to easy answers, and assessors may want to take into account the emotional demands of this work. Child welfare cases can be fascinating, but during assessment practitioners must often review difficult case history information and interview children about traumatic life events. Some clinicians are uncomfortable with abuse and neglect issues, particularly when clients are young and vulnerable, and must be able to manage their personal reactions to such information (Pearce & Pezzot-Pearce, 1997). Likewise, foster and adoptive situations can evoke feelings of sadness and distress. Children who are considered for foster care or adoption often have difficult life histories and have experienced many types of trauma. Even in custody/access cases, discomfort emerges when seemingly high-functioning clients act as if the needs of the children do not matter. Indeed, professionals may begin to view the impact of the ongoing disputes and pressures as being emotionally abusive to children. Furthermore, they must frequently interview children about potentially traumatic events that include verbal and physical fights between parents, neglectful parenting associated with withdrawn and depressed caregivers, allegations of physical and sexual abuse, campaigns of vilification, and abduction.

   Assessors should decide to specialize depending on their clinical skill and knowledge base as well as their personal preferences. Clinicians who take on child welfare cases require familiarity with such areas as child maltreatment, risk and resiliency factors, and family violence. Foster care and adoption parenting assessments necessitate specific knowledge about the impact of child maltreatment and children's reactions to family loss. Children's reactions to divorce and parental dynamics are a necessary component of the knowledge possessed by clinicians in custody/access cases. However, there is much overlap between these areas. Many children in the child welfare system have experienced parental separations and divorce, while children in separating families may have experienced abuse and family violence. Nonetheless, if assessors intend to do work in areas outside of their usual practice area, they must obtain more training and supervision in the new practice domains. Ironically, assessors may clearly be aware that their skills are deficient, but people who contract with them, particularly those who do not have expertise in the area and thus are not cognizant of the requisite skills and knowledge, can pressure assessors to undertake these assessments. In such cases, assessors must be prepared to inform these people about the specific requirements for practice in this area, negotiating with them to obtain the necessary preparatory training.

Legal Considerations

As already mentioned, parenting assessments often are ultimately used in the legal arena. Assessment reports may be entered as evidence, and assessors are examined and cross-examined. Judges review this information as part of a wider body of evidence and then issue orders under various legislative acts.

PRACTICE ALERT #1
Learn how courts work and become familiar with the laws that affect parenting practices and assessments in one's particular jurisdiction.

As readers may be aware, many different laws affect the care and control of children by their parents. Minimally, these include child welfare laws and those statutes governing divorce and separation. As well, legislation governing confidentiality, dangerousness, and other issues can be critical in parenting assessments. The specifics of this legislation can vary significantly across states, provinces, and countries. Therefore, we will not review the laws in various jurisdictions. It is incumbent on assessors to familiarize themselves with the pertinent laws in their particular jurisdictions. Furthermore, as evidential rules vary across legal proceedings, different evidence might be admitted in child welfare as opposed to criminal cases. Assessors must be aware of such differences and be familiar with common legal terminology and procedures that likewise vary across jurisdictions.

Given the legal context of most parenting assessments, assessors must recognize the role they and their assessments play in this process.

PRACTICE ALERT #2

Be very clear that your role is one of an *assessor* who may ultimately provide *expert opinion* to the court.

The role of the clinician is that of an assessor and not a counsellor or therapist. While a therapist can give expert opinion if summoned to court, assessor and counsellor roles differ. The role of an assessor in a parenting assessment is to collect information and use his or her expertise to arrive at reasonable and workable recommendations in a fair and balanced manner. It is difficult and likely impossible for a person who has been a counsellor in a specific case to then assume the role of assessor in that case. Because of the close and supportive work that counsellors do, they usually form particular opinions about their clients. They listen repeatedly to client concerns and see their emotional reactions and their attempts at change. They also may become emotionally invested in the situation, thereby precluding a completely objective stance. For example, if a counsellor works extensively with parents to improve their skills or process various painful psychological issues, it is difficult to step back and objectively evaluate the risks involved in their continued parenting. Additionally, clients might feel betrayed if counsellors see no hope for change and recommend they never resume parenting. Similarly, when a clinician has worked closely in counselling with one spouse prior to a separation, it is very difficult to then assess both spouses fairly. The clinician would already have spent more hours with one spouse, resulting in significantly more exposure to that person's point of view and thereby potentially biasing the assessor against the other party. Greenberg and Gould (2001) discuss another role that may create confusion for practitioners. They call this role the 'forensic expert': these practitioners must function within their therapist role but remain cognizant of many issues that emerge because of their clients' involvement in the legal system. They must stay focused on treatment and place the children's interests and well-being first, and they clearly cannot provide opinions and testimony that involve such psycho-legal issues as recommendations about custody or comments on parental capacity. Such tasks remain firmly within the functions filled by parenting assessors and the court.

Although therapists cannot become assessors in specific cases, assessors, after completion of an assessment and closure of legal processes, may be able to assume the therapist role. However, they cannot revert to the formal assessment role at a later point. Occasionally, therapists must assume an assessor's role with certain clients, particularly in child welfare cases. For example, in isolated areas other clinicians may not be available to do assessments. Consequently, assessors need to recognize that issues of bias might be raised about their opinion, and they need to use procedures that limit this as much as possible. For instance, objective psychological test results might be particularly helpful.

Assessors must be clear that their role is to provide expert opinion to the courts. Although they may undertake thorough assessments that provide reasoned recommendations and opinions, it is important to recognize their conclusions are simply 'opinions.' Courts do not always accept their recommendations, and assessors should not consider themselves triers-of-fact; as expert witnesses, assessors provide information and guidelines to the court. The court then weighs this opinion along with other facts and expert opinions to render decisions. None of these facts detracts from the seriousness and importance of the assessors' job as expert witnesses.

PRACTICE ALERT #3

Adopt a neutral, open-minded, and professional stance and use objective procedures with all parties during the assessment process.

Assessors must be extremely objective in their dealings with all parties involved in an assessment. Fair and even treatment and a neutral stance do much to add credibility to assessors' opinions. Especially in situations where the parenting capacity of two separated parents is compared, as in child welfare cases where each parent is seeking a return of the children to him or her, parallel procedures and equal investments of time with both parties avoid allegations of bias. Assessors may in fact be open-minded and neutral, but marked differences in procedures or a significant difference in the number of hours spent with each individual contributes to a perception of bias; these differences must be explained and justified. Despite a lack of concerns about one parent, it is important to undertake the same assessment procedures with both. If one parent is unreliable and reportedly goes to work inebriated, an assessor should contact both person's employers to ask about these specific behaviours. Similarly, if concerns about one parent's intellectual functioning arise, an assessor should administer the same intelligence test to both parents. A neutral stance must be maintained with all people involved in specific cases, including clients and their attorneys and other references. For example, assessors may appear to be 'hired guns' if they do not communicate equally and neutrally with various lawyers in a case. Overall, assessors can eliminate bias, whether real or perceived, by adopting a professional and objective stance in their interactions with all concerned parties.

PRACTICE ALERT #4
Recognize the limitations in your opinions and base them on concrete information and behaviour.

In order to enhance the validity and credibility of opinions, assessors need to clearly understand the assessment questions and the limits of the opinions they offer. It is easy, either in reports or under examination and cross-examination, to offer opinions without adequate or appropriate data. For example, a common error occurs in child welfare cases when only one parent participates in an assessment. Assessors cannot draw conclusions about the parenting abilities of an unexamined parent. Similarly, they cannot comment on an unexamined parent's need for therapy or on unexamined children's needs for specific living arrangements or interventions. Likewise, in unilateral custody/access assessments, assessors cannot make recommendations about custody and say the examined parent is preferable to an unexamined parent. In either context, assessors cannot comment on optimal custody arrangements because they have no first-hand information about the other parent. Moreover, where psychologists undertake testing for other professionals, such as social workers, who are conducting parenting evaluations, psychologists must clearly understand they are assessing psychological functioning only and cannot comment on custody issues. The same applies to psychiatrists who are asked only to assess a parent's mental health status.

PRACTICE ALERT #5
Obtain appropriate training and supervision prior to independently undertaking parenting assessments.

Validity and credibility of opinions can be undermined when assessors undertake parenting assessments without adequate preparation. Parenting assessments are complex and require specialized knowledge. If important factors are unexplored, the validity of conclusions and the credibility of assessors are greatly reduced. For example, in a child welfare case where family violence is an issue, it is foolhardy to ignore or inadequately follow up documentation from a women's shelter or police. Clinicians must ensure their personal preparation to practice and avoid the many pitfalls that exist. Improper preparation results in poor and sometimes worthless or even destructive recommendations that cost all participants time and money. Further, it invites a difficult time on the stand in court and possible ethical complaints to an assessor's professional association if clinicians exceed the limits of their competence.

PRACTICE ALERT #6
Keep *complete records* and *document* all observations and information collected during the assessment.

Since parenting assessments are commonly used in the legal arena, it is particularly critical to document thoroughly all observations and data in this practice area. Careful documentation ensures all information is available when assessors formulate conclusions and write reports. It is easier to understand the basis for conclusions if records are complete and organized. Such documentation also permits easier preparation for court testimony and allows assessors to be more credible witnesses who can withstand cross-examination. Additionally, if other professionals or expert advisors review the assessor's files during the course of litigation, careful documentation enhances the credibility of the assessor's opinions. Finally, thorough documentation may protect assessors if an ethical complaint is lodged, a not uncommon occurrence, particularly in custody/access parenting assessments. Thus, files should contain observations, quotes, and testing results. Additionally, they should include information regarding referral sources and initial agreements, as well as various consents, releases of information, and other information collected during the assessment process.

Necessary Considerations Due to the Involvement of Children

Developmentally sensitive thinking and assessment methodology are critical. Since children develop and change relatively quickly, their needs can vary dramatically over relatively short periods. Observations and recommendations may need to be qualified by noting this factor. For example, an assessor may need to recommend that an update be undertaken if a case is likely to take longer than a year to be heard in court. Children require an assessment that is child-friendly and developmentally attuned. While parenting assessments tend to occur at stressful times in children's lives, the physical characteristics of the assessment environment and the clinician's manner can do much to alleviate children's stress. Thus, the presence of child-sized furniture and toys may help set children at ease, and assessors who know how to interview and speak with children enhance their comfort level during the assessment.

Additionally, assessors must recognize their opinions can profoundly alter the course of children's lives. These assessments are a serious responsibility that cannot be taken lightly. For example, if assessors do not accurately identify risk factors and children are returned to violent and abusive parents, they may be hurt or killed. Likewise, a recommendation to terminate contact with extended family members cannot be made lightly, as children might lose contact with relatives with whom they have significant relationships. Whereas adult clients can choose to disregard a clinician's opinion, minor children cannot, nor can they actively choose the directions of their lives. If parents or the court agree with an assessor's recommendations, then children's lives can change. For example, an assessor might recommend that a child be allowed to move to another state or province with one parent or a grandparent. This child might lose contact with his or her other parent, various extended family members, and friends. In the new home, the child might need to cope with a caretaker who is now stressed by caring for children without the support of important others in his or her life. While some children might adapt well, others could be irreparably harmed by such a recommendation. The thought of such a consequence should be sobering.

Issues about consent to treatment and confidentiality merit close attention. As parenting assessments must focus on children's needs, children's involvement is critical, but as minors they cannot give either formal consent for assessment or directions around confidentiality. Children may or may not wish to be involved, they may say little, or they may demand secrecy regarding their comments. Regardless, assessors negotiate confidentiality with parents or legal guardians, although children should be informed about the limits of confidentiality.

Finally, assessors must realize they are mandated to report concerns about abuse or neglect when they work with children. If concerns arise regarding a child's need for protection during the assessment period, clinicians are required by law to report these to child welfare authorities. Even though some assessors are loath to make such a report, as they think it is likely to inflame the situation further and perhaps even jeopardize their ability to finish gathering data in the assessment, a report is mandatory if concerns exist. When unsure whether reporting is required in a specific case, clinicians can call the authorities anonymously to consult with intake workers and determine whether a full report is necessary. Similarly, assessors must recognize they are compelled to report significant risk of suicide and homicide, taking appropriate action as necessary. While rare, such concerns may emerge in any parenting assessment. Risk of abduction may also need to be addressed by suggesting safety and supervision plans even prior to completion of the assessment.

Selecting a Model to Guide Assessment

Finally, before beginning any assessment, clinicians must select a model to guide procedures and interpretation of data so assessments are truly comprehensive and attuned to the needs of children. In order to assess parenting capacity, we require an understanding of those factors that contribute to the behaviour of parents. While a number of theoretical orientations describe the influence of parents upon their children's development, few actually speak to the impact of various factors on parenting behaviour. In order to identify important factors for evaluation, we have found it useful to employ a model that is similar to Belsky and Vondra's (1989). Their model evolved through an examination of research findings about parental dysfunction, particularly the etiology of child abuse and neglect. It also incorporates findings from nonabusive families and uses a systems approach that focuses on interrelated processes. This **multifactorial model** assumes parenting behaviour is influenced by three groups of factors that interact with each other. It applies well to assessments for children from the child welfare system as well as to parenting assessments in other contexts.

The three general sources of influence described in Belsky and Vondra's (1989) model are those arising from child factors, parent factors, and contextual sources of support and stress. Child factors involve an array of characteristics, including typical developmental issues as well as specialized needs that result from such factors as premature birth and intense temperament. Although Belsky and Vondra do not mention child resiliency, this is another related consideration, as some children cope well with adversities such as weak parenting and family loss, while others do not. Children who are resilient may not require the same type of parenting as those more susceptible to stress. Parent factors include personality characteristics, psychological and psychiatric dysfunction, and their own developmental histories, including the adequacy of the parenting they experienced in childhood. We discuss these parent influences in Chapter 6. Contextual sources of stress and support for parents, such as the marital relationship, social network, and work, comprise the third source of influences on parenting and are discussed in Chapter 7.

Perhaps the most significant contribution of this model to understanding parenting is its emphasis on the interaction of these factors in generating parenting behaviour. No one factor is paramount, and interactions can vary over time. For example, a parent who has a problem-free developmental history, was parented well, and now exhibits numerous strengths in his or her functioning may cope well with the birth of a premature infant who has cerebral palsy. However, his or her competence may drop significantly if a spouse becomes unemployed. The family might not be able to afford babysitters and might even need to relocate to get work, leaving their supports behind. Likewise, death of a spouse or desertion by a partner might exacerbate stress and decrease the resources available to the family, thereby resulting in poorer parenting. The remaining parent no longer has the practical and emotional support of his or her partner and experiences feelings of grief, loss, and distress. In some families parenting deteriorates when children reach adolescence, while in others it improves. **Parenting competency or inadequacy arises from these types of interactions and the balance of stresses and supports**. A weakness in one area may be buffered by strengths in another. For example, a low-functioning parent with a difficult personal history may meet the needs of his or her children if he or she has a supportive spouse and family or if the child is easy-going and relaxed. This complexity of interactions adds to the challenge of parenting assessments.

3 Child Factors: Typical Development

The Needs of Normal Children

Since children and their needs are the focus of parenting assessments, we will describe child factors that can affect parenting behaviour in the next three chapters. We begin with a description of normal developmental issues and the parenting required to support healthy development. There are many ways to describe the development of children. These vary from simple descriptions of physical attributes and skills to more complicated psychological accounts of language development and the establishment of relationships with other people. It is helpful to examine the developmental tasks that children face because good parents support children in mastering these life tasks. Much of the writing and research that focuses on these issues tends to be concentrated in an area of study called developmental psychopathology. As described by Cicchetti and Rogosch (1994), developmental psychopathology views child development as being influenced by a number of factors wherein children change and reorganize their biological and behavioural systems as development proceeds. Numerous factors can affect development, and information from many disciplines, such as clinical and experimental psychology, psychiatry, sociology, and the biological sciences, is integrated to identify the influence of these variables. These factors are in dynamic 'transaction' or interaction throughout the lifespan, and no single factor is sufficient to explain development. Such biological, behavioural, and psychological factors and the broader factors of environment, society, and culture all interact to influence each other and the subsequent development of an individual.

Cicchetti and Rogosch (1994) describe the stage-salient tasks children confront as they develop. At a particular age, children confront one developmental task that remains primary for a time. Another task then takes on more importance, although the first task still is active and influences mastery of later tasks. In this model, children who are developing optimally negotiate each stage successfully and demonstrate increasing competency and adaptation to their family and wider society. Thus, children move from developing a secure attachment to a primary caretaker as their first childhood task to eventually achieving autonomous functioning as an older teenager. However, Cicchetti and Rogosch make the point that, while children are affected by early experiences, they are not controlled immutably by them.

Basic Physical Care

Prior to reviewing stage-salient tasks that focus on psychological needs, assessors must describe the quality of physical care parents provide, an absolute prerequisite for normal development. To develop well, children require good nutrition, sleep, cleanliness, and safety. **Nutritious food,** both prenatally and postnatally, is critical for proper physical growth and energy for daily activities, as is **adequate rest**. Physical care includes ensuring children are not exposed to inappropriate medications, drugs, and other toxic substances in both prenatal and postnatal periods, as well as the provision of **routine medical care**. Reasonable **cleanliness** is essential to prevent the spread of disease. Ongoing **safety** in the living milieu pertains to both the home and its immediate neighbourhood. We must always review children's basic physical needs, as these may be salient and important issues, particularly in child welfare and foster and adoption cases. For example, children may become so preoccupied with scarcity of food that they cannot focus on other developmental tasks, even when subsequently placed in a situation where food is plentiful. It is common for such children in foster care to hoard food or be unable to regulate food intake. Unless others control food intake, they may eat until they vomit repeatedly. Physical neglect, as manifested by inadequate nutrition, clothing, and shelter, can have a profoundly negative impact on development (Pearce & Pezzot-Pearce, 1997).

The following questions are designed to evaluate the **quality of physical care**, particularly in child welfare cases. In addition to asking if these aspects of physical care are being provided, assessors should also, where relevant, begin asking why parents cannot supply these basic necessities to their children. The reasons may contribute significantly to understanding the dynamics in the family and consequently affect the recommendations of the assessment.

1. Does the family have a home or does it live in shelters or on the street? Has it moved often?
2. Is the home relatively clean, particularly in the kitchen and bathroom?
3. Is there adequate furniture, particularly beds for sleeping? Do children have their own beds or must they sleep with others?
4. Is the home adequately serviced, such as being heated, cooled, lit?
5. Are there adequate bathing and toilet facilities?
6. Is the home tidy so that accidents are unlikely due to falls, electrocution, and burning?
7. Are steps taken to ensure safety, especially for small children, regarding such things as stair gates, covers on radiators, electrical socket covers?
8. Are there safe areas for play and appropriate toy materials?
9. Do parents provide adequate physical supervision of young children in the home and in its immediate vicinity?
10. Are children left in the home unattended?
11. Is there food in the home and can parents provide food reliably?
12. Do parents rely on food banks and social agencies to feed their children? Do they run out of food before their next paycheque or welfare payment?
13. Is the food that is provided to the children nourishing, such as milk, meat, fruit, and vegetables, or are available financial resources spent on snack foods rather than healthy foods?
14. Do parents ensure that their children have adequate rest?
15. Do parents provide basic medical care or do children receive medical care only in crisis situations?
16. Are the parents able to provide adequate clothing for their children and is it kept clean and in good repair?

Attachment

After surviving pregnancy, birth, and the initial weeks of life, children confront their first stage-salient task: the formation of a secure attachment to a primary caretaker or caretakers (Sroufe & Rutter, 1984). Children usually master this task in the latter half of their first year, although the process of developing an attachment begins much earlier. The importance of attachment as a childhood task was first identified by Bowlby (1973, 1980, 1982). Attachment refers to an affectional bond of caring and craving wherein the child seeks security and comfort in his or her relationship with the caregiver (Cassidy, 1999). It ties the child to the caregiver, and attachment behaviour serves to keep the infant in close proximity to one or a few principal caregivers. Attachment evolves from the early interaction between children and caretakers. Early infant behaviours, such as crying and smiling, serve to elicit behaviours in caregivers. In turn, caretakers who recognize and respond to infant cues in a sensitive and immediate manner allow children to reduce their arousal and calm themselves. Sensitive caregiving also involves the provision of physical safety. If parents can recognize and take appropriate measures to meet their children's needs sensitively and reliably over time, children come to expect that their caretakers will help them to regulate distress. Children develop a sense of security vis-à-vis their caretaker(s) and subsequently discriminate between people, establishing an attachment to one or a few select individuals. These initial attachment organizations serve as templates for later relationships.

Bowlby (1973, 1980, 1982) described the mental representations about themselves and their parents that children develop through this process. He called these *internal working models*. If infants are provided with reliable and sensitive care, they come to expect that parents will take care of them and that they are indeed worthy of care. Children then use these models to help them interpret other events in their social world. For example, a well-parented child anticipates that other children will treat them well on the first day of school, but a poorly parented child may expect other students to act harshly towards him or her. Through the use of their internal working models, children become 'active constructors of reality,' differentially attending and reacting to diverse information in their social world to essentially create their own experiences. This is exemplified in the case of Gary, whom we described in our earlier book (Pearce & Pezzot-Pearce, 1997). This physically abused, neglected, and psychologically maltreated youngster interpreted a playground game of tag as potential abuse. He stated, 'They were screaming at me and chasing me, and they were gonna hurt me!' (p. 44). Given his previous experiences with his mother, he not only fully expected other students to assault him, but he ignored their obvious enjoyment of the game. By the end of their first year, children often derive a strong sense of security from their parents. If they can depend on parents to meet their needs reliably, they can then devote attention to other childhood tasks such as mastering language and exploring the environment.

Early research using the Strange Situation paradigm developed by Ainsworth, Blehar, Waters, and Wall (1978) to study mother-infant attachment in the laboratory identified particular patterns of attachment organization. In the Strange Situation, infants and toddlers are stressed by primary caretakers leaving the room and then rejoining them a short time later. Of interest is children's use of their parents during the reunion to modulate their distress. Securely attached infants positively greet their parents, actively seek proximity and interaction, and readily accept comfort if they are distressed, as they have learned to expect their parents will meet their needs. They soon begin to explore their environment again. Parents of these infants have been accessible and sensitive to their children's needs.

Children with avoidant attachment patterns exhibit little distress at separation and on reunion avoid their parents, look away or ignore them, and show little preference for parents over strangers. Parents are insensitive, avoid physical contact, and are intrusive in their interactions with their children, or are hostile and rejecting. Children may suppress or falsify their feelings because they have learned that a display of distress does not elicit comfort from parents. Parents will not be responsive, or they might even become angry and rejecting. However, parental disregard is painful, and some children idealize their caregivers to ease the feelings of anger, sadness, and anxiety that would accompany an accurate perception of their relationship with their parents.

Children with ambivalent-resistant attachment patterns react differently. These children are highly distressed on separation. At reunion they seem ambivalent about interaction. They seek proximity but then push parents away angrily. These children seem to be trying to provoke reactions from their inconsistent parents and in doing so overexpress their feelings. As parents respond only after the child's affective arousal is pronounced, these children become preoccupied with parental unavailability, which in turn compromises their ability to explore the environment. Besides overexpressing feelings to engage parents, such children also become clingy and dependent.

Main and Solomon (1990) subsequently identified a third insecure attachment classification. Disorganized-disoriented attachment does not represent an organized strategy to maintain closeness to an attachment figure in times of stress. Instead, these children appear to be confused about their caregivers' responses. During reunions, children may strongly seek proximity but then strongly avoid it, express fear and distress in a rather indirect manner, present as dazed and disoriented, and seem apprehensive. Children with this attachment pattern have been exposed to confusing parent behaviours, such as threatening behaviour from a previously positive parent, or subtle behaviours where parents are overtly positive but covertly threatening.

Bowlby (1973, 1980, 1982) credits security of attachment with far-reaching protective qualities in children's development. He views secure attachment as an organizing factor that provides children with dependable bases of security and support in times of stress. It fosters explorations of the environment, predisposes children to interpersonal relationships wherein they feel they can trust others, and nurtures a positive sense of self. It also contributes to children's ability to regulate and modulate feelings. Secure attachments thus promote resiliency in children and help them master life's challenges. It is important to note that security of attachment can change over time. Securely attached children may become insecure if exposed to toxic interpersonal events and insecurely attached children can develop secure attachments if provided with appropriate care-taking. For example, the latter might occur in children who have been neglected in early months but then are placed in the homes of sensitive and responsive caretakers.

While the above discussion may seem somewhat esoteric, it has direct applicability to parenting assessments. Children will have a greater chance of developing well if they form secure attachments to primary caretakers, a process clearly dependent upon the parenting they receive. For example, Greenberg (1999) notes that insecure attachments are one of several risk factors that may increase the probability of psychopathology in children. Parents must be available to their children and they must respond in sensitive ways to facilitate secure attachment. Questions concerning security of attachment would arise if parents are often emotionally unavailable to their children, or physically abuse or neglect them. If children involved in parenting assessments are infants or toddlers, assessors can observe the sensitivity with which parents respond to them. Furthermore, assessors can observe children's responses to parents, as is evident in the adoption case example that follows.

CASE 2: An assessor undertook a parenting evaluation in a case where a twenty-one-year-old woman named Janis had placed her daughter at birth with adoptive parents, Sylvia and Steve. The child's birth father, Jim, was married and had teenage children. His wife became aware of her husband's affair and the baby when Wendy was three months old. With his wife's support, Jim applied to the court to assume care of his daughter. He argued that moving Wendy to his home at the age of five months would have no detrimental impact, as she was too young to have formed any bond with her new parents. The assessor was asked to evaluate the adoptive parents' capacity to care for the child, with specific questions regarding the nature of the attachment between them and Wendy. In addition to interviewing and psychologically testing Sylvia and Steve, the assessor observed Wendy in her home. The adoptive parents were clearly knowledgeable about her needs and described her reactions to various routines and activities. During the home observation, Wendy interacted comfortably with her parents, and she both noticed and interacted somewhat with the assessor. When both parents left the room to go to the kitchen, Wendy followed their exit with her eyes and stopped chewing her toy, but did not become highly distressed. This changed when the assessor approached her closely. Wendy became acutely distressed but settled immediately when Sylvia re-entered the room and picked her up. She again began to explore her toys and interact with parents. Both interview data and observation indicated Wendy was indeed securely attached to her parents. This was not surprising given their high responsiveness and sensitivity to her.

Although formal assessment of attachment will be discussed in more detail in Chapter 10, assessors can begin to review **attachment** by asking some of the following questions (Pearce & Pezzot-Pearce, 1997):

1. Did the parents look forward to the birth of the children or were they unwanted?
2. Did the parents prepare for the birth of the children?

3. Were the parents and children separated for long periods during the children's first year of life, perhaps due to such factors as illness or disappearance of a parent?
4. Did the parents use a limited number of reliable caregivers during the children's early years?
5. Did the caregivers ensure safety for the children at home and in alternate child care arrangements?
6. Were the children easy to care for and who provided the basic care?
7. Were the children easy to calm and who calmed them easiest?
8. Did parents respond quickly to infant cues?
9. Did parents immediately respond to their infants' distress or did they let the babies cry for long periods of time?
10. Did the parents have routines for the infants and were these rigidly enforced?
11. Did the children protest separations from their parents?
12. Did the parents talk to their babies and was it in a reasonable manner?
13. How did the parents handle frustration with their infants?
14. Were the parents' expectations appropriate for the age of the children?
15. Did the parents think their infants liked them?
16. Did the children and parents seem to enjoy each other?
17. Have the parents abused or neglected their infants?

Emotional and Behavioural Regulation

Another stage-salient task of toddlerhood and early childhood is development of the ability to regulate emotion and behaviour. According to Cicchetti, Ackerman, and Izard (1995), the central function of emotions is to motivate and organize behaviour. Affect regulation thus refers to the way in which emotional arousal is redirected, controlled, modulated, and modified in arousing situations so that individuals can keep it at acceptable levels, thereby permitting them to optimize performance and function adequately. Parents begin to regulate their children's arousal and emotional levels in the early months of life. When infants are distressed, parents determine the cause and perhaps feed, change, warm, rock, or cuddle their children as the situation demands. They may stimulate infants through social interaction or reduce stimulation if children appear overaroused, thereby consolidating the attachment relationship and regulating arousal. Infants may suck their fingers and cuddle favourite stuffed animals to soothe themselves as they get older. Sensitive parents also reliably talk and sing to their infants, demonstrating their interest and enjoyment, as well as labelling items and events in the environment. Perhaps one of the most important things parents can do to help children regulate feelings and behaviour is to verbally identify emotional states and describe subsequent action plans. Even in early weeks, parents will say, 'Oh, you are so sleepy (or wet, hungry, etc.). We need to put you to bed.' Although an infant may make little sense of this initially, over time such verbalization helps toddlers begin to recognize and label their emotional states rather than acting them out impulsively. Thus toddlers may rub their eyes, say 'sleepy time,' and then get a favourite blanket to lie down. It is worrisome during an assessment if four- or five-year-old children demonstrate limited abilities to label their own and other people's feelings. Concern is heightened if much older children demonstrate minimal capacity to label feelings, as in the following case:

CASE 3: Randy was an eleven-year-old child who was referred for assessment and therapy. An only child, he had been apprehended from the care of his single mother, June, when he was ten years of age due to concerns about neglect and emotional abuse. In a prior evaluation, his mother was psychiatrically assessed as having a borderline personality disorder. Her social functioning had been marginal for numerous years, and she could not maintain employment or a stable living milieu. Some of her parenting skills were very poor: not only did she base her expectations of Randy upon unusual reasoning, but she erratically applied what few rules existed in the home. When Randy entered foster care, he was an unsocialized and impulsive waif who was unaware of normal social expectations. Randy proved to be a verbal child who scored in the gifted range in formal intellectual testing. He spoke of many complex intellectual topics, but labeled only a few feelings, including anger, fear, sadness, surprise, and happiness. Furthermore, Randy was preoccupied with anger. He described feelings in little detail and had tremendous difficulty identifying those of other people, thereby contributing to his proclivity to act out his anger in harmful and antisocial ways. Before Randy's feelings about events in his life could be explored in therapy, the therapist helped him learn to identify and verbalize an array of feelings, behaviours that June should have developed years earlier.

Emotional and behavioural regulation also develops in response to the limits parents impose on children when they are toddlers. While sensitive parents tend not to place behavioural expectations on infants, they begin to put limits on children once they are mobile and start to understand language. For example, parents tell children not to touch things and prohibit various behaviours. Many reasonable parents physically remove children from a situation or divert their attention to settle them rather than verbally abusing or physically punishing them. However, unrealistic parental expectations are worrisome, such as a parent who expects a ten-month-old child to sit still for half an hour or be fully toilet trained. In such a case, questions should be raised about parental motivations and sensitivity or even basic knowledge of children's growth and development, given that these tasks are impossible for most children of that age.

Young children can become overstimulated relatively quickly in many circumstances. The capacity to regulate emotion and behaviour is a critical development, as it allows children to relate well to other people and explore their environment, either physically or socially, while still knowing they can seek help from parents if they get into difficulty. For example, preschoolers who are trying to build block towers and who are developing a good capacity to regulate behaviour might engage in self-talk to manage their frustration, saying, 'I can do this. I'll do it slowly.' Children without this capacity might knock the blocks off the table, throw them at a nearby child, or have a full-fledged tantrum. Others might give up and withdraw completely by staring off into space. The capacity to regulate emotion and behaviour is a strong advantage in learning and socializing. Children who can modulate their reactions in social situations stand a much better chance of being accepted by peers than do children who are constantly reactive and act out their distress impulsively or by withdrawing. For example, Randy (Case 3) had tremendous difficulty interacting with peers, who shunned him because he reacted impulsively and out of proportion to provocations.

In order to assess parents' abilities to help their children learn to **modulate their feelings and behaviour**, the following questions may be useful:

1. Do parents provide a predictable home life with regularity in activities such as meals, bedtimes, and bathing routines?
2. Do parents have knowledge of appropriate expectations for children of different ages?
3. Do parents apply appropriate limits consistently and do they talk to their children about these limits?
4. Do parents label feelings and help children solve situations so they can calm themselves and feel better?
5. Do parents use physical punishment, verbal degradation, shaming, bribery, and isolation to control their children's behaviours?
6. Do parents demonstrate an awareness of factors that make emotional and behavioural control more difficult for their children, such as fatigue, hunger, and new situations? If they are aware, can they respond appropriately to help their children or do personal factors such as being overwhelmed or depressed prevent them from doing so?
7. Do parents appear to be sought out by their children when the latter feel frustrated or overwhelmed?

Development of the Autonomous Self

Another task of childhood is the development of an autonomous self. Again, parenting behaviour can strongly support children to develop a sense of themselves as persons who are lovable, capable, independent, and confident. As noted earlier, Bowlby (1973) asserted that through sensitive and reliable parental care, children begin to develop mental representations of themselves as being lovable people who are worthy of the good care they receive. When care is less than adequate, children may not view themselves as lovable because no one has responded positively to them. Instead, they may have been ignored or maltreated. As noted earlier, children who do not have secure attachments may be unable to actively explore their environment, thereby restricting their physical and cognitive growth and exacerbating their negative sense of self-worth or self-esteem. This poor sense of self-worth is compounded if caretakers have not provided limits and structure that facilitate the development of emotional and behavioural regulation.

By the time many children are two or three years old, they have developed a good sense of themselves as capable and independent persons. Of course, during times of distress or threat, they still depend on caretakers for security and support. On other occasions, they assert their independence with vigour and demonstrate their developing competencies to all people who will listen or watch. Furthermore, they delight in themselves and their new competencies. During this stage, it is critical for parents to accept a toddler's self-assertiveness and the 'I can do it by myself' attitude. It is indeed normal for children at this stage to say 'no' and to refuse suggestions from parents when they had accepted them just weeks earlier. The appearance of this self-assertiveness in previously dependent children is healthy and does not indicate that children no longer love parents. Clinically, it is common to see parents with their own insecure attachment histories have profound problems tolerating a toddler's push to independence. Although we will return to this issue later, it is critical for assessors not only to inquire how parents handle the increasing independence of their toddlers, but also to ask about the relevance of parents' own attachment history and childhood.

While parents have to accept toddlers' independence, they must also impose appropriate behavioural limits. The latter is best done in a positive manner with consequences appropriate to children's developmental levels. Parents not only describe and follow through with rules, but they recognize their children's reactions to the imposition of rules and structure. Labelling children's internal feeling states may have a profound impact on their developing awareness of self. By labelling their feeling states, children begin to differentiate themselves from others. Bretherton and Beeghly (1982) showed that by twenty-eight months, most middle-class children can use a number of verbal labels, including words for perception (i.e., the five senses), physiological states, goals, intentions, and abilities. More than half can discuss basic feelings, such as anger, sadness, and happiness. The ability to use this language permits children to communicate their feelings without acting them out and allows them to clarify misunderstandings in social situations. Thus, a child who puts soap on the floor can tell parents that he or she was 'helping,' and sensitive parents might give the youngster another task so they can 'help' with house cleaning. Children without such language cannot explain their motivations when insensitive parents tell them they are bad because they 'wanted to make a mess.' Such parental reactions might invoke feelings of inadequacy and helplessness, thereby compromising exploration of the environment, intellectual development, and self-esteem.

Questions that can be used to assess parents' support for children's development of a **positive sense of self** follow:

1. Do parents recognize their children's unique personalities, being able to describe them in detail with caring and appreciation?
2. Do parents provide clear, consistent, and appropriate expectations and limits for their children, adjusting them to each child's unique characteristics as described in question 1?
3. Do parents use positive consequences and choices to guide their children's behaviour rather than harsh, punitive, and demeaning consequences?
4. Do parents continue to talk to their children, label feelings, and help them solve problems in difficult situations?
5. Do parents encourage their children to develop new skills and competencies or do they treat them as if they were much younger?
6. Do parents take pride in their toddlers' new skills and independence or are they threatened by this development?
7. Even though children assert their independence in many ways, do they appear to again rely upon parents when they become frustrated or stressed?

Language and Play Development

As children progress through the toddler and preschool years, they develop increasingly differentiated symbolic capacities evident in their language, play, and processing of social information. During their third year of life, most children begin to use language in more complex ways. While younger children often have relatively stronger receptive than expressive language, many do not use speech to directly communicate about their needs and observations until they are over two years old. Then children begin to speak increasingly of their own and other's internal states and ask questions about the environment, not only labelling objects and behaviours but asking such questions as 'why?' and 'how?' Although such questions sometimes are tiring to caregivers, they signal that children's thinking is becoming more complex and sophisticated. Parents can do much to encourage language and cognitive development by labelling, explaining, questioning, and clarifying concepts using developmentally sensitive language.

During assessments, assessors must be cognizant of the quality of children's verbalizations and thinking and of the interaction between parents and children. Concerns arise if children and parents do not communicate and ignore each other, if communication is primarily unidirectional, or if parents spend all of their time explaining and teaching with no elements of playfulness. Children delight in the playful use of language and humour, as it is another way to explore their environment and to exercise increasingly sophisticated cognitive skills. When assessing older children, we ask about the development of children's verbal skills and observe their current use of language.

It is important to assess children's play development, particularly at younger ages. As children develop more sophisticated symbolic capacities, their play likewise becomes more sophisticated. In infancy and the toddler years, play tends to involve manipulation of objects as children experiment and learn about their physical world. Parents can support both play and language development by playing and interacting with their children. Young children take delight in the elements of predictability and surprise involved in games such as 'Pat-a-cake.' In their second year, toddlers often begin to demonstrate play that is representative of daily life experiences. For example, children might feed dolls or stuffed animals and put them to bed, essentially replicating their own experience. As language develops, children use it as an integral part of the play, imitating caregivers' behaviour and words. During the toddler years, parents still often sing and play the fun games of infancy with their children. They also enhance development by engaging in some of the more elaborate play scenarios with their children. Most children are delighted if parents help feed dolls or allow a doll to accompany them on a walk. Parents also support play development through the provision of age-appropriate and safe toys.

Between three and four years, children often begin to involve other youngsters in dramatic play. In this play with other children, they assume different roles, such as the good person/bad person or child/adult. This emerging sophistication demonstrates children's increasing awareness of the attributes, feelings, and motivations of other people and themselves. Many children will dramatize extremes in these roles for fun, such as taking the role of the wicked stepmother or helpless baby. Children's use of roles in play with peers or in role play with adults can also be representative of their internal working models, that is, expectations about themselves and others. Thus if children depict parental figures as harsh, demanding, and non-nurturing, observers might question the children's previous experiences with parents and caretakers. Of course, in an assessment one must corroborate such observations with interview and test information and reports by parents and other references. Evidence of an emerging capacity to be empathic regarding the feelings of others is often found in dramatic play as well as in daily interactions with others. Parents participate less frequently in this play, which typically involves peers from outside of the family. However, parents must remain available to provide some of the physical props, support, and structure that are needed to make this play go well. At the same time, they should not intervene in every squabble, as children often sort out differences if left alone. Parents do need to intervene if children are out of control or are in danger of being hurt.

By entry into elementary school, some children still greatly enjoy dramatic play, where they assume various roles, while others no longer engage in this activity. Children may also use constructive play to master materials, producing various creations, such as arts and crafts. Considerable organization and planning may be employed in such activities. Games, sometimes with elaborate rule systems, also become part of play in the school years. At this age, children require less active play support from parents, although most still enjoy parent participation in some play activities. This may be in organized games, such as board games, physical activities and sports, and creative play such as crafts and Lego. Parents can be particularly helpful when they play competitive games with their children to ensure they abide by the rules so as to learn to win fairly and lose with grace. These are critical skills in good peer relationships.

Given the importance of play for children's intellectual and social development, this is an important area to assess. With very young children, you may need to observe independent play as well as child-parent play. Observing the child's play, including that with the assessor, may be quite informative, as are descriptions of children's play skills by references. Babysitters and day care workers often offer comprehensive descriptions of language and play development and opinions about whether children have any unique needs in this area.

Assessors can employ the following questions to assess parental support of **language and play development**. However when parents are not appropriately supportive, then we must explore the reasons for this.

1. Do parents and children enjoy talking with each other or do parents avoid communication, perhaps being too busy, overwhelmed, or lacking in verbal and cognitive abilities?

2. Is the communication between parents and children primarily unidirectional, with children trying to engage uninterested parents or vice versa?
3. How much television do even very young children watch? Does watching television take the place of interaction with parents? How much time do older children spend watching television or playing computer and video games versus interacting with parents and peers?
4. Do parents have the financial resources to provide children with basic toys and play equipment and do they choose age-appropriate and safe materials?
5. Do parents provide appropriate supervision and guidance when children play with peers, neither intervening too much nor allowing potentially dangerous situations to develop?
6. Are parents aware of their children's play interests?
7. Are parents aware that children sometimes use play to deal with personal issues?
8. How often do parents and children play together, using fairness and humour in their activities?

Peer Relations

Another stage-salient task that emerges during childhood is the establishment of relationships with peers outside the immediate family circle. This task first becomes important in preschool years. Infants are focused on their relationships with primary caregivers and perhaps with siblings. While they may notice other infants, they are not oriented towards them. Toddlers begin to show interest in peers, but as the preceding discussion indicates, usually they do not have the language, emotional and behavioural controls, or play skills to relate well to other children their own age. While toddlers may say they play with peers, they tend to play in a parallel rather than interactive manner. As preschoolers, children demonstrate stronger interest in interacting with other children of their own age. Interaction with peers initially involves considerable negotiation over the use of toys and materials. In the preschool and school years, children must increasingly accept responsibility for their behaviour in social interactions and recognize the impact of their actions on other people. Children are more able to do this if they have negotiated previous stage-salient tasks relatively successfully. For example, if parents have consistently enforced limits, children can more readily accept responsibility for their actions and better regulate their feelings. They will understand consequences, recognize when they make mistakes, and have developed a sense of competence regarding their own skills.

A crucial development at this stage is the emergence of **empathy**, wherein children can take the viewpoint of others and recognize how those others are feeling. For example, they recognize when a peer is hurt, offer consolation, and get help. If they have hurt the other children, they may feel badly and attempt to make amends. While toddlers may show recognition of the distress of other children and attempt to make them feel better in a perfunctory way, older children increasingly use empathy to guide their behaviour. By school age, they are likely to anticipate the reactions of others to their behaviour and thus change it to take these factors into account. Children who have not learned to modulate feelings and behaviours and who have poor self-confidence have great difficulty in peer situations. Randy (Case 3) is typical of such a child. Despite excellent verbal capacity, he was so self-centred, insecure, and unable to modulate his feelings or behaviour that he could not recognize the impact of his behaviour on others. Although he occasionally controlled his reactions, he was easily overwhelmed and provoked by normal peer interactions. He always felt wronged by others and reacted constantly to real or imagined rejection. Despite therapy and strong school support, his peer relationships remained poor.

As children begin to extend themselves in peer interactions, parents still have significant roles to play, although these diminish as children get older. With preschoolers, parents can support interactions by arranging opportunities for their children to interact with other youngsters. Parents with good social networks are more able to provide this opportunity, as they live reasonably close to extended family members and friends. Interactions with same-age cousins or other family members may be easy to arrange. When families are more isolated, parents may need to encourage interactions by placing children in play groups or play schools. Such peer interaction should not be excessive, as young children still require and enjoy interaction and time in their families. Of course, concerns arise if parents do nothing to encourage peer interactions at appropriate ages or if parents are so isolated they keep children at home to meet their own needs for companionship. June (Case 3) could not maintain her own social relationships and thus kept Randy at home, watching television or having long discussions with her. He did not learn to interact well with peers and instead became focused on meeting the needs of his volatile mother.

Once children begin to seek out other children in preschool years, parents can be supportive by occasionally arranging to have another child over to play and by helping structure the play if needed. Young children sometimes require active support to develop ways to share, particularly if they have no siblings with whom they can practice these skills, but parents do not need to hover about and intervene constantly. Parents also need to monitor the safety of the homes their children visit. For example, parents should ensure an adult supervises very young children on playground equipment or that an adult is in the home when children are present.

Parents generally need to intervene less as children enter school or become adolescents, but they must continue to monitor the children's whereabouts and safety and they must still be aware of their children's peers and the children's reactions to such relationships. School-age children cannot single-handedly manage all situations that arise with peers, such as bullying; in these situations, they often require guidance from parents and other people such as teachers. While children do not always want their parents to intervene, they learn from this process and indeed may be more likely to utilize their parents as supports when future difficulties arise. If parents help children in elementary school years through open but sensitive discussion, their youngsters will be more likely to bring issues to parents during adolescence. Parents need to anticipate issues and actively initiate discussions. Concerns arise if parents are completely unaware of children's peers and activities or if they constantly intrude and permit children no opportunity to solve problems themselves.

Questions to ask about parent support in children's **peer relationships** follow.

1. Do parents encourage children to form relationships with peers or do they isolate them? What concrete steps do parents take to ensure that their children have contact with other youngsters?
2. Can parents identify their children's friends and judge the appropriateness of specific friends?
3. Do parents ensure that an adult is supervising when the children are visiting at friends' homes and that the environment is a safe one?

4. Do parents know where their older children are, what they are doing, and with whom they are associating when the children are away from home?
5. Can parents allow their children to negotiate and resolve some issues with their friends on their own or do they intrude and control these relationships?
6. Do parents discuss relationships with children as needed, focusing on how to be a good friend and on how to solve the normal problems that arise?
7. Do parents disregard children's reports that they are being bullied or school reports that their children are bullies? What action do they take?

Cognitive Development and Adaptation to School

As children confront and increasingly master stage-salient tasks, they move towards increasing independence across all areas of functioning. By the time they enter formal schooling in kindergarten or grade 1, most children can undertake many routine self-care tasks and relate well to family members and peers. They think in relatively complex ways and use language to describe many aspects of their environment, themselves, and others, but their worlds are still quite narrow and centred on activities with family and friends. This changes considerably when they begin grade school and establish relationships with unfamiliar children and adults; they must learn to function in a structured situation that has clear demands regarding behaviour and learning. Until this time children have not had to adhere to such strict rules and schedules. Even in day care, where routines usually exist, younger children are provided with many opportunities to choose play activities and playmates. Furthermore, sensitive caretakers may have modified the day's schedule to accommodate the child's current emotional status; for example, a parent might decide against grocery shopping if a child is irritable because of an illness. Adapting classroom schedules and activities to the needs of an individual child is much more difficult. Children must learn to maintain behavioural control despite their emotional state, and they are considerably disadvantaged when they have not learned to modulate their feelings and behaviour. As well, they must begin to comply with requests and demands without constant one-to-one attention and guidance, and they must undertake tasks that are not always fun or interesting. The latter can generate considerable frustration that may be exacerbated by various perceptual and learning disabilities. Children who perceive and use teachers as sources of support are at a significant advantage when attempting to master these challenges.

School entry also can be a trying time for parents, as they must now relinquish some control of their children to strangers. Concerns arise if parents cannot do this and find either overt or covert ways to maintain or even increase their children's dependency. For example, some parents subtly encourage somatic complaints and keep children home needlessly. It is equally concerning if parents do not recognize the significance of school entry and do nothing to support children with this transition. Parents must speak with children about entering school, familiarizing them with the physical characteristics of the school milieu and some of the routines and behavioural expectations, as well as reassuring them of their continued emotional availability. During assessment, it is important to inquire how children and parents handled this major event, including asking about what parents say to their children regarding teachers. For example, if parents denigrate teachers or make fun of them, children might do the same and thus have difficulty following their teachers' directions.

The ongoing language and cognitive stimulation in the home helps prepare children for school entry. Children who have been exposed to the use of language for problem solving and information sharing will be better prepared than those who have not been so exposed. For example, if parents read to children, they provide considerable advantages. Children learn basic pre-literacy skills: where the top of the page is, that people read from left to right, and the ability to sit and listen to stories. These are critical classroom behaviours and skills essential for successful literacy development. Parents also contribute to their children's ongoing school adaptation if they talk about school, read notices, follow through with homework, and communicate with teachers; these behaviours indicate interest and ongoing support. Parents also can support their children's adaptation to school by ensuring adequate study materials, food, rest, and medical aids such as corrective lenses. Even if parents have little money, they must demonstrate an awareness of these needs and take steps to meet them, accepting support from agencies if necessary. Parents also need to recognize when children are not doing well academically. They must explore the reasons for such problems, take appropriate steps to remedy them, and advocate with schools to ensure that their children receive the help they need. It is concerning if a parent ignores a child's frustration in coping with a learning or attention problem, commenting that 'it's not an issue. I had the same problem in school and I turned out just fine.' Conversely, parents who overemphasize difficulties, make excuses, do their children's work, or place excessively high expectations upon their children may be equally problematic.

To assess parental support of **cognitive development and adaptation to school**, ask the following questions:

1. Do parents read to young children, talk with them, and encourage learning in children of all ages?
2. Did the parents take steps to support their children's entry into school with activities such as visiting the school and teacher ahead of time and talking positively about school, or did they send them unprepared or with a negative view?
3. Do children attend school regularly or do they miss inordinate amounts of school and for what reasons? Do children arrive at school on time and are they prepared for learning?
4. Do parents provide the necessary materials the children require, such as books, lunches, and eyeglasses?
5. Are parents aware of school activities, taking the time to read notices, review report cards, and attend parent-teacher conferences?
6. Do parents provide time and space for children to do homework and do they ensure it is completed? Do they do the homework for their children?
7. Do the parents have expectations of their children's academic achievement that are congruent with the children's abilities, being neither too high nor too low?
8. Are the parents aware of frustrations or problems their children are having with learning? Have they sought out assistance and do they advocate for services for their children?
9. How have parents tried to help their children with school problems and how effective have these attempts been? Are parents hampered in supporting their children due to their own cognitive limitations, learning disabilities, or attention problems?
10. Can parents cooperate with school staff to remediate any learning or behavioural problems?

Autonomy

Relatively few parenting assessments are undertaken with adolescent children because many jurisdictions take adolescents' wishes into account when deciding about their care. Even when parents and the courts make decisions, many adolescents chose their own living situations, sometimes leaving home to live with friends or on the street. Nonetheless, assessors must be aware of the tasks that confront teenage children and their parents. A useful monograph that reviews many of the issues confronting adolescents is Volume 4 of the series *The Course of Life*, edited by Greenspan and Pollock (1991).

If teenagers have already mastered the previous stage-salient tasks and developed competence across several areas of functioning, they are likely to move through adolescence more easily than those teens who have struggled along the way. Even so, this process is not always easy, as the transition to adult emancipation presents several challenges. One of the greatest challenges involves relationships. Children have been forming more relationships with others outside of the home for several years, but during the teen years relationships become more emotionally intense. Early adolescence often involves the development of close connections with friends of the same sex followed by romantic relationships with friends of the opposite sex. When adolescents have mastered earlier stage-salient tasks, they enter relationships with the capacity to trust and share. Relationships may be more difficult for those who encountered earlier difficulties in forming secure attachments to others. Teenagers' peer relationships often occur outside of the range of direct supervision, so parents are much less involved, but they must still be familiar with their children's friends and provide limits around activities and curfews. While teenagers often object to such limits, as they believe they are grown up and impervious to harm, limits continue to provide safety and security much as they did when children were younger.

Parental awareness and open communication about relationships are critical because of the numerous risks adolescents face, such as premature sexual relationships with accompanying possibilities of sexually transmitted disease, AIDS, and pregnancy, as well as smoking and drug and alcohol use. Rather than simply avoiding issues or providing simplistic advice ('don't do it'), parents need to initiate dialogue regarding the risks involved and review how teenagers could handle various situations. Of course, parents should continue to support school progress and participation in extracurricular activities, such as sports, hobbies, and clubs, to facilitate the continued development of competency and self-esteem. As parental ignorance or avoidance of their adolescents' relationships and extracurricular activities can be problematic, assessors must include this area in their evaluations.

Teenagers also must adapt to the tremendous physical and hormonal changes that accompany puberty, learning to take control of some aspects of their feelings and behaviour much as they did when they were younger. Parents can do a great deal to help by providing information and open discussion of these changes. Humour often eases this for both teens and parents, but ridicule and sarcasm limit communication about this and other issues. Related to the physical and emotional changes of adolescence is the emergence of significant identity issues. Not only do teenagers continue to address issues of sexual identification that began years before, but they rework their general belief systems. As teenagers are often intensely idealistic, they may challenge a wide range of their parent's beliefs, mores, and values. These challenges occur around such mundane issues as why clothes should be picked up off the floor and range to much broader issues such as religious beliefs and politics. Debate and defiance are common and pose real difficulties for some parents, who may view these challenges as a rejection and repudiation of them rather than as a normal developmental progression. It is important for assessors to ask how families are managing these issues.

The ultimate task of adolescence is emancipation from parental control and care and the assumption of adult activities, responsibilities, and relationships. This happens successfully if teenagers have learned to make decisions and have practiced the needed skills prior to their departure from home. This can be facilitated by parents through allowing teens more opportunities to make decisions and, gradually, to assume more responsibility for their lives as they near the age of emancipation. Many cultures have set rituals that ease this process, but Western cultures tend not to have clear rites of passage that signify adult status. While legal adult status is set by statute, some argue that Western cultures have other, less formal rites of passage: high school graduation, obtaining a driver's licence, a first vote in an election, or a first legal visit to a bar. Since these vary depending upon family and community standards and expectations, assessors must take such cultural differences into account. Assessors must therefore determine whether both parents and teens are managing emancipation appropriately as defined by their cultural group or community.

While a relatively small number of parenting assessments directly involve teenagers, teens can be of significant collateral interest when the care of younger siblings is at issue. In some families, older siblings are expected to provide the majority of the childcare, essentially raising their younger siblings. Even when this is not the case, it is worthwhile to inquire how parents have managed adolescent issues with older siblings, as this may be representative of their skill and sensitivity in subsequently guiding their younger children through adolescence. Similarly, if siblings have left home, assessors should inquire how this happened and if they maintain good relationships with parents and younger siblings. Observations and findings pertaining to these older children must not be automatically generalized to parents' interactions with younger ones; parents handle issues differently with different children, and they also change as they progress through their parenting careers.

A final point concerns adult children who have never left home. It can be worrisome if seemingly competent teenagers and young adults never achieve autonomy. Assessors should explore the reasons for this situation while remaining cognizant that, in some cultures, one child is expected to remain home to care for aging parents. In other situations, children have various physical, mental, or emotional problems that preclude the usual emancipation from parental care. These children present special parenting needs and will be discussed in the following chapter, as will other issues that require more specialized parenting and knowledge.

The following questions explore the abilities of parents to support the **increasing autonomy** of their teenage children:

1. Can parents and teenagers discuss important issues or are most important topics off-limits?
2. Do parents and teenagers communicate in a respectful and responsive manner? For example, do parents use biting and sarcastic humour that discourages communication or do they infantilize their children?
3. Do parents adopt a rigid authoritarian stance or do they discuss issues and allow more choices and flexibility as teenagers demonstrate an increased capacity for responsible behaviour?

4. Do parents encourage school achievement and extracurricular activities that enhance the self-esteem of their teenagers?
5. Do parents have curfews for their teenagers and do they set boundaries regarding the activities in which their teenagers can participate?
6. Do parents allow their teenagers some privacy, such as around bathing, phone calls, and mail?
7. Can parent's identify their teenage children's friends?
8. How do parents handle problems such as substance abuse and sexual promiscuity? Do they seek out appropriate help when problems arise?
9. Do parents understand that teenagers need to challenge and disagree with them or do they take this as a personal affront?
10. Do parents keep their teenagers dependent for too long or do they eject them from the home before teenagers are ready to leave? Why?
11. Do parents maintain good relationships with older, emancipated children?
12. Have older, emancipated children become estranged from the family or do they remain enmeshed in the family's daily concerns?

4 Child Factors: Atypical Development

Most children do well through childhood if they receive sensitive and reliable parenting that supports their mastery of the tasks outlined in the preceding chapter, and most parents are reasonably able to meet their children's needs without undue stress and difficulty. Although the interaction among variables is complex, Belsky and Vondra (1989) note that children's characteristics and the resulting demands upon parents are one of several factors that contributes significantly to parenting behaviour. As assessors, we must not only be aware of the needs of children during the typical course of development, but be cognizant of unique child characteristics and circumstances that may make parenting more difficult. Knowledge about specific problems or conditions that require specialized parenting enhances the thoroughness of any assessment. At the same time, assessors do not need to be experts in every possible problem or condition. For instance, we do not need to be medical specialists, but we must be able to access specialized knowledge about specific medical disorders and incorporate it into our assessments. The following overview addresses some of the common child factors that place unique demands upon parents, but it is not meant to be an exhaustive list.

Difficult Temperament

Perhaps one the most basic child characteristics that influences parenting is children's temperament. The hallmark research into temperament was the New York longitudinal study, beginning in 1956, that followed a number of people from infancy into adulthood (Thomas & Chess, 1977).

Temperament is usually described as an inborn style of behaviour and reactivity; while it can be influenced somewhat by environment, it is not primarily a function of parenting practices or environmental events. In essence, temperament simply describes how a person acts or reacts along several behavioural dimensions. Thomas and Chess (1977) describe **nine basic temperamental traits** or dimensions that are evident at birth and persist over time: activity level, distractibility, intensity of reaction and behaviour, regularity, persistence, sensory threshold, approach/withdrawal to new stimuli, adaptability to transitions and change, and mood. Children vary on these dimensions, and the more intense their characteristics are, the greater the challenges they present to parents. Children with easy and flexible temperaments are generally easier to parent. For instance, a calm infant who sleeps regularly, is easily comforted when distressed, and is generally happy will probably be an enjoyable baby who is relatively easy to parent. Conversely, a child who reacts strongly to light, activity, and sounds, cries loudly and long, cannot be comforted, never sleeps through the night, and is constantly unhappy will likely be exhausting to parent and may provide much less positive feedback to caregivers. Furthermore, these temperamental dimensions persist and affect children's abilities to regulate their emotions and behaviour for many years. Even basic parental duties, such as shopping for clothes, can be trying when children cannot tolerate seams, tags, tightness, or certain textures on their skin. Beginning play school or kindergarten can be challenging because children may react poorly to disruptions in their daily routines and cannot tolerate activities like finger paints, clay, and sand play. During grade school, children with difficult temperaments may still be reacting with tantrums when their peers have already learned to modulate their emotional reactions and transition between activities. Their coping abilities may be significantly disrupted by illness, lack of sleep, room temperature, holidays, or small changes in classroom routine and instruction. Sensitive parents must persist in helping and supporting children to recognize and modulate their reactivity in a positive manner, even though the process can be exhausting. They must also work cooperatively with others who interact with their children, such as teachers and coaches.

Turecki (1989), in a volume often recommended to parents of temperamentally difficult children, describes several levels of temperamental problems that depend on both children's characteristics and the difficulties such behaviours pose to the family. Children may be 'easy' or they may be 'basically easy with some difficult features.' Parents may cope well with the latter or they may encounter problems; for instance, sedentary parents who are sensitive to sounds may have difficulty tolerating a loud and active child. 'Difficult' children have more intense traits and present many more challenges, stressing both parents and other family members. Siblings often feel short-changed in families where parents spend considerable energy managing children who are 'difficult' or 'very difficult'; they often feel as if these siblings control the situation and get away with bad behaviour, and these feelings engender much tension among family members. 'Impossible' children severely stress parents and siblings. It is common to find parents disagreeing about managing the child, with one or both blaming the other. Within a marriage and/or family, this can create marked stress that is exacerbated when extended families make disparaging remarks about the parenting the children receive.

Parents must take steps to help children with difficult temperaments modulate their responses. We must always be aware of the interaction between temperamental factors and parenting behaviour. Consequently, assessors must identify if less-than-adequate parenting is partially a function of a child's difficult temperamental qualities. If children are temperamentally difficult, then we must evaluate parents' understanding of their children's behaviour as well as actual parenting behaviour. For example, some parents may think their children are purposefully bad and may employ punitive practices when the children's behaviour results from temperamental factors that are not easily controlled. Parenting must be altered to take these factors into account, and therefore assessors should examine practices, such as the use of routines and warnings regarding activity changes and pacing of activities, so children do not become overstimulated. Parents need to reinforce good choices rather than merely punish negative behaviour, accompanying this with reasonable and sensitive verbal direction and explanation. Management of tantrums is also critical. For example, implementing a time-out may help calm both children and parents. Parents who can identify the stresses generated by their children and develop coping strategies, such as relieving each other when dealing with difficult situations, are likely to be more sensitive and effective. They may better handle this issue with siblings and may effectively use supports and guidance in managing difficult children.

However, many of these interventions require insight and energy. They may be particularly difficult for those parents in child welfare cases who begin parenting with minimal personal resources.

Assessors should, in history taking, survey the temperamental qualities of all family members. As temperamental dispositions appear to be biologically determined, often other family members have similar intense temperaments. This knowledge can be critical: difficult children can stress parents, but difficult parents can stress children. The concept of 'goodness of fit,' discussed in Chapter 2, is critical when the care of children with very difficult temperaments is at issue. This was the situation in the following custody/access case.

CASE 4: Neil and Flora were referred for a parenting assessment after a recent separation when they could not agree on living arrangements for their children, Larry (five years) and Grace (four years). Although the family had previously sought both marital counselling and consultation regarding Larry's behavioural difficulties, neither counsellor had specifically addressed Larry's extremely difficult temperament. Flora described Larry as a difficult infant who could never be comforted. At five years, he was still loud, active, and reactive, experiencing upwards of eight major tantrums a day. He had difficulty settling at night, and during the day he resisted any activity change that he did not initiate. As Flora provided most of the daily care, she had adapted schedules to Larry's reactivity. She gave several warnings prior to activity changes, enrolled him in afternoon play school to allow for a more relaxed morning wake-up, built active and quiet times into his days, and was always attuned to his emotional state.

Flora found Larry exhausting and was worried about his impact on Grace. She also was concerned about interactions between Larry and Neil. Flora viewed Neil as being just as intense and difficult as Larry, and Neil's mother described nearly identical behaviours in his childhood, however, Neil did not believe he had any problems, always felt justified in his decisions, and believed he coped well. He did not regard his battles with Larry as problematic. He and his son would yell at one another for up to half an hour, and he reported spanking Larry and angrily throwing him into bed. Of course, none of these strategies settled Larry. Neil was unwilling to change his parenting and blamed Flora for favouring Larry and creating a spoiled child. These differences in perspectives directly led to their separation. Although many other factors were taken into account, the assessor recommended that Larry and Grace live primarily with Flora, given the better fit of Flora's parenting style to Larry's needs. The assessor also identified the risks associated with the escalating physical altercations between Larry and Neil, which were partially a function of Neil's lack of insight and unwillingness to develop more sensitive parenting practices.

This case illustrates the importance of parents' abilities to accommodate to children's temperamental characteristics. If parents recognize their own intense temperaments and manage their reactivity well, then they can understand similar temperaments in their children. They also can model and discuss ways to manage reactivity and behaviour, making them powerful role models who demonstrate the very positive qualities that come with temperamental intensity. Once these children and adults achieve emotional and behavioural regulation, they often have high energy, intensity, sensitivity, and persistence that allow them to undertake many activities.

When assessing the impact of **children's temperament** on parenting behaviour, assessors can explore some of the following questions:

1. Does the child display a difficult or easy temperament, according to the nine temperamental dimensions described above?
2. If children have difficult temperaments, do parents recognize this as an inborn quality rather than as purposeful behaviour?
3. Do parents recognize the situations and demands associated with their children's intense reactions?
4. Do parents ensure adequate levels of sleep and nutrition so their children can better cope with their own intensity?
5. Are parents able to adapt routines to ease their children's reactivity, especially if they have several children or if they are parenting on their own without a partner?
6. Do parents pace activities and warn children of changes in activities?
7. Do parents use positive reinforcement of appropriate behaviour and choices?

8. Are parents overly punitive with these children?
9. Do parents manage tantrums appropriately and do they use time-outs to help calm their children rather than as punishment?
10. Have parents developed coping strategies to help themselves when they become exhausted or overwhelmed by their children?
11. Do parents have informal supports available, such as family and friends who can help them in their parenting? Are parents able to ask for and accept this assistance when they require it?
12. Do parents take time for the other children in the family so they do not devote all their energies to children with difficult temperaments? Do they have resources and supports that allow them to do this, perhaps using alternate caregivers to look after their children who are temperamentally difficult?
13. Do the parents have difficult temperaments themselves and how have they learned to cope?
14. Has the family sought professional assistance and was it helpful?

Alcohol- and Drug-Impacted Children

Children exposed to the effects of alcohol or drugs prior to birth can be profoundly affected. Depending on the extent of the effects, parental awareness of these problems and specialized parenting are necessary to optimize children's progress. Given the ubiquitous use of alcohol in most Western societies, it is common for some children referred in parenting assessments to be affected in either subtle or obvious ways. Hence we must always inquire about maternal alcohol and drug use during pregnancy and identify any sequelae. Because some of these children have significant problems, they often have been seen by other professionals before a referral was made for a parenting assessment. It is necessary to access this information, explore the issue with parents, and formally evaluate the child, as well as exploring ongoing alcohol and drug usage by parents. This risk factor will be addressed in Chapter 6.

Although 'alcohol-related neurodevelopmental disorder' is now the more formally accepted name for the difficulties that alcohol-affected children display, the more common name used is *fetal alcohol syndrome* or *fetal alcohol effects*. Fetal alcohol syndrome is a medical diagnosis requiring both physical and functional findings in children and an assumed maternal history of significant alcohol consumption in pregnancy. Effects on the fetus depend on various factors, including the amount of alcohol consumed and timing of exposure during fetal development, the additional intake of other substances and drugs, and specific characteristics in both the mother and the child. Dr. Ann Streissguth and her colleagues in Oregon are some of the more prolific researchers and writers in this area. A book often suggested as reading for caregivers is *Fetal Alcohol Syndrome: A Guide for Families and Communities* (Streissguth, 1997). As indicated by the term 'alcohol-related neurodevelopmental disorder,' children's neurological functioning is often affected. This, when combined with other possible medical and functional difficulties, creates lifelong difficulties that range from mild to severe. When difficulties are severe, eventual independence and emancipation are unlikely.

These difficulties can affect children's mastery of all of the stage-salient developmental tasks. While all possible effects will not be mentioned here, it is useful to note that children who have fetal alcohol syndrome or fetal alcohol effects often are born with characteristics that make parenting more challenging. Low birth weight and prematurity are common, and head and chest circumferences are often below average. Infants have difficulty regulating themselves physiologically and are often irritable, have difficulty feeding, and cannot be comforted easily. Fetal alcohol syndrome is anywhere from the first to third most frequent cause of mental retardation (Behnke & Eyler, 1993). Attention, memory, language, intellectual, and learning problems become apparent during school years, as do difficulties with abstraction and time and number perception. As children get older, difficulties with motor and impulse control, social judgment, peer relationships, and planning are evident. Given these deficits, children often experience their most pronounced difficulties in adolescence, with many encountering problems with the criminal justice system (Streissguth, 1997). As this brief list indicates, problems can emerge in many skill areas and at many ages. Parental responses can help these children, even though basic neurological and psychological deficits do not disappear. It is critical for parents and caregivers to recognize difficulties, identify problems, intervene, and obtain support as early as possible. For example, parents may need to ensure their infants are not overstimulated through touching or overexposure to sights and sounds. With older children, it is necessary to establish clear and predictable limits and expectations that are accompanied by activities and specialized services to enhance the development of various skills.

Many children are exposed to nicotine, caffeine, and various other drugs (illegal and prescription) prior to birth. Children exposed to illegal drugs such as cocaine also experience significant negative effects. They may have characteristics similar to alcohol-affected infants such as low birth weight and small head circumference, and they are at risk for strokes and seizures. They also may have various deformities in limbs and other body systems, although no consistent pattern of congenital abnormalities has been identified (Behnke & Eyler, 1993). Children with prenatal exposure to opiates can experience symptoms of withdrawal if their mothers used drugs actively just prior to giving birth. Irritability, sleep problems, and continuous crying are common (Kenner & D'Apolito, 1997), all of which make caring for these infants difficult. They do not calm easily, and they require environments with low sensory stimulation. For example, the cuddling and rocking that calms most infants heightens rather than lowers the distress of these infants. As drug-exposed infants develop, they may encounter difficulties with coordination, language, thinking, distractibility, and learning, again necessitating early recognition and intervention (Kenner & D'Apolito, 1997).

Given these profound impacts on children and subsequently on parenting requirements, it is always critical to inquire about maternal use of drugs or alcohol during pregnancy, even with high-functioning parents who are involved in custody/access cases. In child welfare cases, parents require thorough interviews and collateral checks regarding substance use as well as careful examination of children for such effects. In foster/adoption cases, complete developmental histories and examination of children contribute significantly to the identification of potential problems and the development of support plans for children and their caregivers. In these cases one must carefully canvass foster and adoptive parents to explore their understanding of the children's problems and the coping strategies those parents might use. For example, parents of children with fetal alcohol or drug-related effects must be aware that these children require strong structure and schedules in their lives, beginning at a very early age. Language and directions must be concrete, broken into small steps, and repeated frequently. Parents must also recognize that, generally, these children are not deliberately malicious. As children begin to associate with peers and attend school, parents need to provide more supervision than they would for the average child: because of their difficulties with social perception and judgement, such children easily get into dangerous situations where they might be exploited or hurt. Parents must also recognize that they may need to advocate for specialized schooling and provide extra academic support and practice at home than they would with the average child. Frequent consultation with teachers and various medical and psychological professionals is likely necessary. Given such uneven and delayed development, parents may have to be involved in active parenting for many more years than is usually expected; in severe cases children never achieve independence, and parents must provide for them on a long-term basis.

The importance of recognizing the impact of these difficulties in parenting assessments is exemplified in the following child welfare case characterized by fetal alcohol syndrome in mother and children and ongoing maternal drug and alcohol abuse. The written parenting assessment report that was produced regarding this case can be found in Appendix D.

CASE 5: When Patty was eight years of age, child welfare personnel requested a parenting assessment to determine if Patty and her one-year-old brother, Gary, should be permanently removed from the care of her mother, Mary, aged thirty-four years. Mary and the two children were assessed, although the children's fathers had disappeared and were not evaluated. Mary participated begrudgingly in assessment sessions with the hope the children would be returned to her from foster care. Patty was an extremely needy child who displayed various learning, attention, and behaviour difficulties. She had already repeated a grade in school. Mary reported a significant history of both heroin and alcohol use during her pregnancy with Patty and of alcohol and prescription drug use during her pregnancy with Gary. Mary said she had difficulty 'bonding' with Patty when she was a baby and had placed her daughter with a religious order for a short period. In contrast, she felt closer to Gary and was more attentive to him. During periods of high drug usage, extended family members or foster parents provided care to both children. At referral, the children were in foster care for the second time in just over a year.

Patty's problems were intensifying due to ongoing instability in her life. She had been sexually abused during drunken parties in her home, her family had moved several times, and she did poorly in school and at home. As she grew older, her deficits became more apparent. Mary was not equipped to recognize or respond to her needs or those of Gary, who was also evidencing various delays. On referral to a pediatric geneticist, he and Patty were diagnosed with fetal alcohol syndrome. Mary's personal history and pattern of deficits suggested she likely had fetal alcohol effects, although she was not medically assessed for this disorder. Even so, Mary was engaging, verbal, and well intentioned during the parenting assessment. It was clear she took adequate physical care of the children when she was not actively using alcohol and drugs, but she provided minimal and unsafe care when she used substances. Furthermore, over approximately the previous fourteen years she had attempted many treatment programs without any long-term success.

During the assessment it was clear that Patty cared about her mother even though Mary did not appear to be particularly fond of her. It was also evident that Mary could not rear Patty to adulthood, and despite Mary's closer bond to Gary, it was unlikely she could rear him to adulthood. Both children required specialized parenting, given the increasing evidence of multiple problems they displayed. The assessor recommended the children be removed permanently from Mary's care with continued periodic supervised access until adoptive placement.

Over the next year, Mary saw her children several times. Patty enjoyed these contacts, which stopped when she and her brother were placed in adoptive homes. Unfortunately, Patty could not tolerate this placement due to attachment and emotional issues. Also, the adoptive parents could not cope with both the symptoms stemming from Patty's fetal alcohol syndrome and the sequelae that emerged due to many years of unreliable care. However, Gary's adoptive parents coped well with his difficulties. Patty maintained some contact with Gary but did not resume contact with Mary, who soon died of medical complications related to alcoholism.

Given the seriousness of Patty's difficulties, child welfare personnel and her therapist expected she might never assume full independence as an adult. Long-term plans included the maintenance of relationships with extended family members and training geared towards supported living and work placements.

This example illustrates the importance of identifying difficulties such as fetal alcohol syndrome, but it also highlights the value of using a multi-factorial model in parenting assessments. Not only did these children have ongoing difficulties and unique needs that placed even more demands on parents; maternal and contextual factors played an equally significant role in the parenting they received. Contextual factors, particularly the willingness of extended family members to offer alternate care in difficult times, likely made it possible for Mary to maintain custody as long as she did. The children's placement with their mother became impossible when extended family members refused to support Mary any longer.

The following questions may help to determine whether parents can meet the needs of **alcohol and drug-impacted** children:

1. Have the children been identified as having difficulties due to maternal misuse of alcohol or drugs during pregnancy?
2. What types of alcohol or drugs were taken, at what dosage, and at what frequency?
3. How have the children been affected and what is the parents' understanding of these problems?
4. What were the children like as infants and how did parents cope with them? Can parents accurately describe their children's past or current characteristics, especially given the parents' drug usage?
5. What further problems have become evident and what strategies have parents developed to help their children cope?
6. What services and supports do parents access to help their children? Do they actively advocate for services, accept only what is offered, or refuse services?
7. Do parents realize their children have organically based brain damage or do they view them as deliberately misbehaving?
8. Do parents provide a structured home consistently or do expectations and rules change unpredictably?
9. Do parents use concrete and practical language when talking with their children?
10. Do parents break directions into small steps and focus on life skills?
11. Do parents provide extra supervision to their children?
12. Do parents provide extra homework support and study time?
13. Do parents demean their children's poor skills and judgment rather than focusing on their strengths?
14. Do parents have realistic long-term expectations regarding their children's abilities to manage independently?

Mental Retardation and Developmental Disorders

Children affected by either mental retardation or various pervasive developmental disorders such as autism and Asperger's Disorder impose more demands on their parents. While parenting evaluations involving such children are not yet that common, they may become more frequent because young children with such difficulties are no longer routinely placed in long-term care institutions. Often, children are cared for at home unless parents place them for adoption. Voluntary adoptive placement is most likely if mental retardation is obvious at birth and if parents feel they cannot cope with the expected difficulties. However, the deficits in some children are not immediately apparent, becoming evident only as the children acquire language and begin to socialize with peers. For example, in children with Asperger's Disorder, speech may have only a marginally late onset. However, the children then use language in a qualitatively different manner, being pedantic and one-sided in their communications (Attwood, 1998). Later, the children may encounter pronounced difficulties in social interaction, displaying limited empathy and marked problems in forming friendships (Attwood, 1998). Their intense absorption in certain subjects and poor abilities to communicate nonverbally impede participation in peer relationships, as do sometimes clumsy and ill-coordinated movements and odd physical postures (Attwood, 1998).

Mild mental retardation or borderline intellectual functioning is frequently an issue in child welfare cases, as many of these children have experienced significant neglect that may negatively affect cognitive functioning. Also, head trauma from physical assaults can result in organically based difficulties in cognitive functioning. Regardless of etiology, these children often exhibit unique needs that contribute significantly to difficulties in parenting and generate family stress. Hodapp and Zigler (1995) offer an excellent review of the difficulties presented by children with mental retardation; their review is based on a developmental psychopathology perspective.

Although children with mental retardation and various developmental disorders almost uniformly require more energy and parenting expertise, the intensity of the demands upon parents depends upon the etiology and the children's individual characteristics. According to Hodapp and Zigler (1995), the issue is not one of quantitative differences when compared to normal children: children vary in their rates of development, patterns of strengths and weaknesses, and the nature of accompanying medical difficulties. Rather, mental retardation and pervasive developmental disorders generally alter how capably children master all of the stage-salient tasks. When such deficits and disorders are severe, they may render impossible complete emancipation in late adolescence.

Hodapp and Zigler (1995) reported that mothers of mentally retarded children tend to be more didactic and initiate interaction with their children more often. These behaviours likely result from both the children's unwillingness to interact and the mothers' anxiety, and may reflect parental attempts to meet their children's needs. As many parents worry intensely about the fate of these children, they attempt to teach skills more actively and are more controlling in an effort to protect them. Developmentally disabled children have a greater need for routine, repetition, and prompts, become more highly dependent on adults, look to others to solve their problems, and generally expect less success and enjoy problem-solving less frequently than most children. Parents may compensate for these characteristics, and assessors must carefully inquire regarding parents' understanding of their children's disabilities and the steps they take to encourage more independence and mastery. In assessments, we must determine if parents encourage the development of practical daily living skills congruent with children's abilities. Problems exist if parents do everything for their children and do not provide them with opportunities to function more independently. Interviews with parents should also explore their progress with mourning the loss of 'perfect' children and their perceptions of their children's futures. For example, it is common for mothers of mentally retarded children to experience some level of depression, and concerns arise if this depression makes parenting difficult or impossible (Hodapp & Zigler, 1995). Finally, it is critical to inquire about the impact of mentally retarded children on the marital dyad, siblings, and the family as a whole, evaluating how parents manage these stresses.

A necessary component of the parenting assessment is the evaluation of the children and a determination of their idiosyncratic needs. Given that these children have greater needs for more intense teaching, interaction, supervision, and possibly medical care, we must examine parental resources for providing such care at home. This includes parents having the necessary physical health and energy to provide extra physical care, as well as the emotional health and energy to cope with long-term and often intense demands. Furthermore, parents require financial resources to suitably equip their homes and vehicles when children have physical problems and to afford necessary support services, such as babysitting and various therapeutic interventions. This evaluation of parental resources applies to both birth parents and foster and adoptive parents. It is necessary to evaluate parents' abilities to work with other specialized systems in the community, such as schools, speech pathologists, psychologists, and occupational therapists. This involvement requires both energy and adequate financial resources, often for many years. Parents do not always anticipate the intensity of these demands and can become worn out. For example, severely mentally and physically handicapped children, although unable to care for themselves, can be physically managed relatively easily when they are small. This changes during adolescence, when even routine chores such as bathing, diapering, and transport require significant physical exertion from often aging parents. Parents' plans for coping with these demands need to be evaluated.

When one is assessing parents' capacity to meet the needs of children with **mental retardation** and **developmental disorders**, the following questions arise:

1. Do the children appear to be mentally retarded or have a developmental disorder?
2. Have these difficulties been formally diagnosed?
3. How do the problems affect the children's daily functioning?
4. Do parents provide adequate safety and medical attention?
5. How do parents understand the children's strengths and weaknesses, and do they have reasonable expectations that are congruent with the children's abilities?
6. Do parents encourage children to undertake tasks independently within their capacity, choosing appropriate activities that ensure some success for their children?
7. Do parents criticize and berate their children when they cannot do various activities?
8. Do parents overcompensate and do everything for their children?
9. Do parents help their children benefit from available therapeutic services by ensuring both attendance and home practice?
10. Do parents both have access to and utilize family and community supports to maintain their energy, and do they devote time and attention to their spouses and other children?

11. Are the parents depressed regarding their child's condition, and does this interfere with provision of adequate parenting?
12. Have parents mourned the loss of 'normal' children and accepted their children as they are?
13. Do parents have a long-term care plan for their children?

Medical Problems

Concerns arise in parenting assessments when caregivers are unwilling or unable to recognize medical concerns and cannot provide the physical care required to keep children healthy. Although Bursch and Vitti (1999) specifically address the custody/access assessment context, they offer a good review of research findings and issues for assessors to consider when children have chronic medical problems. They specifically address factors affecting the use of health services and treatment adherence.

While assessors cannot be aware of all the possible medical problems that afflict children, they must inquire about both routine and unusual medical conditions, seeking information specific to the management of particular medical problems. For example, parents of children with juvenile-onset diabetes must become expert at dietary and exercise programming and stress management if their children are to remain healthy. They may also need to learn to give insulin injections and to monitor blood sugar levels, as few young children can carry out these critical tasks independently. However, parents must then relinquish this control as children get older. Furthermore, parents need to understand and support their children's psychological adaptation to such diseases, and they must manage their own emotional reactions. These include a sense of loss regarding their children's good health and apprehension regarding medical emergencies. For example, adolescence is a particularly trying time for parents of diabetic children because many adolescents feel invincible and consequently may take a cavalier attitude to the management of their disease, including regulation of insulin levels.

Assessors must also recognize when normal behaviours in young children become problematic as they get older, necessitating medical attention. For example, wetting and soiling are expected of infants and toddlers but become problematic if they continue well beyond the typical age for toilet training. Continued problems could suggest parental negligence if parents avoid medical and/or psychological consultation, as occurred with Randy (Case 3), who was not fully toilet trained at eleven years old. His mother had treated him very harshly around this issue, making him sleep in the bathtub wrapped in a urine-soaked quilt. She felt he was deliberately being bad, thought this punishment would make him 'smarten up,' and did not seek medical consultation. Once he entered a foster home, Randy was medically examined and placed on mineral-oil supplements and a high-fibre diet for the encopresis. These medical interventions were combined with regular bathroom habits and medication to reduce enuresis. Significant improvements followed when foster parents took reasoned steps to explore and respond to Randy's problems. They did not take his behaviour as a personal affront, easing the situation considerably.

Concerns also emerge in assessments if parents are so preoccupied with medical problems that they overcompensate and overprotect children. For example, parents may worry so excessively about seizures or allergies that they never let children participate in various physical activities. While supervision of play and appropriate safety gear such as helmets are required, parents must balance safety concerns with supporting children to develop skills, independence, and a sense of competence. This is a difficult task that generates considerable stress in parents and families.

As medically fragile children are often ill, sometimes critically, living with them can alter the lifestyle of families and affect other children in the home. Parents must deal with their own emotions and the ill children's feelings and adaptation to disease, and they must help siblings understand the medical problems without worrying them unduly. Parents must also have sufficient energy to devote attention to siblings, even if this involves the use of respite care for medically fragile children. The potential impact on family functioning also varies depending upon whether children have chronic problems or acute difficulties that resolve relatively quickly. With the former, children might remain dependent for years.

Finally, assessors need to be aware of a rare condition where parents actually create physical symptoms and illness in their children, give fraudulent medical histories, or alter medical samples (e.g., putting blood in a child's urine sample), resulting in needless and harmful medical investigations and treatments and repeated hospitalizations. Bursch and Vitti (1999) offer a good review of the behaviours and considerations necessary to identify Munchausen syndrome by proxy as well as guidelines for psychotherapy for these parents. This fascinating problem may present in child welfare cases because children can be clearly at risk in such circumstances and may require removal from parental care. Considerable consultation among medical personnel and other professionals is required to determine the presence of Munchausen Syndrome by proxy (Bursch & Vitti, 1999). In these situations assessors need to access information from medical personnel and seriously consider this possibility in arriving at their recommendations.

In order to determine if parents are adequately caring for their children with **medical problems**, the following questions require answers:

1. Are medical problems exacerbated by or the result of parents' failure to provide basic medical care, such as where parents fail to comply with the recommended treatment regimen for a child diagnosed with cancer?
2. Did parents recognize initial symptoms and seek medical consultation in a timely manner?
3. Do parents bring their children to required medical appointments?
4. Do parents understand the children's medical problems and what they must do to support treatment recommendations? When they do not, is this because of cognitive and learning problems?
5. Do parents comply with treatment procedures at home as recommended by medical personnel?
6. Do parents have the finances to obtain appropriate medicines and other medical materials needed in the treatment of their children?
7. Are parents overprotective, maintaining children in a 'sick' or 'invalid' role?
8. Do parents take steps to reduce the risk of children developing medical problems or crises when they are not directly supervising them, as where they must educate other caretakers about the children's problems, such as dietary restrictions for diabetes, and where caretakers must provide appropriate medication as needed?
9. Have parents tried to help their children to adapt psychologically to their disease or medical problem? (Assessors must realize this is often an overwhelming task for higher functioning families, let alone some families in the child welfare system.)

10. Have parents resolved their own issues regarding their children's loss of health or mobility, particularly if the problems will have long-lasting impact on the children's functioning? How do these unresolved feelings and issues affect parenting?
11. Do parents have sufficient energy to relate to their spouses and to parent other children in the family, using respite care and outside services as necessary?
12. Have parents developed a long-term care plan for those older children whose medical problems are so severe and chronic that complete autonomy as an adult will be impossible?
13. Has Munchausen syndrome by proxy been considered in cases where children have presented for repeated investigations and procedures for medical problems that puzzle medical personnel?

Attention and Learning Problems

Attention Problems

Many children have varying degrees of attention and learning problems. These may have little impact on children's functioning and there may be no need for specialized input, or the children may require significant alterations in parenting practices. Attention and learning problems often occur together or are co-morbid with many other problems such as conduct disorders. Parental understanding of such difficulties and interventions to support their children are critical for their youngsters' growth and development. There is considerable debate regarding the nature of attention problems and the need for medical treatment in particular. Much has been written in the popular press and other media, and it is common for assessors and parents to hold strong views about the need for diagnosis and treatment with stimulant medications, such as Ritalin or Dexadrine. As an assessor, one must be aware of recent scientific findings and treatment modalities so that one can evaluate children as objectively and accurately as possible.

Assessors always need to inquire about the existence of attention problems. Barkley (1998) has written a useful handbook on attention deficit hyperactivity disorder (ADHD); assessors might also find Brown (2000) informative. Table 4.1 presents some of the characteristics of children with ADHD. For many children, difficulties are evident early

Table 4.1
Characteristics and Parenting Needs of Children with Attention Deficit Hyperactivity Disorder

Primary symptoms: inattention; behavioural disinhibition or impulsiveness; hyperactivity; deficient rule-governed behaviour; greater variability in task performance

Presentation: apparent in early childhood; chronic; not due to gross neurological, sensory, or language impairment, mental retardation, or severe emotional problems

Daily functioning influenced by:
- Demands of setting – more difficulty when behavioural inhibition is required, such as in school, team play, games
- Physiological factors such as fatigue, sensory stimulation
- Nature of how directions are provided – best with short directions that are broken into steps
- Nature of behavioural consequences – best with frequent and immediate reinforcement

Daily parenting needs:
- Predictable routines and expectations
- Clear and concise directions with cues and reminders
- Immediate and frequent feedback and positive reinforcement
- Focus on positive behaviour – not only on negative behaviour
- Effective strategies to manage children's frustration and anger
- Effective strategies to manage parent's frustration
- High energy

Broader parenting needs:
- Consultation with medical and school personnel, including making sound judgments about medication issues
- Responding to complaints from children and adults in the community
- Educating others about how best to respond to their children
- Emotional support from others, opportunity for respite, availability of effective babysitters

in life, but for others problems become more apparent once they enter a structured educational situation. If attention problems exist, one must undertake closer scrutiny of parent's abilities to respond to these difficulties. However, children may respond differently to each of their parents, given the various demands parents place on their youngsters and the different roles they assume in caring for them. One parent may encounter considerable difficulty in managing a child while the other experiences fewer problems because of different parenting styles or because he or she is in charge of different aspects of the child's life. For example, a parent who needs to get a child through morning routines and homework may encounter many more difficulties than the other parent, who has responsibility for taking the child to dance lessons.

Parenting children with ADHD can be exhausting, especially when parents must balance the needs of these children with siblings' needs and the busy lives that some families lead. Parents must often cope with guilt when others in the community complain about their children and blame the parents for their children's misbehaviour. Parents of children with ADHD must also help their children to better understand their problems, manage their frustration, and engage in activities that enhance an ongoing sense of competence and mastery. These demands are more difficult during adolescence, when teenagers are less open to adult direction and support while simultaneously needing to cope with more complex social and academic expectations and to accept more responsibility for their behaviour. In contrast to previous thinking, ADHD does not appear to disappear with time, although many teenagers and adults learn to cope and function well in their daily lives. Demands on parents can be compounded if siblings and parents also have ADHD. When parents have learned to cope well with their own attention problems, they may serve as excellent role models for their children, especially by teaching them effective strategies the parents have successfully employed. If parents are not coping well with their own ADHD, they may well struggle with providing an optimal or even adequate milieu for their children.

Cases where children have ADHD are seldom simple and easy. Diagnosis is difficult. For example, many children in child welfare cases display apparent symptoms of ADHD. Assessors must be careful to ensure that this is truly the case, because such inattentive behaviours might be due to other factors such as preoccupation with violence at home or lack of adequate food and sleep. Additionally, many children often have comorbid disorders, such as learning disabilities. We must be particularly alert when parents ignore repeated concerns raised by school personnel regarding poor attention and hyperactivity in the classroom. Although the diagnostic process is long and involved and interventions are complicated, parental disregard for others' opinions and such comments as 'It is not an issue. They are just like me and I survived' raise real concern. Of course, we must ascertain whether such assertions are defensive in nature, occurring because parents feel judged or are socially uncomfortable in forums such as school meetings. Parents must help identify the exact nature of the difficulties and then help children develop coping strategies. However, it is also problematic if parents consult a myriad of professionals until they find one who tells them what they want to hear. For example, some parents are adamant that they want medication for their child and will consult many professionals until they find a supportive opinion. Parents must gain accurate knowledge about ADHD and be critical of the opinions they are offered, questioning professionals to clearly understand the reasons for the diagnosis and the recommended treatment plans.

While parents can do a great deal to help children cope with ADHD, assessors must be aware of the contribution other parenting practices make to children's adjustment. This is not an easy task, but a detailed developmental history does much to ascertain whether children's inattentiveness is exacerbated by parenting practices. For example, children with ADHD require structure and predictable routines, and directions that are broken into steps and are given only after the adult has the child's attention. These children may also require a calm, distraction-free environment in order to focus on tasks such as homework. Parents who raise their youngsters in chaotic and neglectful homes may exacerbate their children's ADHD because the children have little parental support to help them learn to modulate their attention and behaviour. Definite answers sometimes emerge only after children are removed from parental care and placed in remedial living and school situations. At other times, the answers are unclear, and parents and professionals must develop a comprehensive intervention program without a definitive opinion regarding etiology.

Learning Problems

As mentioned above, attention problems often coexist with learning problems that can create apparent distractibility because children cannot understand or learn certain information. The presence of learning difficulties must therefore be explored, although assessors need not themselves be expert in undertaking learning assessments. Instead, they must be aware of the difficulties associated with learning disabilities and be able to access and understand information provided by others who have assessed and diagnosed children. This may include having an understanding of neuropsychology, given the possibility that some children display specific brain dysfunction. In particular, assessors need a good appreciation of the particular needs of specific children. When children have not been diagnosed but parents and school personnel report significant difficulties, formal evaluation should be considered in order to elucidate the nature of these problems and offer recommendations regarding intervention. Formal assessment is critical when parents disregard professional concerns or when two parents have widely opposing views of their children's problems. Assessment of potential learning disabilities may be an essential part of preplacement work in adoption, as prospective parents must be aware of the high demands their children may place upon them and the school system. In parenting assessments of foster parent applicants, the prospective parents must be appraised of necessary diagnostic and follow-up appointments. Even if questions about attention and learning problems do not arise, we should explore parents' awareness of children's learning styles. Many children have preferred ways of learning, and the ability to describe these styles may be representative of overall parent sensitivity and another reflection of parents' capacity to meet their children's unique needs.

Although professionals agree that learning disabilities are a significant problem in children, they often disagree in how they conceptualize, assess, and treat these difficulties. The APA *Diagnostic and Statistical Manual of Mental Disorders* (4th ed.) (1994) lists four learning disabilities: reading disorder, mathematics disorder, disorder of written expression, and learning disorder not otherwise specified. It also describes diagnostic criteria of a motor skills disorder and several communication disorders. Learning disabilities are diagnosed according to the following general criteria: (1) achievement levels in specific areas are significantly below levels expected given the child's chronological age, measured intelligence, and age-appropriate education; and (2) the disturbance interferes significantly in school performance or use of educational skills in everyday life. Thus children with moderate mental retardation would not be diagnosed with specific learning disabilities because their skills are commensurate with their measured ability levels.

Unless children exhibit significant language or motor difficulties when they are very young, they are usually not diagnosed with learning disabilities until they have begun formal schooling. Furthermore, unless the difficulty is pronounced, parents are usually encouraged to give children several months or years of school experience before formal assessment is initiated. This is typically prudent advice because children must be given some time to adapt to classroom demands rather than being immediately labelled as having learning disabilities. However, children can be harmed by experiencing repeated failures that generate feelings of frustration, low self-esteem, and, sometimes, behaviour problems in the classroom, making assessment and intervention more complex. For example, children may become anxious about their poor classroom performance and develop strong avoidance strategies. Assessment must tease apart the influence of learning disabilities and avoidance strategies, and treatment may need to address the avoidance before the disabilities can be properly remediated. Consequently, parents must voice concerns and advocate for assessment early on in their children's school careers. Parents also have the difficult task of setting appropriate expectations and supporting children as they try to cope with frustration and failure. Many parents want to help children by doing homework for them, but this is detrimental because their children do not learn to apply alternate learning strategies. Parents and teachers must help children to understand their disabilities and develop the motivation and drive necessary to use remedial strategies. For parents to do this, they must have at least some understanding of the learning problems and have the energy, motivation, and skills to help their youngsters. This is particularly so if children have multiple problems.

Many of the points we have raised above in regard to ADHD also apply to situations where children have learning difficulties and to the strategies we have already described. Parents must help children use remedial strategies during homework periods so the latter develop the confidence to persevere when frustrated. Self-confidence can be enhanced when parents encourage children's participation in other activities that build on their areas of interest and strength. Additionally, parents often must consult with various professionals and work closely with school personnel. If parents can intervene and support youngsters to develop good habits and self-confidence early on, as adolescents they may better cope with school frustration. If learning disabilities are identified during adolescence, when teenagers are often more unwilling to accept direct parental help with homework, parents may need to arrange for tutoring at school or through other avenues. When we are attempting to ascertain the needs of children with learning disabilities, it is important to ascertain the specific nature of the difficulties. This is undertaken by direct evaluation of children or through consultation with others who have already assessed them. It may also be useful to explore learning difficulties in the extended family. Similar difficulties in parents or siblings may sensitize parents to these issues and augment their abilities to support children, or may engender even more stress. Both of these situations existed in the following case, where a father initially denied difficulties but then strongly supported his son to master significant learning and attention problems.

CASE 6: Martha was referred for a parenting assessment when school personnel raised concerns about a neglectful home environment with child welfare authorities. At the age of seven years, Martha's son, Paul, had exhibited many problems in Grade 2. He was often out of control behaviourally, could not settle enough to complete school work, did not read, and soiled his pants daily. Martha functioned at a low level intellectually and socially. She also displayed significant psychiatric problems, and both Paul and his nine-year-old sister, Amanda, were considered at significant risk for ongoing neglect in her home. Martha could not recognize or respond to Paul's multiple needs. During the assessment, Paul clearly displayed ADHD symptoms, a severe reading disability, and emotional problems. He had daily temper tantrums, was aggressive with peers at home and school, smoked cigarettes he stole from his mother, and often did not come in until late in the evening. Amanda performed adequately at school but seemed to bear too much responsibility in the home: she cooked the meals and took care of her mother and brother.

When it was evident to Martha that she could not care for her children, she asked that they be placed with Paul Sr., her estranged husband. He had married a woman named Bertha, and this couple's capacity to parent Paul and Amanda was subsequently evaluated. Paul Sr. and Bertha had been together for five years and parented Bertha's teenage children. The family lived on public assistance, as Paul Sr. could not hold a steady job. He had been volatile and irritable when he worked as a janitor. He had occasional contact with Paul and Amanda but had not actively parented them for many years. He blamed Martha for Paul's difficulties and had relatively high expectations of Paul, asserting that the boy should just work harder at school. The results of the psychological testing revealed that Paul Sr. had a marked attention deficit disorder and a significant reading disability. He was illiterate and avoided jobs and situations where he needed to read. After displaying some initial defensiveness, Paul Sr. acknowledged these difficulties and those of his son. Despite rather low and rigid functioning, he accepted help from Bertha in filling out job application forms and enrolled in adult literacy courses. He also accepted some help and guidance regarding his parenting skills when he regained custody of his two children. He became Paul's strong supporter and modelled the perseverance required to confront significant learning difficulties. Paul Sr. agreed to medication for his son that subsequently improved Paul's capacity to concentrate, but he refused to take it himself.

Since the parenting demands presented by children with attention and learning problems have some similarities, the following questions help identify whether parents are dealing adequately with their children's **attention and learning problems**:

1. Do the children appear to have attention problems or significant learning problems?
2. When were concerns raised and by whom?
3. Have attention and learning problems been formally diagnosed and did parents facilitate this process? What is the specific nature of the problems?
4. Do parents understand their children's difficulties and frustrations or do they dismiss them?
5. Have parents followed through with recommended medical and/or behavioural interventions?
6. With attention problems, do parents manage their children's behaviour appropriately or do their parenting practices compound the children's difficulties?
7. Do children exhibit less difficult behaviour with one parent, and what are the factors contributing to this differential response?
8. Do parents work cooperatively with school personnel to facilitate their children's adaptation to this setting, or do they appear to undermine the efforts of professionals?
9. Do parents support children in using remedial strategies during homework periods, or do they overcompensate and do the homework for their children?
10. Do parents set appropriate expectations for school achievement?
11. Do parents support their children in developing other areas of interest and strength, such as sports and hobbies?

12. If other family members have attention problems or learning disabilities, do they model appropriate attitudes and coping strategies that encourage children to persevere rather than give up?

5 Child Factors: Specific Life Events and Parenting Needs

In our previous discussions of developmental variations that require extraordinary parenting practices, sensitivity, and knowledge, it was apparent that these conditions can have a significant impact on children's mastery of stage-salient tasks and engender frustration and inadequacy in affected children. Even with strong support from parents, siblings, and others, some children develop secondary emotional difficulties. For example, depression is common in adolescents with fetal alcohol syndrome (Streissguth, 1997). This is not surprising; it is intensely frustrating for children and teenagers affected with such conditions to experience repeated failures despite their best efforts and intentions. The likelihood of secondary emotional difficulties increases if parents are not sensitive, responsive, and supportive. Parents must recognize difficulties, obtain help as needed, and respond appropriately in daily interactions with their children.

Of course, emotional problems are not always a reaction to developmental, cognitive, or physical disabilities. Children have mental health problems as a function of life stresses and adverse events, such as maltreatment. We must always inquire about parental concerns regarding children's emotional health. It is important to ask about the time of onset of these concerns, what precipitated them, and the steps parents have taken to help children. In order to evaluate the validity of parent concerns, we must complete thorough evaluations about the specific nature of these difficulties using a variety of assessment methods. If other consultants and therapists are involved, their observations should be considered.

Since the range of children's emotional difficulties is broad, this chapter does not review specific emotional disorders, diagnostic categories, or treatment modalities. Instead, it reviews several life experiences associated with emotional sequelae, such as child abuse and neglect, adoption, and family separation and divorce. These experiences often surface in the lives of children whose parents are undergoing parenting assessments. The following sections describe the known impact of these events on children and the key factors that support adaptation. The latter is critical, as assessors must determine if parents are appropriately supporting their children. Given that children display varying abilities to cope with similar adverse life events, the chapter ends with a discussion of resiliency factors that influence children's coping capacities.

Child Abuse and Neglect

Some of the most complex and demanding specialized parenting needs children can present are those arising from physical, emotional, and sexual abuse and physical neglect, especially if the maltreatment has been severe and chronic. In an earlier volume, we offer a comprehensive review of the impact of abuse and neglect on children's development, as well as assessment and intervention strategies (Pearce & Pezzot-Pearce, 1997). Table 5.1 summarizes these psychological and developmental problems associated with maltreatment. In examining this table, it is critical to note that not all maltreated children exhibit these effects: maltreated children are a heterogeneous group, and many factors contribute to children's adaptation to maltreatment.

Attachment organization can be profoundly affected by maltreatment. As noted in Chapter 3, attachment security is directly related to the early parent-child relationship. Unless parents can be helped relatively quickly to respond more sensitively to young children and thereby enhance their security of attachment, children often have difficulty with subsequent developmental tasks. They develop expectations about relationships and then act and react in ways that are congruent with these working models of relationships. For example, some insecurely attached children expect people to respond to them in harsh, disregarding, or unpredictable ways, and subsequently develop strategies (e.g., avoidance or clingy, dependent behaviour) that in turn inhibit exploration of their world and undermine their capacity to relate to other people in an open and trusting manner.

While these strategies seemingly allow maltreated children to cope in the home, they create significant difficulties in other settings. For example, children with an avoidant attachment pattern will ignore

Table 5.1
Known Effects of Abuse and Neglect on Children's Development

Attachment organization:
- Physically abused and neglected children are less likely to develop secure attachments, with estimates ranging as high as 70 % to 100% of infants.
- Maltreated children's attachment security can change over time, with some becoming more secure and some less secure.
- The relation between childhood sexual abuse and attachment security has not been studied empirically.

Emotional and behavioural regulation:
- Higher levels of externalizing problems (aggression and antisocial behaviour) and internalizing problems (depression, anxiety) are exhibited by children who experience various types of maltreatment.
- Increased sexual behaviour is more likely in sexually abused children.
- While some sexually abused and physically abused children exhibit higher rates of post-traumatic stress disorder, it is not shown by the majority of maltreated children.

Development of an autonomous self:
- Maltreated youngsters use fewer words that describe their internal states and feelings and are less likely to talk about negative affect and feelings; maltreated children with insecure attachments are likely to have the most compromised internal state language.
- Maltreated children have more difficulties with developing an autonomous sense of self.
- Maltreated youngsters may develop poor self-esteem over time, although some research evidence suggests these children may exaggerate their sense of competence in early grades, and only in later elementary school do they begin to describe themselves as less competent than their peers.
- Severe maltreatment, particularly severe physical and sexual abuse, has been linked to increased incidence of dissociative disorders such as multiple personality disorder.

Language development:
- Physically abused and neglected children have an increased likelihood of language delays, particularly in expressive language, with those of neglected children being the most severe.
- Maltreated children exhibit less play overall and more repetitive and simplistic play.

Cognitive development and adaptation to school:
- Maltreated children are at risk for decreased levels of cognitive functioning even after children with neurological damage are excluded from research studies.
- Maltreated youngsters have lower levels of academic success and demonstrate more social and behavioural problems in the classroom.
- Findings are least definite for sexually abused children.
- Severe neglect, particularly emotional neglect, may lead to situations of nonorganic failure-to-thrive and psychosocial dwarfism, both conditions where intellectual and academic functioning are compromised; increases in intellectual functioning and

physical growth are possible with removal from the neglectful or abusive environment.

Peer relations:
- Maltreated youngsters exhibit more aggressive interactions with peers, particularly unfamiliar peers, and they may react aggressively in response to both aggression and distress in their peers.
- Maltreated children, including both physically abused and neglected children, demonstrate increased social withdrawal and avoidance.
- Maltreated youngsters tend to be rated as less popular by their peers and exhibit more negative interactions with their peers.

Note: Adapted from Pearce and Pezzot-Pearce (1997, pp. 17–40).

new caregivers, such as foster parents or adoptive parents, because they expect harsh treatment. Unless the new parents understand that children are using this strategy for self-preservation, they might prematurely stop trying to engage a newly placed child in a close relationship. Alternatively, they might overwhelm the child with excessive affection that is too threatening and results in the child's making even more efforts to avoid such intimacy. Children with ambivalent-resistant attachment organizations may present quite differently in foster or adoptive homes, sometimes being dependent and clingy and at other times intensely provocative. Again, unless the new parents understand the underlying reasons, they might become confused or even hurt by the children's behaviours. They might personalize the children's reactions and think they are doing well as parents when the children appear dependent, only to feel betrayed when the children are hurtful and emotionally provocative. Assessors must clearly understand such dynamics, which are evident in many maltreated youngsters, so they can carefully interview prospective parents about their knowledge of children's coping strategies and plans to respond to such difficulties. It can be worrying when foster or adoptive parenting applicants express the attitude that 'love can cure all' without demonstrating any knowledge of these issues. In many cases, assessors may need to make specific recommendations regarding how parents should respond to children with insecure attachments.

As well as assessing foster or adoptive parents' awareness and knowledge base regarding attachment problems, assessors also must frequently evaluate biological parents' abilities to recognize such issues. We must ask parents about their beliefs regarding the reasons for their children's behaviours, perhaps suggesting alternate interpretations to determine if parents have the capacity to understand and respond to their children differently than they have in the past. Parents may personalize their children's problematic behaviours, in part because they contributed significantly to their children's development. Thus assessors must determine whether parents can overcome their guilt and defensiveness in order to acknowledge their children's behaviours and put their children's best interests first, so they can learn to parent differently.

It is important to identify if children have difficulties with **emotional and behavioural self-regulation**, and to examine parents' abilities to help children learn alternate ways to manage their feelings and arousal levels. As Pearce and Pezzot-Pearce (1997) described, abused and neglected children frequently display numerous difficulties in this area through externalizing and internalizing problems. For example, parents of children exhibiting physical aggression or sexualized behaviours must clearly demonstrate a capacity to keep both maltreated children and other children safe, to provide clear guidelines for expected behaviour and consequences for inappropriate behaviour, and to model and teach healthy ways of expressing anger or sexual feelings. Concrete rules such as no unsupervised contact with younger children may be necessary when children present with sexually intrusive behaviour. Parents require a somewhat different skill set when they must help maltreated children with internalizing problems, such as depression and post-traumatic stress disorder. They may need to help identify sources of anxiety; support children in learning anxiety-reduction strategies, such as relaxation and self-talk; and develop concrete routines that help children feel safer and less anxious. Such strategies are often complex and require close work with various therapists and other professionals. Additionally, caregivers often need to support children to use psychotherapy to ameliorate these difficulties. Not only must they ensure children attend therapy sessions regularly, but they may also need to follow through with discussions and behavioural limits at home. Such requirements can be very demanding for parents. Furthermore, their children's participation in psychotherapy may be threatening for those parents whose child-rearing practices likely contributed to the children's difficulties, and who may need to examine their roles. Parents may worry about censure and be hesitant to truly support the child's active participation in sessions, or they may become jealous of the child's growing regard and affection for the therapist. They may need counselling for themselves as well.

As indicated in Table 5.1, maltreated children often display difficulties with their **sense of self** and **internal-state language**. They may have problems labelling their own and other people's feelings, and they often feel incompetent, particularly in later elementary years. In extreme circumstances, children may experience marked disturbances in their sense of self, perhaps using dissociation to cope with overwhelming anxiety and threat. As assessors, we must carefully evaluate whether such problems exist in individual children, and determine if parents can work towards helping children label and understand feelings and develop a sense of self-efficacy. For example, parents need to recognize and build on their children's strengths rather than denigrate them and focus on their weaknesses. If children are dissociating, parents need to recognize this and realize that it is a coping strategy. They can then help their youngsters to rely less on such strategies by acknowledging the abuse, by encouraging them to realistically express their feelings, and by accepting the children's feelings.

Deficits in **receptive and expressive language** and in **play skills** are another common problem. Unless parents are willing and able to recognize difficulties and alter their behaviour to better respond to their children's needs for stimulation, those children's cognitive development may well be jeopardized. This is not to suggest parents must change their parenting in a matter of weeks. Rather, as assessors we want to see parents be willing to acknowledge problems, and we need to determine if they are capable of making the necessary changes.

Since child maltreatment can have disastrous effects on **intellectual development** and **academic performance**, it is critical to evaluate the cognitive and academic status of these children. This is particularly important for those youngsters who have low intellectual functioning, are mentally retarded, or have fetal alcohol syndrome or fetal alcohol effects. Establishing parental understanding of these deficits and willingness to support children in school and social functioning requires careful query. Many of the questions and areas of inquiry outlined throughout Chapters 3 and 4 must be explored.

Peer relations are often problematic, particularly for physically abused and neglected children. Some of these children are physically aggressive in social interactions, while others avoid or withdraw from peer interactions. They are often considered unpopular and have few friends. Assessors must explore the reasons for these behaviours, including the children' internal working models of relationships, and identify the specific actions parents can take to help them, such as discussing appropriate interactions or even role playing so children develop alternate ways of thinking and responding in relationships. Parents also may need to work closely with teachers so children are guided and encouraged to use these new strategies in their daily interactions. Clearly, as assessors we must determine if parents have the capacity to work collaboratively and cooperatively with teaching staff.

Even though the assessment of children will be discussed in Chapter 10, readers are referred to Pearce and Pezzot-Pearce (1997) for a detailed outline regarding how to clinically assess maltreated children. By the end of a parenting assessment, evaluators should know how abused and neglected children express their thoughts and feelings about what has happened to them, how they understand what has happened to them in their family, how they coped with the maltreatment, and what they exhibit in terms of their emotional and psychological needs. Since maltreated children are such a heterogeneous group, each child deserves a comprehensive assessment. Clinicians cannot assume that every maltreated child will demonstrate all of the characteristics presented in Table 5.1. Likewise, parents must be canvassed regarding their perceptions of their children's behaviours and functioning and the steps they have taken to help their children. Parents will need to be able to talk with their children about the maltreatment, acknowledging that the abuse happened and their children's feelings about it. They must effectively manage children's problem behaviours, such as physical aggression and sexually intrusive behaviours as well as anxiety-related symptoms and post-traumatic stress disorder. Parents also need to cooperate with various agencies in the aftermath of disclosure and through the process of treatment.

These supportive behaviours are critical regardless of whether parents just became aware of the maltreatment or witnessed ongoing abuse but were unable to stop it. Recommendations might be very different in cases where parents are insightful but ineffectual as opposed to cases where they have no comprehension of their children's reactions. For example, it is worrisome when a parent strongly asserts that completely indiscriminant social interaction is positive, friendly behaviour. It may be less worrisome when another parent recognizes that such behaviour is inappropriate and places the child at risk for further victimization, but does not know how to stop the child from walking off with strangers. Likewise, foster and adoptive parents must demonstrate some understanding of the difficulties if they are not only to successfully cope with the children's behaviours but also to help them understand and deal with their history of maltreatment. Of course, the evaluation of risk of further maltreatment by parents is a critical task in child welfare cases. Additional factors that may contribute to heightened and lowered risk are discussed in Chapters 6 and 7, and the weighting of these factors is dealt with in Chapter 11.

The following questions can be used to review the needs of maltreated children and parents' ability to meet them:

1. Who is the perpetrator? Were the children abused and/or neglected by the biological parents or by others in their lives, and are these people still active participants in the children's lives?
2. What type of maltreatment occurred and what was its duration and frequency?
3. What, for the children, are the sequelae of the abuse and neglect?
4. What are the children's needs regarding these problems?
5. Do parents and other caregivers recognize these needs and understand why the children behave as they do?
6. Do parents personalize the children's behaviours?
7. Can parents respond appropriately to support their children to cope with their abusive experiences, such as keeping children safe, providing appropriate limits, and verbalizing appropriately with them?
8. Can parents respond appropriately to children's problems with attachment, emotional and behavioural self-regulation, self-esteem, internal-state language, receptive and expressive language, play skills, intellectual development, academic performance, and peer relationships?
9. Are parents supportive of required counselling and other specialized programming?
10. Given the children's current status, is there an ongoing risk of maltreatment by the parents or others in their lives?

Adopted Children

Routes to Adoption

Many adopted children also require specialized care from their parents. Children generally follow one of two routes to adoption. Children who have entered the permanent custody of child welfare authorities due to abuse and neglect follow one route. Since these children have usually been taken away from their parents, they tend to be older than those placed in adoptive homes by biological parents, and only a small number of them are placed with the knowledge and involvement of biological parents. The second route to adoption generally involves newborns or infants placed for adoption by biological parents who have decided they cannot provide adequately for their children. Some ask child welfare agencies to select adoptive homes for their children. Others opt for private adoption and assume a more active role in selecting adoptive parents. In these situations, some birth and adoptive parents maintain communication between themselves, including direct contact between birth parents and adopted children. While most people assume that adoption of a newborn or very young child is apt to be relatively problem free, this is not always the case. Sometimes, significant temperament, learning, attention, medical, and emotional problems develop and engender as much stress for adoptive parents as they do for biological ones. Adopted children in general are at somewhat greater risk for developing psychological problems. For example, Howe (1995) reported that those who are later-adopted with a history of abuse, neglect, and/or multiple placements had increased difficulty forming relationships, displayed indiscriminate behaviour towards others, and had poorer developmental outcomes.

The Importance of Family History

In order to develop a better understanding of adopted children's needs, it is necessary to obtain as comprehensive as possible birth and developmental histories, including various medical, learning, and emotional difficulties in the members of the immediate and extended biological family. Although this information is unavailable in many cases, more detailed histories permit professionals and potential adoptive parents to be aware of some of the specialized needs children might subsequently develop. Prospective adoptive parents must be assessed regarding their willingness and ability to care for such children, and they must be told of the risks associated with accepting for placement children who have little documented information about birth families or early history. For example, such information would have been helpful to Bruce and Karen in the following case.

CASE 7: At twelve years of age, Joseph was brought to therapy by his adoptive parents, Bruce and Karen. He had been with them for one year, and all struggled with his entry into the family. Joseph was withdrawn and showed no interest in the activities in their cultured and academically oriented family. Although Bruce and Karen had two other children, they applied to adopt Joseph after reading about him in a newspaper column. He had lived in foster homes since the age of eight months following his removal from the care of his biological mother, who lived in an isolated rural community. As Bruce and Karen wanted to give Joseph love and opportunities, they were highly disappointed by his lack of interest. They had undergone a brief home study during the adoption application and had the distinct impression that Joseph was placed with them because they were the only family who wanted him. At placement, they were told Joseph needed love because he had been in a foster home with several other children where he did not get much attention. Otherwise, they were given little information, and they were not told what they could expect from him, nor were they given any follow-up support.

Before counselling began, the therapist fully assessed Joseph and found significant learning and attention problems, as well as the presence of severe attachment and emotional difficulties. When his file information finally arrived, his early history was such that many of these problems were quite understandable. It documented neglect and repeated physical and sexual abuse in several of his previous foster homes. Bruce and Karen were appalled when they received this information and realized the depth of Joseph's needs. They said they would not have adopted him had they been fully informed of his history and significant risk of developing serious psychological and emotional problems. Although they attempted to meet his needs over the following year, this time with support, they eventually returned him to the care of the child welfare department. Bruce and Karen, along with their natural children, and Joseph, were saddened by this step.

Detailed information regarding birth families and children's histories is essential at placement, but it also has a secondary benefit when adopted children begin to confront some of the identity issues that later emerge. Adoptive parents can expect many children to ask about their origins throughout childhood, but questions may become more salient and critical during adolescence. Information about birth parents, including even such basic characteristics such as hair and eye colour, height, weight, need for eyeglasses, medical problems, interests, and talents, may be helpful to adopted children; adoptive parents need to be open and share such information as required. During parenting assessments, it is important to determine if applicants are willing to be open about the children's adoptive status and any available historical information. Assessors need to determine whether parents will be able to display a respectful attitude to children about their birth parents; if adoptive parents speak in a degrading manner about biological parents, this may compromise their children's abilities to accept their histories and develop positive feelings about themselves. Steinhauer (1991) reports that adopted children have a somewhat more complicated process of identity formation than do nonadopted children. This process is not necessarily more stressful but depends, in part, on the parents' understanding and support. If parents have openly acknowledged children's adoptive status from their early years and have been open and responsive to questioning, then relationships will be predicated on truthfulness and trust, thereby enhancing development.

Parents' Reasons for Adoption

In all adoption parenting assessments, applicants need to be asked about their reasons for wishing to adopt a child. Winkler, Brown, Van Keppel, and Blanchard (1988) discuss several common motivations, such as the wish to create a close family despite infertility, a desire to provide a permanent family for children who might otherwise remain in institutional or temporary care, a wish to prove to themselves that they can parent well even though they are infertile, a response to family or social pressures, and a need to replace a child that has died. In cases where infertility is a factor in the decision to adopt, Winkler et al. stress that parents need to grieve the loss of their infertility so they can better support adopted children to cope with their own sense of loss. For the adopted child, adoption almost always means a loss of relationships with biological family members, including a loss of roots and genetic identity. If adoptive parents have not mourned their inability to have children biologically – perhaps shown in an inability to discuss infertility and their sense of loss, an outright denial of any sense of loss, or an ongoing preoccupation with infertility – then they may truly have difficulty supporting their children. If infertility is not a reason for adoption, such as in the case where parents want to provide a disadvantaged child with love and opportunities, we must explore their expectations to ensure that potential adoptive parents do not have a naïve and unrealistic view of the challenges they might face. This is especially so when children have come to them with a history of abuse or neglect, as was the case with Bruce and Karen described above.

Adoption Failure Risk Factors

Given their previous negative life experiences and associated problems, children from the child welfare system make vastly higher demands on adoptive parents and placements are at higher risk of failure. In addition to the sequelae of maltreatment, they are usually older at adoption and may have stronger memories of biological parents. Consequently, they may feel disloyal to biological parents when they start feeling comfortable with adoptive parents. It is worrisome when adoptive parents comment negatively on or condemn biological parents because this exacerbates children's loyalty conflicts, which are akin to those experienced by children in separated families when one parent condemns the other.

Steinhauer (1991), in a survey of the research literature, identified several factors that are related to unsuccessful adoption. Child characteristics include a higher number of previous placements, longer periods in care prior to adoption, high levels of aggression, previous diagnoses of conduct disorder, and a strong attachment to biological mothers. Characteristics of adoptive parents that increase risk of placement breakdown include low levels of self-esteem, flexibility, and capacity to manage their own anger, as well as poor relationships with their own parents. Obviously, assessors need to examine such issues as part of any pre-adoption parenting assessment.

International Adoption

Children who have been adopted internationally represent a small proportion of adopted children. They have often been severely neglected and sometimes abused overseas. These children bring another specialized set of needs to their adoptive families, as they have often spent a significant period of time in institutional care. Not only have they often had minimal physical care, but perhaps more importantly, they were probably exposed to limited psychological stimulation. Currently, many international adoptees come from countries such as Romania, Russia, and China. These children exhibit medical problems and delayed growth (Ames, 1997), and many also have difficulties with the childhood tasks outlined in chapter 3. Some children also have difficulties associated with fetal alcohol syndrome if they come from countries where the rate of alcohol consumption is high, such as Russia.

Ames (1997) reviewed outcomes of Romanian orphans adopted into Canada and found generally that early-adopted children (under four months of age at adoption) had fewer long-term problems than those adopted after spending more than eight months in an orphanage. As a result, parents of later-adopted children must attend not only to their children's medical problems, such as parasites and malnourishment, but also to their rather complex and ongoing psychological needs, especially difficulties with attachment. When examined after approximately three years in their adoptive homes, all children who had been adopted after spending eight months or more in an orphanage were found to have formed attachments with their new parents. However, a third displayed secure attachments, a third displayed insecure patterns typical of Canadian-born children, and a third displayed atypical insecure patterns (Ames, 1997). Furthermore, the children with atypical insecure patterns of attachment had lower IQs and more behaviour problems, and their adoptive families had somewhat lower socio-economic status, although differences in income were not large and none of the adoptive families were living in poverty. Ames speculated that, in general, children fared better if families had the emotional and financial resources to respond to their special needs. When extra money was not available, they could not afford the things that would ease the demands of parenting these youngsters, such as high-quality day care. This study suggests that many factors interact to eventually contribute to the adoptee's developmental progress.

Evaluations must assess parents' expectations about these adopted children; their ability to cope with multiple problems, including sufficient financial resources and the availability of supports (both informal, such as family and friends who can babysit, and formal, such as developmental pediatric evaluations and therapy); their capacity to seek such help; and their potential to act as strong advocates so their children can acquire necessary services. The importance of considering child, parent, and support factors in these types of adoptions is evident in the following case.

CASE 8: A preadoption parenting assessment was undertaken for Doug and Nancy, who had applied to adopt a child from Russia. They had debated the risks of overseas adoption for several years after they could not have children following Nancy's surgery for cervical cancer. Both appeared ready for this step, as they had actively sought information about the problems adopted children face, and both appeared to have the emotional and financial resources to provide good parenting to a child from overseas.

They travelled to Russia, to an impoverished orphanage located just outside of Moscow, where they met Sophia, a petite three-year-old with blonde hair and blue eyes, and immediately fell in love with her. They successfully managed several medical problems such as scabies, pinworms, and chronic diarrhea. They immediately had Sophia assessed for fetal alcohol syndrome and were relieved when this proved negative. Sophia learned English relatively quickly and seemed to thrive with them, and they thought their worries were over. Unfortunately, this was not the case. Sophia was always distant with them, and she avoided affection and physical closeness. When distressed, she retreated to her bed or a chair where she rocked and stared blankly. After two years, she sometimes sought out Doug and Nancy if she was hurt, and she tolerated some hugging, but only if initiated by her. Her parents were frustrated by the fact that she spoke indiscriminantly with strangers, sometimes giving them hugs in the shopping mall.

The situation escalated when she entered school; Sophia had difficulties with academic tasks, particularly reading. Although she became a good oral reader, she often did not understand subtle meanings. Even more problematic were her relationships with teachers and peers, as she remained aloof and seemed baffled. Parents sought therapeutic help for Sophia during her kindergarten year, and her therapist found pronounced attachment difficulties. Sophia clearly expected others to either ignore her or react negatively. Even when other children made friendly advances, she thought they disliked her. Therapy with this child challenged her beliefs and expectations in relationships and supported Doug,

Nancy, and Sophia's teachers to do the same. Over the next three years, Sophia's social functioning improved significantly, although in any stressful situation she retreated to her old ways of handling stress. Doug and Nancy worked diligently to address Sophia's learning problems. They received strong support from professionals and nearby members of their extended family and, most important in their view, they had the support of other parents who had adopted children from similar circumstances. They still met with these parents years after the adoption and found that the validation of their experiences and reactions helped them to cope with the challenges they continued to face.

The following questions can guide a review of the needs of **adopted children** and parents' capacities to respond to them:

1. Have parents decided to adopt for appropriate reasons and do they have reasonable expectations about the parenting challenges that they may face?
2. If parents are adopting due to infertility, have they resolved their feelings about this issue?
3. Do parents recognize the added risks of adopting children from overseas?
4. Do parents have the emotional and financial resources and support necessary to parent effectively if their children have significant difficulties?
5. Why have the children become available for adoptive placement? What is their history? Are they infants or are they older children, and do they have histories of abuse or neglect?
6. How many previous moves and placements have the children had?
7. If historical information has not been provided, can this be obtained?
8. Does the history of the biological family and the children's birth and early developmental histories suggest any possible areas of difficulty that might emerge?
9. What problems are already evident in the children's functioning?
10. Do the children still have strong memories of and attachments to biological mothers?

11. When do adoptive parents plan to tell their children they are adopted?
12. Are the adoptive parents willing to consider the involvement of biological parents in their children's lives, providing it is appropriate or even safe? When do parents expect this to happen?

Family Separation and Divorce

Perhaps one of the most disorganizing and emotionally painful events that happens to children is the breakup of their families through separation and divorce. Emotional distress is intensified if children sense the animosity some parents feel towards one another. Children also must learn to divide time between parents, and frequently they must adapt to modified physical and financial circumstances and to the entry of other significant adults into their lives and those of their parents. Children also experience these adjustments when parents are not legally married or when parents are gay or lesbian couples. Given the relatively high current divorce rate, thousands of children must cope with these reactions each year, including many who are involved in the child welfare system. Consequently, assessors need to be aware of the phases of family adaptation and the challenges and reactions children face in the process of adapting to parental separation and family dissolution. This knowledge helps assessors determine whether parents are truly keeping the best interests of the children in mind.

Phases of Adaptation

Over the past quarter century, researchers have focused increasingly on the impact of separation and divorce on children, and much has been published for both professionals and parents. Wallerstein and Corbin (1999) confirm that adjustment to separation and divorce is not an easy or quick process; it can continue for many years, and each stage of adaptation can be brief or lengthy. For example, some families might remain in the initial phase for a long time if one parent unilaterally leaves a relationship, engendering highly intense feelings in the deserted partner that make adaptation more difficult for all family members.

Table 5.2
Sequential Tasks for Children Adapting to Parent Separation and Divorce

1. Acknowledge the reality of the marital rupture
2. Disengage from parental conflict and distress so they can resume usual activities
3. Rework the resolution of losses, including the loss of one parent from the home
4. Resolve their anger and self-blame (sometimes takes several years)
5. Accept the permanence of the divorce
6. Develop some realistic hope regarding relationships

Note: Adapted from Wallerstein (1983, pp. 233–42).

According to Wallerstein and Corbin (1999), separations entail three **phases**:

1. initial acute phase, often lengthy, marked by short-term diminished parenting capacity, during which, some parents develop a short-term dependency on their children
2. transitional phase, in which parents begin to disengage from each other and move into new relationships, and there is some flux in living arrangements, activities, and feelings;
3. stable post-divorce household.

Wallerstein (1983) also offered a useful outline of six tasks children confront over their years of adaptation; these are presented in Table 5.2. An awareness of these tasks can help assessors to determine how children are progressing in resolving issues around the separation of their parents. For example, Wallerstein suggests it is critical for children to master the first two tasks within the first year after separation in order to maintain good academic and developmental progress. Parents might have to facilitate this by putting some of their own feelings aside in order to also acknowledge the breakup and ensure children are not involved in the conflict, perhaps by refusing to fight in front of them.

If parents understand these tasks and actively support their children, they can do much to attenuate the potential negative impact of separation or divorce. Of course, if parents are still lodged in the acute phase of adaptation several years after separation and if children continue to be involved in the parental conflict, especially if they have not resumed their usual interests and activities, there is significant cause for concern. Clinicians can use this model to determine children's and families' progress in adapting to separation and divorce. This was the goal in the following case:

CASE 9: Anna, Mike, and Joyce and their parents, Della and Tyler, were referred three years after the family's breakup. The separation occurred when Tyler left the home following his threatening and physically assaultive behaviour towards Della. While he had not physically abused the children, who were now four, six, and nine years of age, Della worried this would eventually happen. Tyler was unhappy with the separation and tried to reconcile many times, although he actively pursued litigation and made many negative allegations about Della. He believed he was adapting well to the marital breakup and that he responded appropriately to his children's needs. During the assessment, it was evident that Tyler hated Della for rejecting him. He was firmly stuck in the initial crisis phase of adaptation, while Della was progressing and re-establishing a new life without him. However, his continued interference in her life made this difficult. She felt overwhelmed by his intrusive and angry behaviour, and while she did not wish to fight about custody arrangements for the children, she believed she had to defend their best interests. The assessment revealed that she was the more sensitive parent who best met the children's needs.

Conversely, Tyler was oblivious to his children's emotional needs, given his ongoing preoccupation with Della. Despite his denials to the assessor, his children were aware of his rage and ambivalence towards his estranged wife. On some occasions he invited her to participate in events as a family and told the children he loved her, but at other times he criticized her and made negative comments, leaving the children confused, ambivalent, and angry. Given their father's behaviour and ambivalence, they could not adapt to the separation. They still thought their parents should and would reunite. Joyce often pretended that her parents lived together, maintaining they never quarrelled. Although the assessor recommended that Della be the primary caretaker, she also recommended therapy for Tyler and the children. Specifically, Tyler needed to resolve his rage over Della's rejection and gain insight into the impact of his feelings on the children, while the children needed to recognize that the family was not going to reunite. The judge agreed and directed family members to attend counselling. However, Tyler disagreed and continued to malign Della. After two years, the situation was essentially unchanged.

Children's Reactions and Coping Strategies

Assessors need to be aware of children's typical reactions to separation and divorce. As family members progress through the above phases, children experience many anxieties. They may worry about who will take care of them and fear that both parents will disappear. They often feel intensely angry, sad, and vulnerable, and believe they are responsible for the breakup. Children may cope by trying to mend the situation, by pretending the separation did not happen, or by pleasing their parents. The latter can occur in highly contentious situations. Children recount different stories, wishes, or feelings to each parent to please both and make each feel better, thereby coping with their own sense of divided loyalties. This sometimes results in divergent reports from parents regarding their children's feelings and wishes. At other times, children side with one parent and reject the other. Others refuse to tell parents or assessors about their feelings for fear of offending or hurting either parent. It is important that we assessors recognize these possibilities; otherwise, we will be confused when conflicting information is gathered in the assessment process. Concerns also arise if parents display no recognition of their children's reactions or dilemmas and if parents report that their children's reactions are identical to their own. This can indicate that parents are still preoccupied with the separation or are insensitive to their children's true feelings.

As well as identifying parents' awareness of children's reactions, assessors need to explore the steps parents have taken to help their children adapt. For example, parents begin to help their children when they first tell them of the separation, reassuring them they are not to blame and outlining the concrete changes that will happen in their lives. Sensitive parents then make residential and access arrangements to ensure contact with each parent in ways that meet the children's needs rather than their own. For example, very young children often need frequent contact with parents to maintain their relationships. Supportive parents also are attuned to their children's reactions, ensure children are excluded from parental conflict, and do not malign the other parent. Finally, they seek professional help for their children and themselves if needed. If counsellors have been involved with families around such issues, assessors are well-advised to contact them.

Factors Influencing Children's Adjustment

It is important to become familiar with the factors that influence the long-term adjustment of children after divorce. The available cross-sectional and longitudinal research regarding the impact of divorce is somewhat equivocal. In their meta-analysis of ninety-two studies, Amato and Keith (1991) concluded that the negative impact of divorce is influenced by several factors, including parental absence, economic disadvantage, and family conflict. Children exhibit better adjustment after parental death than divorce. Children who live with a step-parent do no better than children living in a one-parent home following divorce, although some boys do better when a stepfather joins the family. Additionally, continued contact with the noncustodial parent does not uniformly improve the well-being of children, although their functioning seems to improve generally with the passage of time.

Bricklin (1995) reviewed studies examining the effects of divorce on children and similarly found numerous factors that affect adjustment, although conclusions are far from clear and unequivocal. **Age at separation** affects adjustment, likely because children process information differently and deal with different developmental tasks at various ages. For example, concrete arrangements and regularity and frequency of contact may help maintain significant attachments with a four-year-old child. A ten-year-old child may focus on broader issues and truly question the motivations and long-term availability of each parent, and a teenager's confidence in relationships may be shaken. In their reactions to separations, infants may experience language and gross motor delays, while preschoolers may be upset initially but then experience variable long-term effects. Young school-age children may regress and have many intense feelings, including sadness and anger. Older school-age children can have a compromised sense of identity and compensate for feelings of powerlessness by engaging in activities where they can develop a sense of mastery. Teenagers and young adults may have difficulties with heterosexual relationships; this is particularly so for young women. Although research findings are equivocal regarding **gender** of the child, some boys in maternal custody or in families with stepfathers tend to do more poorly, while girls in paternal custody may not do as well. Differences in adjustment between boys and girls tend to decline during adolescence, although girls sometimes have more adjustment problems than do boys, as noted above.

Other variables that influence child adjustment include continuing **parental maladjustment** and **interparental conflict** after divorce. Psychologically well-adjusted parents likely maintain healthy parent-child relationships that support children in dealing with the divorce and other life tasks. Maladjusted parents are less likely to maintain good parent-child relationships, thereby increasing the risk that children will develop problems. Amato and Keith (1991) and Schroeder and Gordon (2002) also found that children whose families experience post-divorce conflict have a lower level of well-being than those where ongoing conflict is low. However, children in separated families with a high level of interparental conflict do better than those in intact high-conflict families.

Custody arrangements may also affect children. Some do extremely well with joint custody arrangements where they live part-time with each parent, while other children do more poorly. Such joint arrangements are more likely to work well if parents actively choose this arrangement and if children are flexible and can easily adapt to changed residences and routines. Generally, however, good outcomes are attributable less to custody arrangements per se than to interactions of factors such as the personal characteristics of the children and parents and other, more contextual factors, such as financial resources and extended family support. For example, flexible, easygoing children may adapt better when parents are maladjusted or have markedly different parenting styles than would intense, inflexible, and reactive children.

Although children's adaptation to separation and divorce may seem to be a minor factor in cases where children have been abused and neglected, it is critical to always ask about adaptation to separations and family dissolution because this can be another significant risk factor that decreases the probability of healthy development. When parents have been involved in several or even many relationships, assessors need to inquire about children's reactions to the entry and loss of these partners in their lives. This is particularly important when children have developed close relationships with these individuals.

The following questions may be used to evaluate children's **adaptation to separation and family dissolution** and parental support for them:

1. How do children understand the reasons for the breakup of their family?
2. How much consideration did parents give to the concrete living arrangements for children prior to telling them of the separation?
3. How did parents tell children about the impending separation?
4. Has the family progressed through the phases of separation or have they not progressed beyond the initial acute phase?
5. Can children acknowledge the reality of the marital rupture and have they disengaged from the parental conflict and distress?
6. Do parents keep children out of any ongoing conflict and distress or do they involve them in the conflict?
7. Have children resumed their usual activities or are they still preoccupied with their parents' ongoing adaptation?
8. Do the children feel responsible for the separation? Do parents recognize their children's feelings of responsibility, and how have they addressed these feelings?
9. Do children maintain active fantasies of reunification well after the separation, and why is this the case?
10. Have parents resumed parenting in a manner similar to that which they used prior to the separation? If parenting was poor, has the family breakup improved parenting in the home?
11. Do parents actively support the involvement of the other parent in their children's lives, except in cases where he or she was truly abusive to the children?
12. Do parents actively criticize the other parent in the child's presence?
13. Do parents recognize children's feelings and dilemmas and support them or are they still preoccupied with their own personal issues?
14. Have parents sought appropriate consultation or counselling if needed for either themselves or their children?

Risk and Resiliency Factors

As the previous discussion indicates, many child characteristics must be carefully considered and assessed during parenting assessments to derive a clear picture of children, their needs, and the challenges they may present to parents. The next step is to consider parental characteristics, both personal qualities and contextual sources of support, that detract from or enhance parents' abilities to meet their children's needs. Here it is important to remember that valid and useful parenting assessments identify the strengths of children and families, not only their weaknesses. This is particularly important because we know that many children who experience adversity in childhood go on to do well. For example, Rutter (1985) estimated that half of the children exposed to severe stress and adversity do not develop symptoms of psychopathology.

This capacity to adapt and develop competence in the face of risk factors and threat is called *resilience* and has been studied for a quarter of a century. Rutter (1993) prefers the term 'resilience' to the older concept of 'invulnerability' because the children are not absolutely resistant to damage. The study of resilience has focused on identifying factors, or moderator variables, that affect developmental outcome. Cicchetti and Rizley (1981) and Cicchetti and Rogosch (1994) classify moderator variables into two broad categories: 'potentitiating factors' that increase the probability of negative developmental outcome, and 'compensatory factors' that decrease that probability. Masten and Coatsworth (1995) indicate that while we still have not identified the specific underlying processes or mechanisms that generate resilience, we do know that, as the number of risk factors to which children are exposed increases, the chance of successful adaptation decreases. Similarly, if buffering or protective factors exist, the chance of successful adaptation increases. For example, a good relationship with one parent has consistently been found to be a protective factor for children whose parents have divorced and where there is a high level of discord between parents (Masten & Coatsworth, 1995).

Assessors in child welfare and foster and adoption cases would be particularly wise to develop an awareness of these factors. Scott Heller, Larrieu, D'Imperio, and Boris (1999) reviewed recent research literature and described protective factors believed to contribute to resilience in maltreated children. These include above-average cognitive abilities, positive self-regard, internal locus of control, external attribution of blame for the maltreatment, spirituality, and ego-control and ego-resilience. According to Scott Heller et al., 'ego-control' and 'ego-resilience' refer to a capacity to control feelings and behaviour, thereby making a person less susceptible to noxious environmental factors.

Thus children who can modulate their feelings and behaviour in response to their personal circumstances are likely to do better. Family cohesion is also a protective factor; this refers to the presence of a caring and supportive adult in children's lives as well as changes in the family for the better (Scott Heller et al., 1999). For example, the latter might include the departure of an extremely abusive stepfather from the home or placement in foster care after living in a highly neglectful and abusive home. The literature on resilience consistently reports that children can derive a considerable sense of protection against later difficulties by having at least one relationship with a significant caring adult during childhood. This adult need not be a parent. Teachers, grandparents, neighbours, relatives, or others may provide this protective influence, providing the child feels valued by this person. Finally, Scott Heller et al. described various extrafamilial supports that can be protective, such as structured school environments, family interventions to stop abuse or change family dynamics, involvement in religious communities, or involvement in extracurricular activities or hobbies. Thus, a child who is a good athlete and is given the opportunity to participate in sports may do better than a child from a similar difficult background who does not have such talents or opportunities.

Steinhauer (1998) identifies certain factors that are essential in promoting resiliency at different ages. The establishment of a secure relationship with a primary caregiver is critical during infancy and toddler years. Through toddler, preschool, and school years, parental capacity to meet the child's needs promotes resiliency, particularly in disadvantaged families. The needs to be met are those arising from normal development as outlined in Chapter 3 as well as those arising from developmental variations as discussed in Chapter 4. Parental characteristics that undermine parents' abilities to meet children's needs must be evaluated. Many of these will be discussed in Chapter 6.

While the above discussion is brief, it is critical to be aware of some of these protective factors, which may contribute significantly to final recommendations. This was the situation in the following case.

CASE 10: Jim was initially referred for therapy at the age of eight years, shortly after the birth of a younger brother to his single mother, who worked in a low-paying retail job. He was seen in weekly therapy for two years to address neglect by his mother, who, while now sober, had binged on alcohol throughout his early years. At the time of referral, Jim performed poorly in school in both the academic and social realms. The initial assessment revealed that he was a bright boy whose difficulties resulted from mild attention problems and his mother's failure to ensure that he completed homework. Besides therapy, Jim was given extra tutoring, and he began do much better academically. His therapist also noted that he was coordinated and strong and had expressed an interest in baseball. He was encouraged to join a community baseball league, where he proved to be a naturally skilled player despite a lack of previous experience. A men's service club provided the necessary equipment, and a mentor from the club was paired with Jim to act in a 'big brother' role.

Jim and his mentor, Jack, participated in many activities together over the next several years and developed a close relationship. Jim became familiar with Jack's new wife and attended various activities with both of them. When Jim was thirteen years old his mother began to drink again, and the care she provided to her son rapidly deteriorated. A parenting assessment was undertaken to determine if he should remain in his mother's care. Given his ongoing good school performance, involvement in baseball, and positive relationships with Jack, his wife, and a maternal grandmother, the clinician recommended that Jack remain in his mother's care, although the situation was monitored regularly by child welfare personnel. His grandmother assumed care of the younger brother pending his mother's completion of a day-treatment program for alcoholics. Jim successfully coped with several difficult months while remaining at home as his mother progressed through treatment. His chances of continued successful adaptation were considered good. Although he married at a young age, Jim maintained regular employment and did not maltreat his wife and children.

The following questions can be used to review factors that may promote **resiliency in children**:

1. Do the children have good cognitive abilities?
2. Does school achievement provide a sense of accomplishment and satisfaction to the children?

3. Do children feel good about themselves and do they think they have some control in their lives?
4. Do children blame others for maltreatment and misfortune or do they feel personally responsible?
5. Can children control their feelings and behaviour in response to events in their lives?
6. Does at least one adult provide caring and support to the children?
7. Have changes for the better occurred in the family?
8. Do the children belong to a community, such as a neighbourhood or religious group?
9. Do the children have any special talents and abilities?
10. Do the children participate in any structured extracurricular activities on a regular basis?

6 Parent Factors: Personal Characteristics That Increase the Risk of Poor Parenting

The preceding three chapters examined many child characteristics that pose real challenges to parents and require their increased sophistication, knowledge, and sensitivity. A careful identification of children's needs is critical because the test in all parenting evaluations is whether parents can meet these needs. Assessors then carefully examine parents to identify the characteristics that make it more difficult for them to meet the needs of their children and those that may enhance their capacities to parent well. These factors include the individual characteristics of parents, the nature of their joint interactions and relationships, and the existing supports for parenting in their lives. Belsky and Vondra (1989) describe these influences as arising from parent factors and the influence of contextual sources of support and stress. If we think of these factors in terms of those that increase the risk of poor parenting and those that attenuate that risk, then we can more easily weigh risk and compensatory factors when making recommendations. Much of the research that examines the impact of these factors on parenting emerges out of the study of child abuse and neglect. However, knowledge of these factors is important in parenting assessments in other contexts. Parents in foster and adoption and custody/access assessments are not immune to addictions, mental health problems, and other characteristics that can negatively affect their parenting.

Parents' History of Maltreatment

One of the most studied parent characteristics that contributes to poor parenting is a childhood history of abuse and neglect. When this was first studied in the 1970s and 1980s, researchers and clinicians noticed that many parents who abuse their children had themselves been abused as youngsters, but Belsky (1993) reported that many of the early studies linking perpetration of abuse with childhood histories were methodologically problematic. Not only did co-morbidity among various types of abuse make it difficult to establish experimental groups, but inadequate and biased sampling added to the methodological problems. Samples were generally small, control and comparison groups were only roughly matched, and severity and chronicity of maltreatment were often ignored as variables. Finally, many early studies gathered information only after the fact, as prospective and longitudinal studies were infrequent. Belsky also reported that results of later, well-designed prospective studies do suggest a link between child abuse and a parental history of childhood abuse, although not as strong a one as the initial studies suggested. The estimated rate of intergenerational transmission is now commonly thought to be about 30 per cent (Belsky, 1993); in other words, only about one-third of children who are maltreated grow up to abuse their own children. Problems with over- and under-reporting of childhood abuse and studies that examine parents at only one point in their parenting careers still create difficulty in estimating the rate of intergenerational transmission. For example, even if parents are not currently abusing their children, they may still abuse one or more of them later in their parenting careers.

Memories of Childhood

Despite the absence of a one-to-one correspondence between a childhood history and abusive treatment of one's own child, as assessors we need to consistently explore parents' memories of childhood with particular attention to any evidence of abuse or neglect. However, we must remain aware that some parents genuinely do not remember much of their early years, while others idealize them to avoid the miserable reality of their upbringings. Given the evaluative nature of parenting assessments, some parents consciously choose to portray an ideal childhood so that assessors form more favourable impressions. Assessors need to be aware of such possibilities, and if parents give consent, they should contact references, particularly siblings and long-term friends, to validate reports of how parents were treated as youngsters. Also, child welfare and other court records may provide pertinent validation, especially when parents do not give consent for direct contact with references. When parents provide global childhood memories such as 'it was fine' or 'my childhood was bad,' we should ask for examples of events that generated their opinions, and specifically how grandparents did or did not show caring and how the parents felt and reacted to their parents.

When parents cannot recall specifics, we need to explore further because they may be idealizing their childhoods or using some other strategy to cope with what happened to them. For example, Jackie (Case 1) asserted that she had a 'rotten' upbringing, particularly because she was sexually abused by her father in her early teens. She also reported 'a bit' of drinking and drug usage by parents and a family environment where she took care of younger siblings because her mother was 'tired.' Jackie minimized these latter circumstances and stated that her family was identical to those of her school friends. Furthermore, she asserted that she had resolved all feelings about what had happened to her. When contacted, Jackie's mother denied her husband had sexually abused Jackie, but she admitted he had physically abused her in Jackie's presence. Also, she described his harsh and arbitrary treatment of all family members. Two other references from early years reported a poor home situation. Not only was her father violent and abusive, but her mother often abdicated her role as parent, and both parents spent most evenings at the local bar. References clearly reported several traumatic family and personal events involving Jackie that she could not remember. When asked about these reports, Jackie discounted them by saying, 'Oh, they never liked me anyway. They just want me to look bad so I don't get my children back.' Interestingly, Jackie was the person who suggested the assessor contact these references.

Without this extra sleuthing to cross-validate reports, the assessor might have accepted Jackie's reports at face value and subsequently discounted the continued impact of her upbringing on her current parenting capacity. Jackie negatively described her upbringing to elicit the sympathy of others, who might then excuse her poor parenting and decision-making. Simultaneously, she minimized and denied the true picture to avoid her feelings about her parents, and she asserted she had resolved her feelings in part because she thought she had done so and in part to avoid a recommendation for further individual or family therapy. She had in no way resolved her feelings about her own abuse and neglect. Essentially, Jackie maintained an ongoing view that the world was so dangerous that she had to keep people distant and manipulate them to survive and meet her needs. Such a stance proved to be incompatible with sensitive parenting, particularly when accompanied by other problems such as addictions. Jackie relied on her children to validate her, and she demanded closeness and love while being overtly rejecting and demanding with them. Besides being unable to recognize or meet their emotional needs, she often had difficulty meeting their basic physical needs because of her transient lifestyle and short-lived relationships with often dangerous men. Jackie repeatedly minimized the emotional, physical, and sexual abuse risks these people posed to her children.

Why Childhood Maltreatment Impacts on Parenting

Belsky (1993) discusses mediating processes that may partially account for why poor childhood care affects parents' later abilities to competently care for children. As youngsters, parents may learn aggressive and antisocial behaviour through processes such as modelling, direct reinforcement, and inconsistency training. The latter includes an escalating series of aversive interactions between parents and children due to inconsistencies in reinforcement and punishment of children. Children do not comply with parental demands because parents do not consistently use consequences; as children do not comply, parents become angry, coercive, and punitive. Similar philosophies of discipline between grandparent and parent homes may also partially account for why some abused children become abusive parents. As youngsters, parents may have been repeatedly told they deserved beatings because they were bad and beatings would teach them to be good. It is thus not surprising when they make the same assumptions regarding their own children; that they are bad and need beatings to be good. Indeed, some may feel they are poor parents when they do not use physical punishment. Another possible reason for intergenerational transmission of abuse and poor parenting includes issues that relate more to how maltreatment shapes children's personality formation and functioning.

Parents' internal working models may also play a role in how they perceive and interact with their children. For example, parents' descriptions of their infants and young children may reflect as much about the parents as about their children (Zeanah & Benoit, 1995). This is not surprising because, as discussed in Chapter 3's section on attachment, children form internal representations regarding themselves and others through their interactions with parents. If provided with unreliable and/or abusive care, they begin to expect parents will not provide good care to them and they view themselves as unloveable. van IJzendoorn (1992) cogently points out that if parents received unresponsive, rejecting, or ambivalent care as children, they may have difficulty responding to their own children. For example, they might expect others, including their children, to reject them, and thus stay disengaged from their children to avoid being emotionally hurt by them. Also, parents might disregard children's signals of needing care, and they might not recognize their children's feelings and perspectives because they are too concerned with their own feelings and viewpoints. Some parents may be coercive and abusive in order to maintain control in their family because they lack feelings of efficacy and control in their lives generally, and still others abdicate their parenting role and neglect their children because they expect to be ineffectual anyway.

Recognizing the potential impact of parents' internal working models on their current relationships, including those with their children, Zeanah and Benoit (1995) developed the 'Working Model of the Child Interview.' This is a semi-structured interview that focuses on several qualities of parents' discourse about their youngsters and is used to evaluate parents' perceptions and subjective experience of their children and their relationship with their infants. It employs eight rating scales to describe parents' or other caregivers' representations of their infants: richness of perceptions, openness to change, intensity of involvement, coherence, caregiving sensitivity, acceptance, infant difficulty, and fear for safety. These qualities may be representative of parents' general modes of interaction with others and are likely derived from their own early experiences as children. Thus maltreatment during childhood can have enduring effects on parenting capacity, as it did for Jackie, discussed above.

Factors Mitigating the Impact of Childhood Maltreatment on Parenting

Specific inquiry about parents' understanding and resolution of early maltreatment issues is critical because one cannot assume that a history of maltreatment continues to negatively influence all parents. Phelps, Belsky, and Crnic (1998) reviewed a number of studies with both clinical and normative samples that concerned intrafamilial transmission of parenting. These studies suggest that both continuity and discontinuity in transmission exist, with some families passing on poor parenting but others parenting well. Two major factors seem to promote discontinuity.

First, parents tend not to re-enact poor parenting if they have developed **awareness of the influence of their difficult childhoods** on their own functioning and well-being and of the potential effect on their childrearing behaviour (Main & Goldwyn, 1984). These parents remember painful childhood events and associated emotions and beliefs rather than either suppressing them or idealizing them, like Jackie did in Case 1. When feelings are suppressed or idealized, parents may act out in response to their inaccurate perceptions and feelings. When parents acknowledge, accept, and understand their childhoods, they are likely to respond more appropriately to others, including their own children. Some may feel badly about their early lives, but may consciously endeavour to respond differently to their children and other people. They are not overwhelmed by reminiscence, and they remain coherent in their recollections of childhood and their descriptions of their children. According to Main, Kaplan, and Cassidy (1985), parents who are coherent display an organized and logical flow of ideas and feelings when talking of themselves or their children. Parents who are still influenced by their early negative experiences are more likely to be confused, contradictory, and even bizarre in their descriptions, making it difficult for a listener to understand what really happened in their early years or what their children are truly like (Zeannah & Benoit, 1995). Phelps, Belsky, and Crnic (1998) found that parents who had developed a coherent view of their difficult childhoods, as assessed using the Adult Attachment Interview (AAI), parented well even when subjected to stressful circumstances, and they parented better than others who had not developed a coherent view.

A second factor that lessens the chances of repeating poor parenting is the **receipt of consistent emotional support from at least one significant person** in either childhood or adulthood. This can be a spouse, therapist, family friend, or other person, as discussed in the resiliency factors section of the last chapter. Such a relationship is compensatory and validates parents in a positive way, making them feel loved and cherished. They may then be less needy and feel more competent, thus being more able to nurture their children and perhaps increasing their chances of parenting their own children adequately or even well.

These and other research findings that parents can develop secure attachments and come to terms with earlier maltreatment provide direction and a degree of optimism in assessments. They suggest that parents who were abused as children are likely to do best if they have had the opportunity to talk about and cognitively and emotionally process what happened to them. Future parenting can be enhanced if interventions specifically target their internal working models and if parents are taught to be sensitive to child cues, particularly from their infants or young children. Approaches such as infant-parent psychotherapy, which helps parents attune to their infants, can thus be helpful. Lieberman and Zeanah (1999) describe several clinical programs that use such an approach. Where parents have not developed a coherent understanding of their maltreatment, assessors need to consider their potential to do so, either on their own or with therapeutic support. Assessors must then estimate how long it will take parents to make these changes. This estimation is particularly salient in child welfare cases, where children sometimes cannot wait for three or five years while parents attempt to change, particularly if the probability of positive change is low. Years of waiting are usually not in children's best interests, as they may not really invest in relationships with new caregivers if they expect to be returning home.

Such predictions of parental response are often difficult. Assessors must strive for as complete an understanding of the parents as possible, given that some continue to be influenced by their pasts while others do not. Understanding of their past and its influence on their lives may indeed make them stronger as parents, as was the situation in the following case.

CASE 11: Gavin and Judy were referred for parenting assessment when they applied to adopt a four-year-old foster child, Mina, who had lived with them for ten months. This child had been horrifically abused and had spent her first three years of life confined to a crib and then to a closet. Child welfare workers requested a formal parenting assessment because Gavin had a similar history. Workers were comfortable with Gavin and Judy as foster parents because the workers continued to serve as Mina's legal guardian. However, they were concerned about the impact that Gavin's personal history might have on his ongoing capacity to make decisions about Mina and parent her adequately in the long term.

Gavin indeed reported a difficult childhood. Until the age of seven years, he had lived with two younger sisters on an isolated farm. Although he did not remember his mother, he understood she had committed suicide when he was four years old, shortly after the birth of his youngest sister. Gavin then continued to live with his father and paternal grandmother. His father was a volatile and controlling tyrant who degraded his family and had abused Gavin's mother. Neither mother nor grandmother could stop his father's abusive behaviour, and Gavin had the profound feeling his father hated him. This intensified after his mother's death. When his father was not beating and shaming him, which he recounted in detail to the evaluator, Gavin and his siblings were usually confined to a bedroom and were always hungry. Occasionally his grandmother smuggled treats or food to them. Gavin stated that he always saw kindness in her eyes even though she could not make things substantially better for him. She also told him his mother had loved him.

Gavin and his sisters were rescued from this situation when his father was arrested for assault of a neighbour. They were placed in the home of a poor but caring couple who raised them to adulthood. In school, Gavin was bright, learned quickly, and participated in school sport activities. He maintained positive feelings about his mother and grandmother but also recognized the terror his father had instilled in him, vowing he would never be like him. Gavin completed high school and consciously chose to be a firefighter because of the structure and security the profession offered. While in training, he met Judy. He was attracted because of her gentle nature, their similar ideals, and her large and close-knit family. They married and had three children together. Even so, Gavin had a strong need to help disadvantaged children, and he and Judy decided to foster abused children. During the assessment, Gavin realistically acknowledged his strengths and weaknesses as a person and a parent. For example, he knew food was an issue for him; indeed, he recognized that his moderate obesity derived from this ongoing anxiety about never having sufficient food. As a result, he consciously ensured his children never went hungry. He also knew that his need for order and control in his family came from his childhood feelings of helplessness. When asked about the high demands he placed on his children, Gavin acknowledged these but reported that he always attempted to be humane in his expectations, explored the viewpoints of his children, talked with them about his own motivations, and supported their involvement in school and other activities in order to ensure their self-esteem was high.

Occasionally, Mina's behaviour and demeanour triggered unsettling feelings for Gavin. He felt better after speaking with Judy and reminding himself that he overcame a poor start in life. He was proud that he was a benevolent father whose children did well. Given Gavin's apparent understanding of his abuse and the strengths both he and Judy displayed, the assessor supported the adoption but outlined difficulties that might emerge as Mina developed. Also, the report outlined possible avenues of support, such as therapy for Mina and for Gavin if he began to feel overwhelmed.

The following questions can be used to help guide inquiry about **maltreatment in parents' own childhoods**:

1. What memories of childhood do parents express?
2. Are these memories positive or negative in nature and do they sound realistic?
3. Can parents give detailed memories, including emotional memories that support these views?
4. Are parents' reports of childhood congruent with the reports of references or child welfare and court records?
5. If parents had difficult childhoods, are they aware of their pain and have they developed a 'more than superficial' understanding regarding how this affects their lives, especially their parenting?
6. Have parents ever formed a close positive relationship with one other person who provided them with support and validation?
7. If parents have not resolved issues around their childhood problems, do they appear open to doing this rather than denying issues or blaming others? What kind of support will they require to accomplish this goal?

Mental Health Problems

Early thinking regarding the etiology of child maltreatment presumed, given the horrific nature of some children's injuries, that parental mental health difficulties were the principal cause of child abuse. However, as Belsky (1993) clearly indicates, no one pattern of personality traits or psychological problems typifies all parents who abuse and neglect their children, although research findings demonstrate some link between general negative emotional states and maltreatment. The lack of consistent research findings linking a specific personality trait and poor parenting is not surprising if parenting behaviour is determined by multiple and interacting factors, as our model assumes. For example, it is possible for parents with significant mental health problems to provide acceptable care if they receive ongoing family support, among other factors (Cassell & Coleman, 1995). The lack of positive research findings may also be due to the use of group comparisons. The quality of care that a particular parent provides comes about because of an interaction of factors that are peculiar to that family alone. It is unlikely that exactly the same factors would be replicated in another family. Consequently, the richness of each family's dynamics may be blurred in group studies. Parenting assessments must delineate salient contributory factors and permit recommendations to be fine-tuned to the specific needs of children and parents.

Depression

Despite the general absence of consistent findings in most group studies, parent depression is one of the few mental health problems that is appears to be linked with poor parenting. This is not surprising based on our knowledge of child development and, in particular, attachment. Low energy levels and depressed affect are characteristic of depressed people; responding attentively and consistently to an infant or young child will be difficult, and this lack of response will impair the development of a child's secure attachment (Cassell & Coleman, 1995). Thompson and Calkins (1996) also speak of the difficulties children have in developing emotional regulation when they are being cared for by depressed parents. Such parents often make tremendous emotional demands on children, who must cope with their parents' sadness, irritability, helplessness, and guilt. Parents may be unable to place limits on their children's behaviour or encourage them to use internal state language to modulate their emotions. Furthermore, parents may model negative self-talk and personal attributions of helplessness.

The burden and demands on children may be intensified if parents discuss their feelings with their children, blame them for the depression, or make them feel guilty if they cannot help parents feel better (Thompson and Calkins, 1996). Children may become overinvolved in their parents' emotional struggles, detracting from their ability to invest in more age appropriate tasks and activities. Given their young age, limited resources, and ongoing need for sensitive parenting and support, children may not cope effectively, and they are likely to remain quite needy. Furthermore, as Thompson and Calkins note, children may become hypersensitive to negative emotional cues, resulting in ongoing difficulty with emotional arousal and regulation as well as other life tasks. Interestingly, Thompson and Calkins report that children of depressed parents are likely to be more empathic than their peers, perhaps because they have had to be sensitive and respond carefully to others in their own homes.

Suspected depression in a parent requires careful assessment of the degree of depression and its impact on parenting responsiveness, as well as an assessment of the strategies children use to cope with their parent's problems. Formal psychiatric or psychological assessment, including psychological testing, may help to determine the severity of the parent's depression, as may reports from collateral references such as counsellors, physicians, friends, and family members. This type of assessment was undertaken in the following case.

CASE 12: A single mother, Isabelle, was referred for a parenting assessment by her child welfare worker when school personnel raised concerns regarding possible physical and emotional neglect of her ten-year old daughter Amy. After a preliminary child welfare investigation, Amy was left in Isabelle's care provided she sought help from a community mental health clinic. Isabelle minimized her difficulties, saying that she was sad because her sister had died and she had lost her job. She provided many logical reasons for frequent family moves and a lack of friends in the neighbourhood. She agreed to go for counselling, but after four months Amy remained needy and unkempt. Isabelle's case worker requested the evaluation because he was confused about family dynamics and the action he should take.

During the assessment, it was apparent that Isabelle had experienced chronic depression since a rape by her brother at the age of sixteen years. Her depression intensified after the birth of Amy when Isabelle was eighteen years old. Although she tried to maintain work as a waitress, her depression made employment difficult. Furthermore, she had been hospitalized twice for severe depression, but she failed to report this to the clinician. In fact, Amy had alerted the assessor when she described being left with a series of 'aunties' when her mother was hospitalized. Various acquaintances also provided care for Amy when her mother tried to work, but, essentially, Amy had been looking after herself since grade 1. Although Isabelle maintained infrequent contact with her own mother, Amy's grandmother reported that Amy had been hospitalized as an infant. A subsequent check of hospital records indicated she had been admitted for failure to thrive at the age of four months. These data indicated Isabelle had periods when she did not provide basic physical and emotional care to Amy. Psychological testing supported interview and reference findings that Isabelle was experiencing clinically significant depression requiring both drug therapy and an inpatient admission.

Isabelle was admitted to a long-term treatment program and Amy was placed in foster care, where she thrived. Given Amy's worries about Isabelle as well as her attachment to her, contact between mother and daughter occurred regularly. Amy's therapist supervised contact so that she could be guided to maintain her relationship with her mother while being helped to not feel responsible for her problems. As Isabelle had never previously persisted with any treatment, predicting her progress was difficult. The assessor suggested scheduling a later update to the assessment. After one year, Amy had made significant progress but Isabelle still struggled. The clinician recommended that Amy permanently remain in her foster home while maintaining regular contact with her mother. This ensured good parenting for Amy and interrupted the cycle of family moves. Child welfare authorities and Isabelle shared legal guardianship of Amy.

Psychosis

Depression is not the only mental health difficulty that deleteriously affects parenting. Cassell and Coleman (1995) discuss the impact of psychosis on parenting, stating that affected parents have many of the same characteristics as those who are depressed. They may be unmotivated and withdrawn, making them unable to attend emotionally and physically to their children. At other times, during florid psychotic episodes, parents may be so agitated that they provide chaotic and unpredictable homes. Judgment may be poor, presenting safety risks due to lack of supervision. At other times, parents may be a danger to themselves and their children. If parents are actively delusional, children may become confused as they attempt to compare their own perceptions with those of their parents. This becomes particularly problematic when the children and others are included in the delusional thinking, as was the case in the following situation.

CASE 13: Alexander was four years old when his parents separated and his father, Andy, moved to a distant city. Andy maintained contact with Alexander during major school holidays. For the following four years, Alexander lived with his mother, Jeanne. Neighbours viewed her as odd as she became progressively more bizarre and reclusive. Although she enrolled Alexander in school and walked him there on a daily basis, she made few other forays into the community.

Andy became concerned about Alexander's care when his son spoke of aliens during visits. By the age of eight years, Alexander could not read and never mentioned friends or outside activities. Eventually Andy sued for custody, and a parenting assessment was done. It was clear that Alexander was being adversely affected by his mother's deteriorating mental state. Although Jeanne had always been somewhat unusual, her coping ability declined as she became increasingly delusional. She did not let Alexander out of their apartment for fear of an alien abduction, and she did not allow friends in because she worried aliens would come in disguise to abduct them. Also, she thought Alexander's teachers were malevolent aliens. Alexander and Jeanne's isolation from the community was reflected in her tendency to draw window shades, avoid phone calls and television, repeatedly wash food to remove alien influences, and often keep Alexander home from school.

Alexander's perceptions of the world became quite bizarre, and other students shunned him. He also had difficulty working despite being bright. Teachers were puzzled by Jeanne's comment that they did not know how to teach such a gifted child as her son. She demanded they use the specially designed teaching methods she used with him at home. For example, to teach him to read, Jeanne read a book into a tape recorder and then made Alexander listen to the tape for hours each day. Given the ingrained nature of her delusions, Jeanne had no insight into her difficulties or the impact they were having on her son. Furthermore, once Andy filed for custody, he became the focus of intensifying delusions of persecution. The danger Jeanne posed for both Andy and Alexander then became a concern, and the assessor recommended that Alexander be removed from his mother's care. This move occurred with the involvement of child welfare workers and the police, due to a risk that Jeanne might kill her son rather than let him live with Andy.

Factors to Consider

Obviously, parents may present a wide range of mental health problems, and not all are as pronounced as those of Isabelle and Jeanne. However, even seemingly more benign difficulties such as anxiety disorders can be problematic given specific circumstances (Cassell & Coleman, 1995). For example, a mother who cannot touch vegetables or meat during food preparation may present significant risks to the health of a young child, but older children might be less affected because they are more able to prepare their own food. Some children of highly anxious parents may attune to their parents' anxiety and develop their own symptoms.

Other parents who display personality disorders may experience sometimes serious difficulties in the provision of sensitive parenting. As described in the American Psychiatric Association's *Diagnostic and Statistical Manual of Mental Disorders* (4th ed.) (DSM-IV) (1994), these people have deviant patterns of experience and behaviour that are pervasive and inflexible and lead to chronic difficulties in daily functioning. For example, June, who was described in Case 3, had a formally diagnosed borderline personality disorder that led to chronic and pronounced difficulties in her interpersonal and job functioning. Her behaviour was so erratic that she provided Randy with an unstable and often bizarre home life. Table 6.1 presents a summary of the characteristics of each of the ten primary personality disorders described in DSM-IV. A category of Personality Disorder Not Otherwise Specified permits identification of personality disorders where a person meets the general criteria for a personality disorder but displays traits that characterize several different ones or traits typical of an-

Table 6.1
Personal Characteristics That May Be Evident in Specific Personality Disorders

Paranoid:
- Pattern of **distrust** and **suspiciousness** where the motives of others are seen as malevolent without sufficient basis for such a view; **lack of trust** in others
- May feel exploited, harmed, or deceived by others
- **Questions the loyalty of others** or the fidelity of partners; may bear grudges
- Reads hidden demeaning or threatening intent into benign remarks and events
- **Reacts angrily or quickly counterattacks** when thinking others are attacking his or her character or reputation even though these attacks are not apparent to others

Schizoid:
- **Detached from social relationships** with an accompanying **restricted range of emotional expression**
- Does not seek or enjoy close relationships, including those with family members
- Often chooses **solitary activities** and may take little pleasure in any activities
- Emotionally cold and detached with flat affect; seemingly **indifferent to reactions** of others
- Lacks close friends or confidants except for possibly first-degree relatives

Schizotypal:
- **Acute discomfort in close relationships** that does not diminish with familiarity and is associated with paranoid fears rather than negative self-evaluations
- Cognitive or perceptual **distortions**; incorrectly interprets casual events as having unusual personal meanings or evidences magical rituals, superstitions, or preoccupations about the paranormal
- Suspiciousness or paranoid ideation
- **Eccentric** or **peculiar** behaviour and mannerisms, may be inattentive to social conventions
- Lacks close friends or confidants except for possibly first-degree relatives

Antisocial:
- Consistent **disregard and violation of the rights of others** beginning in childhood or early adolescence
- Fails to conform to social norms, exhibits **unlawful behaviours** that are grounds for arrest
- **Deceitful**, such as in chronic lying, using aliases, or conning others for profit or pleasure
- **Impulsive** and lacks planning; chronic **irresponsibility** in work and financial areas
- **Reckless disregard for the safety** of the self or others
- **Irritability** and **aggressiveness** with repeated physical fights or assaults
- **Lack of remorse**; indifferent to hurting others or provides superficial excuses for hurting, mistreating, or stealing from others

Borderline:
- **Instability** in interpersonal relationships, self-image, and affects
- Makes **frantic efforts to avoid real or imagined abandonment**, intense fear of abandonment; anger when faced with even minor separations or changes in plans

- Sudden and dramatic shifts in views of other people – extreme idealization to marked devaluation
- Marked and persistent unstable self-image
- **Marked impulsivity** in areas that are potentially self-damaging, such as eating, sex, substance abuse, reckless driving
- Recurring suicidal behaviour, gestures, or threats; or self-mutilation
- **Unstable affects** due to marked reactivity of mood, chronic feelings of emptiness
- **Anger management problems,** such as constant or frequent angry outbursts or recurrent physical fighting
- Transient, stress-related paranoid ideation, possibly shows dissociative symptoms

Histrionic:
- **Attention-seeking**; discomfort when not the centre of attention
- Interaction with others may involve inappropriate sexually seductive or provocative behaviour; may use physical appearance to elicit attention from others
- **Excessive emotionality** wherein emotions shift rapidly and are shallowly expressed
- Emotions may be self-dramatized, theatrically expressed, or exaggerated
- Style of speech is impressionistic and lacks detail
- **Easily influenced** by suggestion and circumstance; views relationships as more intimate than they are

Narcissistic:
- **Grandiose sense of self-importance**, overestimates personal abilities and accomplishments and expects to be recognized as superior regardless of achievements, feels special and privileged
- **Need for excessive admiration**, often with a sense of entitlement
- **Lacks empathy** for the feelings and needs of others, may be interpersonally exploitative
- May envy others or believe others envy him or her
- Arrogant, haughty behaviour and attitudes

Avoidant:
- **Social inhibition**, unwilling to get involved with others unless certain to be liked, restraint in intimate relationships for fear of shame or ridicule, reluctant to take risks or do new activities due to potential embarrassment
- **Feelings of inadequacy**; preoccupation with criticism or rejection of self, may be inhibited in new interpersonal situations; views self as socially inept, unappealing, or inferior
- **Hypersensitivity to negative evaluation**, may avoid occupations involving significant interpersonal contact due to fears of criticism, disapproval, or rejection

Dependent:
- **Submissive and clinging behaviour** related to an **excessive need to be taken care of**
- **Difficulty in making decisions** without considerable advice and reassurance from others
- Needs others to take responsibility for most areas of his or her life
- **Problems expressing disagreement** for fear of loss of support or approval;

difficulty initiating or doing things independently because lacks confidence in personal abilities and judgement

- Goes to **excessive lengths to obtain nurturance and support,** such as volunteering to do aversive activities
- Feels **uncomfortable or helpless** when alone; seeks a new relationship immediately after a previous one ends, unrealistically preoccupied with fears of being left to fend for himself or herself

Obsessive-compulsive:

- **Preoccupied with orderliness, perfectionism, and control** at the expense of flexibility, openness, and efficiency
- May **lose the purpose of an activity** due to preoccupation with details, rules, lists, etc.; **perfectionism interferes with task completion**
- Devotion to work and productivity such that leisure activities and friendships are excluded
- **Overly conscientious**, **scrupulous**, and **inflexible** about morality, ethics, and values
- Cannot discard worn-out or worthless objects even when sentimental value is absent
- **Difficulty in delegating tasks** unless can control their exact execution
- **Miserly** with money, particularly for fear of future catastrophes
- **Rigid** and **stubborn**

Note: Adapted from American Psychiatric Association, *Diagnostic and Statistical Manual of Mental Disorders, Fourth Edition* (1994).

other personality disorder not included in DSM-IV. Readers should refer directly to DSM-IV for a more detailed description of specific personality disorders and criteria for diagnosis.

Obviously, the **chronicity** and **severity** of mental health problems must be considered in parenting assessments. The long-term impact on children might be very different if a parent is temporarily depressed due to job loss or a separation as opposed to a parent who has had life-long difficulties. Even acute psychosis in a parent might be quite manageable if the other parent or family members can support the child through the crisis period and if the parent's difficulties can be treated and settled relatively quickly. Of course, assessors must consider availability and adequacy of treatment interventions as well as the willingness of parents to comply with therapy and/or medication regimes. For example, a parent with an entrenched paranoid belief system might have difficulty taking the necessary medication given suspicions that others are poisoning him or her. Cassell and Coleman

(1995) stress that **prognosis** for parental improvement is a critical issue and that the potential for 'significant' harm of children must always be considered. In other words, does the mental health problem so impair parents' abilities to respond to children that the latter's developmental progress is at risk?

While the wide range of **mental health problems** cannot be reviewed here, the following questions can help to delineate the impact that problems can have on children's development.

1. What is the nature of the parent's mental health problem?
2. Is the problem likely to be brief or chronic?
3. How does the nature of the parent's mental health problem affect parenting? Can the parent take care of the physical, safety, and emotional needs of the child?
4. Are the parents at risk of hurting or killing themselves or other family members, and are they likely to do this in front of the children?
5. Are the parents likely to hurt the child, either as part of a suicide or if they are delusional?
6. Is the home milieu so bizarre that children will be confused and have difficulty relating to peers and others in the community?
7. Do the parents have insight into their mental health problems?
8. Is the prognosis for parent change good or poor (e.g., a parent with a severe personality disorder might have a very poor prognosis)?
9. What is the parent's history of treatment compliance and progress, and are these reports cross-validated by mental health professionals and others who interact with that parent? If the history is poor, what has changed to make compliance more likely?
10. Are alternate caregivers or other supportive people available to care for the children during hospitalizations and to monitor the children's safety when they are in the care of their parents?
11. Have repeated separations of parents and children occurred due to parent hospitalizations, or will they be likely, especially when the children are very young?
12. Did the children have several good years with the parents prior to the onset of the mental health problems, years that might contribute to their resiliency and capacity to cope?
13. What do the children understand about their parents' mental health problems?

14. How do the children cope with the parent's mental illness and do they provide care to the parents rather than the reverse?

Alcohol and Drug Misuse

Although some children of parents with significant mental health disorders can manage well, the situation is different for those whose parents misuse alcohol or various drugs, including prescription drugs. While little is known about the effects of recreational alcohol and drug use on parenting proficiency, it is clear that alcohol and drugs have wide-ranging effects on the behaviour of those people who use them. Obviously, these substances affect feelings, perceptions, energy levels, and general health. When they are used regularly and in higher doses, their potential for detrimental impact increases. Few of us have not known of someone who does poorly because of drinking or drug use. Jobs and family life suffer significantly. Therefore it is not surprising that parenting is significantly affected by chronic misuse and that any parenting assessment needs to question alcohol and drug use by parents or others in the home.

Direct Effects

Coleman and Cassell (1995) offer a brief review of the effects of various types of drugs. The DSM-IV also offers a comprehensive list of criteria to be used in diagnosing substance dependence, abuse, intoxication, and withdrawal. Essentially, dependence is diagnosed when a maladaptive pattern of use exists that leads to clinically significant impairment in daily functioning. Thus tolerance may develop, withdrawal effects occur if usage is reduced, and use continues despite wishes or attempts to cut back. Considerable time and effort may be devoted to obtaining the substance, including illegal means, and social, occupational, and recreational activities may be curtailed because of the substance use. Users may also continue to utilize the substance despite known negative effects on psychological or physical functioning. Substance abuse is more serious, as users often cannot fulfil major role obligations, use substances in hazardous situations such as while driving an automobile, have associated legal problems, and continue use despite deleterious impact on their interpersonal functioning and health. Table 6.2 offers a summary of the effects of several types of substances that are most likely to be misused by parents who are involved in parenting assessments.

Table 6.2
Effects of Drugs and Alcohol

Depressant Drugs: includes alcohol, sedatives, tranquilizers, solvents
- Effect: depressed functioning of nervous system; impaired mental and physical performance; disinhibited behaviour; tension and anxiety decreased; drowsiness and unconsciousness at high levels of intake
- Prolonged usage: tolerance develops and higher dosages required for same effect; stopping use results in irritability, overarousal, difficulty sleeping, disorientation, medical difficulties such as seizures, nutritional deficiencies

Opiates: includes such drugs as heroin, methadone, codeine
- Effect: reduced emotional responsiveness, discomfort, and anxiety; feelings of warmth, contentment, and tranquillity; sedation and perhaps unconsciousness only at high levels
- Prolonged usage: tolerance and physical dependence; lethargy, apathy, and withdrawal from others with chronic use; withdrawal symptoms less severe than those evident with depressants

Stimulants: includes drugs such as cocaine, amphetamines
- Effect: increased wakefulness; delayed sleep and fatigue; increased performance; elevated mood
- Prolonged usage: agitation, anxiety, and sometimes depression when use is discontinued; sometimes paranoia with continual use

Hallucinogenic Drugs: such as cannabis, angel dust (PCP), LSD
- Effect: cannabis results in euphoria and a sense of emotional and physical well-being; PCP and LSD affect sensory phenomena with unpredictable and varied distortions of reality
- Prolonged usage: no withdrawal, although flashbacks may occur with LSD

As is evident in Table 6.2, the misuse of alcohol and others drugs can have a significant influence on the general emotional and behavioural responses of parents, and it may aggravate existing mental health issues. Defining the influences is complicated because many parents use several drugs rather than a single one (Behnke & Eyler, 1993). As discussed in Chapter 4, misuse can also have direct physical impact on children if mothers use substances during pregnancy. For example, children may be born with fetal alcohol syndrome, or they may contract HIV infection if their mothers have been infected due to their drug usage. As Coleman and Cassell (1995) report, substance misusers are also more likely to have difficulties maintaining their pregnancies, and children are more likely to have low birth weights, among other problems.

Indirect Effects

Alcohol and drug misuse can also have a number of indirect effects on family functioning and children. Some of these existed in the case of Patty and Mary, whom we described in Case 5 of Chapter 4. Mary invited strangers home to drink or use drugs and could not, when intoxicated, adequately protect her daughter. Patty was raped while Mary was passed out in another room during a drinking party. Mary did not believe Patty's report because she could not recall the evening or the identity of the strangers whom she had brought home. When intoxicated with alcohol or drugs, Mary repeatedly 'forgot' Patty at daycare, and she often 'forgot' where she had left her car the night before. Relatives picked Patty up, but the car was impounded many times. Mary also lost various jobs when she could not get up to go to work. Violence was common, as her partners frequently physically and sexually assaulted her. Patty sometimes witnessed these assaults and had intrusive memories about them, although Mary usually could not remember them.

In order to buy expensive drugs, Mary resorted to defrauding her drug plan. Using aliases, she would visit upwards of twenty to thirty physicians over a few days. These physicians provided prescriptions for various fictitious ailments. A number of male friends also supplied alcohol, usually in exchange for drugs or sex. Although Mary had periods of drug and alcohol abstinence where she parented quite adequately, she was preoccupied with alcohol and drug availability when she was actively using them, and her energies and financial resources were then devoted solely to obtaining these substances. At these times, Mary did not buy food or clothing, resulting in periods of neglect where Patty was often hungry and unkempt; she missed school and was left on her own for hours. Mary's alcohol and drug usage was cyclical in nature; Patty came to dread the difficult times, and she learned to recognize the signs of drinking and drug-use cycles. She attempted to divert her mother's attention away from drug use, poured beer down the toilet when she found it, begged her mother to stop drinking alcohol, and tried to take care of her intoxicated mother, making her coffee and cleaning the home in the morning.

This example clearly identifies many of the indirect effects that occur in families where alcohol and drugs are misused. When parents do not have steady, legal incomes, they may engage in illegal activities such as selling drugs, prostitution, fraud, and theft. Because such activities usually involve others, children may be exposed to an array of individuals who engage in antisocial activities, provide poor role modelling, and sometimes actively harm or threaten the children. Basic physical care and safety concerns may arise, and accidents are common. For example, a very young child can easily fall down the stairs when a parent is intoxicated with cannabis or alcohol and unable to supervise or monitor the youngster. Additionally, parents may demonstrate poor judgment and undertake such activities as driving a car while intoxicated. Children may also be at risk if parents leave used needles around the home or let children roam hallways and alleys where such dangerous materials abound. Generally, children are at risk for abuse and neglect, because intoxicated parents may have real difficulty supervising and monitoring their children's safety.

Children's physical and emotional needs also are neglected as alcohol or drugs become the priority in their parents' lives. Over time, children learn to take care of themselves and their parents, like Patty did in Case 5. They learn to attune to signs of substance use, and they may avoid the home when people are intoxicated so they cannot be hurt or verbally attacked. Unfortunately, the children are deprived of so much care that they cannot master the developmental tasks outlined in Chapter 3. For example, they may have difficulty modulating their affect and behaviour, and their social, cognitive, and academic progress suffers because parents cannot provide the necessary guidance, support, and stimulation. Children often begin to model the behaviour they see around them. Given their milieu, this may include not only aggressive and illegal activities but experimentation with alcohol and drugs. Mary, who was described above, reported she first began to drink alcohol at the age of five years when adults attending parties in her grandparents' home offered her sips of their beer or left unfinished drinks, which she consumed. As Coleman and Cassell (1995) point out after reviewing various studies, the outlook for children in families where parents misuse substances is generally poor. Although not all of such children are directly abused, development is often compromised.

Factors to Consider

Of course, not all children raised in families where substances are misused have such dire outcomes. Other factors in the children's lives can compensate for the poor care parents provide. Relatives or friends may provide sensitive care, such as happened with Patty (Case 5). If only one parent has an alcohol or drug problem, the other parent may compensate for that parent's inadequacies. Some parents also have long periods of abstinence between relatively short bouts of alcohol or drug use, thus meeting the children's needs for the majority of the time. Clearly, during assessments we must explore these **compensatory factors** and the known **factors that enhance resiliency** in children. Examples include having a significant caring adult involved in their lives, having various talents and skills, or being involved in positive school and community situations (see Chapter 5).

In regard to the actual substance dependency and misuse by parents, we must consider factors that are similar to those used to evaluate the impact of mental health problems on parenting. Thus, the **chronicity** and **severity** of the alcohol and drug problems should be assessed. Recommendations might be different for a young mother just developing a dependency on alcohol and becoming alarmed when she drinks alone during the day, versus another mother who does the same but is completely unconcerned about her behaviour. The first might actively seek treatment and respond well, but the second might not seek treatment at all. **Prognosis** is thus a critical factor. Parents who enter programs and maintain abstinence for lengthy periods are viewed more positively than those who repeatedly enter appropriate treatment programs but relapse soon afterwards. Likewise, insightful parents who are genuinely motivated to enter and follow through with treatment are viewed more favourably than those who do not regard their alcohol or drug abuse as a problem. If parents have no social supports or relationships with people outside of their alcohol- or drug-using social network, the prognosis is likely poorer (Coleman & Cassell, 1995). Overall, we must evaluate the degree to which substance misuse affects parenting, the likelihood that children can be safe, the degree to which parents can actively meet their children's needs, and the extent to which parents can overcome their problem. This assessment is complicated by the fact some users have co-morbid mental health problems that may in part precipitate substance misuse. For example, a parent with post-traumatic stress disorder arising from sexual assaults as a teenager may use alcohol to forget his or her pain.

In order to assess the impact of **alcohol and drug misuse** on parenting, the following questions can be employed:

1. What is the specific pattern, frequency, type, quantity, and manner of alcohol and/or drug usage in the home?

2. Does substance use divert financial resources away from the provision of basic needs for food, clothing, and housing?
3. Are parents so regularly intoxicated they cannot meet their children's basic needs for physical care, supervision, safety, boundaries, and stimulation?
4. Do parents engage in illegal activities to support their alcohol or drug usage and do these activities occur in the home?
5. Do visitors to the home have difficulties with alcohol or drug usage and do they display behaviours that directly or indirectly threaten or harm the children? Can parents supervise and protect the children in these situations?
6. Do parents view their substance use as a problem in their lives and families?
7. Have parents sought treatment for their substance use and has this been effective? If previous treatment has been ineffective, what has changed to make progress more likely?
8. Do parents have other mental health problems besides their substance misuse?
9. Do parents have any family or friend supports that are not involved in substance use and illegal activities? Do parents recognize the negative impact of the drug/alcohol lifestyle and the concomitant need to make new friends, having a plan about how to do so?
10. What is the long-term prognosis for the parents in regard to their alcohol or drug usage?
11. Are the children already using drugs and are they involved in illegal activities?

Family Conflict and Spousal Abuse

The presence of conflict and violence within the family is another factor that limits parents' abilities to care for children. In Chapter 5, we discussed the marked negative impact that direct abuse and neglect can have on children. In some families, violence is directed towards children. In other families, children are not the targets of violence but a spouse may be beaten and threatened or parents may engage in aggressive verbal and physical interchanges. These situations can be terrifying and upsetting for children. Thompson and Calkins (1996) report that marital conflict generally creates anger, distress, and anxiety in children, who subsequently may have difficulties in regulating their own emotions. This effect is exacerbated if arguments are intense and ongoing, if they are not resolved, if they centre on the children, and if they culminate in violence (Thompson & Calkins, 1996). After undertaking a meta-analysis of 118 studies, Kitzmann, Gaylord, Holt, and Kenny (2003) found that children who witness domestic violence are more likely to experience significant disruption in their psycho-social functioning than children who are not witnesses, with a higher risk for preschool children. Domestic conflict vitiates the sense of emotional security that children feel because of threats to the provision of care to the children, the children's actual physical well-being, and the integrity of the family (Cummings & Davies, 1996). Over time, children who remain in intact high-conflict families do more poorly than children in families that have separated but continue to be embroiled in conflict (Amato & Keith, 1991). The latter finding is noteworthy because, as reviewed in Chapter 5, ongoing post-separation conflict significantly decreases children's abilities to cope following family breakup.

Children's Coping Strategies

When marital conflict is accompanied by physical assaults, children may fear for their own and their parents' well-being (Thompson & Calkins, 1996). This can be truly terrifying, particularly for young children, who cannot flee the home or fight back. Children try to cope in various ways. Many become hypersensitive to cues of impending conflict, sometimes reacting even when no conflict is imminent. For example, a child whose parents regularly have heated arguments or fist fights may flee a room when parents loudly comment on a television program. Children may also attempt to stop arguments between parents by stepping into the fray to plead with parents to stop, or they may divert parents' attention to themselves through bad behaviour. For example, Mike (Case 9) was highly attuned to the intense marital conflict that occurred prior to his parents' separation. Whenever he sensed that a fight or an assault was imminent, he acted up by hurting his sisters or the family pet. This usually postponed the parents' fighting because Tyler yelled at Mike and spanked him. Parents then resumed their fighting, now additionally blaming each other for Mike's negative behaviour. Mike continued to demonstrate this hypervigilance after the separation and still used negative behaviour to avert fights between parents. Mike's sister, Joyce, used a different coping strategy in that she attempted to please both parents and make them feel good so that they would not fight. She also often hugged or clung to them, comforted Della after assaults, and insisted on sleeping with her parents so they would not fight. Joyce often felt sad and guilty when these efforts failed to prevent disagreements. Anna, the youngest child, retreated to her closet and buried herself under a blanket until the fighting ceased. All three children were preoccupied with parental fights and family tension, diverting energy to coping with their feelings and fears rather than engaging in age-appropriate activities.

Parent Reactions

Authors such as Johnston and Campbell (1993) point out that various dynamics may contribute to the development of conflict and violence in families. They have developed a typology of the kinds of interparental violence seen in high-conflict divorcing families that has some applicability in child welfare cases because these families also may experience both violence and separations. Their classifications include ongoing or episodic male battering, female-initiated violence, male-controlled interactive violence, separation and post-divorce violence, and psychotic and paranoid reactions. Although the resulting violent interactions vary in terms of dynamics, intensity, and frequency, they inevitably affect all family members. Austin (2001) offers a different typology of variables regarding partner violence that can be surveyed to predict further violence and developmental outcomes for children. The six factors he includes are a temporal dimension, the sex of the perpetrator and the causal direction of the violence, the severity of physical harm, the type of aggression, the presence of major risk factors, and whether the children are exposed to the violence. He offers various suggestions for collecting and using information about violence in families during the course of parenting assessments.

Johnston and Campbell's (1993) first classification, ongoing or episodic male battering, closely resembles the battering spouse/battered wife syndrome as described by Walker (1984), wherein women are commonly the abused partners. As a cycle of marital and violence becomes established in these families, female partners often bear the brunt of the physical assaults, which are frequently accompanied by considerable verbal denigration. Over time, abused spouses feel increasingly ineffectual and perhaps even deserving of their abuse. These feelings intensify as they often become increasingly isolated from their usual social supports when abusive partners limit opportunities for interaction with others. Children are likewise isolated from outside people, with abused partners and children sometimes feeling like hostages. By the time this cycle is well established, abused spouses and children may be truly terrified of what might happen if they tried to reach out and tell others. As abused parents are often isolated and thus dependent on the abusive spouse for emotional and financial support, it is difficult for many victims to take steps to stop this cycle and protect themselves or their children. Some abused spouses attempt to leave on several occasions, only to return to abusive partners who promise the behaviour will not reoccur. However, the abuse, control, and terror often intensify with each return to the family, and children may worry that one parent will eventually kill the other.

While some parents remain in such violent situations indefinitely, others do manage to escape and take both their children and themselves to safety. Sometimes this is achieved by entry into a shelter, or they flee to another jurisdiction; this occurred in the case that follows. Even when parents flee, the situation is not always resolved. Abused parents and children worry that they will be found and that the abusive parent may seek legal recourse to have the children returned because they were taken without parental consent. Parenting assessments may be initiated, as was the situation in the following case.

CASE 14: Laura and her five children, aged three years to twelve years, arrived in a city after fleeing her abusive marriage with Bob, who remained in another state. After she and the children had lived under assumed names for three months, Laura called extended family, and against her wishes, they informed Bob of her location. A parenting assessment was court-ordered when Bob applied to have the children returned to him.

Laura described a marriage replete with escalating verbal and physical abuse. She claimed Bob had broken her arm and wrist, thrown hot coffee on her during arguments, pulled her hair out, and knocked her senseless numerous times. He also raped her several times, resulting in two unplanned pregnancies. She was afraid for her life and said she finally left when he began to beat her oldest son. Bob denied ever abusing Laura or the children, although he admitted to having a short temper and said he had 'pushed' Laura around a couple of times. He justified his actions by saying he was suspicious of her relationship with a man who lived next door. He said Laura was exaggerating their conflict, and he portrayed himself as a hard-working and long-suffering spouse. Despite these reports, Bob became upset when asked to sign consents so the assessor could obtain various records. He was unwilling to sign consents for a criminal record check for himself; the assessor eventually obtained a court order to access this information. Bob's record indicated one conviction for assault against Laura, but he had been allowed to serve sentences on weekends so he could work to support his family. When he was younger Bob had been charged and convicted on several occasions for impaired driving and physical assault. Records also indicated the police had attended at the family home several times to settle domestic disputes.

As information emerged about Bob's history of violence and job losses due to his volatile and aggressive nature, the assessor became concerned about using the usual assessment process. Nick, the oldest child, presented as a frightened child who vomited when questioned about his father; he could not sleep because of worries that Bob would kidnap them. He also said that, for the first time in his life, he experienced occasional periods where he could relax and did not need to be ready to protect his mother. The younger children were also anxious and described fears that their father would kill Laura and Nick if he found them. Although it is common practice to see children with each of their parents, the assessor found that the degree of the children's terror of their father argued against such contact during the assessment. Furthermore, given the extensive documentation of Bob's violent nature, his minimization of his behaviour, and his unwillingness to enter treatment, the assessor recommended the children have no ongoing contact with him.

Bob was incensed by these recommendations and raised questions about the procedures used in the assessment. However, the judge ruled that the interests of the children would be best served if they had no contact with him. Laura and the children then moved to another city, where they lived under assumed names as they attempted to develop a life free of terror. Unfortunately, Bob remained angry with the assessor and for several months made threats towards her. She changed her office location to improve security measures. Bob's threats decreased somewhat once he became involved in a relationship with another woman.

In rare circumstances, children are removed from violent family situations because one parent kills the other. The remaining parent is usually charged and incarcerated, and the children are placed with alternate caregivers. These situations are tragic because children often have very conflicted and confused feelings. For example, they may feel guilty if they are relieved when their victimized parent kills an abusive partner, but then they must grieve the loss of both the parent who has died and the remaining parent who is incarcerated. If the abuser is freed, children must grieve the loss of their dead parent but may still experience apprehension about the release of the other parent from jail. In such circumstances extended families tend to become polarized, and children may not have the support of various relatives just when they need it most. Occasionally, parenting assessments are undertaken when a parent is released from jail, and decisions must be made about the return of the children to a parent who has murdered his or her spouse.

Factors to Consider

Even though all family conflict does not lead to the degree of violence just described, parenting assessors need to consider several factors when determining the degree to which conflict and violence impede the ability of parents to care adequately for their children. Some disagreement is inevitable in any home, and assessors must clearly determine the **modes of conflict resolution** used among family members. If parents disagree regularly, then assessors must determine their ability to insulate the children from some of the conflict. In families where parents experience high conflict, cannot insulate the children from the dissension, and engage in physical violence, then assessors must assess the **severity** and **chronicity** of the abusive cycle in the family. In these situations it is critical to determine the **dangerousness** of the situation. In the typology Austin (2001) proposes, the presence of major risk factors such as alcohol and drug use during the violence, ongoing alcohol and drug abuse as a mental disorder, existence of a major mental disorder, and history of violent behaviour in other settings may increase the likelihood of violence in a family. Abusers' histories of anger management problems and violent behaviour need to be considered; risk is heightened if abusers have previous charges or convictions for assault against family members and other people in their extended families and communities. Police and court records can be accessed to verify such behaviour. Even without formal charges, concerns increase if the abuser has demonstrated difficulties with anger management in school, work, and other settings. Within the home we may want to examine whether violence is threatened or directed to more than one family member, including pets, and we will need to ask about the nature of violence. For example, pushing and grabbing at a person may have different implications than choking or holding a knife or gun to a person's head. References are critical in validating such reports, and child abuse registries can provide cross-checks on some of these events. Concerns are attenuated if parents can both admit and take responsibility for their behaviour, and if they enter treatment programs and actually utilize the strategies they are taught to manage anger and frustration in more adaptive ways. Of course, there is significant risk if parents continue to deny their abusive and violent behaviour or blame their spouses or children.

If the risk of violence is high and increasing, then we must also determine the capacity of the non-offending parent to **protect themselves and their children**. One must consider whether they have attempted to leave the situation previously and whether they have any supports in the extended family or the community. As leaving a home is particularly difficult if an abusive cycle of family violence is well established and victims are isolated and terrorized, assessors may need to determine what supports are needed to help the family take steps to become safe and whether non-offending parents can utilize them. For example, some parents verbalize appropriate plans of action but then do not follow through with them. Also, the **risk of violence towards assessors** must be evaluated, and assessors need to take steps to protect themselves if such risks exist. This may include interviewing potentially violent clients in locations where other people are present and can be summoned to help; home visits may require the presence of another person. Certainly if assessors go to meetings alone with potentially violent people, they should let others know of the address and their expected time of return. It can be helpful to carry a cell phone so help can be summoned quickly. However, the latter procedures are prudent in any assessment situation.

Finally, assessment procedures may need to be altered so children in the family are not further traumatized by them, such as occurred in the case discussed above. Assessors may need to dispense with some of their more routine assessment procedures if risks exist, and they must work within the legal constraints imposed by existing restraining, no contact, and supervision court orders. For example, an assessor may need to obtain a specific order to permit joint sessions between a parent and child when a no contact order already exists. Also, safety precautions regarding logistical issues may be necessary to protect clients, particularly if allegations of assault, threats, and stalking have been made. For example, sessions with separated parents may need to be scheduled on different days to ensure clients do not inadvertently meet in a waiting room.

The following questions can be used to guide assessment of the impact of **family conflict** and **spousal abuse** on parenting capacity:

1. How do the family members resolve disagreements and conflicts?
2. What is the frequency and intensity of conflict between parents and does fighting centre on the children or other issues?
3. Are the children aware of the conflict and how do they cope with it?
4. Does the conflict ever end in violence or threats of violence and are physical injuries documented by medical personnel or other people?
5. Has a cycle of family violence been established where one parent tends to be controlled and isolated by the other?
6. Have police ever been called to the home to settle domestic disputes and have charges ever been laid?
7. What efforts have victimized parents made to try to protect themselves and their children? Have parents failed to protect their children when involved in subsequent relationships?
8. Have family members attempted therapy and was this successful?
9. Does an ongoing risk of assault or homicide exist in the family?

Adolescent Parenthood

Effects on Adolescent Parents

Adolescent parenthood is another factor that can compromise parenting abilities. Levine Coley and Chase-Lansdale (1998) reviewed recent evidence regarding teenage pregnancy and parenthood and the consequences for both teenage parents and their children. The majority of the existing research has focused on teenage mothers rather than fathers. As this book discusses, it is clear that parenting requires considerable energy and sophistication in responding to the needs of children. Parents must often delay the gratification of their own needs and goals so they can meet those of their children; this means teenage parents often must put aside their own developmental needs. They may not be able to direct energy to the normative adolescent tasks of autonomy and individuation from the family, identity formation, and the establishment of mature intimate adult relationships. Stress may be high, and they may experience considerable conflict between wanting to provide for their children and wanting to participate in teenage activities. Friendships, dating, schooling, leisure activities, and career choices can be significantly affected. When compared to peers who postpone childbearing, teenage mothers experience more negative consequences (Levine Coley & Chase-Lansdale, 1998). They complete school less frequently, have less stable employment rates, and have higher rates of poverty and welfare use. If they marry they are more likely to divorce, and they spend more of their parenting careers as single parents. They are also more likely to have additional nonmarital births, experience more pregnancy and delivery problems, and have less healthy babies. However, these physical problems may be more related to factors such as poverty than to maternal age per se. Factors that enhance the likelihood of more positive outcomes for adolescent mothers include a higher grade level when they become pregnant, a smaller family of origin that is not on public assistance, and higher expectations about life experiences from both teenage parents and their families.

Very little is known about teenage fathers. Levine Coley and Chase-Lansdale (1998) report that the sparse existing data suggest teenage fathers tend to be two to three years older than teenage mothers. Although marriage rates are low, approximately 50 per cent of fathers live with the mothers of their children after the birth, but usually not for long. Many see their children regularly in the first few years, but rates of contact decline over time. Few are able to provide financial support on an ongoing basis, although many have good intentions about doing so. They often are poor and have low education levels that limit their overall ability to provide for their children.

Effects on the Children

It is not uncommon for the parenting of adolescents to be negatively impacted by the conflict they experience between meeting their own needs versus those of their children, as well as characteristics such as poverty and lack of supports. Levine Coley and Chase-Landsdale (1998) report that while some teenage mothers may be just as warm with their children as older mothers, they are less verbal, sensitive, and responsive to their infants. Some studies suggest they provide less stimulating home environments, perceive their infants as more difficult, and harbour unrealistic expectations about their children. For example, they may treat their infants as dolls or toys, take their babies to unsafe places, and plan poorly, expecting babies to manage without food and diapers. Even so, in infancy few differences exist between children of adolescent and older mothers, although there is a higher risk for attachment problems. Differences become evident in the preschool years, when children tend to exhibit more delays in cognitive development and show more behaviour problems, such as aggression and poor impulse control. It is also thought that parenting adequacy may decline as children get older, particularly when they reach adolescence. Adolescent children of teenage mothers tend to have more school problems, delinquency, incarceration, and early sexual activity and pregnancy, although there is great variability and some children do well (Levine Coley & Chase-Landsdale, 1998).

Few teenage mothers are equipped emotionally or financially to parent single-handedly, and most require support from other people to raise their children without compromising their youngster's development. Since teenage fathers seldom can provide the needed emotional and financial support, mothers' extended families often fulfil this role. In particular, maternal grandmothers and sometimes grandfathers often end up providing for both their daughters and grandchildren; adolescent mothers and children may even cohabit with the grandparents. The most optimal arrangement for older teenagers appears to be one where the grandmothers provide support and modelling for their daughters but do not live in the same household (Levine Coley & Chase-Landsdale, 1998). Thus, mothers are permitted some autonomy but grandmothers are available to provide support. Open communication between mothers and grandmothers is necessary in such situations. However, these arrangements might be problematic if the grandparents also experience serious problems, such as low cognitive abilities, drug or alcohol addictions, or serious mental health problems. When adolescents become mothers earlier in their teens, cohabitation may contribute to better outcomes. However, their children are at risk of attaching to grandparents rather than parents if care is not taken to enhance mothers' parenting competencies. This occurred in the following case.

CASE 15: Grandparents Ellen and Sidney and their daughter, Jessie, were referred for assessment when they disagreed about ongoing plans for Maxine, who was born when Jessie was fourteen years old. Her fifteen-year-old boyfriend broke up with Jessie when he found out she was pregnant, and he never met Maxine. The grandparents and Jessie shared guardianship of Maxine, and Jessie and Maxine lived full time with Ellen and Sidney for the first four years after Maxine's birth. Ellen babysat while Jessie attended high school and worked at a corner store. After high school, Jessie met and married Dave and they rented an apartment two blocks away; Ellen provided babysitting and considerable childcare for Maxine, who sometimes slept at her grandparents' home and sometimes at her mothers' home. This arrangement continued after Jessie had another baby, although this child always slept at his parents' home. Maxine did well and came and went easily between homes. The family was thrown into conflict, however, when Dave wanted to seek work in another city. Dave and Jessie wished to move so they could become independent of Ellen and Sidney, who they thought meddled in their affairs. The grandparents objected to Maxine's move because they believed Jessie and Maxine were not closely bonded and they could not trust Jessie to provide for her daughter. Jessie and Dave had difficulty maintaining steady employment, and the grandparents recounted many occasions when they had to provide groceries for their daughter's household. They also felt Dave favoured his son over Maxine.

The assessor recommended that Maxine live with her grandparents, in part because she clearly derived her sense of security from them rather than from her mother. In many ways, Jessie was more like an older sister than a mother to Maxine. Jessie had been involved with friends, work, and parties with her peers through high school because Ellen always cared for Maxine during Jessie's absences. Ellen also enjoyed caring for her granddaughter and did not insist that Jessie assume more responsibility for her. The assessor noted that Jessie and Dave's parenting and life skills were generally poor and they were clearly quite self-centred, spending the money they earned on themselves rather than on basic family expenses. Much of Jessie's behaviour appeared geared to provoking distance between herself and her parents and, in many ways, she was still dealing with adolescent issues at the age of 22 years. Counselling was recommended so Jessie could work towards providing better parenting to both of her children, but she declined such input. Within a year child welfare contacted the grandparents to ask if they would care for Maxine's brother because he had been apprehended due to neglect and abuse.

The following questions can be used to guide inquiry about the impact of **adolescent parenting** on parenting competency:

1. How old were the parents when the girl became pregnant?
2. At what stage are the mothers in their mastery of the developmental tasks of adolescence? Have the mothers developed good capacities to regulate their own emotions?
3. Do the mothers have any difficulties, such as low cognitive functioning, that might jeopardize their capacities to parent sensitively?
4. Do the mothers place their child's needs before their own and how do they balance these opposing sets of needs?
5. Are grandparents able to support the mothers to parent adequately and to develop maturity and independence? What are the mothers' views of the grandparents and can they accept support from them?
6. Are the mothers at risk for neglecting or abusing their children?
7. Are the fathers involved and, if they are, are they supportive and positive influences for the mothers and children?
8. Can the mothers financially support themselves now or do they demonstrate the drive to gain the necessary skills so they can do so in the future?
9. Are positive role models available who can help guide the mothers in acquiring sensitive and responsive parenting behaviours?
10. Are adolescent parents accepting of support and instruction about parenting?

Cognitively Limited Parents

As discussed in chapter 4, children with cognitive limitations that arise from mental retardation and developmental disorders place increased demands on parents and can contribute to parenting difficulties. Similar difficulties in parents themselves can contribute to parenting problems and, at times, can make good and safe parenting problematic. This is clearly the case when parents are profoundly or even moderately affected, although Gath (1995) reports that few people with this degree of impairment become parents. However, mildly mentally retarded people may be referred for parenting assessments, and it is common for assessments to be undertaken when parents function at the low average or borderline levels of intelligence. Tymchuk (1992) notes that while there are many similarities between parents with diagnosed mental retardation and those with borderline IQs, differences are evident and may affect parenting. Many people with such cognitive levels are integrated into the community and may have partners who are more cognitively able (Gath, 1995).

Cognitive limitations may affect different aspects of parents' general daily functioning. Employment may be problematic given generally low levels of educational attainment and, if parents are employed, jobs often involve low skills and low pay, resulting in meagre living conditions unless a partner has higher skill and income levels. If unemployed, parents tend to receive public assistance, either through month-to-month welfare payments or on a more stable basis through funding for handicapped persons; in either case incomes are low. The stresses of low income are exacerbated by limited planning and management skills that make managing finances and running a household difficult. Impulsiveness and an inability to anticipate consequences and to plan ahead may compromise everything from daily nutrition to relationships; much of everyday life can be quite overwhelming unless support and supervision are available. However, parents may be defensive and resist such input, requiring a slow and painstaking process of engagement.

Cognitive limitations also affect parenting abilities. Tymchuk (1992) reported that the risk of child neglect is higher when a parent is mentally retarded. Parents with mental retardation may have difficulties with parenting knowledge and skills, the provision of health care and a safe environment for children, general decision making, the learning and generalization of parenting knowledge, and parent-child interaction. Although the existing research is in some ways flawed, mentally challenged mothers do tend to be less supportive, reinforcing, and varied in interactions with their children. They also may be more directive, and some are more punitive. While they can identify their children's negative behaviours, they may have more difficulty identifying and reinforcing desirable behaviours.

Life can become even more overwhelming if people have been living in supported situations such as institutions or group homes and then leave these to establish their own households when they meet a new partner. New partners may be supportive, but sometimes they are abusive and controlling. When children arrive, some cognitively limited parents cannot cope, and they may not provide a safe and stimulating environment despite their love for the children. This occurred in the following case.

CASE 16: Sally and Ken were referred by their child welfare case worker after the third apprehension of their two boys, who were three and five years of age. Ken was thirty-two years old and worked as a trucker while Sally, aged twenty-seven years, stayed home to care for the children. Child welfare concerns had arisen periodically since the birth of the first son, but both parents always complied with parenting programs and in-home supports. Sally was thought to be of limited cognitive potential, but workers had always recognized that Ken functioned adequately and likely provided considerable stability in the home. Sally's mother, who managed a large office, helped with childcare and provided emotional and occasional financial support to the family.

An assessment was requested given the confusing picture the family presented. Both parents clearly said they wanted to care for the children, and Ken appeared to relate adequately with his sons. He spent time with them and read to them when he was home. He thought Sally did similar things when he was at work, although he recognized she could not manage the household finances, do the grocery shopping, or prepare good meals. The assessment revealed that Sally functioned in the borderline range of intelligence and, despite reasonable verbal interaction, she was limited in her ability to plan and make sound judgments about herself or her children. It was common for her to spend the day watching television and eating while her children were left in their rooms without food. When the boys became mobile, they sustained several injuries when they fell down stairs or wandered outside. Both had been hospitalized with failure-to-thrive as infants, and records indicated that Sally seemed uninvolved with her infant children. She was overwhelmed by the task of caring for them and had not bonded with either child.

Over the years Ken had tended to take over when he was home, and he had not recognized the poor care and attachment issues regarding Sally and the boys. Sally's mother excused her daughter's behaviour and did not recognize the severity of the situation. School personnel expressed considerable alarm when Sally clearly could not reliably feed or clothe her eldest son or get him to kindergarten on a daily basis. The assessment concluded that the children were at risk in the care of their parents. Although Ken had some parenting skills, he had not recognized the problems with his children and was unable to take steps to protect them or provide a healthier environment. Ken chose to stay with Sally after the assessment rather than attempt parenting by himself. The boys became permanent wards and were subsequently placed for adoption, although both had significant learning and emotional difficulties.

Cognitively Limited Parents: Effects on the Children

As the above case demonstrates, parents with limited cognitive abilities often struggle with caring for themselves, let alone children. Such basic tasks as cooking and supervising children may be impossible or be done poorly, so children are indeed at risk for neglect of their basic physical needs. Even prenatal nutrition can be affected if mothers do not eat well. Medical appointments may be forgotten, and cognitively limited parents may be unable to intellectually stimulate their youngsters. Abuse may occur if parents are frustrated and cannot develop solutions to problems or have no one to help them do so. They may have limited understanding of the normal growth and development of children and are not cognizant of their children's needs. Parents may not have sufficient judgment to protect their children from possible abuse by others in their families or the community, or they may be unable to advocate for their children with their spouses or other people. Children are at more risk if both parents have cognitive limitations. Risk also increases with each additional child in the family (Gath, 1995; Tymchuk, 1992). Increased awareness of their compromised functioning may lead many cognitively limited people to develop mental health problems such as depression. If a dual diagnosis exists, children's risk of poor care increases. The emotional and physical development of children being raised by mentally retarded parents has received little research attention. However,

Tymchuk (1992) indicates that the most common outcome for such children is cognitive delay, although some of these children appear to be resilient and develop adequately despite the negative parenting styles.

Factors to Consider

Tymchuk (1992) identified both historical and current factors that increase the risk of poor parenting. He indicated that the risk of inadequate parenting rises if parents have been in institutions or special education programs, if they were abused as children, if their own parents had significant difficulties, and/or if they had lifelong medical or emotional disorders. Factors such as poverty, inadequate support agencies, and multiple agency involvement increased the risk, as did a lack of familial support, from either a spouse or extended family. Having an abusive partner or partner with a significant medical and emotional problem also heightened risks of poor parenting. Risk increased if there was more than one child, if children were over six years of age, and if children had medical, emotional, or behavioural problems. Finally, the following maternal factors contributed to increased risk of poor parenting: emotional problems and high stress; cognitive problems such as an IQ below 60; reading recognition and comprehension skills below grade 4 levels; limited or no parenting skills; health problems; poor coping and decision-making styles; and a punitive and nonempathic parenting style.

It is critical to note that risk consistently decreases if parents have supports and are willing to rely on these supports. Not all parents with limited cognitive abilities and various learning problems do poorly. Outcome depends not only on parent abilities but also on child characteristics and contextual sources of support, as discussed in our initial model of parenting behaviour. An assessor should never assume that specific scores on intellectual testing preclude the capacity to parent. Instead, the following questions can guide inquiry into the impact of **limited cognitive abilities** on parenting:

1. What is the capacity of the parents to care for themselves on a daily basis?
2. Do parents demonstrate good self-help skills; are they able to anticipate problems and find concrete and workable solutions to everyday problems?

3. Do parents have any ongoing and severe medical problems that further limit their capacity to care for children?
4. Do the parents exhibit good judgment about relationships and in the other decisions that they make?
5. Are parents able to comprehend the nature of the care their children require and do they understand the nature of their children's problems?
6. Do parents have the capacity to learn to provide care for their children? If exposed to previous teaching about parenting, did they improve their skills, and if they were not so exposed, did they profit from other types of training? Are parents likely to accept such training regarding their parenting skills?
7. Are parents able to provide for their children's basic physical needs, their need for structure and predictability, and their need for cognitive and emotional stimulation?
8. Can parents ensure safety by providing appropriate supervision?
9. Do parents exhibit good impulse control so they will not hurt their children when frustrated?
10. Are other people available who recognize the risks and are willing to provide the necessary support so risks for the children are lessened? Will these supports remain stable over time?

Poverty

Although many assessors tend to minimize or even disregard poverty as a factor that contributes to poor parenting, it cannot be ignored. Many poor parents care adequately for their children, but for others this factor contributes significantly to difficulties. As Erickson, Egeland, and Pianta (1989) indicate, in the literature poverty has been linked to poor developmental outcome. At a basic level, minimal monetary resources limit the home environment. In extreme cases that are unfortunately becoming more common across North America, whole families are homeless and parents live from day to day attempting to find shelter either on the street or in temporary shelters. Koblinsky, Morgan, and Anderson (1997) found that homeless mothers provided less positive physical environments, reduced learning and academic stimulation and variety in social and cultural experiences, and less warmth and affection to their children than low-income parents who had stable housing. Such findings are not unexpected given the worries and stresses in such families. Even if families have homes, if income is limited worry and stress may still be high. One or both parents may need to work long hours for minimal pay and thus not be physically and emotionally available to provide interaction, guidance, and stimulation. Consequently, young children may be left to care for themselves and younger siblings. When parents are home, they may be tired and stressed. Food and clothing are limited and of poor quality, and families members may become preoccupied with finding food at the expense of other concerns. Children may quit school early to find work, or they may gravitate to peer groups or gangs for social contacts and income.

Poverty is often a risk factor in child welfare parenting assessments. Assessors clearly need to inquire about income and debts, hours spent working, childcare arrangements when parents are working, and whether they are both available and have sufficient energy to provide good care when they are home. They should also examine personal factors, including those discussed earlier in this chapter, that have led to the parents' poverty and may affect their subsequent financial situations. Home visits permit assessors to determine if parents provide safe and stimulating homes that have the basic necessities of food, a place to sleep, adequate cleanliness, and clothing. Some questions follow that may allow assessors to gauge the impact of **poverty** on parenting; they can be combined with those regarding physical care in Chapter 3.

1. Do the families have homes?
2. Are the homes safe and do they provide for the basic physical needs of the children? How often do the families move and who else lives in the homes?
3. What is the source of income for families and is it stable?
4. Is the income sufficient to provide adequate food for families, or do family members often go hungry and are they preoccupied with their next meal?
5. Do parents go into significant debt just to fulfil the basic needs of their children? Do they manage the financial resources they have at their disposal well?
6. Are parents at home to nurture and supervise their children or do they work long hours and leave their children unattended?
7. What is the quality of alternate childcare provided to children if parents work?

8. Are parents exhausted by the task of providing the basics of physical survival for their children? Is any money available for fun activities that might lessen the stress that families endure?
9. Do parents have access to transportation so they can attend medical and other appointments or go to a workplace?
10. Are the financial situations of the families likely to improve and are parents taking active steps to make this happen?

7 Parent Factors: Contextual Sources of Support or Stress

Assessors in child welfare cases are confronted with the task of identifying and weighing factors to determine if individuals can provide good enough parenting. Just as our discussion of resilience in Chapter 5 indicated that various factors contribute to the positive adjustment of children despite poor parenting, numerous factors contribute to parents' abilities to meet their children's needs in sensitive and appropriate ways. For example, Brodsky (1999) identified a number of factors that contributed to positive parenting: the neighbourhood, the parenting role, financial status, family, friends, men as significant others, personal characteristics, and spirituality. Also, authors such as Reder and Lucey (1995) emphasize the need in parenting assessments to focus on positive aspects of family functioning along with problems and risk factors. However, there is no unequivocal list of positive influences that may attenuate the risk of poor parenting, even in adverse situations, and we cannot review all possible factors that may compensate for negative circumstances. As assessors we must remain aware of the factors contributing to the resilience of parents as individuals as outlined in earlier portions of this book. Assessors should also examine environmental factors that support good parenting.

Income and Residence

As discussed in the last section of Chapter 6, poverty is clearly a factor that increases the risk of poor parenting. It contributes to neglect of both the physical and emotional needs of children, and it increases the life stresses that parents must manage. Many elements contribute to poverty by limiting the ability of parents to find gainful and steady employment. Quite a few of the factors discussed in Chapter 6, such as mental health problems, alcohol and drug misuse, teenage parenthood, and cognitive limitations, can compromise the abilities of parents to find steady and well-paying jobs. Circumstances that generate **steady and adequate income levels** are thus compensatory and may attenuate the effects of other negative factors. For example, parents who have mental health problems may parent better if they qualify for a steady pension. Even a small pension that provides only the basics, such as shelter, clothing, and food, relieves these people of the stress of worrying about work and money. Given less stress, they might actually encounter fewer mental health problems and thus provide better care to their children, who might otherwise need to enter the foster care system. Work training programs might also increase the chances that some parents and their children will break out of the cycle of poverty. In cases where divorced parents consistently withhold maintenance payments to punish ex-spouses, children's circumstances can be improved through maintenance enforcement programs. Assessors can recommend such actions if withheld and unpredictable payments lower income and generate high stress for the parents who should be receiving this income. For example, maintenance enforcement programs can appreciably improve the circumstances of single, teenage mothers who are attempting to parent their children.

We also need to explore the **stability of parental employment.** Even if parents do not earn high salaries, those who maintain steady employment with one employer and report that they feel good about working or enjoy their jobs may experience enhanced functioning as individuals and parents. They are likely to be more reliable employees than those who often switch jobs, and such reliability may extend to parenting; if valued by employers, they are more likely to have an increased sense of self-worth that may have a positive impact on parenting. Finally, if they maintain employment for long periods, they are more likely to form relationships with co-workers and perhaps derive a sense of support from them. At the same time, various personal characteristics contribute to their abilities to maintain stable employment and function better in other areas of their lives. Assessors must ascertain if such synergy exists or whether it can be developed in particular families.

Stable jobs also increase chances that families will remain living in the same neighbourhoods and perhaps even in the same residence. **Stability of residence and neighbourhood** is another compensatory factor. Many families must live in often overcrowded and unsafe buildings where they might need to move on little notice. In Chapter 6, we mentioned the stresses faced by homeless families. Families with a stable residence avoid many stresses that come with frequently needing to find and change shelters; subsidized or other types of stable housing can lower stress. Families may be more likely to attempt to make their residence more 'homey,' and they are more likely to establish relationships with neighbours and develop a sense of community. Residing in a stable neighbourhood, where parents have friends and family members nearby who can offer emotional and pragmatic support, contributes to better parenting. Frequent housing changes or residing in dangerous and transient neighbourhoods clearly adds stress, as families may never establish a sense of community or feel safe. Canino and Spurlock (2000) report that area of residence can be a pronounced environmental stressor and that living in the inner city of large cities can reduce social cohesion and integration. Likewise, DePanfilis (1996) reports that certain neighbourhoods clearly do not promote social connections and can increase the likelihood of neglect in some families. Assessors thus need to inquire about these broader **employment and physical environment factors** and can use the following questions:

1. Do families have reliable incomes and from what source?
2. Can parents maintain steady employment in the same job and do they derive a sense of self-worth from their employment?
3. Do employment choices contribute to instability or introduce untoward influences into the home (e.g., mother is a stripper and socializes with a bar crowd)?
4. What factors prevent parents from maintaining steady employment?
5. How long have the families lived in their current residence?
6. How many times have the families moved during the children's lives and why did the moves occur?
7. Do the parents own or rent their own home and is the housing subsidized?
8. Is the neighbourhood safe? If not, do parents recognize the risks? If the parents keep children inside the home because of worries about safety, can they cope with the increased stress that results from having the children underfoot constantly?
9. Do parents and children participate in community activities and have they made friends within their neighbourhood?

Social Supports

Regardless of the physical circumstances, social supports are a factor that can ease or exacerbate the normal difficulties and stresses of parenting (DePanfilis, 1996). 'Social support' is a general term referring to the varied types of connections that exist between people. DePanfilis (1996) outlines several functions filled by social supports. Emotional support includes love, caring, and empathy, while instrumental support encompasses both the material and behavioural assistance given to families. Cognitive support involves information, guidance, or feedback that is useful in problem solving in child management situations, and appraisal support is information provided to parents relevant to their self-evaluations. Finally, social companionship involves spending time with others in various leisure or recreational activities. DePanfilis (1996) describes other properties of social support that contribute to its compensatory benefits for emotional and behavioural functioning of families. Reciprocity in social connections, longer-term availability of supports, and stability of people in the support network enhance the benefits, as does a network of people that are relatively homogenous in regard to factors like economic status and values. Finally, parents need to have the motivation and skills needed to use the supportive relationships and, as noted by Brodsky (1999), nonreciprocal social relationships can be draining and add to the stress of parenting.

Assessors need to keep these various functions and characteristics in mind as they examine the social supports available to a specific family. We next describe several specific parts of the social support network.

Stability of Relationship with Partner

In Chapter 6, we discussed the protective effect that consistent emotional support from at least one significant person in either childhood or adulthood had in preventing abused parents from abusing their own children. Similarly, in Chapter 5, we discussed the importance of caring relationships in promoting resilience in children. Therefore, it is not surprising that the **stability of a supportive relationship with a partner** can do much to compensate for adverse life circumstances. Regardless of whether partners are the biological parents of the children, their support can do much to ease stresses in parenting. They can provide extra income and can help with many routine tasks such as shopping, cooking, cleaning, and tending to children's needs. Perhaps most importantly, a supportive partner is likely to be empathic about the frustrations of rearing children and to provide positive feedback about a parent's self-worth independent of his or her parenting role. Even though some tension and disagreement are likely in all relationships, partners who have evolved adaptive ways to resolve disputes will derive security and acceptance from their partners. If parental partners are also the biological parents, they may feel more closely connected to the children and invested in actively parenting them. Lebow, Walsh, and Rolland (1999) report that stepparents may have weaker emotional bonds with their stepchildren and often adopt a more laissez-faire parenting style.

Of course, some parents have unchanging and long-term relationships with unsupportive partners who are critical of them as partners and as parents. Such partners may indeed add to the stress of parenting. As discussed in the last chapter, physically abusive partners engender significant difficulties in families. If parents change partners frequently, stresses are exacerbated for both parents and children; all must adapt to the addition of new persons to the family system, often without knowing just how long the 'new' daddy or mommy might be part of the family. In these circumstances many children are reticent to get emotionally close and, instead, become behaviourally provocative to perhaps drive away the new person or test his or her commitment, as occurred in the following case.

CASE 17: Sue and her son, Jay (nine years), travelled through several states as she worked as a stripper in small towns. In each new community, Sue rented a motel room and immediately found a boyfriend. Her stays were only a few months long, and just as Jay settled into school, his mother moved on. Consequently, Jay had to constantly adapt to new surroundings and live-in boyfriends whom he resented; not only did he keep his distance from them, but he often acted atrociously to make them leave his mother alone. In one town Sue picked yet another boyfriend but found reasons to stay, prolonging her relationship with him. Although Mark slowly made efforts to engage the boy in a caring relationship, Jay consistently rejected his overtures, thereby angering his mother. He was even more perturbed when Sue quit working and moved them into

Mark's home. Mark proved to be a stable person who cared for Sue and, despite Jay's provocations, persistently tried to relate warmly to him. Only after several years did Jay come to realize that Mark would be an ongoing part of his family and no longer acted out to provoke his departure.

In order to assess the quality and **stability of the parents' relationships with partners**, the following questions might prove useful:

1. Are the children's parents still together or have they separated, and for what reasons?
2. If no longer together, have parents entered new relationships? How and when were these new partners introduced to the children?
3. How long have the current partners been involved in the children's lives?
4. How many partners have been involved in the children's lives? If the children have different fathers, what is the nature of the continuing relationships with these people?
5. Do parents over idealize or make naïve assumptions about their partners, especially new partners, that may affect their abilities to safely and adequately care for their children?
6. Do the partners share concrete and emotional tasks or do these responsibilities fall mainly on one partner?
7. Do the partners offer emotional support to each other or is one partner overly needy or highly critical?
8. Do the parents have congruent attitudes and expectations about parenting, their relationship, and life in general and can they resolve differences?

Family and Friends

Just as a stable partner can be compensatory, parents do better if they have stable and supportive relationships with extended family members and friends. Conversely, relationships can add stress if, for example, they are one-sided or intrusive. For example, an uncle who brings his friends home to use or trade in illicit drugs may engender considerable stress and even danger within the home. Parents' anxiety or preoccupation with these influences or their becoming embroiled in constant quarrels with such extended family members may detract from the time and attention they can devote to their children. On the positive side, both family and friends may provide emotional support, childcare, and even economic support. For parents without partners or with unreliable partners, friends and family can be important sources of support as occurred in the following case.

CASE 18: Eve married young and had four children with her husband, who worked away from home. Because of limited income, the family lived with his elderly parents in a rural community. They were highly critical of Eve, but even they became concerned when their son did not earn sufficient money to support his family and rarely came home. These events severely stressed Eve, who felt like a beggar and had to cope with parenting her children under her in-laws' critical eyes. She grew despondent and later indicated that she considered suicide and would not have survived had a neighbour woman not provided emotional support. She unburdened herself to this friend, who listened to her concerns in a sensitive and nonjudgmental way. While this other woman could not offer any instrumental supports, Eve decided to change her life because of their daily chats. She left her husband and moved nearer to her extended family. She realized her friend had given unselfishly of her time in what had been a one-sided relationship. The relationship became more reciprocal after her move.

To evaluate social supports from **family and friends**, ask:

1. Do the parents have contacts with members of their extended family and friends?
2. Who are these people and are they dysfunctional?
3. What is the nature of their contacts? Do they live in the homes of the families?
4. What is the nature of the support that family members and friends provide, such as daily childcare, evening babysitting, emergency childcare, money, food, emotional validation, advice or guidance regarding child management?
5. What aspects of their relationships with family and friends do the parents appreciate?

6. Do family members and friends place additional stress on parents by demanding ongoing physical, emotional, or monetary support for themselves? Do parents allow others to routinely take advantage of them and can they recognize this and change it?
7. Are family and friends critical of parents and children?
8. Do family and friends introduce untoward influences into the children's lives, such as illegal activities and violence?
9. Do parents belong to a criminal subculture, such as biker gangs?
10. Do parents recognize the potential impact of negative peers on their families, or are they so desperate for contact that they continue their involvement despite this?
11. Do parents know how to set limits regarding inappropriate behaviour of family and friends that might negatively affect their children?
12. Do parents know how to make new friends?

Religious Beliefs and Spirituality

Spirituality is another factor that can contribute to enhanced parent functioning (Brodsky, 1999). Religious beliefs can provide support even when parents are not members of organized religious congregations. Some parents maintain strong beliefs in God that provide acceptance and guidance to them although they do not attend services; others attend services and observe religious practices in their homes. When parents are part of a religious community, they may have the opportunity to establish supportive relationships with congregation members, they may develop friendships that extend to other parts of their lives, and they may receive clothing and food from their congregations. Religious services and group meetings provide outings for parents and children, thereby decreasing isolation, particularly if families have no money for other types of community involvement. Some congregations even provide transportation for such outings. Religious affiliation may also ease adaptation when parents move to a new neighbourhood because they may have automatic acceptance in a new social group that likely maintains similar values to theirs.

Even though religious beliefs and participation may be positive for a number of parents, such involvement may stress some families. This is especially so if congregation members are critical of the parents' life choices and provide acceptance and support contingent on specific behavioural demands. For example, a congregation may frown on sexual relationships outside of marriage and thus be critical of single mothers or cohabiting partners who are not married. Such expectations engender guilt and, rather than enhancing a sense of belonging, actually exacerbate parents' feelings of worthlessness. Given such possibilities, it is important to ask if parents have religious beliefs and how these affect their daily lives, especially their parenting. We must guard against allowing our own religious beliefs to bias perceptions of parents either positively or negatively. When an assessor is unfamiliar with a specific religion, a good first step is to find out more about it in order to gain an overview of its principle beliefs and their implications for parenting. However, it is absolutely critical to identify the particular beliefs of individuals and how they actually influence parenting. For example, some parents who espouse a 'God will provide' attitude may have no concrete plans to enhance either their marriages or their parenting skills. Other may appeal to religious beliefs to justify the use of severe physical punishments in parenting. Still others use their religious views to help them respond kindly to their children.

Given the strong views many people have about the importance of religion, as well as the rights to freedom of religion that many countries guarantee, it is not surprising that parenting assessments can be challenging when religion is raised as a major issue. Remember the basic question of parenting assessments in these cases – 'Can this parent meet the needs of this particular child?' – and do not become sidetracked by religious issues per se. Focus on whether parents can meet the children's needs and whether the children are at significant risk of abuse or neglect while in the parents' care. This was the situation in the following case:

CASE 19: A child welfare intake office responded to a complaint by a mother who reported concerns because her ex-husband had joined a 'cult.' Not only was she concerned that her children were being inducted into a bizarre belief system, but she reported that they often had bruises and welts when they came to see her for weekends. She was also concerned because the children came to see her less frequently, and whenever she tried to speak with her ex-husband, fellow sect members disallowed contact. The group did not have a phone, and she was not allowed inside the residential commune when she picked up her children. The mother took the children to a hospital to document the bruising, but they would not disclose how they had been hurt. Investigators were met with silence when they attempted to interview commune members, although the leader indicated that the children helped with farm work and often were bruised or bumped in this process.

After bruising was repeatedly documented, child welfare personnel obtained a court order for the assessment of both parents. The father complied minimally and would not discuss much about his religious beliefs, aside from saying physical punishment of children and adults was necessary if they transgressed against God. The children continued to be mute about commune activities, but they exhibited nightmares and apprehension in their mother's home. Home schooling supervisors who regularly visited the children in the commune indicated that, while the children appeared to have adequate physical care, their school progress was poor. School subjects were selectively taught, and many units were omitted for 'religious reasons.'

In contrast to a typical parenting assessment where children are interviewed in a few sessions, the assessor decided to see these children for seven sessions each. He always interviewed them individually, exerted considerable effort to make them feel comfortable and engage them in play, and did not immediately inquire about their home life. While the nine-year-old boy remained reticent, the seven-year-old girl began to depict beatings and talk of the devil in her doll play. Eventually she gave a brief but coherent account of the degradation and abuse she experienced at the commune. Given documented physical findings and this specific report, a court order placed the children in their mother's care and permitted only supervised access with their father but not with other commune members. The assessor had recommended supervised access because he had identified a moderate risk of abduction as well as a concern that the daughter would recant her report if permitted unsupervised contact.

To evaluate the supportive influence of **spirituality or religion** in the lives of parents, assessors can use the following questions:

1. Do the parents see value in religion or spirituality and do they plan on introducing religion into their children's lives? How do they plan to introduce such beliefs and what steps, if any, will they use to enforce compliance with religious beliefs and values?

2. What aspects of religion do parents find helpful or not helpful, especially in regard to parenting?
3. How have these beliefs affected their parenting, such as beliefs in regard to corporal punishment? Can parents think parenting issues through independently of their religious beliefs, relying on known information regarding child development and parenting?
4. Do parents demonstrate the importance of their beliefs to their children by following various religious observations at home?
5. Do parents belong to an organized religious congregation and what is the nature of their participation in it? Do they attend regularly or sporadically?
6. Is religion or spirituality a long-standing or relatively new part of life in the families? If religion is new in parents' lives, is it part of an existing pattern of behaviour where parents seek new and immediate solutions to their problems?
7. Do parents ever receive concrete help from their congregation, such as food, clothing, or money?

Cultural Identity

Just as a spiritual community may support parents, identification with a cultural group may be supportive and lessen isolation. This applies not only to broader cultural memberships such as nationality, but also to identification with narrower groupings such as Afro-American, Hispanic, or First Nations peoples. Recent immigrants are likely to be more strongly identified with the culture in their country of origin and bring many child-rearing ideals and practices to life in their new country. In most instances, identification with and pride in cultural membership exert a positive influence on sense of self. Parents maintain social ties to family and friends in their cultural group, and cultural identification enhances self-worth and decreases feelings of isolation. Cultural beliefs may provide guidelines for parenting, and members of the cultural group may provide both support and censure regarding appropriate parenting practices. In a broader society where many people can become alienated and feel disenfranchised, such contacts may indeed have compensatory influences.

However, adherence to various cultural expectations can also create difficulties for some parents. For example, Belsky (1993) speaks to the influence of the broader societal-cultural context on increased the likelihood of poor parenting and child maltreatment. He cites the acceptance of violence in North American culture, the sanctioning of corporal punishment as a child-rearing technique, and the perception of children as parental property as factors that will make the elimination of child maltreatment difficult if not impossible. Although state and provincial laws may say hitting that leaves bruises is child abuse and unacceptable, it is common for some parents to be adamant that corporal punishment is a completely acceptable method of child discipline. They cite not only their life experiences but the parenting behaviours expected and sanctioned by their cultural norms, sometimes strongly asserting that they are good people and their children are not harmed by such behaviour. In these circumstances assessors must clearly be aware of the laws in their jurisdictions so they can determine if disciplinary strategies constitute child abuse and neglect. Assessors also need to examine many other aspects of parenting behaviour to identify compensatory factors and parents' willingness to adopt other discipline practices that are less abusive.

Canino and Spurlock (2000) further caution about the identification of abusive parenting behaviours in specific cultural groups. Common examples, as many assessors who have work with parents of South East Asian origins recognize, are 'cupping' and 'coining' or 'coin rubbing,' healing practices used in these cultures. These procedures can leave welts or bruises that may be erroneously classified as child abuse even though they are intended as healing and caring acts. Clearly, emphasis must be on careful evaluation of the specific practices within the family, rather than on making automatic assumptions of abuse. Likewise, various behaviours or symptoms in either parents or children that could be classified as psychiatric disorders in North American culture might be accepted ways of showing emotions in other cultures (Canino & Spurlock, 2000; Cuellar & Paniagua, 2000). Canino and Spurlock describe several such culture-specific syndromes. For example, they cite 'ataque,' evident in people from the West Indies, where people collapse in response to specific emotions and cannot move or speak while still understanding what others say. Appendix I of the DSM-IV (1994) provides descriptions of various culture-bound syndromes that Paniagua (2000) has summarized in a table format. Paniagua also discusses how cultural contexts can be used in applying DSM-IV criteria to diagnose psychiatric difficulties, specifically reviewing many diagnostic categories.

In culturally diverse cases, parenting assessors must be cautious when diagnosing either abuse or serious mental health problems that can affect parenting. It is critical to acquire information about the cultural context of specific families to avoid such errors. Even within a specific country, behaviours can have dramatically different meanings from region to region. Cuellar and Paniaga (2000) have developed a useful handbook to educate professionals about the impact of culture on mental health problems, provide information about assessment in specific groups, and then adapt treatment interventions. Geissler (1998) also has developed a guidebook for cultural assessment that outlines information such as social customs, touch practices, birth and death rites, perceptions of time, and child-rearing practices for many countries of the world. Besides using such references, assessors can further explore the meaning of many behaviours and practices by asking the parents themselves or by consulting with colleagues who are either from the same cultural group or work extensively with clients from that group. The importance of this exploration is evident in the following case:

CASE 20: Child welfare personnel requested a parenting assessment in a family of three young girls whose family had immigrated from a Southeast Asian country. The children were apprehended when school personnel noted repeated bruising. The girls, who were in kindergarten and grades 1 and 2, indicated they had been hit with a stick by their parents for not doing homework. Child welfare concerns intensified during supervised visits. Parents showed little affection for the children, bossed them around, and made them sit at a separate table to eat. Parents were initially hostile, but relaxed as the assessor took considerable time to ask about their cultural expectations and the reasons for their parenting choices. For example, they indicated that children ate at a separate table to show respect for all elders; eating together was markedly disrespectful, and the parents felt the supervisor undermined their authority and insulted them when he chose to eat with the children rather than with them. Likewise, the parents felt strongly that they were poor parents if they outwardly showed strong affection to their children. They explained that parents in their culture were physically affectionate and indulgent with children in their first three years of life, but became much sterner when their children grew older. They also said that children were expected to do their parents' bidding without question. For example, if the father wanted a drink of water, then the child should get it without

> hesitation. Parents were distressed by the prospect that their children might favour and adopt a more North American style of relating where they were much freer to openly disagree with parental demands.
>
> When discussing the bruising, the parents said they had been hit with sticks as youngsters, but neither recognized that this was unacceptable in North America. Both agreed to try alternative discipline methods, as they had resented the beatings they received. However, neither would relax their demands for high academic performance because they viewed education as a way for their children to succeed in their new country. Given the somewhat different understanding that emerged regarding the family during this assessment, the children were returned to their parents. Care was taken to pair the family with a family support worker from their own cultural group. Other supports helped parents to secure job and language skills, as well as a reliable income while they gained these skills. Child welfare personnel remained involved for several months on a supervisory basis.

As this case shows, we must carefully explore the attitudes and behaviours parents view as acceptable in their culture to understand the meaning of the observed behaviours. Unless parents are truly hostile and unco-operative, they and some of their references are excellent sources of this information during the history taking part of the interview process. Canino and Spurlock (2000) report that assessors can facilitate this process by asking about such things as religious practices and holiday celebrations, dietary habits, community activities, and recreational and music interests. Attitudes about school and educational expectations, child discipline, parental involvement in teaching, and interactions with children can be investigated. Division of labour and participation in childcare by parents, elderly family members, and community members may be defined by cultural norms. Even the importance of time can be influenced by culture (Canino & Spurlock, 2000). For example, American Indians and Latinos share a present-time orientation rather than a focus on the past or the future. This may have an impact on such basic assessment activities as their ability to arrive punctually for appointments. Styles of emotional expression also may be influenced by cultural norms and traditions (Canino & Spurlock, 2000). For example, people from some cultures may be very reserved and polite in assessments while people from others interact in an immediately familiar manner.

The impact of culture on parenting is variable and depends upon the time that has elapsed since immigration and the homogeneity of the community in which the families live; both factors merit attention. Additionally, assessors need to be particularly attentive to situations where clients are not fluent in the assessor's language, because accurate interpretations of interview responses may be compromised. While interpreters or translators may be used to facilitate communication, assessors must recognize that various translation errors can significantly alter the meaning of communications. As Musser-Granski and Carrillo (1997) indicate, errors of omission, addition, and substitution may occur. Errors can be reduced if translators share clients' racial and ethnic backgrounds and if they have levels of acculturation similar to clients' (Paniagua, 1998).

Recognition of cultural differences enhances the validity of a parenting assessment, as more appropriate interpretations of the meaning of various statements and behaviours are possible. An assessor who does not take the time to consider such differences and respond appropriately may indeed make errors that lead to inappropriate or even harmful recommendations. For example, in the case just discussed, an assessor who did not take the time to inquire about cultural differences might easily have concluded that the parents were inadequate and abusive with few redeeming features, when they actually were motivated and responsive if engaged appropriately. At the same time, assessors cannot attribute all variations in parenting to cultural variables, nor can they dismiss practices that are clearly detrimental to children's development. Also, assessors must be cognizant of the impact of their own culture on their conduct and interpretation of data, ensuring it does not bias their opinions.

As assessors inquire about extended family, friends, community participation, and religion, they will begin to derive a sense of the importance of **cultural membership** in families. The following questions can be used to guide further inquiry:

1. Do the parents identify themselves as belonging to a specific cultural group?
2. Do parents come from the same cultural origins? If not, are they respectful of each other's heritage or is this a source of conflict and criticism, especially regarding parenting practices?

3. Is cultural identification a source of pride or embarrassment and shame for various family members?
4. When did parents, grandparents, great grandparents, or other family members immigrate? How has this affected the strength of their adherence to their cultural norms and traditions?
5. Do parents display an idiosyncratic interpretation of their own cultural norms and expectations?
6. Do parents have any friends outside of their cultural group, especially those that might provide exposure to other parenting viewpoints?
7. How does their culture impact on parental attitudes and childrearing behaviours? Do parents recognize the impact?
8. Does culture exert an influence on educational and employment expectations?
9. How does culture affect the participation and presentation of the parents and children during the assessment process?
10. Does culture create differences in how the parents and children relate to professionals such as child welfare and school personnel and lawyers?

Gay and Lesbian Parents

Just as assessors must guard against their own biases and preconceived notions regarding factors such as culture and religion, they must do the same when one or both parents are gay or lesbian. Although sexual orientation is a factor that does not generally impact negatively on parenting adequacy, it is sometimes raised as a possible negative influence in parenting assessments given the political, social, psychological, and moral assumptions of many people. It may be raised in child welfare cases in regard both to parents of children and to gay or lesbian persons who apply to become foster or adoptive parents. It can also arise in custody/access assessments when parents have been involved in heterosexual relationships and then establish gay or lesbian relationships. Buxton (1999) offers an excellent review of research findings regarding the impact of this factor on parenting, particularly in custody/access cases, and King (1995) likewise addresses this issue.

COMMONLY RAISED OBJECTIONS

Objections to parenting by gay or lesbian parents are often based on one or several assumptions. These include the beliefs that children are more likely to be sexually molested by gay or lesbian parents, they will be encouraged to become homosexual, or they will be teased and ostracized by others. As Buxton (1999) concludes, after reviewing two decades of research, there is little evidence to support such assumptions. Although the exact mechanisms through which sexual identity, orientation, and roles are established are still unclear, current research suggests biological rather than environmental factors may play the somewhat larger role (Buxton, 1999). Living with a homosexual parent is unlikely to be a major factor that generates a homosexual orientation in children. Buxton could find no research literature or court records supporting the view that gay or lesbian parents were likely to abuse their own children, but children may become hurt when they encounter either implicit or explicit negative responses towards homosexuality in their extended families or communities. However, she states that most children learn to cope with these negative views, perhaps even becoming stronger and more understanding in the process. The possibility of such reactions from others outside of the family should never be a reason for removal of a child from a home or for lack of access to a parent. This context is analogous to situations where one would never deny access to a parent just because he or she belonged to an oppressed minority cultural or religious group.

Another objection often raised about gay or lesbian parents is the possibility that they have serious mental health problems. This is clearly not the case; as Buxton (1999) indicates, homosexual parents have rates of mental health problems similar to those of the rest of the population. Homosexuality is not a psychiatric disorder. Indeed, gay or lesbian parents who have accepted and disclosed their sexual orientation generally evidence more positive adjustment than those who have not done so (Buxton, 1999).

EFFECTS ON THE CHILDREN

The research clearly reveals virtually no differences between children raised by heterosexual versus homosexual parents on variables such as psychological adjustment, separation-individuation, gender identity and role, sexual orientation, peer relationships, and self-esteem (Buxton, 1999). This is not to say that having a parent that is gay or lesbian poses no challenges. Children may struggle, particularly during adolescence, but as Buxton points out, most have positive attitudes and feelings by the time they achieve autonomy in their late teens. Reactions to learning of parental homosexuality depend on age and developmental stage (Buxton, 1999). Preschoolers accept the information matter-of-factly, while school-age children may be somewhat embarrassed and can be upset by other's remarks. Adolescents may experience additional confusion about their own identity because they normally confront issues of sexuality and identity at this stage. They may attempt to keep their parent's homosexuality secret to avoid being stigmatized by peers. Older teenagers tend to be less affected because they have usually worked through their own identity and sexuality issues.

When children live in heterosexual families where one parent later acknowledges and discloses his or her homosexuality, resulting in family breakup, children are likely to experience the family separation as being more traumatic than the discovery of their parent's sexual orientation. Similarly, in families where children are born to or adopted by gay or lesbian parents, subsequent family breakups are likely to be provocative and hurtful. Children with gay or lesbian parents also experience feelings similar to those of other children when parents introduce new partners after a separation.

EFFECTS ON PARENTING

Because sexual orientation is only one factor that contributes to a person's sense of identity as an individual and as a parent, it is not surprising that Buxton (1999) found that gay and lesbian parents are similar to others in parenting attitudes and behaviour. They value children, and some research suggests they are more child focused than other families. They provide appropriate toys, involve adults of the opposite sex in the children's lives so that appropriate role models are available, and communicate in appropriate ways with their children. Many participate in stable and long-term relationships where both partners assume various childcare roles. Generally, gay and lesbian households are organized like most other homes, and children come to accept partners and can develop close and caring relationships with them.

Because of these similarities in parenting and an overall absence of detrimental effects on the children, assessors clearly need to evaluate the same factors and use the same standards in making recommendations concerning gay or lesbian parents as they do in other families. For example, issues such as violence, drug abuse, serious psychopathology, and indiscriminant and dangerous relationships with people who are brought into the home are significant factors in families where parents are homosexual just as they are when parents are heterosexual. Similarly, overt and indiscriminant sexual behaviour in front of the children is an issue in all families. The quality and reliability of care and the parents' abilities to meet children's needs are therefore the critical variables, although assessors need to additionally ask how the issue of parental homosexuality has been handled with the children. Assessors can then gain an understanding of how parents respond to and support children and of how children have handled the issue for themselves. Assessors also need to ask how extended family members and people in the broader community have responded to the parents' disclosures regarding sexual orientation, thereby providing information about the extent of support available to families. This was a significant factor in the decision making during parenting assessment in the following case:

CASE 21: Jan and Rick were referred for parenting assessment by the courts when they could not agree on custody and living arrangements for their children, aged eleven and fourteen years. Jan alleged that the children were neglected and possibly abused when their father took care of them, and Rick alleged that Jan was an unfit mother because she had begun to live with a female partner a year before the assessment. He thought Jan had significant mental health problems and that she and Marie would encourage his son and daughter to become homosexuals. During the assessment it became very clear Rick had been hurt when Jan acknowledged she was lesbian and left their relationship. Although he and Jan had shared parenting following the separation without excessive animosity, this changed when Jan began to openly cohabit with Marie. He decided to seek sole custody and moved to a nearby town, where his extended family resided, so he could secure their help in raising the children.

Transitions of the children between homes became conflict ridden, and the children suffered immeasurably from Rick's open displays of hostility to Jan and her partner. Additionally, members of his family often told the children their mother was 'evil' and 'perverted' and they left negative and threatening messages on her answering machine. Their comments added to the children's distress. Not only were the children still dealing with their parents' separation, but they were adapting to hearing of their mother's homosexuality and to the entry of her partner into the home. Although they liked Marie, who was caring and responsive, they never brought friends home and tried to hide the relationship. Jan and Marie appropriately explained issues and accepted the children's feelings. Marie was thoughtful in how she slowly increased her parenting involvement. Given Jan and Marie's ability to recognize and respond to the children's issues and concerns and their provision of an ordered and stimulating home, the assessor recommended they assume full care of the children. Their behaviour contrasted significantly with that of Rick and his family, who clearly did not recognize the children's concerns and compounded rather than attenuated their distress. Furthermore, Rick found single-parenting to be difficult; when stressed, he abused alcohol and become physically threatening with the children. He also derided Jan even more intensely.

Contacts with other gay or lesbian parents provide strong social support to parents and children as they deal with regular parenting issues as well as those specific to gay or lesbian families. The following questions can be used to guide questioning about these supports and the impact on children of having **gay or lesbian parents**:

1. When and how did parents come to recognize they were gay or lesbian?
2. How did the parents come to have children, such as through previous heterosexual relationships, adoption, or artificial insemination?
3. Are the parents involved in stable relationships or have the children been exposed to a series of partners?
4. When and how were the children told of the sexual orientations of their parents?
5. How did the children respond to hearing this information and how have parents subsequently responded to the children's questions and feelings regarding this and other issues?
6. Do parents ensure that the children have appropriate opportunities to interact with people of both sexes?
7. Are members of extended families, former spouses, and friends accepting of the sexual orientations of the parents or do they comment negatively and add to the children's distress?

Summary regarding Social Supports

Social supports can provide considerable compensatory benefits that help parents develop and maintain good parenting skills; these supports must be surveyed in any comprehensive parenting assessment. General questions follow that help evaluate the **overall social supports** available to families.

1. Do families receive support from an informal social network, or do they derive their primary support from professional caregivers such as social workers and therapists?
2. Are parents overly dependent on their support network?
3. Do parents believe they have enough support?
4. Are families completely isolated, and what are the contributing factors, such as abusive and controlling partners, personality dynamics, lifestyle choices, irritating personal qualities, or situational changes and moves?
5. Do isolated families have the skills that might allow them to contact and subsequently utilize either formal or informal social supports?

When families have not developed informal social supports, the risk of poor parenting increases. We must then endeavour to determine if such families can accept and respond to various community support services and if these relationships are likely to become more informal and self-maintaining over time. These predictions are difficult, but by examining the parent's previous capacity to respond to input and their strengths as well as factors that might preclude good responses, assessors can make such a determination.

8 Referrals, Contracting, and Defining the Assessment Steps

One of the most important steps in any parenting evaluation is the initial structuring of the assessment process. However, before this can begin, a referral must be made and it must be accepted by an assessor. Thus both the referral source and the assessor play significant roles in this initial step of the assessment process. Here we focus on the tasks that both referring parties and assessors must consider. This process is critical because it not only begins the assessment, but establishes the questions and sets the tone for the entire process.

Information for Referral Sources

Guidelines for Making a Referral

As the preceding chapters indicate, a multitude of factors must be considered in parent assessments. Often social workers and other professionals involved in specific cases have already collected significant information concerning these factors prior to the referral. A logical question that is often asked by these professionals is, 'When do I make a referral for a parenting assessment, especially if I have already collected considerable information regarding a family and have a good idea of what is happening?' This can be a difficult question, and sometimes pragmatics generate referrals. Agencies may have competent staff persons who could undertake parenting assessments, but they are often so busy with case management that they do not have the necessary time to undertake these complex and time-consuming assessments. Other agencies may not have sufficient financial resources to afford assessments or lack staff with the requisite skill base.

Several general guidelines can help referral sources make decisions about when to refer clients for parenting assessment:

1. *Refer clients for formal parenting assessments when staff within agencies do not have the requisite skills or are not admissible as expert witnesses in court.*
   Given that many parenting assessments are ultimately used in court, it is often worthwhile to refer parenting assessments to practitioners who can be admitted as experts. Normally this means they are certified to practice independently in their profession and they have expertise in parenting assessments. Assessors who can qualify as experts in court are permitted to offer opinions about their behavioural observations rather than simply stating those observations, i.e., the facts. In other words, they can explain and interpret their observations and draw conclusions about parenting based on the information they have gathered. These opinions are often of assistance to the court, as most lawyers and judges do not have formal training in these more psychological matters.

2. *Refer clients for parenting assessments when cases are complex and involve a multitude of contributing factors and/or when the family presents with discrepant and sometimes confusing dynamics.*
   While many assessors would say most cases are complex, some cases are more complex than others and some families present with confusing dynamics. For example, it is not uncommon for parents to present well and say all of the right things to child welfare workers while their children continue to act very disturbed or distressed in response to their 'reasonable' behaviour. This was the situation in Case 1. The mother spoke well and appeared to be sincere and motivated, but the children appeared to be damaged and behaved in unusual ways. The child welfare worker referred the family for assessment given this incongruity and her uncertainty about returning the children to Jackie's care. The referral was appropriate as it ultimately furnished information that was used in planning for the children's needs. The assessment indicated that the mother had significant drug and alcohol addictions, was highly narcissistic, lied pathologically, had not resolved her own childhood history of abuse, and was clearly unable to protect and nurture her children. Their behaviour was understandable in light of these variables.

3. *Refer clients for parenting assessment when specialized issues are apparent.*
   Although many factors should be reviewed in all child welfare cases, some involve rather specialized issues that are not routinely confronted by most child welfare workers. For example, workers may not routinely work with psychotic parents or have even had previous exposure to people with such difficulties. It might be difficult for them to understand the nature of these parents' problems and how these affect parenting. Similarly, child welfare workers may know little about the evaluation of risk for homicide or abduction and the impact of such risks on children. While child welfare workers can often ask consultants to give specific opinions and guidelines regarding immediate decision making in cases where these factors exist, a parenting assessment can clarify the longer term impact for children's care and development. Assessors who have this knowledge and can thoroughly evaluate the situation are able to offer useful guidance regarding planning for these youngsters.

4. *Refer clients for parenting assessments when long-term planning issues exist regarding the best interests of the children.*
   Knowledge of children's current functioning, their past history, and the type of parenting they received can contribute significantly to long-term planning for their care. Although file history information and a current individual assessment can help in long-term planning for children under the guardianship of child welfare authorities, the process is more accurate when formal parenting assessments are available. Usually parenting assessments are undertaken to help in long-term planning when decisions are needed about whether children should remain in permanent care of the authorities or be returned to parents. More infrequently, some are undertaken when children are permanent wards and questions arise about the advisability of contact with parents or if children should be returned to parents after spending several years in care.

5. *If you are a lawyer, refer clients for parenting assessments when you need to know the strengths and vulnerabilities of your clients.*
   This guideline is applicable for lawyers who represent parents involved in child welfare court actions. In order to adequately advise and represent clients, lawyers need to have accurate information

about them, and when the issue focuses on parenting capacity, parenting assessments are an avenue to gain pertinent information. However, given the necessary involvement of parents and children in this process, it usually cannot proceed without the knowledge of child welfare authorities, as they normally have at least temporary guardianship of the children. Thus lawyers must negotiate the parenting assessment with child welfare personnel. If child welfare staff are the legal guardians, then lawyers need to release the results of the evaluation to them.

Commonly Asked Questions

In addition to using the above guidelines to decide when to refer a family for a parenting assessment, referral sources should expect assessors to ask a series of questions about the specifics of the referral during their initial contacts with each other. It is likely that assessors will want to know what particular questions are being asked in the assessment. When referral sources are unclear on their specific questions, most assessors will help them delineate these as they negotiate the referral, a process discussed later in this chapter.

To further explicate the decision-making process used in making referrals, it is helpful to review some questions that commonly arise in parenting assessments:

1. If a history of child welfare concerns exists, what can be done to remedy the situation and how much time should be given to the parents to improve their parenting before beginning proceedings to permanently remove the children from their care?
2. Will this parent ever be able to adequately care for his or her child or children?
3. How significantly do mental health problems and other difficulties affect parenting, and what sequelae do the children display?
4. If parents are unlikely to ever adequately care for their children, what kind of contact, if any, should they have with those children?
5. If parents cannot ever parent adequately, should adoption of the children be considered and what kind of home should be sought for them?

Common questions that may arise in foster/adoption cases include the following:

1. What types of children with what kinds of problems can be placed in these homes?
2. What are the potential difficulties these parents are likely to face in the task of parenting?
3. What supports are needed to ensure these parents function well?
4. How will these parents manage the needs of their other children if emotionally damaged and demanding children are placed with them?
5. What are potential risk factors that could jeopardize subsequent placements in their homes?
6. How valid are allegations that foster parents have sexually abused or otherwise harmed children placed in their care? How do such allegations affect their continued status as foster parents?

Although custody/access issues are not the focus of this book, it is interesting to note how different are some of the questions that may arise in these cases. As is evident in the following questions, it is not surprising that these situations tend to generate animosity and tension:

1. Which of the two parents is likely to provide the best day-to-day care for the children?
2. How should the children's time be divided between the parents' homes?
3. Should one parent essentially raise the children and should the other have contact? What specific arrangements are needed during transfer times if the relationship between parents remains highly conflicted?
4. Did one parent sexually abuse the children, making contact dangerous? Under what conditions should parents and children have contact?
5. Is one parent alienating the children from the other parent and what should be done, including the possibility of moving the children to the home of the other parent?
6. Is there a risk that one parent will abduct the children and never allow them to see the other parent again? What can be done to prevent this?
7. If one parent wants to move away, who should care for the children? Should the children move with that parent? What arrangements should be put in place regarding access?

tional questions during assessments when they identify critical issues. In these preliminary discussions, it is crucial to document the issues that are discussed. Clear documentation allows assessors to keep specific issues in mind during the course of the assessment and facilitates the initial stage of report writing. The questions that follow help potential assessors to derive a sense of the context and the salient issues, so they can then decide whether they wish to proceed with establishing a contract to begin an assessment.

1. *Who is making the referral?*
   This may sound like a silly question, but it is critical in determining the assessment's context and ensuring that, as assessors, we treat all involved parties fairly. For example, in situations where one parent is battling another for custody of children, it is critical to communicate the same information to both parents and/or their lawyers. If an assessor communicates primarily with one side in this initial phase, bias may later be raised as an issue in the proceedings. Furthermore, one side may actually be attempting to bias the assessor's opinion even at this stage by making the initial call and presenting only certain information. It is also important to determine if the parents and their lawyers agree with the referral. For example, if parents do not agree and feel coerced into the assessment by child welfare workers, they may present differently than those who seek an assessment of their own volition. The same applies to parents who are referred for assessment by the courts; if assessments are court ordered, one should ask for copies of the orders to see what the judge has specifically requested and whether he or she has imposed any limitations on the assessment. For example, a judge can prohibit the use of psychological testing. Such testing is informative and its exclusion might be ill-advised, and assessors can then decide if they are willing to proceed under such conditions.

2. *Why is this case being referred for parenting assessment now?*
   This question allows assessors to gain some sense of what has preceded the referral. Normally referral sources give some short history of the case. They may indicate when parenting concerns first arose, how many times the children have been under the care of child welfare authorities, what efforts were made to support the parents to care for their children, and why the decision has been

made to obtain a parenting assessment. In foster/adoption cases, the referrer can give a brief history of the application, perhaps saying that approval or rejection depends on the results of the assessment. In cases where concerns have arisen about the quality of care being provided by foster or adoptive parents who already have children in their homes, a short history regarding the concerns sets the context, as does an outline of efforts to resolve the concerns. The same applies in custody/access cases where previous efforts to resolve issues by mediation or arbitration are part of the history. Besides providing information about the context, the answers to these questions begin to delineate what further questions merit attention.

3. *Who is being referred?*
   The answers to this question allow some estimation of the scope and complexity of the assessment process that will be required and permit a more accurate prediction the amount of time and fees needed for the assessment. The primary people and other important people who may need to be interviewed should be identified. For example, if the care of young children in a family is at issue, they and their parents require interviews. However, older siblings, step-parents, and sometimes even the parents' new partners have to be interviewed in order to obtain a broader view of the children's environment. These interviews may add valuable information, but they also entail additional hours of assessment time: when assessment funding is limited, assessors may need to weigh the clinical costs of omitting these important interviews with donating their own time to do them. If the assessment will be weakened too much through such omissions, the assessor may need to decline doing the entire assessment. When some of the clients have been involved with other mental health professionals, assessors may be able to get information about them without undertaking more elaborate interviews themselves. For example, if reputable practitioners have formally assessed children recently, one can review their reports and consult with these clinicians, personally undertaking only brief individual child interviews before seeing the children jointly with their parents.

4. *What type of assessment is wanted and what are the specific questions that require answers?*

These important questions begin to clarify the assessment questions and procedures that are to be used. For example, referral sources may request a full parenting assessment or individual psychological evaluations of the parents or the children. In the latter situation, assessors would want to explain the more limited opinions about parenting and planning for children that can be drawn from individual assessments rather than full parenting assessments. Similarly, in situations where parents live apart and seek custody, the advantages and disadvantages of unilateral and bilateral assessments can be discussed with referring parties. Issues around the confidentiality of the assessment results need to be reviewed, particularly in child welfare cases where workers must give consent for children's participation if they are their legal guardians. Such discussions allow parents, their lawyers, and other referral sources to make informed decisions about whether to proceed. Specific questions should evolve during this stage that begin to set the structure and goals for the assessments. Samples of common questions are provided in an earlier section of this chapter.

PRACTICE ALERT #7
Always clarify and confirm the guardianship status of the children who are being referred.

Although this seems like an obvious thing to do, assessors sometimes fail to ask about the guardianship status of the children involved in particular cases; this is a critical question, as it is unethical to see children without the consent of their legal guardians. Furthermore, it is upsetting to begin an assessment only to discover that a parent is bringing children to assessment sessions without the knowledge of a legal guardian. For example, a parent may suspect the children's other parent is abusing them and seek assessment without the consent of that parent. The information presented may be biased, and the children may be placed under considerable pressure to support the parents' views. To avoid such a situation, it is wise to ask to see a copy of the guardianship order or to speak with child welfare authorities so appropriate consents for assessment are obtained. It is also important to be cognizant of exceptions in some jurisdictions to the rule that legal guardians must give consent for assessment. For example, in the Province of Alberta, a clinician could see a child in the above example if he or she highly suspects abuse is occurring. However, such a case is reportable to child welfare, and a prudent clinician would consult with child welfare personnel prior to undertaking such an assessment.

5. *What time lines exist for completing the assessment?*
   As part of the initial contact, one must inquire about any existing time constraints. Often court hearings are already scheduled, and as these are sometimes imminent, an assessor should specifically ask for dates of upcoming hearings and/or the duration of temporary guardianship orders. If a temporary guardianship order expires during an assessment, children may be returned to their parents regardless of the status of the evaluation. If time lines are so short that a thorough assessment is impossible, one will obviously need to decline involvement to avoid producing an evaluation that has been compromised by insufficient time; it is sometimes possible to negotiate a delay of court hearings. A related issue concerns the hours required for an assessment. This is often a significant issue in child welfare cases, where agencies have limited financial resources that result in strict limits on the hours and/or amount of remuneration that can be expended in any particular assessment. Without initially clarifying this issue, assessors are left with the choice of producing a compromised assessment because of time insufficiency or investing extra unpaid hours to complete a thorough evaluation.

6. *Are police interviews of the children planned regarding the alleged abuse to determine if criminal charges will be laid?*
   Finally, assessors need to ask if the children have been or will be interviewed by police regarding the alleged abusive incidents. If such interviews are yet to occur, estimates for the completion of the parenting assessment may be affected because assessors usually must wait until police interviews are completed before they can initiate interviews. Furthermore, when charges or trials are pending, authorities in many jurisdictions frown on other people interviewing the children about the abuse for fear that such additional questioning will taint evidence. Assessors must inquire about this possibility, as it may preclude specific questions about the alleged maltreatment during the assessment, especially given the lengthy time periods that usually elapse between the imposition of charges and the onset of trials.

While these initial questions may appear simple, they do much to begin defining the assessment process for all concerned parties. Both parents and assessors can make informed choices regarding whether they wish to proceed further with establishing a contract.

Defining the Contract for the Assessment

After clarifying the referral questions in the initial contacts, assessors then decide if they wish to accept the referral. If they do, they begin to outline the specifics of what will occur during assessment, including both the clinical aspects, such as ways in which data will be collected, and the pragmatics of the assessment, which include matters such as fees, scheduling, and release of the report. These details are specified in initial telephone contacts and are then reviewed with parents in their first sessions. Documentation of these details may prevent later disagreements. Some assessors prepare specific written outlines of these issues and forward copies to parents and/or their lawyers. Of course, parents may decline participation at this stage. Even if they are ordered to participate by the court, they may choose not to do so, thereby becoming accountable to the judges who ordered the assessments.

Essentially, the initial contract outlines the assessment process, although the actual content of clinical interview questions and psychological tests is not specified. The assessor indicates a willingness to proceed and gives **estimated start and finish times**. The work to be done includes interviews as well as contacts with references, scoring and interpretation of any psychological testing, and preparation of the report. Clearly, assessors must have a good command of their schedules to free time from other activities for these tasks. Underestimating time frames increases frustration for clients, lawyers, and assessors themselves. If delays in the process are likely to be created by an assessor's holidays or out-of-town trips, these are identified so clients realize there will be no sessions during these periods. Similarly, evaluators should ask clients about their anticipated periods of unavailability, and this information is taken into account when estimating completion dates.

Based on initial information, assessors reiterate **who will be seen** in the assessment. Certainly parents who contest guardianship issues and the children involved will be included, and, as already noted, the existing guardianship status of these children should always be confirmed. As assessors initially do not always know the degree to which parents' new partners are involved in children's lives, they usually indicate that these people may be interviewed. When new partners live with families and assume parental roles, full assessment is prudent. Dating partners require less in-depth assessment unless relationships are long standing or the partners are actively involved with the children. When such partners are new or unknown to the children, it may be sufficient to briefly interview them, in particular asking them to describe the role they expect to play in the children's lives. It can be worrisome when parents constantly introduce many new but short-term partners into the family. While these partners would likely not be interviewed, clearly the parents should be queried about their perception of the potential impact of these people on the children. Similar information is given about possible interviewing of other children or stepchildren in families. The full extent of their involvement is not decided until somewhat later in the assessment process, because their participation depends on both the nature of their involvement with the children at issue as well as their willingness to participate.

Related to this, assessors indicate how parents should **schedule the initial sessions**. This can be handled in one of several ways: assessors outline their availability and leave it up to the parents to come to sessions at predesignated times; they provide several options and ask clients or their lawyers to confirm their attendance; or they ask clients to call to negotiate initial appointments. None of these options is decidedly preferable, but permitting some choice may increase clients' level of comfort with the examiner and the assessment process because they feel their schedules and opinions are respected. Clients need to know if evening or weekend appointments are unavailable because they must then take time off work and, since they will have individual appointments, they will need to arrange for childcare during these sessions.

Assessors then begin to **outline the assessment process**. While assessors vary in the assessment tasks they use and how they order the assessment steps, clients need to know what is expected of them during the assessment. For example, it is unfair and likely upsetting if an assessor does not indicate ahead of time that formal psychological assessment procedures are part of the required process. Identifying general procedures allows parents to give informed consent for their participation. Thus, assessors might indicate that they begin with interviews of parents followed by interviews of the children as well as possible joint interviews and home visits. Finally, clients need to know that assessors plan to contact various references and that this is done only after they have signed formal releases of information. Parents should also be informed that, to help the assessor understand the situation, they can submit various other types of information as well as copies of previous orders, assessments, and other documentation. Such notification allows parents to prepare for the assessment prior to the initial appointment.

Related to this is a discussion regarding the preparation and release of a **final report**. Clients should be told that a formal report will be prepared as a way of communicating the assessment's findings. In some circumstances, assessors agree to meet with lawyers prior to the release of the report. This plan should be identified ahead of time and should only be undertaken after careful consideration, as there are both positive and negative reasons for such meetings. For example, they can be particularly helpful in situations where plans may need to be put in place to ensure the safety of various individuals. This is especially so if a recommendation is to be made that may well provoke an individual who is deemed to be at risk for volatile or aggressive behaviour. On the other hand, such meetings allow lawyers an opportunity to argue their cases more strongly as they attempt to sway the assessor's opinions, even if the assessor has already made up his or her mind. Assessors should also let a client know ahead of time if they have agreed to share preliminary information over the telephone with child welfare workers during the course of the assessment.

Since parents and their lawyers clearly need to know how they will be informed of the results, this needs to be specified prior to the assessment's initiation. Many different courses of action are possible. For example, in child welfare cases some assessors simply forward one copy of the report to the referring agency, while others simultaneously send another copy to the parents' lawyers and/or the parents themselves. In the first instance, the agency normally forwards a copy to the parents' lawyers; if a court hearing is scheduled, they are required to do this by a specific date. Other assessors not only forward a copy to the agency but also meet with parents and possibly agency workers to review the findings. Such a step depends upon the context and initial referral questions. Obviously, if a case is highly adversarial, an assessor might choose not to meet because client reactions could be so strong that discussion is ineffective. Assessors might want to meet for feedback in a case that is more therapeutically focused, so information is communicated in a way that further engages parents in the treatment process. For example, an assessor may focus on parent strengths in examining what can be done to safely reunify a family. Even so, parents may be unhappy because their children are not being returned immediately. In custody/access cases it is common practice to release the report simultaneously to both lawyers by courier so no bias occurs because the courier determines the first recipient of the report.

PRACTICE ALERT #8
Determine payment arrangements ahead of time.

Payment arrangements require prior agreement. Early negotiation reduces clinicians' frustration and helps ensure that invoices will be paid. Furthermore, frank discussion about this issue allows clients and referral sources to plan their budgets accurately, and essentially it allows any concerns to be raised and treated respectfully by all parties. Arrangements vary depending on the referral source and context. In child welfare cases, it is common for the referring child welfare agency to be responsible for fee payment. Costs are established through either a standing contract arrangement regarding provision of a specific number of assessments for set fees or individual contracts on a case-by-case basis. Both are likely to specify the maximum allotted hours for interviews, testing, and report writing, the expiry date, and how payments are to be made. Often payments are remitted once the report is released and the agency is invoiced. Thus assessors might provide all of the service before they receive remuneration because they are reasonably assured of payment. When parents or their lawyers make the referral for assessment, different arrangements are necessary. Sometimes, contracts are arranged through Legal Aid lawyers if parents are represented by such counsel; in this situation, predetermined limits according to a set fee schedule are usually present. When parents do not have access to such funding and have limited financial resources themselves, assessors may need to consider either reducing rates or referring the parents to agencies that may be able to provide assessment at reduced or minimal cost.

The situation is different in foster and adoption cases, particularly if parents are paying for the assessment. If the assessor recommends approval as foster or adoptive parents, payment is usually not an issue, but if an assessor draws other conclusions, prospective parents might not pay and may search for reasons to discredit the assessment. In such contexts, it is wise to demand a retainer fee before beginning, followed by full payment before the report is released. Assessors are thus assured of payment for their time and effort regardless of their opinion. Similar procedures are usually employed in custody/access cases because nonpayment is more likely after release of the report: one or even both parents may dislike some of the findings and therefore refuse to remit their portion of the fees. In such circumstances, assessors should demand retainers before they begin and then require full payment before releasing the report.

Defining the Assessment Steps

After establishing an agreement to undertake a particular parenting assessment, clinicians must clearly think through and establish the assessment methodology they plan to use. This varies somewhat depending upon the referral questions, the structure and context of the family being referred, and the theoretical and professional orientations of the assessors. For example, an assessor who is a psychologist is likely to undertake formal psychological testing, but a psychiatrist or social worker is less likely to incorporate such procedures. Given the complexity of parenting assessments, it is wise to develop a checklist of important tasks to ensure they are done; nothing is more disconcerting than to discover the omission of an essential step late in the process, as assessors might then need to call clients back to collect missing information. Such omissions, whether intended or not, call the assessors' credibility into question and may limit the validity of their conclusions. A sample checklist of the most common steps in the assessment process can be found in Appendix B.

INITIAL APPOINTMENTS

We already reviewed the two first assessment steps in the preceding section. During the initial contact with a referring party, assessors establish an assessment contract and clarify referral questions. These critical steps provide a framework for the assessment regarding both the pragmatics of the assessment and the clinical questions that must be addressed. Assessors can now set appointments with the parents. In child welfare cases, assessors may begin with a joint session followed by individual interviews or they may interview parents individually and then see them together. The nature of the referral questions sometimes helps in determining the particular sequence of interviews. For example, in a case where concerns about family violence exist, an assessor might choose to begin with separate interviews given the possibility that one spouse will be so controlling or intimidating that the other does not feel free to express his or her opinions. Separate interviews can also reveal gross discrepancies in how parents understand the problems and the salient issues to be addressed by the parenting evaluation. In child welfare cases where parents are separated and each seeks a return of the children to their care, separate interviews are usually the chosen approach, much as they are in custody/access cases. Joint initial interviews are most common in foster and adoption assessments.

PRACTICE ALERT #9

Ensure that parents give informed consent for participation by clearly outlining the parameters of the assessment process.

Initial interviews focus on a few main tasks, such as obtaining informed consent for participation in the assessment. Here assessors may point out possible risks and benefits of assessment, letting clients know they have a right to refuse assessment and a right to seek another assessor. Initial interviews also focus on gathering such basic information as the legal names, birth dates, and addresses of the adults and children and asking parents about their understanding of the reasons for a parenting assessment. Parents may offer simple explanations such as, 'The judge said I had to come so I could get my children back,' or they may offer long and complex explanations regarding how the assessment came about. Assessors then clarify their own understanding and, through discussion, assessors and parents agree on the questions that will be addressed in the assessment. It is important to be clear about the assessment's purpose, neither sugarcoating nor avoiding the real reasons for assessment. For example, a parent may have had repeated hospitalizations for suicide attempts. An assessor might say that the case worker is concerned about the parent's ability to safely care for the children, his or her choices of alternate caretakers during hospitalizations, and the impact of repeated absences and mental health problems, including the suicide attempts, on the children's functioning. If the goal is to make recommendations regarding how to best support the family, then this should be stated. If it also involves a question about permanent removal of the children from parental care, then this should be identified as an issue. By being clear that permanent removal is a possible recommendation, assessors decrease the sense of betrayal parents might feel if such an option is eventually recommended, and ensure that parents are fully aware of the assessment's significance. Any marked parental lapses in judgment and behaviour that then occur during the assessment process become even more significant.

PRACTICE ALERT #10
Review the limits of confidentiality that exist in the assessment process.

In order to ensure informed consent, it is important to explain confidentiality limitations regarding the information parents provide by telling them that any information gained during the assessment may be incorporated into the final written report; no information is off the record. This is a different confidentiality agreement than that used in therapy or counselling situations, where client confidentiality is maintained. However, in both situations confidentiality can be broken if clients become a danger to themselves or others, as in cases of child abuse and suicidal and homicidal risk.

In initial interviews assessors need to speak with clients about formulating a list of references who may be contacted later in the assessment. This list comprises people who can comment on the functioning of family members and may include extended family members, friends, employers, teachers, physicians, and childcare personnel, among others. Of course, one must explain that these people will be contacted only with the parents' written consent. However, if children are under the guardianship of child welfare authorities, case workers must give consent for obtaining information specifically about the children. Parents can refuse permission for assessors to talk to these people regarding the parents' behaviour. Assessors also need to speak with parents about providing any other documentation that could help them arrive at their conclusions. This may include previous legal documents such as affidavits and court orders. Other information could be such items as diaries, photo albums, children's report cards, and letters. If items such as diaries, taped phone messages, and e-mail messages are given to the assessor, the information cannot be used unless the author is informed of this and gives consent for use of the materials in the assessment.

Finally, in initial interviews with parents, and particularly if children are in the care of their parents or will be seeing their parents extensively before the children come to their first appointments, assessors should ask what parents plan to say to the children about the assessment. Their responses may reflect the parents' sensitivity to their children's worries and needs. If parents do not know what they will say or if they verbalize an intention to say something that may constrain children, requiring them to reiterate the parents' views rather than their own, then assessors should instruct parents to say something such as, 'We are trying to decide how we can be the best parents for you, and the assessor will be talking to everyone to help us make a plan.'

REVIEW OF CHILD WELFARE FILE AND OTHER LEGAL DOCUMENTATION

When the context involves child welfare concerns, it is useful to review either the entire child welfare file or documents from these files that outline previous child welfare involvement. Many agencies include summaries and information consolidation reports in their files that document child abuse reports and investigations, judges' orders, child placements, and previous assessments regarding the family. Agency files frequently include historical information that parents provided in earlier contacts and generally include reports regarding the children's behaviour in current and previous foster homes. Information gained from these file reviews offers a broader context for the assessments, and allows assessors to compare previously collected information with current data to help determine if there have been any changes in the functioning of children or parents. Although assessors vary in the timing of this file review, it is a critical part of the process. Some prefer to review this information early in the assessment, while others prefer to begin interviews and form some working hypotheses prior to perusing file information. Still others do not review this information until after they have formulated preliminary opinions, so the written documentation cannot be an alleged source of bias. Since child welfare files may exist in both foster and adoption and custody/access cases, assessors should take steps to review them.

In some assessments, serious questions arise about such issues as drug and alcohol use, drunk driving convictions, and criminal records. Assessors should not hesitate to ask for certified copies of drunk driving convictions and criminal records. Immediate drug testing without warning can be arranged when drug and alcohol use is a significant concern.

FURTHER INTERVIEWING OF PARENTS

We review the assessment of parents in detail in Chapter 9. However once the review of the referral questions and the pragmatics of the evaluation has been completed in an initial interview, we can then begin to collect assessment information, although parents' actions in the initial steps are also diagnostic. By this point assessors have usually only briefly questioned the parents about their understanding of the reasons for assessment, and most now go into more depth regarding both current and previous child welfare concerns. The personal and family histories of both parents are questioned, usually in individual interviews, and if answers are short and glib, we inquire about specific instances and events that contributed to their feelings and opinions. For example, in Case 1 Jackie asserted that her childhood was 'rotten' but then minimized this statement; she could not elaborate, although references yielded specific information suggesting a childhood replete with neglect and abuse.

Interviews also focus on the parents' current functioning and life circumstances as well as the children's developmental histories and current functioning. These specific areas of inquiry will be reviewed in Chapter 9. If two parents are involved in an assessment, we should try to devote relatively equal amounts of time to each parent's individual interviews. This is particularly so if they disagree about many matters, and especially if they are contesting custody. At some point, parents may be interviewed together to determine how they relate and communicate.

Finally, interviews focus on what the parents see as the ideal solution to their situation and their plans to improve it as well as their concerns about their own or their children's functioning.

INTERVIEWING CHILDREN

Once parents recount personal and family histories, describe the current functioning of all family members, and outline their concerns, one can begin the children's interviews, although some assessors prefer to meet children before their parents. We prefer the former arrangement because many children are reassured when told the assessor already knows their parents. Some overlap in schedules for parent and child sessions allows assessors to ask parents about specific behaviours or concerns that are suggested or observed in children's interviews. For example, if speech or motor difficulties are evident, assessors can ask parents if they have noticed or taken any steps to respond to them. Generally, children's interviews are undertaken individually, as every child has a different perspective of the family and his or her role in it. When children are only seen together, the most dominant child's point of view tends to be the one heard. However, some joint sibling interviewing allows observations of their interactions that may later contribute to decisions about whether they should stay together or be split up.

PSYCHOLOGICAL TESTING AND CHECKLIST COMPLETION

Regardless of professional affiliation, many assessors use various checklists or questionnaires to collect information about family members. Social questionnaires and behavioural checklists are used by psychologists and other professionals, but only psychologists can use formal psychological tests. Some of these, such as IQ tests, are directly administered by psychologists, while clients can complete others by themselves. With the latter, one must provide a comfortable and quiet milieu for parents who are completing such forms. It is advisable to have parents complete testing in the office rather than allowing them to take various forms and test materials home. Not only do many tests need to be administered under standardized conditions but, given the high stakes, some parents seek the help of other family members or even other professionals to complete them. This invalidates results and produces inaccurate scores, wasting the effort of both parents and assessors.

PRACTICE ALERT #11

Ensure that you have the knowledge base and expertise to administer and interpret any questionnaires and/or formal psychological tests.

Professionals who are not psychologists cannot use formal psychological tests but may wish to include some psychological testing in their assessment. In this case, a psychologist may formally psychologically assess clients and provide the results, usually as written reports. Assessors must choose these psychologists carefully, using many of the same guidelines that referral sources use in choosing the assessors themselves, and these psychologists must recognize the role of their assessments in the overall parenting assessment. The psychological assessments should only comment on the parents' psychological functioning and not on custody or access per se. Assessors can enhance the usefulness of these supplementary assessments by posing specific referral questions. For example, testing may help identify the presence of such factors as psychopathy, psychosis, depression, or paranoia.

JOINT OBSERVATIONS IN THE OFFICE

Once most of the individual interviews and testing are completed, joint office observations usually occur. Although brief interactions between family members were observed in the waiting room, parents and children are formally observed together in the controlled office milieu, at which time assessors can observe both structured and unstructured interactions between various family members. These observations are reviewed in more detail in the next chapter.

OBSERVATIONS IN HOME VISITS AND OTHER SETTINGS

Another step includes observations of families in more natural settings. Depending upon their theoretical and practice orientations, assessors vary in the amount of these ecological observations they include in their assessments. For example, some assessors who work from a more social work perspective may very well conduct the majority of their interviews and observations in the homes of families or their immediate environs. Minimally, however, at least one visit to the home permits observation of the physical aspects of the home and neighbourhood and evaluation of the home's emotional tone. Although the assessor's presence changes the situation and adds an artificial element to observations, scheduling visits during busy times such as the dinner hour often provides more valid data. Again, specifics are included in the next chapter.

CONTACT COLLATERAL REFERENCES

Most assessors contact references towards the end of the evaluation. While some are contacted earlier, assessors often do not know enough about the family members to ask germane questions until they are well into the assessment. Also, assessors cannot anticipate the most useful information sources until they become familiar with the lives of family members. To become familiar with references, it can be helpful

PRACTICE ALERT #12
Always obtain signed releases of information before contacting references for family members.

to have parents describe the context in which they know the references on their list. For example, references may be friends, family members, teachers, or physicians. You can also ask permission to contact references parents do not have on their reference lists, although parents can, of course, withhold consent. In all circumstances obtain written releases of information from parents before you contact references. If parents identify many references on their list and you do not plan on contacting all of them, inform the parents you will only be calling a selection of the people and perhaps have them identify the most critical references. Ask parents to tell references you will be calling so references clearly know they have the parents' permission to speak with you. Alternatively, one can tell the references of the parents' consent, but be prepared to provide them with copies of the written consent, if requested.

FINAL PARENT INTERVIEWS

Near the end of the assessment process, it is worthwhile to schedule relatively brief parent interviews to ensure they have a last opportunity to add any further information or comments before data analysis and reports are completed, and so the assessor can ask any remaining questions. Offer parents the option of calling with more information during the period of report writing. Parents commonly ask assessors about their conclusions and recommendations during these last interviews, but because assessors have not integrated their data and written their reports, it is inappropriate to provide such information at this point. Reassure parents that you have appreciated their cooperation and you will be seriously considering all of the collected information as you develop your recommendations and prepare your report.

DATA INTEGRATION, CASE FORMULATION, AND REPORT PREPARATION

Once interviews and testing are completed, analyse and integrate all of the collected information. This is often one of the most challenging and fascinating parts of the whole process. Chapters 11 and 12 review the process of integrating data and presenting the assessment's findings.

RELEASE THE REPORT AND PREPARE FOR POSSIBLE COURT TESTIMONY
When the final report is ready, release it in the manner agreed upon at the start of the investigation. While the parties in some cases now settle and child welfare personnel and parents agree about the children's status and begin to develop plans for the children and the family, many cases remain unresolved and proceed to litigation. Assessors involved in these cases must prepare for court testimony. Although all assessment steps should have been undertaken as if the matter were going to court and there would be a thorough examination and cross-examination of the assessors' conclusions, preparing for court is still a challenging and sometimes intimidating experience for many professionals. Preparation for court testimony is discussed in the final chapter of this book.

Alterations in Standard Assessment Steps

While not all assessors undertake the preceding steps in the order outlined, most incorporate the majority of these steps in parenting assessments. The steps allow assessors to gain information from multiple sources and thereby enhance the validity and reliability of their observations. For psychologists, this use of multiple sources is recommended by the American Psychological Association in their *Guidelines for Psychological Evaluations in Child Protection Matters* (1999). However, occasionally it is acceptable to omit some of the steps. We will describe a few such circumstances, but the list is not meant to be exhaustive; one must very carefully weigh the risks and benefits of omitting any of the major steps.

Perhaps one of the most commonly omitted steps is joint observation of parents and children. For example, even though the American Psychological Association's guidelines recommend that evaluators make efforts to observe the child and parents together, particularly in natural settings, they make two exceptions. The first occurs when parent contact with the child is prohibited by court. The other occurs when the safety of the child is in jeopardy. This is most likely in situations where significant family violence or physical and sexual assaults on children have occurred. Children's marked fear and anxiety and possibly their expressed reluctance to see an abusive parent may increase the risk of further traumatization even if contact is closely supervised. The existence of violence and abuse per se does not preclude joint sessions, but this is a difficult judgment call. Clearly, assessors need well-documented evidence of previous abuse and observations of significant fear and anxiety in the children. Assessors need to speak with any therapists who are involved with the children, as these professionals can speak to the children's previous trauma and the likelihood that additional contact might re-traumatize them. In Case 14 in the Family Conflict section of Chapter 6, the assessor opted to dispense with joint sessions involving the father and his children for just such reasons.

Another circumstance where joint interviews might be omitted is in situations where children and parents have not had contact for years and are essentially strangers. If separation occurred when children were very young and they now have no recollections of their parents, joint sessions for the sake of assessment might be unwarranted. Assessors may evaluate both the children and parents separately and, if contact is appropriate, then they may recommend this with specific directions regarding how the plan is to be implemented. In these instances a child's therapist may be a useful reference.

Home visits, essentially a type of joint session, may be precluded if the assessor's safety is likely to be jeopardized. Also, they might be precluded by high travel costs to a distant home. When this occurs, parents can supply pictures and floor plans of their home, maps of their neighbourhood, and the names of references who have been in their homes.

Joint sessions with parents and children also are omitted in assessments of potential adoptive and foster parents simply because they have not yet been approved to either adopt or foster children. However, if parents already have other children, joint observations and individual interviews are undertaken with these children. Usually, other clinicians have conducted assessments of children who are candidates to be placed in a particular home.

Joint parental sessions often are omitted in assessments where high animosity exists between parents. This sometimes occurs in child welfare cases with separated parents who both want to assume the children's care or in cases of domestic violence where one parent is frightened of the other. It is important to ensure parents attend sessions at different times to avoid negative verbal interchanges and physical altercations in waiting rooms or even on office steps.

In-office interviews may not be possible when parents are incarcerated, necessitating interviews and testing in that setting. Prison administrators must give consent for these activities, and usually very specific arrangements must be made ahead of time. Assessors also may need to travel to other jurisdictions to interview parents and children. Rather complex arrangements may then be necessary: assessors can rent office space from other practitioners so that interviewing occurs in a neutral setting; interview schedules are compressed into a few days; and complex travel arrangements are made. Besides regular assessment fees, assessors can expect reimbursement for their travel time and expenses. Caution is advised regarding such work, because assessors may not be licensed in other jurisdictions and work visas may be necessary if assessors cross national borders. Fortunately, while prison visits are a possibility in child welfare cases, most assessors do not need to travel to other jurisdictions and make such cumbersome arrangements.

9 Assessment of the Parents

Engaging the Parents

Successful engagement of family members does much to increase the validity of the information collected during any parenting assessment. Parents are likely to engage in the assessment process, providing more complete information and truly revealing their perceptions, if they are treated with respect and honesty. This begins with the first phone contact and extends throughout the remainder of the assessment. For example, if we have clarified with clients the information noted in Chapter 8, discussing the assessment's purpose and general procedures, how and with whom findings will be shared, and our ethical obligations to report issues such as child abuse, parents know the existing ground rules and can engage in the process accordingly.

PRACTICE ALERT #13

Approach all parenting assessments with an open mind and do not make early assumptions that may affect your interactions with family members or your interpretation of the data.

The mind-set we as assessors bring to the process is critical to engaging family members and significantly contributes to a comprehensive assessment. When we have preconceived notions about clients or recommendations, we may alter our interactions with those clients and selectively collect information. Instead, we must strive to assess parents' strengths and weakness objectively, as both individuals and parents, and to identify children's idiosyncratic needs and perspectives.

At the same time, we clearly need to recognize that the job is assessment, where a broad array of data must be collected efficiently. We cannot wait months for information to spontaneously emerge; control of the data collection process is essential, as it can easily get out of hand. For example, some parents are so anxious or verbose their discourse becomes repetitive and overwhelming. By maintaining an awareness of information already collected, we can stop reiterations that provide no new data. Such an approach was necessary in the following case.

CASE 22: A family with two children, aged five and seven years, was referred for assessment when the mother did not return from caring for a dying relative in another city. Graham, a bright professional, cared for the children during his wife's absence but became stressed because of the excessive demands of his career. Neighbours called child welfare authorities when he sometimes left his children on their own before and after school. Although a willing participant in the assessment, Graham was so anxious about the complaint and the assessment's outcome that he constantly repeated himself. He also faxed reams of materials to the assessor. Graham recognized his inappropriate response to anxiety but could not control it. Consequently, the assessor limited his repetitive verbalizations and avoided wasting many interview hours by identifying which points had been already been covered. This not only lowered costs, but also reduced the likelihood that others such as lawyers or judges would allege bias in the assessment. Furthermore, such limits allowed Graham to become more focused. When he also recovered from the shock of his wife's permanent departure, his overall coping capacity improved. In the final analysis, Graham had more strengths than were evident initially.

Other clients have little to say, and assessors must draw information out. It is tempting to accept 'yes,' 'no,' or 'I don't know' answers when clients are not talkative, but then they do not really voice their opinions. At these times it can help to carefully word inquiries, give adequate time for responses, and work to increase the client's comfort level. Simpler language and a relaxed and patient interview style facilitate interviews of relatively nonverbal or hostile clients. Always be alert to signs of confusion and provide opportunities for family members to ask questions, conveying an attitude of openness and respect. Sarcastic and condescending comments, bored responses, and constant interruptions by people and telephones have no place during sessions. When clients are antagonistic or critical, avoid verbal power struggles with them. Particular sensitivity is required when family members are recent immigrants, speak a language other than English, or are members of a distinct cultural group. Then we should make every effort to clarify differences in language usage, utilizing translators as needed while remaining cognizant of potential problems that this may entail, as discussed in Chapter 7. Also, we may need to explore the use of specific idioms and gestures to ensure we do not inadvertently respond disrespectfully. Obviously, this adds complexity to both preparations for assessment sessions and the interpretation of the information.

Additionally, the office milieu itself may augment the comfort levels of family members, and should be tidy, clean, and comfortable. Assessors create a better impression of themselves if they are organized and prepared for all meetings rather than disheveled, disorganized, and unprepared. Provision of juice, water, or coffee as well as short breaks in the interview process allow clients to have brief pauses in the sometimes intense interview process.

Appendix C contains sample content checklists for each family member that can be adapted as needed to ensure complete data collection.

Parental Understanding of the Reasons for the Evaluation

Once parents are engaged, we must evaluate their understanding of the reasons for child welfare involvement and whether they think these reasons are valid. Parents occasionally have sought child welfare input themselves; at the other extreme are parents who negatively speculate about the people who filed the 'malicious' reports. Insight into child welfare concerns is positive, especially when parents acknowledge them, can identify the impact on their children, and display a sense of responsibility. In contrast, many deny difficulties and blame others or see the situation as unfair, referring to other families they know who parent poorly and yet have had no child welfare involvement. Jackie in Case 1 speculated about who reported her. Since she felt there were no grounds for apprehending her children, she accused others of gross errors in judgment. Such lack of insight spoke poorly for her ability to identify and respond to her children's needs. In this inquiry, one must also try to derive a sense of how parents perceive the impact of their behaviour and child welfare experiences, such as foster care placement, on their children.

As part of the discussion of the reasons for child welfare involvement, assessors may discuss the specifics of the abuse allegations with parents, specifically their behaviours that have raised concerns. Some parents may vehemently deny their behaviours, others state that their intentions or behaviours were misinterpreted, and still others may discuss their behaviours in some detail. It is worrisome when parents report clearly inappropriate behaviour without recognizing why others are concerned about it. Discussion of specific abuse allegations is likely not advisable if criminal charges or trial dates for such charges are pending, or if parents are about to be investigated by either police or child welfare personnel.

Since the accuracy of parental reports is important, we can begin to assess this by asking parents to specify dates and descriptions of various family events such as moves, children's apprehensions, and court hearings. These details can be compared to those noted in other documentation such as court or child welfare files. For example, parents who are abusing drugs or alcohol and those with cognitive problems, such as low intellectual functioning, severe attention deficit disorders, or psychotic disorders, may provide nebulous or wrong dates. Similarly, parents who are experiencing multiple and severe life stresses, or were during the periods in question, may have difficulty accurately remembering such detail. When their account of sequences and dates of events is accurate, reports may be more credible.

To further gauge parents' insight and willingness to sensitively respond to their children, it can be useful to ask them to justify their perceived ideal solutions. Some request that their children be returned immediately because they have little understanding of why their children are in care or are unable to acknowledge their difficulties with parenting, while others realistically recognize their weaknesses and strengths as parents and offer reasonable solutions. For example, they may truly recognize the deleterious effects of family violence and child abuse. It is sometimes easier for parents to do this when interviewed individually, particularly if spouses are controlling and critical.

Personal and Marital Histories

When taking personal and marital histories, we must constantly evaluate the accuracy and reliability of parental reports. As discussed in

Chapter 6, parents can have much invested in making poor histories seem better, while others cope with their childhood maltreatment by altering their accounts. Although references may validate some reports, we should request specific and detailed accounts of events and feelings. For example, we might ask for descriptions of specific incidents that made them feel loved or hurt by their parents. Not only does this allow us to gauge the quality of care they received in childhood, but it may give an indication about the internal working models they had at the time and that still may influence their relationships and parenting. Thus, one might ask about how they expected their parents and others to respond to them and how they felt about their own personal value. These are both components of **internal working models** (Bowlby, 1973, 1980, 1982).

A structured interviewing protocol called the *Adult Attachment Interview* (AAI) was developed by George, Kaplan, and Main (1984, 1985, 1996) to formally assesses the attachment organizations of adults, and is described well by Hesse (1999). It is a semi-structured hour-long protocol consisting of eighteen questions about childhood relationships and separations and their associated memories. It also questions the impact of these experiences and memories on development and current personality functioning and relationships. After the interview responses are transcribed, the interviewee's attachment organization is rated as evidenced in his or her discourse. The current classifications include secure/autonomous, dismissing, preoccupied, and unresolved/disorganized and correspond to patterns of Infant Strange Situation behaviour. They have implications for the quality of parenting individuals provide to their children. Although the validity and psychometric properties of the protocol are being constantly studied and updated, the AAI is not currently available for routine use in clinical or forensic circumstances. Not only is it used primarily in research, but extensive training is needed to score and interpret the subject's responses. However, some of its questions can inform our practice by suggesting salient avenues of inquiry we can use in assessment interviews. For example, the protocol asks individuals to produce five adjectives describing each of their parents and then recall specific memories that led them to choose those adjectives. It also asks individuals to talk about separations from their parents, speak of times they felt rejected or threatened by their parents, and describe other people to whom they felt close in childhood. While this is only a sample of questions, they are instructive. Additionally, if parents experienced childhood abuse or neglect, we can ask how they now understand these experiences, and specifically why they were maltreated and what allowed them to adapt and survive.

A thorough review of personal history can be structured around the parents' management of the stage-salient developmental tasks outlined in Chapter 3. First, of course, is the **physical care** that parents received as children, including the family's financial status, the moves they made, and the structure of the family. It can be helpful to construct a **genogram**, particularly if circumstances are complex. For example, parents may have full and half-siblings as well as several children with different fathers who may or may not be involved in their lives. While these genograms may not be included in final assessment reports, they can help identify patterns that occur within and across generations in specific families, and they can facilitate communication with other professionals who work with the family (Stratton & Hanks, 1995). For this reason, it is wise to use relatively standard symbols and conventions in drawing them, such as those described by McGoldrick and Gerson (1985). Given the complexity of some child welfare families, several attempts may be necessary to produce a comprehensive and understandable genogram. In the case that follows, a genogram clearly allowed the assessor to begin making sense of the rather chaotic and destructive nature of the parenting.

CASE 23: Two children were apprehended from their mother, Tammy, when nursing staff became concerned about her interactions with a newborn son in hospital. As a teenager Tammy had been in the care of child welfare authorities due to neglect and sexual abuse by family members. Likewise, several of her siblings and half-siblings were maltreated and had been apprehended. During Tammy's parenting assessment, her mother was interviewed and three generations of maltreatment and inadequate parenting were identified, as is evident in the accompanying genogram. Tammy's mother was also neglected and sexually abused as a child, and her two brothers spent time in foster care. Furthermore, two suspicious infant deaths occurred in the extended family, with both infants reportedly dying from Sudden Infant Death Syndrome. An accident had taken the life of Tammy's first common law husband and Tammy's uncle died in a shooting, indicating the lack of safety in which generations lived. Psychiatric illness was common in the extended family, and Tammy's brother developed schizophrenia as a teenager. Finally, incest was common: not only had Tammy given birth to a daughter sired by her father, but Tammy's mother cohabited with her uncle and had two children by him. These intergenerational family patterns of abuse and psychopathology helped identify significant risk factors that argued against the return of the children to Tammy's care.

When asking about **parents' childhoods**, specifically inquire about early caretakers and the importance of other extended family members in their lives, noting in particular any enduring, positive relationships in which the parents say they felt truly valued, as these may contribute to their positive self-esteem and resilience. Due to the possibility that parents may overidealize these early relationships, we will need to make sure to evaluate the accuracy of the parent's perceptions through contacts with collateral references as well as in the parent's responses to formal assessment measures. Similarly, the type and importance of early and later peer relationships and the parents' subsequent involvement with members of the opposite sex contribute to understanding how they relate to others and their expectations in relationships. Included here is their participation in any antisocial groups during school years or afterwards.

Another important avenue of inquiry concerns parents' school achievement and learning difficulties. Placements in behavioural classes and treatment programs for emotionally or behaviourally disturbed children and youth suggest childhood problems with emotional and behavioural regulation that may have continued impact into adulthood and now affect parenting. When these experiences are seen as routine parts of life, it is not surprising that parents do not recognize their own or their children's problems. Strengths and problems in school achievement as well as participation in extracurricular activities and sports provide a sense of the parents' talents and areas of competence. For example, a parent might have had learning and friendship problems in elementary school, but have excelled in sports. Alternatively, with such problematic profiles, parents may never have developed a positive sense of themselves as children, particularly if they were also abused or neglected. We must also specifically inquire about any medical or emotional problems parents experienced in early years. Not only might these have impeded their participation in family life

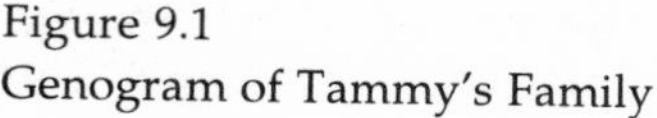

Figure 9.1
Genogram of Tammy's Family

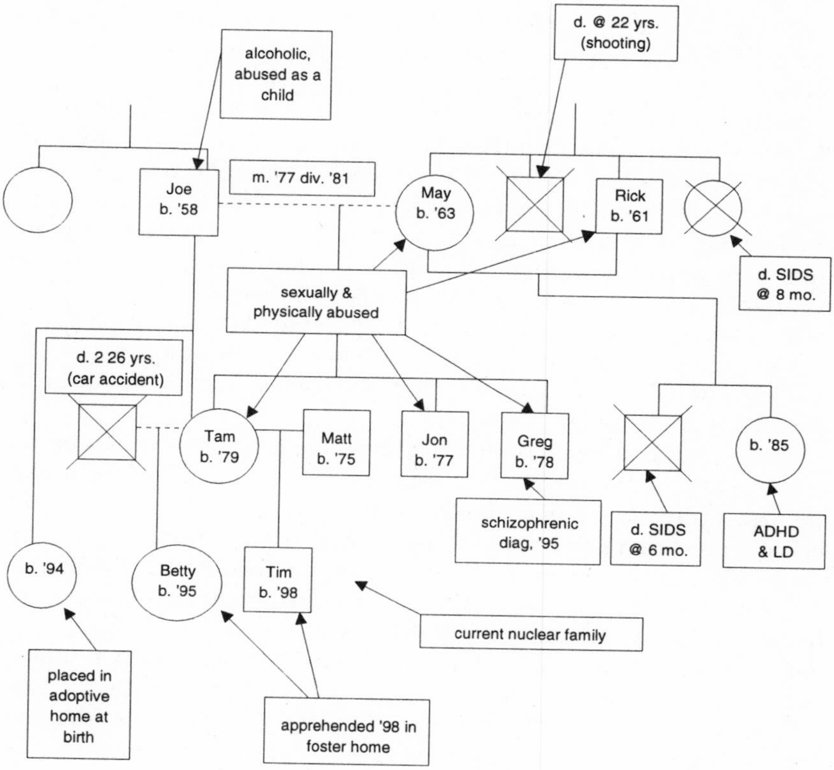

and school and community activities, but they may have lowered self-esteem and affected life-choices. Similarly, **educational choices** and **employment history** deserve careful inquiry because independence and economic self-sufficiency are two of the hallmarks of positive adult functioning. However, we must remember that some parents who are hard workers live in poverty because they are poorly paid or cannot budget efficiently. We must be alert to parental dependence on their own parents' emotional and financial support or on social service agencies for social contact and financial support, carefully exploring the reasons for dependency, because the implications for parenting might be very different for a parent who cannot work due to a physical/medical problem than for another who cannot work because of psychiatric difficulties. Concerns also arise when parents depend on criminal activities or are immersed in a criminal subculture for their income.

As discussed in Chapter 3, the process of teenage emancipation deserves inquiry, particularly if this occurred precipitously, as when parents fled a difficult home or abusive situation or because of intense unmet needs for emotional nurturing. Tammy (Case 23) was a dependent young mother who had never had her needs for security and attention met when she was a child or teenager. After surrendering her father's child for adoption at the age of fifteen years, she fled the care of either of her divorced parents and entered a relationship with a man who was ten years her senior. When he was abusive and controlling, she became pregnant in hopes a baby would meet her needs for love and affection.

As forming relationships and having a family are tasks often undertaken in early adulthood, relationship and marital histories are a critical area of inquiry. **Early dating relationships**, particularly those involving physical or emotional abuse, require inquiry because they may have implications for parents' expectations in relationships generally. For example, Tammy began dating and sexual activity in her mid-teens, repeating her mother's pattern. Not only did early boyfriends date her to use her sexually, but they commonly beat and intimidated her to ensure her compliance with their demands, such as their expectations that she have intercourse with several of them in an evening. Tammy expected and accepted these experiences and could take no steps to protect herself and perhaps later her children.

It is important to next inquire about the specifics of **later relationships** that form after adolescence, noting their duration and the modes of conflict resolution and presence of abuse within these relationships. How the partners met and what attracted them to each other can provide insights. Reasons such as emotional neediness (i.e., 'I needed someone to take care of me'), a need to escape an abusive family, and ready opportunities for indiscriminate sexual relationships provide information about the emotional maturity of the partners. This information helped ascertain patterns of dysfunction in the following parenting assessment.

CASE 24: Martin and Barb met at a party and Barb immediately fell in love with Martin, knowing she would marry him. He felt she was the most beautiful woman he had ever met and was overwhelmed by her avid sexuality. Within three months Barb was pregnant, and they married. Still in the glow of their early relationship, both overlooked behaviours that later created huge difficulties in their relationship. Martin despised both Barb's habit of smoking marijuana and her 'low-life' friends. She despised his rigidity and constant criticism. The birth of four girls in quick succession generated further stress in their relationship. Barb managed the stresses of parenthood poorly and continued her drug use during and between pregnancies. Martin further objected to her parenting methods. When disgruntled, neither brought up issues maturely or sensitively. Instead, each physically and verbally attacked the other and had extramarital affairs to hurt the other spouse. Eventually they separated when neighbours filed child welfare complaints about untended children during the working day. Despite this, their violence escalated and their functioning declined. The children were briefly apprehended while a parenting assessment was completed.

Parents' general **expectations of relationships** may help explicate dynamics. For example, Martin and Barb were naïve and immature. While both recognized some potential problems early on, each expected the other to change following marriage. Even when aggravations arose prior to the birth of their first child, neither addressed them because both expected parenthood and love would offer the best solution. Tammy (Case 23) expected mistreatment from her partners and love and affection from her children; when her children failed to meet her emotional needs, Tammy ignored them and occasionally hit them. Other parents may expect relationships to be short lived and invest little energy in making them work. For example, a mother who grew up in a father-absent and violent family may have similar expectations of her own relationships, especially if the same situation prevails for relatives and family friends. As we saw in the case of Martin and Barb, parental expectations about the expression of anger can also affect the subsequent resolution of disagreements and eventual dissolution of relationships. Since expectations can profoundly influence behaviour, patterns evident in earlier relationships may characterize current relationships, making it important to inquire about the continuity of such and their amenability to change. For example, many clients leave one horrific relationship only to pick new partners that result in continued dysfunctional relationships. This may continue even when they recognize the existence of problems, vow never to repeat the same mistakes, or participate in therapy or counselling to address these issues. Dysfunctional patterns that are chronic and seemingly impervious to modification may have grave implications for recommendations about the ability of adults to parent their children.

The process of obtaining such detailed personal histories is not always easy, particularly when it is emotionally provocative, as in Tammy's case. Clients may become agitated and upset because of the feelings that surface. This is particularly so when they have not dealt with childhood events or integrated them into their lives. Phelps, Belsky, and Crnic (1998) report that parents who can acknowledge childhood problems and maltreatment and can express accompanying feelings in an integrated fashion are likely to be less affected by a poor early history in regard to their own parenting. Although one is tempted to stop inquiry when difficult issues provoke anxiety, one must endeavour to ask questions in a direct but sensitive manner that is neither intrusive nor disrespectful. Often we can help clients recount history by simply noting the topic's difficulty and using momentary diversions to other, less provocative topics. However, we must be alert to garbled, vague, incoherent, and incomplete reports, to assertions that the information is irrelevant, and to blasé and muted reactions that seem disconnected from the interview's content. In such instances, we need to make adequate formulations as to why parents cannot recount their histories more coherently.

While this interviewing requires more specific inquiry than that undertaken in general personal and family histories, the detail is needed given the profound influence of early experiences on later personal and relationship functioning. This is particularly so in child welfare cases, where earlier parental difficulties may be more likely. The same areas must be reviewed in foster/adopt and custody/access cases, although sometimes parent backgrounds are less problematic. Detailed histories not only help establish a context in which to evaluate current functioning, but serve a particularly useful function for those children who become permanent wards of the child welfare authorities without ongoing contact with their birth parents. These histories, assessment reports, and genograms may be the only available detailed and coherent records of their families, perhaps eventually facilitating their understanding and acceptance of their backgrounds.

Current Functioning

Many of the current factors that potentially influence the risk of poor parenting are reviewed here. The questions in Chapters 6 and 7 can provide guidance for inquiry; here we will detail more specific areas of inquiry. Given the profound impact poverty and social supports can have on parenting, as discussed in Chapters 6 and 7, it is critical to inquire about the current physical circumstances of the family, asking about the location of their **residence** and the family's source of **income**. For working parents, we must ask detailed questions about the nature of their **employment**, job stability, relationships with fellow workers, and happiness with employment prospects; stability and contentment can offer significant compensatory benefits to them in their functioning as individuals and parents. We need to contact employers for verification of their reports, particularly if there are any suggestions of problems. A reason for contact must be provided to employers during these calls; this is simply accomplished by indicating that we are undertaking an assessment and, as part of this process, are contacting employers to ask about work. No details of family problems need to be given, since it is clearly inappropriate to give information that may jeopardize the parents' continued employment or violate confidentiality. The Collateral Contacts section later in this chapter provides detailed information about contacts with references. When parents do not work outside of the home, we can still ask for descriptions of a typical day and verify as needed by contacting appropriate references.

Current **physical** and **mental health** is another area of inquiry. This includes medical problems, particularly any that are chronic and induce children's anxiety or impede the provision of adequate physical or emotional care. For example, a parent's uncontrolled seizure disorder can generate considerable anxiety for children and limit mobility because parents cannot operate a motorized vehicle. Similarly, chronic fatigue syndrome may so drastically limit a parent's energy that children must be placed in daycare. When asking about medical problems, we want to know specifics, such as symptoms and what treatment is required. We can also ask how parents have explained the problems to their children and whether they have inappropriately involved them in treatment measures. It is very important to verify such reported problems by contacting the attending medical personnel, particularly in regard to issues such as treatment compliance and whether parents either deny or overemphasize their difficulties. Attending medical personnel may also be helpful references when concerns are raised about parental neglect of children's medical needs.

Mental health personnel often offer useful information if they have provided services to help parents or children cope with various emotional problems. Clearly, assessors must determine if parents have any diagnosable, clinical mental health problems such as depression or psychosis as well as any underlying personality disorders that might affect parenting. Since many daily activities are stressful, including parenting, we must also ascertain how parents cope with stress. We can ask them to identify their sources of stress, specify how they recognize when they are stressed, and describe what they do to make situations less stressful and to control their reactions. For example, some parents realize they are stressed when they begin to scream at their children, but they may have limited insight into the reasons for this behaviour and cannot take steps to lessen their frustration. Furthermore, when parents cannot outline specific coping strategies and are constantly overwhelmed, question how their stress is expressed to those around them. For example, some yell at their children, as noted above, while others fight with their spouses, eat, watch television, gamble, sleep, or use drugs or alcohol. Since alcohol and drug use is always a critical area of inquiry in any assessment, parents must specify amounts and frequency of use rather than providing general statements such as 'I drink occasionally.' Drug testing and records of impaired driving convictions may be needed to validate concerns because they can indicate both problematic use and poor judgment. Finally, if parents have been in treatment about mental health issues and problems such as drug and alcohol abuse, treatment personnel may offer valuable information about the extent of the problems, the course of and response to treatment, and the long-term prognosis and ongoing need for treatment. Reports from other professionals and people in the community provide corroboration of both medical and mental health problems even when assessors undertake comprehensive psychological testing and psychiatric interviews with the clients themselves.

Related to stress management is inquiry about **recreational interests**. Even in poor families, parents may find visiting with family and friends or attending religious activities to be both relaxing and enjoyable. Concerns arise if they have no time, interest, or energy for such participation, or if they chose recreational activities that are likely to detrimentally influence their children. This occurred in the following case.

CASE 25: A rural family was referred for assessment when residents of the town reported that Jan and Bill left their children unattended in their van when they went drinking in the local bar. The complaints annoyed Jan and Bill, who agreed to a parenting assessment to prove they were good parents. They viewed their weekly trip from their remote ranch to have several beers as well-earned relaxation. They felt that no one should begrudge them this enjoyment because they always bought treats for the children and locked the van doors to keep them safe. During assessment it became evident that while parents worked long hours, five-year old Meg was left to care for her two-year old sister. They received accidental burns on several occasions when Meg tried cooking. Jan and Bill applauded Meg's efforts at self-sufficiency and saw nothing wrong with her responsibilities. They clearly did not recognize the children's needs and jeopardized their safety on many occasions.

It is important to ask how families relate to each other. Since **family interaction** spans across several areas, it is sometimes useful to begin with **pragmatic roles**, as this may be the least threatening to parents. Identify the routine tasks of different family members by having parents describe a typical day at home. For example, one parent may miss the morning routine due to an early departure for work. Others miss meal preparation and homework periods due to late shifts, perhaps leaving these parenting tasks to their spouse, an adolescent child, or even a very young child. By asking who does the cooking, cleaning, shopping, washing, scheduling, and homework, one may identify inequalities that generate family stress. Resentment may grow if one parent receives little recognition for assuming the majority of the housework and childcare, or if he or she cannot ask for help, expecting the other to notice and volunteer assistance. Likewise, responsibility for less routine tasks, such as scheduling and keeping medical and dental appointments and attending parent-teacher conferences, merit investigation. One sometimes derives a sense of a parent's resentment about bearing the brunt of responsibility for child-rearing tasks, as well as the parents' insight and problem-solving abilities, by asking how parents would change things to make their families run more smoothly.

This may be followed by a discussion of the **needs of family members**. In any family parents set priorities depending upon the needs they perceive from each member. Some parents place their needs ahead of those of their children, while in other families the reverse is true. Needs can be identified by asking questions such as 'What does ... need to have happen in your family to be happy (healthy, develop well, etc.)?' or 'If ... could change your family, what do you think (he or she) would wish?' Such questions can often identify differences in perception, and even resentments, that clearly affect how family members relate to each other. Further questioning about how members express their needs (i.e., 'How do you know when ... wants this to happen?') begins to provide some insight regarding how family members negotiate having their needs met. When parents are inarticulate and uninsightful, specific scenarios may need to be presented to facilitate their discussion. Also, family interviews sometimes provide a good venue for such a discussion because children may correct parents when perceptions are not accurate.

Discussions of needs often lead directly into a discussion of sources of friction and disagreement and consequently to **modes of conflict resolution and emotional expression** as well as roles adopted by family members in this process. Different family members may have varied styles of managing difficult feelings, with some assuming roles such as 'bad boy' or 'peacemaker' to maintain emotional equilibrium in families. For example, in Case 9, Joyce vacillated between being the peacemaker who made everyone feel good to living in a fantasy world. Mike acted up to divert parents away from fighting and unite them to deal with his negative behaviour. Since it is common for family members to show approval, tenderness, and emotional closeness differently, it is import to ask specifically about the expression of positive feelings. In one family a parent may show love and approval by playing checkers with a child, while in another a parent may view corporal punishment as the ideal way of showing their love and investment in a child. Finally, one should ask how decisions are made in family, including whether children have a voice and who makes the ultimate decisions.

The nature and quality of the **marital relationship** deserves careful inquiry regardless of whether parents are legally married or live common law. Here some of the questions asked in the marital history extend to current relationships. Thus, an assessor would inquire specifically about the satisfaction parents derive from their relationship, and identify their needs and expectations and the degree of support they feel from their spouses. If difficulties are occurring, then parents need to speak to their efforts to remedy these issues.

Patterns of communication are another line of inquiry. Do the family members communicate directly and openly about needs and expectations or is communication obtuse, where they wait for other family members to recognize and respond to their feelings and needs? Are there rules about who talks to whom and who can bring up certain topics? For example, in some families true feelings and needs are stated only in the heat of an argument. Arguments seem to happen because people connect only during them, albeit hurtfully. In other families certain topics are taboo. For example, children cannot talk about a parent who deserted them because the issue is too painful for the remaining parent. Some families are much more open to including other people in their lives, while others keep issues to themselves. Tammy's family in Case 23 was very insular. Not only did they avoid discussion of issues within their family, but they remained aloof in the community to ensure their incestuous relationships would not be revealed. All family members were suspicious and mistrusting when child welfare personnel first became involved. It took concerted effort on the assessor's part to slowly break through the family's implicit pact of silence.

In adoption or foster care assessments, assessors must carefully query how parents communicate and cope with issues regarding their **infertility**. An assessor would thus ask about the duration of the parents' attempts to have children, how and when they realized they were infertile, steps they have taken to medically remedy the problems, and their acceptance of this aspect of their lives. (This issue may be more resolved for applicants who know they are permanently infertile than for those where infertility is unexplained and the possibility of biological children still exists.) We should ask these couples why they still want to parent children instead of devoting energies to other activities. Finally, we need to ask them to anticipate their feelings if they do not become parents and to describe the reactions of family and friends to their application.

Broader relationships within the community and extended families must be clarified to gauge the immediately available supports to the parents. Parents should be asked about the type and frequency of activities with others and the benefits and supports they gain from these interactions. Other questions focus on how friends are made, including the duration and progression of friendships and how disagreements are resolved. Friends may fill many roles, such as being sounding boards during coffee chats, drinking buddies for the parents, or babysitters. Some friends are integrally involved in the lives of each other's families. Extended family members also fill variable roles ranging from providing strong, positive, pragmatic, and emotional support to being intrusive and critical to being completely uninterested. For example, a sister might be a sounding board for a new mother, offer constructive suggestions about caring for a newborn, and reassure that feelings of being overwhelmed and inadequate are normal. Another might criticize the new mother for not knowing what to do with an irritable infant, suggesting she should have thought of this before she became pregnant; others might say, 'Don't bother me now. I have my own problems.' The messages and derived support for proficient parenting are completely different.

During this inquiry we must not accept glib assurances that parents have many close relationships. Their reference lists sometimes indicate the quality of parents' friendship and family networks. Concerns arise when parents cannot think of any friends to serve as references, or when parents report many 'very good' friends who, when contacted, know virtually nothing about the parents and indeed are surprised to be regarded as friends. Sometimes supposedly friendly references are hostile, attesting to the parents' poor judgment and erratic relationships. This was the case with Jackie (Case 1), who provided a list of several 'good friends' whom she said supported her and would attest to her parenting skills and personal stability. When contacted, some indicated they had little to do with Jackie, and they provided rather damaging information about her. Furthermore, in the two weeks between the time Jackie signed releases of information and the time her 'best friend' was contacted, the two had a falling out; Jackie had only met her 'best friend' two weeks earlier in a bar and their entire friendship lasted a month. Jackie had sex with her friend's boyfriend, used her car without permission, pawned her television, and reported her to child welfare. Contacts with other references indicated this was a common relationship pattern. Jackie made friends easily but tended to use and abuse their goodwill, and she generally picked people who had significant problems.

Psychological Mindedness

A final facet that requires inquiry is parents' insight into their personalities and parenting abilities. For both themselves and their spouses, we request them to describe their personalities, outlining personal strengths and weaknesses as well as their strengths and weaknesses as parents, and asking for examples and elaboration as needed. These descriptions are informative, particularly when compared with your own observations and psychological testing results. Parents who give accurate descriptions and who identify both their own and spousal strengths and weaknesses may be more likely to accurately recognize their children's reactions and needs than those whose thinking is inflexible or unfocused. For example, Martha in Case 6 was inarticulate. She could not describe her strengths and weaknesses although she critiqued those of Paul Sr. Initially, he focused exclusively on his strengths and his children's weaknesses, but he became less defensive and demonstrated more flexibility and balance in his opinions as the assessment progressed.

In addition to current descriptions, it sometimes helps to understand the parents' broader expectations if you ask them to turn the clock ahead five, ten, and even twenty years. Some have specific expectations while others have no plans; some are optimistic while others are pessimistic, expecting to die shortly or be deserted by their children. When parents are pessimistic, we can ask what they can do to alter expectations and make remaining years better. Even when they have not previously considered such a question, some parents can actively and accurately respond. Furthermore, this may generate insight that can alter their expectations and propel them towards a more active approach to the problems in their family.

The Children's Developmental Histories

Earlier we reviewed child factors to be surveyed in parenting assessments. Because the primary task of parents is to support children in negotiating the stage-salient tasks of childhood and to meet their children's needs, the entire development of children is reviewed with parents. Instead of reviewing these in any detail here, we refer readers back to Chapters 3, 4, and 5 for a discussion of salient factors. The necessary inquiry is summarized in Table 9.1, which was also included in Pearce and Pezzot-Pearce (1997). These factors are surveyed by interviewing parents and/or having them complete developmental history forms that are then supplemented with additional interview questions. Screening questionnaires and inquiry about specific behaviours ensure information is not missed. The Aggregate Neurobehavioral Student Health and Educational Review (ANSER) (Levine, 1985) is one example of a commonly used developmental history form. However, it is important to ensure that parents read well enough to understand the questionnaires.

In a developmental history assessors must be alert to situations where parents have marked difficulties recalling their children's histories, possibly suggesting parental problems that must then be verified. They may have problems with intellectual functioning and memory or be unable to recall details because of alcohol or drug problems or psychiatric difficulties. They may also be uninterested in their children, possibly reflective of an insecure attachment, or have experienced such significant stress that they did not attend to developmental milestones. In still other situations, their cultural origins result in better or poorer memories for specific details. In some cultural groups, children spend significant periods in the care of extended family; parents may not recall details of all these episodes because they are too numerous. Others do not note or report details because they are viewed as insignificant. For example, when asked about problem behaviours, a parent may omit behaviours typical of children with attention problems because the parent exhibits the same behaviours and does not see them as problems. Paul Sr. (Case 6) did not recognize his child's problems as significant for this reason.

Descriptions of the Children's Current Needs

As assessors delve into developmental histories, they move to inquiry about current functioning and needs. The areas to be covered are outlined in Table 9.2: an assessor reviews the children's status in meeting stage-salient tasks and asks about current living arrangements, medical status, and attachments. Children's capacity to modulate feelings

Table 9.1
Developmental History of the Child

1. Pregnancy and delivery
   a. Was the pregnancy planned?
   b. Was this the mother's first pregnancy?
   c. What were the parents' feelings about the pregnancy?
   d. Did the mother have medical care and consultation during the pregnancy? When did this start?
   e. Health of the mother during the pregnancy
      (1) Weight gain
      (2) Medications taken, including substance abuse
      (3) Medical concerns and treatments
   f. Was the child born preterm or postterm?
   g. Labour
      (1) Were both parents present?
      (2) Duration
      (3) Medications administered
      (4) Special procedures used
      (5) Was the baby healthy at birth?
      (6) Baby's weight and apgar scores
      (7) Was the baby held immediately? What were the parents' first thoughts and feelings on seeing the baby?
      (8) Did the baby require time in the intensive care nursery?
      (9) How long did the mother and child stay in the hospital?
      (10) How and when was the name selected?
      (11) Was the baby breastfed? Why or why not? How long was the baby breastfed?
2. Neonatal period and infancy
   a. Constitution and temperamental style (e.g., activity level, reaction to stimuli, general responsiveness, reactions to change and transitions)
   b. Growth patterns
   c. Establishment of eating, sleeping, toilet routines
3. Developmental milestones
   a. Parents' general memory regarding whether concerns were apparent
   b. Specifics regarding approximate age at first smile, sitting, walking, first words, good communication understandable by others outside of the family, day and night toilet training achieved, sexual maturity and puberty
4. Quality of early relationships and attachment history
   a. What is the pattern of the child's early relationships with caregiver(s)? Were these relationships consistent or changing?
   b. Were there extended separations of the child from a primary caretaker or caretakers and at what ages did these occur?
   c. What were the child's reactions when separated from primary caretaker(s) and how did he or she relate to them when reunited?
   d. Who did the child seek out when he or she was hurt or distressed?
5. Stresses
   a. Physical illnesses/injuries (acute/chronic)

b. Emotional (e.g., separation/divorce of parents, death of significant family members or pets, family moves, poverty, family violence, physical and mental illness of family members)
c. History of maltreatment
   (1) Type of maltreatment
   (2) Age at onset
   (3) Duration
   (4) Perpetrator(s)
   (5) Child's reaction (behavioural, emotional, physical) to the maltreatment
   (6) Response of the environment to the maltreatment (e.g., parents/caregivers, siblings, wider community [including teachers, legal/justice system])
   (7) Previous or concurrent treatment or other services to the child and family and their outcomes

6. Other placements
   a. Number of placements and duration: types of placements
   b. Reasons(s) for each placement (e.g., maltreatment, breakdown in placement because of the child's behaviour)
   c. Feelings and attitudes of previous caretakers towards the child
   d. Child's behaviour in each placement (e.g., any significant difficulties: if so, obtain as full a description as possible)
   e. Were alternative childcare arrangements used when parents worked? Who were the caregivers, and what was the child's response to them?
7. Response to discipline and nature of discipline used with child
8. School history
   a. Emotional reaction
   b. Progress at school (review report cards if available)
   c. Behaviour with teachers and classmates
   d. Special class placements or other educational and psychological assistance (review reports and speak to program personnel)
9. Hobbies, interests, sports, chores
10. Peer relationships
   a. Number of friendships
   b. Nature and intensity of friendships (e.g., Has the child been detached or overly dependent upon peers? Did the child take all the initiative to establish and maintain peer relationships, or did other children initiate contact?)
   c. Problem areas in relationships with peers (e.g., fighting, withdrawal, sexually intrusive behaviour)
   d. Issues and attitudes about sexuality (e.g., sexual maturity, identification as a male or female, sexual interest – age at first interest; dating habits, attitudes, and feelings about sexual behaviour)
11. History of any other previous problems
   a. Nature of the problem
   b. Onset, frequency, duration
   c. Treatment or other services

Note: Portions of this table are from *Psychotherapy of abused and neglected children* (pp. 79–80) by John W. Pearce and Terry Pezzot-Pearce (New York: Guilford Publications, 1997). Copyright 1997 by Guilford Publications. Reprinted with permission.

and behaviour is reviewed, as is their cognitive and language development, with attention to current school functioning if they are of school age. Their relationships with peers are questioned, as are preparations for and attempts at emancipation. Through this inquiry, one must ask about any special needs children exhibit, perhaps using the questions in Chapters 4 and 5 as a guide. Given that most children in child welfare cases have been somehow maltreated, parents should be asked how they became aware the children were being maltreated if they were not the abusers, as well as how the children reacted to maltreatment and the steps parents took to protect their children and facilitate recovery. Table 9.1 describes the salient information that should be gathered. Again, one must be alert to times when parents cannot describe their children accurately and note if their observations agree with one's own and with the results of formal psychological testing. Parents who provide coherent and accurate descriptions of their children's behaviour are perhaps more likely to recognize the children's needs and respond appropriately. If descriptions are grossly inaccurate, then one would seriously question parents' sensitivity and attunement to their children and needs. This was the situation for Randy (Case 3), whose mother provided a disjointed developmental history and a grossly inaccurate description of his current functioning. For example, she said he had several good friends when his interviews and reference contacts showed these to be fleeting relationships that lasted only days because he behaved inappropriately and impulsively. June did not know what constituted normal relationships for an eleven-year old boy. Furthermore, she complained that Randy was immature and self-centred because he did not recognize and respond to her needs; she expected him to comfort her and discuss her worries and problems. While Randy was indeed immature, it was not for the reasons June described. Her expectations were clearly inappropriate and arose from her egocentricity and personality dysfunction. Given her inappropriate expectations and extremely poor knowledge of normal child development, she could not recognize or respond to his needs.

Assessors need to constantly evaluate the parents' **knowledge of normal child development** as they present it in general discussion and in response to specific questions and scenarios. Parents sometimes have a good understanding of typical development but have unrealistic expectations, perhaps because they believe their children are gifted or special. It is therefore important to clarify parents' **expectations regarding their children**. Assessors can ask parents to speak

Table 9.2
Current Functioning of the Child

1. Attachment relationships
   a. Does the child rely on any one or more people for security and calming?
   b. Is the child overly dependent on this person(s)?
   c. Do relationships seem to matter to this child?
   d. Does the child exhibit empathy regarding the feelings of other people?
   e. Does the child exhibit affection and is this in an appropriate or indiscriminant manner?
   f. Does the child accept displays of kindness and affection from other people?
   g. Does this child behave in ways that keep people emotionally distant?
2. Emotional and behavioural regulation
   a. Is this child able to regulate expression of feeling and behaviour in a manner that is age appropriate?
   b. Does the child have behaviour problems at home, in school, or in other settings, and what are the circumstances of these difficulties?
   c. Is the child in a special school class or specialized living placement due to behaviour problems?
   d. Has the child been in trouble with the law?
3. Self-view
   a. Does the child like himself or herself?
   b. Does the child see himself or herself as doing well or poorly, and is this congruent with actual behaviour and achievement?
   c. Does the child initiate new and challenging activities or does he/she not take risks, doing activities that are typical of younger children?
   d. Does the child exhibit independence in a typical manner for children of that age?
   e. Does the child have interests, hobbies, and sport activities that he or she enjoys?
4. Language and play development
   a. Is the child's level of language development age appropriate?
   b. Does the child play in an age-appropriate manner and does he/she exhibit sportsmanship?
5. Peer relationships
   a. Who are the child's friends?
   b. How often does the child see these friends and in what context?
   c. Who initiates these contacts (e.g., child, friends, parents)?
   d. Do other children seek to have contact with this child (e.g., invitations to birthday parties, phone calls, knocks on the door)
   e. What difficulties does the child have in current relationships with peers?
6. School functioning
   a. Does this child like school and attend reliably?
   b. Does the child achieve at a level that is commensurate with his/her ability?
   c. What problems hold the child back from achieving more competently at school?
   d. Is the child in any special programming and is he/she responsive to it?
7. Physical functioning
   a. Is the child physically healthy (e.g., growing well, well fed, well rested)?
   b. Does this child have any chronic medical problems (e.g., HIV, diabetes)?
   c. Is the child receiving and responding to medical treatment?

8. Current stresses
   a. Is the child coping with any ongoing stresses (e.g., ongoing maltreatment, separation from family, foster care, institutionalization, family fighting and violence, divorce of parents, family moves, homelessness, poverty, pregnancy)?
   b. Is the child receiving ongoing support from parents and/or other people regarding these stresses? What is its nature and is it helpful?
9. Emancipation
   a. Is an older child gaining skills that will allow him/her to be appropriately emancipated in early adulthood?
   b. Is the child prematurely threatening or attempting to emancipate himself or herself from parental care or are parents threatening to emancipate the child prematurely?
10. Other current problems
   a. Nature of the problems as defined by others. Does the child define the problems in a similar manner?
   b. Onset, frequency, duration
   c. Treatment or other services; outcome

---

of what they expect for their children in five, ten, and fifteen years. This simple task reveals broader expectations, priorities, and the importance attached to various life tasks. Thus some parents focus on careers and income while others stress the importance of caring relationships. Parents' knowledge of child development and expectations for children are equally important in foster and adoption assessments. Even when unmatched with specific children, parents can talk generally about these issues. Furthermore, assessors can inquire about how parents expect to cope if subsequently placed children do not meet their expectations. They can also query parents' **values**, as some hold strong opinions about the importance of issues like education, religion, premarital sexual activity, and drug usage. Although assessors must be aware of their own values and ensure these do not negatively influence a parenting evaluation, some parental beliefs and values provoke concern. When parents see no problem with antisocial activities such as robbery, rape, or physical assault, their values may well conflict with the provision of adequate parenting; clearly one would be concerned about the likelihood of parents with such values placing firm limits on their youngsters, thereby increasing the risk for the development of serious conduct disorders.

Actual parenting behaviour demands both inquiry and observation because many challenges for parents occur in these daily interactions with children. Although behavioural expectations should vary depending on the children's ages, we will want to know specifically how parents react when children do not want to eat their dinner, do their homework, get ready for school, clean their rooms, or go to bed. We also should ask what parents do when children have temper tantrums, either at home or in public, and what they do when children misbehave, such as when they have a fight, hit someone, smoke, or get drunk. Additional inquiry focuses on how parents endeavour to meet more specialized needs, such as learning problems. Assessors can explore any number of specific situations and should not be satisfied with glib assurances that children present no challenge or with glossed-over responses that lack detail. When parents respond with seemingly rehearsed and ideal answers, the assessor should ask for descriptions of recent incidents, cross-validating by asking other family members or even references about the same incidents. Later in the assessment, you will make direct observations that can further validate reports.

As parents describe their children, inquire about how they try to help the children with the behaviour and emotional issues that present challenges to them. This may include descriptions of what parents have learned and used from previous courses and therapy, as well as what they hope to learn now or in the future. Even when children are in the care of child welfare authorities, parents can be supportive. Thoroughly clarify whether parents recognize their children's feelings of separation and loss and the steps they are prepared to take to learn to respond to their children needs, such as courses or therapy. For example, parents can respond by reliably visiting their children and maintaining contact with the children's workers. While the latter may be threatening, particularly when parents view child welfare personnel in a negative and adversarial manner, parents must put their own feelings aside to work cooperatively for a safe return of the children to their care. If parents are having difficulty approaching the child welfare workers or visiting the children, we must inquire about the reasons. For example, sometimes workers are indeed hostile in their interactions with parents, or the parents may not have transportation. Parents must realize that reliable and consistent contact helps children to recognize that their parents do care about them. Missed visits compound feelings of abandonment and confirm children's perceptions they are indeed unworthy of care, further rigidifying negative internal working models. When June unpredictably missed visits, Randy's sense of betrayal by his mother intensified (Case 3). Not only was he more provocative in his next visit with her, but he regressed in his foster home and strongly tested his foster parents' patience. For example, he urinated in the bathtub and on their daughter, gave or threw away some of their belongings, and tortured the family's pet. June usually gave Randy convoluted reasons for missing visits that increased rather than decreased his anger and sense of betrayal, especially as he slowly realized his foster parents calmly persisted in caring for him while his mother was emotionally demanding and disregarded his needs and feelings.

Accurately recognizing and responding to children's needs is an essential task for both biological and foster/adoptive parents, especially when children have difficult histories with an ongoing multitude of problems. Parents must realistically anticipate difficulties and problem-solve, as is exemplified in the following case.

CASE 26: Anna arrived in a foster home at the age of six years after living in her neglectful and sexually abusive biological family. She had been her father's sexual partner for four previous years, which included intercourse for the last two. Unfortunately, the workers who apprehended Anna were unaware of her history of sexual abuse. Believing that she was only grossly neglected, they placed her in a foster home recognized for its ability to meet the needs of neglected children. Mildred usually cared for two of her biological children and three to four neglected children at any one point in time, generally accepting placements of children under the age of five years. Despite being slightly older, Anna was accepted without much trepidation. She roamed the home at night to steal and hoard food, behaviours that Mildred expected. When she did not know how to use the toilet or eat with cutlery, Mildred worked to remedy these problems. However, Mildred was unprepared for her eleven-year old son's report that Anna had come to his room and fondled his penis while he slept. Mildred increased supervision but, even so, Anna roamed at night, tried to fondle younger children, and started two fires in her bedroom. Mildred became exhausted, but an absence of alternate placements meant she had to persist in caring for Anna. Finally, with the consent of Anna's worker, an alarm was placed on her door so that her nightly movements were monitored; Mildred began to sleep again. Over time, with support and firm behavioural limits, Anna began to internalize ways to modulate her behaviour. In therapy she disclosed her sexual abuse, began to understand that her father's behaviour was inappropriate, and was guided to find other, more appropriate ways to seek closeness with others. When she became a permanent ward, she was successfully adopted and weathered a stormy adolescence to become a competent adult.

When foster parents describe the needs of children who are about to be or are already placed in their homes, it is important to inquire about some of the more common needs foster children display. As foster children struggle to adapt to new homes, they often must deal with a sense of loss and abandonment by their parents. Despite the trauma they experienced in their parents' care, most foster children still love their parents and consequently experience feelings of loss when removed from their care. It is, therefore, critical for foster parents to refrain from criticizing biological parents, so children do not need to defend them. This is similar to the situation in separated and divorced families wherein children pick sides when one parent criticizes the other. Foster parents must recognize this and not challenge the children's loyalties to their biological parents. In our experience, when foster parents are extremely negative about biological parents children almost inevitably chose to defend their biological parents and distance foster parents, often through defiant or destructive behaviour. Similarly, foster parents must accept children's ongoing love for their biological parents. They must recognize this caring and, like assessors, be willing to search for both the strengths and the weaknesses of biological parents. In circumstances where children may be returned to biological parents, foster parents must strive to have them maintain a sense of connection to their parents. Finally, foster parents must recognize that it is not their job to prove they are better than biological parents; their task is to support children to maintain connections and help those children to realistically appraise their own lives and parents. Children require consistent care and support as they confront the realities of their lives, not just the blunt 'truth.' Similarly, adoptive parents must be open to viewing biological parents positively and not be threatened when adopted children express interest in their origins. This includes being supportive when adult adopted children wish to search for biological parents.

To accurately evaluate the **appropriateness of parent plans** for meeting children's needs and their **capacity to make changes**, assessors must form clear perceptions of the children's needs themselves. These should steadily emerge as parents outline the history and current functioning of all family members. Verification of these reports through observation, child interviewing, testing, and collateral contacts is, of course, necessary. Since past behaviour is one of the best predictors of future behaviour, previous therapists and other helpers who have worked with parents may offer good information. Even when parents are well intended and truly want to improve their children's situation, they may not have the capacity to alter their behaviours to parent better. Past responsiveness to intervention is a good indicator of future responsiveness, although assessors must always judge whether previously offered programs were a good therapeutic 'fit' for the parents in question. Additionally, in situations where parents were not responsive to a therapeutic intervention, assessors must determine if environmental or personal factors have so changed that therapeutic progress is now more likely. Steinhauer (1991) uses a past history of using help successfully as one of several factors that help differentiate families who are likely to improve their parenting capacity from those where a positive change is unlikely regardless of attempted interventions. He notes that when parents are open to and seek help, form a treatment alliance, and derive significant benefit, they are likely to increase their parenting capacity. When they refuse help or have repeated unsuccessful involvements, form no alliance, and derive no real benefit, their prognosis for positive change is limited.

Mental Status Examination

During initial interviews with parents, assessors may undertake formal mental status examinations of individual clients based on their physical and verbal presentation as well as their reported subjective experiences. According to Rosenthal and Akiskal (1985), these can range from relatively brief overviews that convey information about the client's basic presentation and are gained from general interview and history-taking, to much more in-depth descriptions obtained through extensive and probing questions. The latter are essential when serious mental health questions exist due to evidence of deviant and severely disturbed behaviour. Rosenthal and Akiskal stress that during this process, assessors must back up more global impressions with specific behavioural examples. General categories utilized in these descriptions vary among professionals and may include such elements as physical appearance, relationship to the examiner, behaviour, cognition, perception, speech, affect, and insight and judgment (Pearce & Pezzot-Pearce, 1997). Rosenthal and Akiskal use somewhat different categories that essentially survey the same characteristics, describing various specific tasks that can be used to determine client skills. Table 9.3 presents several categories and descriptions that are often included in mental status exams and can be used to communicate information about both parents and children in parenting assessments.

Psychological Testing

By now most assessors will have formed a relatively complex picture of the history and current functioning of the families being assessed. Psychological testing is another tool that can enhance the validity of observations. As in any assessment, more credence is given to observations and conclusions when the same information arises consistently in psychological tests, clinical interviews, *in vivo* observations, and reference reports. Assessors from disciplines other than psychology may strengthen conclusions if they include psychological test results in their deliberations. However, automatic administration of a standard battery is seldom worthwhile, and psychological testing should be used for specific reasons. Furthermore, the majority of psychological tests must be administered and interpreted by psychologists, although some available tests can be used by non-psychologists. These tend to be surveys and questionnaires that require less stringent user qualifications. Most test suppliers clearly indicate the required qualification level at time of sale. When practitioners plan on using surveys and questionnaires in the assessment process, they should familiarize themselves with development information about the instrument, and they should be cognizant of the limitations on conclusions that can be drawn from it, being able to justify its use in examination and cross-examination in court. Since this book is intended for the use of assessors from various disciplines other than psychology, we will review psychological testing more generally before we discuss the specific use of testing.

What Are Psychological Tests?

Given their emphasis on scientific knowledge in understanding human behaviour, psychologists have developed a number of 'tests' to measure personal qualities. Some tests directly measure behaviour such

Table 9.3
Mental Status Examination

1. Physical appearance
   - aspects such as age, gender, race, height and build, level of grooming, clothing, posture, and facial expression
   - commentary regarding whether appearance was unremarkable for someone of the client's age, socio-economic level, educational level, and cultural background
2. Relationship to the examiner
   - observations regarding how the client related, such as open, fearful and anxious, closed and guarded, wary, indiscriminate, hostile and aggressive, sexualized
   - observations regarding working alliance or degree of co-operation with the interview or assessment process
   - quality of social skills evidenced in interviews
3. Behaviour
   - activity level, including such behaviours as restlessness, agitation, excitability, hyperactivity, and hypoactivity or psychomotor retardation
   - degree of behavioural organization may include comments on impulsiveness, compulsiveness, and disorganization
   - client reactivity to such factors as probing questioning, challenge, and failure
4. Cognition and thought
   - estimated level of intelligence based on quality of discussion as well as client's capacity to think in abstract or concrete terms
   - attention and concentration levels
   - memory capacity for immediate, short-term, long-term, and remote information
   - thought processing or comments regarding how ideas are put together, including sequencing, coherence, and speed, and possibly using descriptors such as loose, perseverative, confabulatory, blocked, and incoherent
   - thought content, including major themes such as delusions, suspicions, and preoccupations with suicide and homicide
   - problem-solving abilities using such descriptors as organized, disorganized, and preoccupied
5. Speech
   - physical qualities such as articulation, fluency, speed, and expressiveness
   - characteristics such as complexity of syntax and vocabulary
   - levels of both receptive and expressive communication
6. Perception
   - orientation to time, place, person, and situation
   - disturbances such as hallucinations and dissociation
7. Affect and Mood
   - affect refers to the general emotional tone as well as the range and intensity of affect, including such descriptors as labile, hostile, constricted, blunted, or flat
   - mood refers to the client's subjective experience of emotion over time, perhaps including such descriptors as elated, depressed, irritable, and anxious
   - commentary if observed affect and reported mood are congruent as well as appropriate to the client's life experience
   - awareness of emotional responsiveness as well as personal capacity to control and redirect emotions

8. Insight and judgment
   - regarding own problems and motives
   - regarding consequences of own behaviour and actions that result in appropriate or inappropriate behavioural choices

---

as response time while others measure more theoretical qualities such as narcissism, psychopathy, and intelligence. Generally, the goals are to describe current behaviour and predict future behaviour and performance levels. When tests accurately predict behaviour and/or produce scores that are in accordance with theoretical models, they are said to be *valid* and are thought to measure what they say they are measuring. When tests result in the same scores or interpretations repeatedly then they are *reliable*. Valid tests are necessarily reliable, but reliable tests are not always valid. In other words, if tests accurately measure a construct they must do this reliably, but tests may repeatedly result in the same scores without actually measuring what they purport to measure. In contrast to data collected through interviews, which can vary considerably depending on the interviewer, tests collect information or data and generate scores using standardized procedures. Thus, the specific test stimuli and directions are constant in all administrations, and set procedures are used to score and interpret responses. However, most inexperienced assessors will need formal training to choose instruments and interpret responses.

Most tests available through publishers or test suppliers have undergone a period of development where procedures are standardized and the collected data from a clinical group are compared to those obtained from a standardization group. Since results are compared to a normative group, statistical comparisons can be made between one client's scores and those from the normative group. For example, scores in intelligence testing allow assessors to determine if the client functions within one, two, or three standard deviations above or below the norm. Similarly, when scores in various tests of psychopathology are above various cut-off levels, the reported behaviour is similar to that found in various clinical groups. Test scores are expressed in various ways, such as age-equivalents, percentiles, scaled scores, and *t*-scores, among others. When test development follows a rigorous and well-documented course, test users place increased confidence in their findings. Once a test's final version is ready for market, test materials and an accompanying manual are made available for clinical use. A manual outlines the entire developmental process, provides validity and reliability data, and defines the administration, scoring, and interpretation procedures. Many psychological tests can be hand scored, but computer programs and test-scoring services are available for some. Computer programs generate test reports that outline significant findings in particular test protocols. These reports are done on a test-by-test basis, and programs to integrate the results of several tests are not available. This task falls to the administering psychologist.

Psychological tests vary significantly. Some are more objective or scientific, with rigorous test development using specific comparison groups, while others are less objective. For example, many projective tests use less standardized instructions and permit wider variability in test responses. In projective tests, test takers are required to produce open-ended responses to various stimuli such as incomplete sentences, inkblots, and pictoral stimuli. Although scoring systems have been developed for some projective tests, the interpretation of their responses depends more heavily on the test givers' observations and interpretations. Generally, with these tests, clients' responses are compared to their other test and interview responses.

Psychological tests also vary in transparency, which refers to the test taker's ability to ascertain the test's purpose and alter responses to present a more favourable impression. This is difficult to do in tests that measure abilities per se, unless people want to appear less capable, but is decidedly easier to do in tests that measure qualities such as psychopathy and alcoholism. For example, in a screening test for alcoholism a client can blatantly lie about alcohol intake, appearing to have no problems. The test's accuracy depends on the client's willingness to be truthful. Consequently, some psychological tests include validity and reliability scales that provide estimations of the truthfulness and consistency of the client's responding. The Minnesota Multiphasic Personality Inventory – 2 (MMPI-2) (Butcher, Dahlstrom, Graham, Tellegen, & Kaemmer, 1989) is one test incorporating such scales. People interpreting this test check these scales to determine whether clients are trying to present an overly favourable, accurate, or perhaps negative impression of their functioning. Some scales also provide information regarding whether test takers have changed responding during the course of this rather lengthy test, i.e., whether their responding is internally consistent. However, even when tests are transparent and are easily faked they need not be automatically eliminated from a test battery, because the information they provide could be validated by other sources.

Use of Psychological Tests in Parenting Assessments

Many psychological tests currently available are useful in exploring various aspects of the functioning of family members in parenting assessments. Unfortunately, some assessors routinely administer the same battery of psychological tests in all assessments without apparent thought about the reasons for the use of specific tests. Such use can result in the gathering of irrelevant and redundant information and adds to expense, wastes clients' and assessors' time, and needlessly increases the stress of the assessment. At the same time, well-chosen psychological tests can enhance or modify possible conclusions. Psychological tests may help clarify confusion and allow a more accurate understanding of the strengths and weaknesses of family members. They were used to good advantage in Case 1, as described below:

Jackie initially presented as a bright woman who gave detailed descriptions of her life. However, her reports were glib and inconsistent and references often refuted their accuracy. For example, references reported that she was an average to poor student who generally worked as a waitress. She said she was an honour student who excelled in several certificate programs after high school. Although poor intellectual functioning per se was not an issue in regard to her parenting abilities, the assessor decided to undertake intellectual testing using the Wechsler Adult Intelligence Scale-Revised (WAIS-R) (Wechsler, 1981) to clarify her confusing presentation. Jackie became agitated when asked to produce specific answers and do tasks rather than simply talk about her opinions and her exaggerated sense of competence and intellect. Despite a quick and bright presentation, Jackie scored in the average intellectual range. While her concrete problem-solving skills placed her at the 50th percentile when compared to other people of her age, her verbal score was at approximately the 30th percentile. These results supported the hypothesis that Jackie had developed a superficial conversational style to compensate for her deficits in abstraction and general learning; she used this rather glib mode of interacting to engage people so she could use them to her own advantage. This was further supported in her responses to the MMPI-2 (Butcher et al., 1989), where she scored significantly into the clinical range on the Psychopathic Deviate scale. Commonly, high scorers are antisocial people who are immature, irresponsible, and unstable, among other descriptors. While other possible descriptors were offered in the manual, the listed ones were congruent with the remainder of Jackie's testing and the data from other observations, interviews, and references. Although this summary is a simplification of the use of psychological tests with Jackie, test results strongly suggested she used people to her advantage and had significant difficulty responding sensitively to others, particularly to the needs of her children.

This example clearly represents an appropriate use of psychological testing. It is important to note that the two tests mentioned in the example were not designed for use in parenting assessments. Indeed, most psychological tests employed in parenting assessments were not designed for use in these situations. They were intended for clinical rather than forensic use, that is, to help clinicians assess individual people so that program placements and treatment interventions could be developed. They were not intended for court use where issues may not centre on treatment planning. While we must always remain cognizant that psychological tests in child welfare assessments may ultimately be used in legal decisions, the line between forensic and clinical use sometimes becomes blurred. Parenting assessments can indeed be used to develop, for both parents and children, interventions that are separate from strictly legal issues. For example, in determining a child's needs, an assessor might identify significant learning disabilities that require specific interventions by parents and school personnel. Similarly, they might identify previously undiagnosed emotional difficulties, such as parental depression, that require medication and psychotherapy. Such interventions might enable parents to begin adequately caring for children. Even when assessments can have positive clinical impact, however, assessors should not lose sight of the fact that they must be able to defend their use of specific psychological tests in the courtroom, including the psychometric properties of those tests.

PRACTICE ALERT #14

Use psychological tests to explore specific issues rather than as routine procedures in all parenting assessments.

GUIDELINES FOR USE OF PSYCHOLOGICAL TESTS IN PARENTING ASSESSMENTS

It is impossible within the context of this book to review all of the psychological tests that can be used in parenting assessments; the following are some guidelines to assessors in their choice and use of these instruments.

1. Always select psychological tests for specific reasons. Several well-chosen tests may provide more useful information than a large, routinely administered battery that produces irrelevant or redundant data.
2. Never base significant conclusions solely on the scores from one test without reference to other interview, test, and reference information.
3. Administer all psychological tests using standardized procedures. Note departures from these procedures and be able to clearly justify them. For example, it might be acceptable to read questions to a blind person so they can respond to a test such as the MMPI-2 (Butcher et al., 1989). However, it is inappropriate to read questions to a recent immigrant who has little working knowledge of English. Similarly, it is inappropriate for a practitioner's secretary to administer intellectual tests or answer substantiative questions about personality tests.
4. Ensure that the client is sufficiently similar to people in the standardization group used to develop test norms. If not, the meaning of scores is changed and the use of standardized scores might be invalid. For example, intellectual test scores from a child who is not fluent in English have limited meaning; a culture-fair test would provide more valid information. These differences in normative groups can be quite subtle. For example, when the Wechsler Intelligence Scale for Children – III (WISC-III) (Wechsler, 1991) is administered, Canadian children perform somewhat differently than do American children, necessitating the development of a separate set of norms based on a Canadian standardization group.
5. Ensure that individuals have the prerequisite reading level for tests that require reading.
6. Use updated versions of tests, as populations change and commonly used tests are regularly revised: dated materials are replaced and new norms are developed on new standardization groups. For example, a psychologist who still uses the Wechsler

Adult Intelligence Scale (Wechsler, 1955) would be using scores that compare a person's functioning to a standardization group that was tested in 1953 and 1954, clearly a significant error.

7. Evaluate whether clients are responding in an honest manner that represents their true characteristics and feelings. Determine if, and possibly why, they are manipulating their impressions and use validity scales to comment on this, where possible.
8. Understand the differences in the confidence that can be placed in conclusions drawn from objective versus projective tests. While this does not preclude the use of projective tests, assessors clearly must understand their use and justify their choice.
9. Use tests with which you have good working familiarity. If you plan to incorporate an unfamiliar test, follow manual guidelines explicitly and obtain appropriate training and supervision.
10. When using computer-generated reports, do not accept these results unequivocally or use them in isolation. Instead, integrate these findings with other information and determine if the results present a consistent and congruent picture of the client.
11. When presenting test results, interpret the scores rather than simply reporting them. It is not accepted practice to report raw scores in formal reports, but verbatim quotes can be used to make a point.

A brief case follows in which the assessor clearly violated many of the guidelines just noted.

CASE 27: An assessor evaluated an immigrant family from an East Asian country. Parents became refugees after the father was tortured while imprisoned by a military regime. Within two years of coming to North America, they were reported to child welfare authorities. Parents admitted to the use of physical punishment but said this was commonly accepted in their country of origin. They also said they were experiencing significant stress in their attempts to adapt to a completely new culture. Communication with the family was labourious given their poor English skills, and the assessor had to rely heavily on an interpreter. To determine the parents' potential for employment and to clarify issues around depression and psychiatric functioning, the assessor administered the WAIS-R and the MMPI, early versions of the WAIS-III and the

> MMPI-2. Because the MMPI was long, she left it to the interpreter, who was also the family's support worker, to administer the test, likely introducing translation errors and subjectivity into the process. The assessor disregarded the validity scales on the MMPI that indicated a random response pattern. Even so, and inexplicably, she proceeded to interpret the profiles. She described the parents as depressed and rigid people, attributing this to their low scores on the WAIS-R. She recommended various supportive interventions but advanced a negative long-term prognosis.

The assessor had a difficult time under cross-examination, and although some of her recommendations were reasonable, they were disregarded by the court because of her inappropriate use of psychological tests. Essentially the assessor undermined her own credibility through poor choices.

SPECIFIC PSYCHOLOGICAL TESTS

As noted earlier, very few tests have been developed specifically for use in parenting assessments, and most of those are designed for use in parenting assessments in custody/access cases rather than in child welfare and adoption/foster cases. Ackerman and Ackerman (1997) surveyed the custody evaluation practices of 201 seasoned psychologists in custody/access cases and found that many routinely employed psychological tests. For example, 92 per cent routinely used the MMPI or MMPI-2, 48 per cent used the Rorschach, 43 per cent used the WAIS-R, and 34 per cent used the Millon Clinical Multiaxial Inventory – III (MCMI-III) (Millon, 1997). Categories of tests employed included intellectual tests (e.g., WAIS-R, WISC-III), objective personality tests (e.g., MMPI-2, MCMI-III), projective personality tests (e.g., Thematic Apperception Test (Murray, 1943), the Rorschach (Exner, 1993), various forms of the Sentence Completion Test (Rotter, Lah, & Rafferty, 1992), and other tests that are more specific to family relations and parenting issues (e.g., Family Relations Test [FRT] [Bene & Anthony, 1985], Parenting Stress Index [PSI] [Abidin, 1995]). Many of these same tests are used in parenting assessments in child welfare cases.

Bricklin (1999) describes two additional systems can be used to help make custody recommendations. These incorporate both observational data and various psychological tests and are used in custody/access cases where comparisons are made between the parenting abilities of two parents. They include the Ackerman-Schoendorf Scales for Parent Evaluation of Custody (ASPECT) (Ackerman & Schoendorf, 1992) and the Comprehensive Custody Evaluation Standard System (ACCESS) (Bricklin & Elliot, 1995). The ASPECT produces three scaled scores and an overall Parent Custody Index (PCI) that is used to compare parents. Overall, it assesses the general appropriateness of the parent's presentation of self, the suitability of the social environment provided by the parent, and the extent of the parent's cognitive and emotional capacity to provide effective parenting. Similarly, ACCESS uses observational and test data to compare parents' abilities. Using well-known tests and some newer ones, it examines factors such as parental awareness of optimum childcare skills and knowledge of a child to distinguish between adequate and inadequate parenting and to develop shared parenting plans. Continued validation work is ongoing with these instruments, and their applicability to child welfare cases is limited, requiring further systematic exploration.

Bricklin (1999) reviews several other tests for use with parents in custody/access cases, and some of these have more applicability in child welfare cases. As noted earlier, the MMPI-2 and the MCMI-III often provide useful information. Although these are well reviewed in their respective manuals and in books and chapters such as those written by Bricklin (1999), we briefly mention some of their uses here. The MMPI-2 is a true-false test that has 567 items and provides validity scales, basic clinical scales, and other scales. This test not only screens for serious psychopathology but provides information about such issues as relationship functioning, impulsivity, flexibility, antisocial tendencies, substance abuse problems, and judgment. Likewise, the MCMI-III includes validity scales that examine test-taking attitudes, but it deals with personality disorders rather than other forms of psychopathology that are addressed in the MMPI-2.

We have personally found the Parenting Stress Index to be useful in child welfare assessments, particularly because it examines sources of stress within the parent-child interaction system. It was developed for use in families where children range in age from one month to twelve years, and parents complete it in reference to a specific child in their family. Some of the sources of stress arise more within the child domain or as a result of the child's characteristics: distractibility/hyperactivity, adaptability, positively reinforcing to the parent, demandingness, unhappy mood, and child characteristics that are unacceptable to the parent. Others arise more from the parent's characteristics: sense of competence regarding parenting ability, social isolation, attachment to child, health, depression, restrictiveness of parenting role, and relationship with spouse. A Total Stress Score and Child and Parent Domain Scores are derived, and life stresses aside from the parent-child relationship are reviewed. A validity scale that assesses defensive responding was included in the latest version, and fathers were also included in the standardization group. The PSI has good congruency with the model of parenting described in this book because it examines child, parent, and environmental factors that contributing to parenting adequacy.

Another test that examines parents' attitudes towards their children and parenting is the Parent-Child Relationship Inventory (PCRI) (Gerard, 1994). The information from this test, completed by parents, is integrated with other qualitative observations and allows exploration of various hypotheses about the functioning of both individuals and the family. Two validity indicators are provided, as are separate norms for mothers and fathers. There are seven scales: level of social and emotional support the parent receives, satisfaction with parenting, parental interaction with and knowledge of a child, parental perception of effectiveness of communication with his/her child, discipline style, parental ability to promote a child's independence, and parental attitudes about gender roles in parenting. Another test that examines parenting behaviours and expectations about children is the Parent Behavior Checklist (Fox, 1994). However, this test is for use with parents who have children between one and four years of age, limiting the cases in which it might be useful. The three area scores are for expectations, discipline, and nurturing.

The Child Abuse Potential Inventory (CAPI) (Milner, 1986) is an additional test that is often worth including in child welfare parenting assessments. It was developed as a screening tool for use by protective service workers during investigations of reported child abuse cases, and is best utilized in specific populations where a higher base rate of physical abuse exists (Milner, 1986). The 160-item questionnaire has a readability level of grade 3, takes approximately fifteen to twenty minutes to complete, and can be either hand or computer scored. It has three validity scales: lie scale, random response scale, and inconsistency scale. In cases where one or more of these scales is elevated, response distortion indexes are computed that include a faking-good index, a faking-bad index, and a random response index. The CAPI yields an abuse scale that is used for predictive purposes and should be combined with other assessment information to determine risk for physical abuse of children. Other factor scale scores are descriptive and may suggest dimensions that contribute to overall risk of abuse. They include distress, rigidity, unhappiness, problems with child and self, problems with family, and problems from others.

The above are some of the more objective tests that examine psychopathology and parenting behaviour, stresses, and perceptions of children; there are also various projective tests that examine some of these same issues. A number of forms of the sentence completion test are available, such as at the Rotter Incomplete Sentences Blank, second edition (Rotter, Lah, & Rafferty, 1992). In this test parents complete the ends of sentences, either writing in their responses or having them recorded by examiners, who inquire further as necessary. Commonly, the sentences address childhood experiences and memories (e.g., I wish my father ..., My most vivid childhood memory is ...), current relationships (e.g., I like my mother but ..., If my father would only ..., If I had sex ..., My feeling about married life is ...), job and self-confidence issues (At work, I get along best with ..., People think I am ...), and wishes and plans for the future (e.g., I look forward to ..., In the future ...). Psychologists examine the responses to discern patterns of perceptions and behaviour, and they compare this information to that obtained in interviews and from other sources. Generally, sentence completion tests have no formal scoring system and are used more like a semi-structured interview.

The Thematic Apperception Test (TAT), developed by Murray in the 1940s, consists of a series of black-and-white drawings that depict one or more people. In his original directions, Murray (1943) recommended that two one-hour sessions be used where ten cards are presented in a first sitting and another ten cards that are more unusual and bizarre are presented in a second sitting. Currently, most assessors present an abridged set of cards in one sitting. Responders are asked to describe what happened before, during, and after the picture, with particular attention to what the people in the pictures might be thinking and feeling. The examiner records the responses verbatim and asks questions for elaboration if needed. Questions are opened ended, and no correct answers exist. The test assumes that individuals structure their stories based on their own experiences and perceptions. The record is examined to identify expressed needs of the characters and the environmental factors that facilitate or interfere with meeting these needs. There are various adaptations of these original guidelines, and many assessors also examine the responder's routine ways of perceiving feelings and handling relationships and emotionally difficult situations, their general expectations about themselves and others, and their defences, among other issues. For example, some parents with difficult lives routinely idealize their childhood and current relationships and consistently avoid any negative emotional content in interpreting the pictures, telling short and idealistic stories. Others not only accurately perceive the emotional content in the pictures, but they tell stories where the characters engage in realistic problem-solving. Still others completely misperceive or cannot resolve the situations that are evident in the pictures.

Clients are likewise thought to bring routine ways of structuring their perceptions to the Rorschach Test. Here the stimuli are inkblots that are not intended to represent anything specific. Hermann Rorschach developed ten inkblot cards that were made public in 1921 in a monograph entitled *Psychodiagnostik* (Rorschach, 1942). He developed this test after noting that schizophrenic patients responded differently to a common inkblot game than did people without schizophrenia (Exner, 1993). The inkblots are presented one at a time so that the responder has an opportunity to say what each might be. The examiner records the responses verbatim and then begins an inquiry phase to gain and record whatever additional information is needed to accurately score the responses. Many different scoring and interpretative systems have been developed. Of these, the one developed by Exner (1993, 2002) has the broadest empirical support and research base. He has systematically developed his system for the past forty years, examining the responses of adults, children, adolescents, and various clinical groups. In three volumes that are regularly updated, he outlines very specific methods for scoring and interpretation. The Rorschach examines coping styles, cognitive styles, management of affect, and self-image, among many other aspects of psychological functioning. As with other psychological tests, it should never be used in isolation, and users are unwise to employ a simplistic and invalid sign approach. For example, few examiners can withstand a rigorous cross-examination if they state that particular responders are paranoid solely because they see many eyes and ears in the inkblots.

Many other psychological tests are available that may have applicability in parenting assessments, but we will not review them here. Instead, assessors must be cognizant of the development, psychometric properties, and appropriate uses of tests because lawyers and judges commonly ask for descriptions and justification regarding their use in any particular case. Careful selection, use, and knowledge lend credibility to other observations and opinions, while inappropriate usage undermines credibility, as shown in an earlier example.

Observations of Family Functioning

Several opportunities for observation of parent-child and whole family interaction occur in any parenting assessment.

The Waiting Room

The most frequent and informal observations occur in the waiting room. Unless children are not in parental care or have only court-mandated supervised access, parents bring children to assessment sessions. An initial observation concerns the expectations and control parents have over their children in the waiting room. Some expect young children to sit still and do nothing even when toys and books are available, others permit play while maintaining appropriate supervision, and still others seem oblivious to their children's activities. For example, in the case of Martin and Barb (Case 24), the assessor's first observations of the children and mother together occurred in the waiting room. Although Barb had presented well in her individual sessions, her children were completely out of control in the waiting room. While she read a magazine, two of her young children balanced on a four-foot high room divider. In such a situation, it can be informative not to intervene immediately, unless it is too dangerous, waiting to determine if parents recognize the inappropriateness of their children's behaviour and enforce limits. Barb simply commented, 'Oh, they're such monkeys,' taking no steps to ensure their safety. On another occasion, Barb thought nothing of swatting her child and roughly yanking her away from a potted plant. It is common for many parents who routinely yell, hit, or berate their children to do so in the waiting room. By behaving like this in front of an assessor, parents demonstrate the automatic nature of their behaviour and a lack of judgment. Since some parents promise big rewards if the children control themselves, repeated observations in various settings permit sampling of more typical behaviours.

The physical interaction among family members is another observational target, although the children's developmental status will contribute to judgments regarding the appropriateness of physical contacts. Thus, it is inappropriate for an eleven-year-old boy to curl up in his mother's lap, as Randy (Case 3) did with June, but it is fine for a two-year-old to sit on a parent's lap. Intrusiveness into the body space of other people may highlight boundary and socialization difficulties. For example, Anna (Case 26) constantly invaded her father's and foster mother's body space in the waiting area. Furthermore, to the astonishment of another male client, she climbed into his lap, putting her hand inside his shirt. Anna's father also invaded her body space. After two months of no contact, he took the six-year-old onto his lap in the waiting room, put his arm around her, and placed his hand on her inner thigh. She responded by melding to his body contours and snuggling into his neck.

While Anna's behaviour was somewhat extreme, needy parents and children may indiscriminantly approach others in the waiting room, being overly friendly, telling their life stories to strangers, and asking inappropriate questions. It is worrisome when indiscriminate youngsters ignore a parent to eagerly seek attention from strangers, particularly when parents see this as mature and friendly behaviour. Separations are also informative. The ease with which a child separates from parents is likely to vary with age; children of two or three years should have more difficulty separating than those a decade older. Since parents may have prepared children differently for the anticipated separation, this is another observational target. For example, to ease the transition with young children, parents sometimes bring snacks or a favourite toy for children to bring into a session. With older children, parents may have reassured the children that they will wait for them. Other parents do not prepare children for the separation and yet become irritated when the children are anxious or hesitant. Others become highly anxious themselves, thus heightening the children's anxiety and making separation more difficult. Through this whole process, we must observe the parent's sensitivity and responsiveness to their children's feelings, and we may later ask them what they were thinking at the time.

In-Office Observations

Most assessors observe various parent-child and whole family combinations in their offices. Even though this can be done in many ways, we find it useful to include both unstructured and structured activities during these sessions, having materials available of interest to children to facilitate interaction and perhaps setting a specific task for family members. For example, one might ask parents and children to pick and read a book, jointly draw a picture of their family, write a short passage about a mutual activity, or play a specific game. More open-ended interaction where they are free to pick an activity might then follow. During the interaction, the assessor can sit to the side, noting interactions among family members. Since it is worrisome if a child seeks attention from the assessor rather than using this special time to interact with a parent, one can direct the child back to the parent. While some parents try to facilitate the child's involvement in a joint activity, others do not. For example, clinically depressed parents or those with serious psychopathology or who are high on drugs may have difficulty responding, as might others who are highly self-conscious.

During these interactions, some parents can appropriately attune to children and follow their lead while still placing appropriate limits and expectations on them. For example, parents could allow children to pick the game, but they should ensure fair play and cleanup. It may indicate a worrisome lack of respect for other people's property and an inability to place any limits on children when parents allow them to leave a playroom in complete disarray, especially if assessors have directed them to ensure the room is tidy. During this observation, it sometimes appears that parents and children have never played together, while other dyads are comfortable and interact easily and still others fight for control. Randy and June (Case 3), both creative and self-centred people, fought over the choice of their unstructured activity until he conceded to his mother's wishes. June became engrossed in drawing, denigrated Randy's picture, and expected him to praise her work. As June took over the activity, Randy sat quietly on the side and occasionally complimented her. June did not notice his muted reaction and commented excitedly about the 'fun we're having.' Sadly, such interactions were commonplace in their relationship.

Again, we direct attention to instances of inappropriate comments, violations of body space, and aggression. Both instances of parental praise and appropriate sensitivity as well as inappropriate teasing, harsh commentary, and unusual or clearly inappropriate comments are targets for observation. For example, June (Case 3) often made unusual comments and discussed inappropriate subjects such as her sexual history in Randy's presence. Likewise, Jackie (Case 1) graphically described a beating by a boyfriend despite Jill's obvious anxiety. This discussion did nothing to allay Jill's constant worries that someone would kill her mother. Jackie did not respond to Jill's feelings even when the assessor pointed them out.

As well as observing dyads, an assessor can gain information from the presence of other family members. If both parents are present, their communication styles and abilities to problem-solve with their children are observational targets. Through having entire families undertake specific activities that require cooperative decision-making, we can highlight how they handle this process. It can also be evident when we simply ask the family to choose one activity out of several that are available. Parents must manage sibling rivalry and address the feelings of their children who dislike the chosen activity. While some parents manage these complex dynamics well, others struggle and still others ignore the children and try to engage the assessor in discussion. Assessors should be careful to not overinterpret observed behaviours, carefully validating them with other observations and reports from collateral references.

Home Visits and Other Settings

As well as interviewing and observing families in an office setting, assessors may often find it very helpful to observe them in more naturalistic settings. Interactions with assessors in family homes, playgrounds, and even shopping malls may be much less intimidating for families who are particularly threatened by the formal office milieu, and may facilitate rapport-building and acceptance. Consequently, it is sometimes helpful to begin the assessment with a home visit to promote engagement of families in the process of evaluation and then undertake other naturalistic and in-office interviews and observations as necessary to obtain multiple samples of family interaction. Although a few specific rating procedures are available to evaluate these various observations, Budd and Holdsworth (1996) report that their use is often problematic: not only were many developed for research use and have little applicability in a clinical context, but most also require extensive training for reliable use. Nevertheless, they suggest that some of these formal systems may inform our practice by suggesting family characteristics as observational targets. However, they caution assessors to not overgeneralize or misinterpret findings from clinical observations. In particular, they suggest that assessors not make definitive assertions without supportive descriptive examples of behaviour, nor should they infer parenting qualities based on selected child behaviours.

Given that most assessors include at least one visit to residences in their assessments, we will specifically discuss home visits here. Many families, in an effort to make a good presentation, prepare for this visit by cleaning their homes; it is worrisome when families take no steps to clean or organize a terribly dirty or messy house. Even when homes have obviously been readied for the visit, an assessor's observations can always be compared with those of others, such as child welfare workers who visit unannounced. Assessors should ask for a tour using the list of questions in Chapter 3, Basic Physical Care section, to guide their examination into whether homes are clean and safe with appropriate sleeping spaces and washing facilities. For example, a home in a tenement where used needles, condoms, and even intoxicated people are found in the hallways may well be a poor environment for children. Even so, the apartment unit may be clean and organized, with the parent(s) obviously taking some pride in it, and the parent may have taken concrete steps to ensure the child is protected from the neighbourhood hazards; such a home is preferable to one that is dishevelled, dirty, and unsafe. During the visit, assessors can see if the children have age-appropriate toys instead of just watching television or wandering about, and they can make a note of obvious priorities in the home, such as money spent on a big-screen television instead of food or clothes for the children. Even during relatively short home visits, one can gauge the integration of families into the neighbourhood by observing if neighbours drop by to chat with parents or play with the children. However, too many visitors and interruptions, especially during the course of planned home visits, may suggest that families have difficulty establishing boundaries.

To gather more information about stress management strategies, it may be useful to visit at a more stressful time of the day, such as at the dinner hour when people are tired and hungry. Parents must manage the children's strident demands for food while preparing dinner and coping with the assessor's presence. We can observe who cooks, how parents get children to the table, the rituals they follow, the strategies used if children refuse certain foods, the meal's nutritional value, and the clean-up process. For example, in Barb's (Case 24) tidy home, dinner and later activities were chaotic. Children climbed on the table, left to buy candy without permission, tumbled down the stairs, and were generally insolent and not heedful of her directions. She resorted to yelling and spanking while verbally minimizing the out-of-control nature of her home; these observations were congruent with previous observations in the waiting room and office. Furthermore, when assessors visit homes later in the assessment process, family members have usually become somewhat comfortable with them. Given this and familiar surroundings, interactions may be more typical of their general functioning levels. For example, Barb's children would likely not have behaved differently had she either threatened them with severe punishment or promised fantastic rewards.

We must explore reasons for any discrepancies in observational data derived from different environments. During one home visit, Jackie and her children (Case 1) were not relaxed and interacted in a different manner than previously observed but denied anything was wrong. It was later discovered that an abusive ex-boyfriend was hiding in the home during the visit and Jackie had sworn her children to secrecy. Again, her judgment was poor and she did not recognize the anxiety his presence generated in her children. A final comment concerns home visits in custody disputes. In such cases, it is prudent to undertake home visits at similar times of the day. For example, it is inappropriate to visit a parent's home during a chaotic dinner hour but to go to a grandparent's home after lunch when the planned activity is an outing to a park or playground.

Collateral Contacts

As described in chapter 8, collateral references are contacted after obtaining written client consent, optimally at times convenient to those references. In the initial contact, you need to explain the reason for your call and the limits regarding the confidentiality of their information so they can give informed consent to their participation and the use of their data. One can explain that their information will be used to eventually formulate recommendations, and that it may be directly referenced in the report, as nothing is off the record. Furthermore, their names will be identified in the report as one of many sources of data and they may be required to testify in court about the informa-

PRACTICE ALERT #15
Inform references about the limits of confidentiality that exist regarding the information they provide to you.

tion they provide. On occasion references decline participation, as in situations where they are fearful of a parent's retaliation or when parents are in conflict with each other and references do not want to anger either side. Another difficult situation exists when one parent gives an assessor permission to contact a particular reference but the other does not. This must be clearly explained to references and questions must be limited to only the behaviour of the consenting parent.

If references agree to participate after this discussion, one then finds out the legal spelling of their names, the duration of their relationships with family members, and the contexts in which they know them. For example, it important to clarify the reference's perception of the nature of his or her relationship with the parents, as it may be at odds with the parent's perception of the relationship (see Case 1 involving Jackie and her 'best' friend, discussed earlier in this chapter). References may be character/personal references for parents, or they may know the whole family and can comment on the parent-child interactions they have witnessed. In the latter situation, we need to ask about the type and frequency of their contacts with family members. Thus, a woman who runs a day home that cares for a child in the assessment might more ably comment on interactions and parent reliability than a professional colleague of the parent. Besides asking about specific incidents and issues that have been identified in earlier interviews with family members, we can ask for general comments about their strengths and weaknesses as well as any other observations references wish to offer.

For those references who are professionals, we must focus on more specific details that are related to good parenting. For example, medical personnel can provide information about whether parents regularly bring children for medical attention or seek medical help only when in crisis. Additionally, they can speak about parents' reliability in following required medical directives at home. Other professionals who work with families, such as speech therapists, occupational therapists, and mental health professionals, can provide similar kinds of information as well as their opinions about parents' response to intervention. Teachers can comment on whether parents regularly send the children to school and come to parent-teacher interviews, if the children are ready and able to work through being fed and rested, and if parents follow up as needed at home. However, all of these references may be unable to comment on issues such as family dynamics, because of their limited exposure to this aspect of the children's lives.

Professional references may be asked if they have ever had concerns about abuse or neglect and, if they did, whether they reported to child welfare authorities and attempted to otherwise help.

Clearly not every collateral reference can comment on the same issues because their knowledge of specific families varies significantly. Some provide considerable validation for the observations of others, while other references contribute little because they know parents superficially or in specific contexts. The information that might be gained from any specific references is not always discernable in advance, and often assessors make several calls that really add little to their knowledge of a specific family. Some parents are isolated and have few references, while others have extensive superficial networks with no close friends who can offer the real-life observations of interest to assessors. Even so, this is valuable information as it speaks to social supports, parents' interest in their children, their judgment, and other factors. Under no circumstances should assessors discuss their findings, deliberations, or the recommendations they are considering, especially with friends and family.

10 Assessment of the Children

Why the Child's Assessment Is Critical

As outlined in Chapter 2, the fundamental question that must be addressed in any parenting assessment is, 'Can *this parent* meet the needs of *this particular child*?' Since no one ideal parenting style exists and different styles may work better with some children than others, assessors must gain a sense of the fit between the styles of particular family members. Both individual assessments of children and joint observations of children and parents facilitate this process; it is therefore critical to assess children thoroughly to identify their needs. Although parents can provide detailed descriptions, assessors need to meet, observe, and assess children individually as part of any comprehensive parenting assessment. This allows assessors to form first-hand impressions of children and to verify parent reports. For example, had the assessor not met with Randy (Case 3) and only believed June's reports as described in the previous chapter, a completely different picture would have emerged. In situations where the children are being assessed by other clinicians, assessors must work collaboratively with those clinicians to ensure adequate collection of information that can be integrated with their own observations.

Engaging Children

As in any assessment, children must be engaged so they become comfortable and understand the process. Obviously this process varies with age, and it is critical to use developmentally appropriate language, play settings and materials, and test procedures. Many of the issues discussed earlier in regard to adults apply here. Although assessors already have some working hypotheses regarding children based on previous discussions with child welfare workers and parents, they should approach children's interviews with an **open mind** rather than assuming they already completely understand them. For example, in cases with abuse allegations, assessors cannot begin children's interviews with assumptions that these reports are valid. Conversely, they must not assume children have not been abused because the family seems nice and the home is clean and tidy. It is important to have an **assessment plan** that includes both assessment tasks and the information to be collected, since a disorganized interview process can unsettle children much as it does adults. The checklist in Appendix C can help to ensure complete data collection.

PRACTICE ALERT #16

Employ developmentally appropriate language, play settings and materials, and test procedures with children involved in parenting assessments.

Just as assessors must keep language and behaviour differences in mind when interviewing adults from different cultural groups, they must employ **culturally sensitive** evaluation strategies and techniques with children. When children speak English well, it is easy to ignore the importance of cultural variables. For all children, especially young ones, families are important transmitters of behavioural norms and expectations, and it is critical to recognize and evaluate the impact and importance of this affiliation. Canino and Spurlock (2000) offer guidance around cultural differences in expectations of children, noting that behaviours such as passivity, dependence, and even language and motor skill development have different meanings in different cultures. For example, Latino Caribbean children are encouraged to be both physically and emotionally expressive, but they also avoid looking directly into the eyes of authority figures. American Indian culture likewise encourages children to avert their eyes from those of authority figures, but it discourages overt verbal expression of feelings, especially anger. Assessors who are unaware of such cultural differences might very well rate a child from one group as excessively labile and the other as constricted, when indeed they are expressing feelings appropriately as encouraged by their cultural group. Canino and Spurlock (2000) describe other cultural differences, and Walker (1999) describes cultural differences in the use of language. For example, she notes that pauses in speech are an integral part of communication for Native Americans, whereas other cultures value rapid speech and welcome interruptions. Assessors also can ask parents, children, and other professionals in the community about the meaning of various observed behaviours. However, we must not automatically assume children will behave in certain ways just because they were raised in a specific culture. Not all members of a cultural group are necessarily homogeneous in regard to their cultural practices/beliefs (Walker, 1999); each family and child must be considered individually.

Assessors must provide a **child-oriented milieu**. For, example child-sized furniture helps children feel at ease. A four-year old child can feel uneasy when interviewed while sitting in a big office chair with legs dangling. Furthermore, toys and a child play area in an office directly convey the impression that a particular assessor knows about children and is interested in them. If assessors are relaxed and use language and tasks that are age-appropriate, children can become comfortable relatively quickly. Assessment tasks should provide considerable opportunities for interaction and discussion. Thus, drawing and creative play facilitate interaction while computer play does not, even though some children are excited by it.

Assessors must also be **skilled at interviewing children**. Much as it is tempting to accept 'yes' and 'no' answers from relatively nonverbal adults, it can be easy to do the same with uncommunicative children, and again we must support children to voice their views. Some children try to please by saying what they think assessors or their parents want them to say. Verbal children may skilfully avoid questions and, unless assessors are organized and aware, may effectively provide no substantive information; assessors may discover that children have not addressed salient incidents or feelings only later, when they are preparing the report. Since some children become silent when they are uncomfortable about discussing certain issues and others say anything to prevent assessors from probing more deeply, we must be alert to their anxiety and take steps to reduce it. For example, it can be useful to let children know it is acceptable for them to identify when they are uncomfortable and do not want to answer specific questions. Be patient, use diversions to allow anxiety to lessen, and employ some of the more structured techniques such as Sentence Completion Tests or play scenarios to more comfortably approach issues. This pacing of inquiries and activities is part of sensitive interviewing. Since children, particularly younger ones, cannot usually focus intently on one task or an anxiety-provoking topic for a long period of time, we can vary tasks and topics to maintain optimal attention and responsiveness. Furthermore, individual child sessions may need to extend over a few weeks rather than being closely grouped in a short time span. This allows children to develop comfort and assessors to get to know children more thoroughly; the assessors may see them on days when the children are happy but also on days when they are overtired, tense, or irritable.

Another component of sensitive interviewing is the use of developmentally appropriate language. Walker (1999) has written a handbook regarding children's linguistic capacities and methods of questioning to ensure clear communication with children. Although originally developed around children's interviews and their testimony in court, it is a particularly relevant reference for any professionals who interview children, as it describes developmental differences in children's use of language as well as various principles that can guide questioning. It also identifies problems that may occur in assessors' questions, special issues to watch for in children's responses, and reasons for inconsistencies that occur in children's testimony.

Sensitive and child-oriented assessors are also aware that children must be treated respectfully in an honest and direct manner. Thus, simple but not condescending language is needed because children, particularly those in the pre-teen and teenage years, are easily offended when others talk down to them; also, some are confused by elaborate language and grammatical constructions. A twelve-year-old may appreciate discussion about courtroom procedures that uses relatively formal language, but a six-year-old more readily understands legal concepts such as 'talking to the judge' rather than 'testifying.' We must also clarify the **purpose of the assessment** without reviewing explicit information concerning parents' skills. Instead, we can say assessments help parents and others to make decisions about what should happen in families and about how to help them. However, before providing such an explanation, it is useful to ask children why they were brought to see you. Some know the reasons, others say they or their parents are 'bad,' others think they have come to play or for medical checkups, and still others have no idea. While these initial responses may reflect children's views and concerns, they may also speak to their parents' sensitivity and capacity to prepare them for assessment. Depending on the children's responses, they may also render information about the parents' overall abilities to keep adult issues to themselves and to the predominant emotional tone in families. Although the following example occurred in a custody/access assessment, the child's response to this initial question attested to the mother's negative feelings about the father and her investment in 'winning' the assessment.

CASE 28: A nine-year-old girl was the focus of a custody/access assessment. When asked why she was seeing the assessor, Lynn stated, 'So my mom can win custody of me.' She proceeded to explain they were doing this because they had previously seen a counsellor who had 'betrayed' them because she said 'Dad was good and Mom was bad.' Lynn occasionally called this counsellor the 'enemy.' Lynn's mother viewed the counsellor negatively because she had supported the father's involvement in Lynn's life. Despite Lynn's apparent alliance with her mother in criticizing her father, it became clear she also loved him but felt constrained to suppress these sentiments. When asked about the ideal solution to her situation, Lynn provided two alternatives: 'be cloned' or 'live in an apartment' with her fifteen-year-old sister, indicating the intensity of her dilemma.

This brief example says much about Lynn's mother's animosity towards her father. She could not acknowledge her daughter's positive feelings, becoming negative whenever Lynn showed any interest in him. This placed Lynn in an untenable situation where she felt pressured to choose one parent over the other. Given her immediate and strict overt adherence to her mother's feelings and perceptions, the assessor interviewed Lynn carefully. She saw her several times to establish a safe relationship where Lynn could express her feelings and, to help her approach her feelings, she used various strategies such as direct interview, sentence completion testing, and projective measures. The assessor also wrote the report in such a way that Lynn's mother could not blame Lynn for the assessor's recommendation to increase contact between Lynn and her father.

Clarification of the assessment's purpose need not always occur in the first few minutes of the initial session. Instead, one must be attuned to children's feelings, help them to feel comfortable, and settle them into the assessment. Some are ready to talk about the reasons immediately, while others prefer an initial general discussion about school, pets, hobbies and interests, and other activities. In child welfare cases, the opportunity to ask about the purpose may emerge quickly because foster parents commonly bring children to assessments. Simply asking why they live in a foster home often elicits information about natural families and leads to discussion of the assessment's purpose.

Once the purpose is clear, assessors must explain **assessment procedures**, such as what they and the children will do together. This need not be complex, and the exact wording varies with developmental status and the assessment's context. You can often reassure children by saying you will talk, play, and do some work together: terms such as 'psychologically assessed' or 'tested' can be threatening, especially for children who do poorly in school and have low self-confidence. You can let the children know you will be talking with their parents, visiting them at home, and calling their teachers. Such explanations, while brief, allow children to predict what will happen when they come to see you, and thereby reduce their anxiety. Encourage the children to ask you questions about these upcoming activities and answer their questions, if you can, while refraining from discussing your deliberations and recommendations. Finally, you can say you will write a 'report' or, for younger children, a 'story' about what happened in the assessment, and that parents and judges will use it to help decide what will happen in their lives.

PRACTICE ALERT #17
Make the assessment environment safe for both children and assessors.

To help children feel comfortable, we must ensure several levels of safety. We have already spoken of the use of interview pacing and direct and honest communication to promote safety in regard to the anxiety provoked by specific emotional issues. Safety also includes concrete issues like ensuring supervision if children must stay in a waiting room alone. For example, one should avoid having them wait where others might harm them or act inappropriately with them, such as in the bathroom. Parents should be asked to help young children with using the bathroom. Children also feel more comfortable if they have access to a glass of water, toys, or a toilet. We can further enhance children's comfort and security by ensuring contact at eye level when meeting or interviewing them. While the influence is subtle, children may be intimidated when adult assessors tower over them, especially if they also speak in loud or confusing ways.

Assessors must be particularly sensitive to feelings of threat or anxiety that certain situations may provoke in maltreated children. For example, some were physically or sexually abused in situations that parallel elements of the assessment environment, such as when an adult male has befriended a solitary child by offering play activities and food. By clarifying the assessment's purpose and plan relatively quickly and by specifying that the situation is different from others in their previous experience, we can ease children's anxiety. Similarly, we can allow an adult to accompany them if they are hesitant to enter our offices alone. As they become engaged, we can then cue the adult to leave. Some children want office doors to be left slightly ajar, an acceptable practice if it helps them become comfortable. When children have trouble separating, this can be diagnostic of various difficulties within parent-child relationships that we should explore. More difficulties are expected in very young children; for example, two-year-old children are more likely to have trouble than are twelve-year-old children.

A final note concerns safety issues for assessors themselves. Since many children in child welfare cases have been maltreated and indeed expect this in their interactions with others, we must ensure our behaviour cannot be misinterpreted, which could increase their anxiety or cause them to make allegations of abuse against us. For example, it is prudent to limit physical touching when seeing children alone, particularly those who are indiscriminant and physically affectionate with everyone they meet. A handshake or 'high five' greeting may be a more appropriate greeting rather than a hug, and it may reduce risk for both children and assessors. As discussed earlier, Anna (Case 26) was indiscriminant and constantly violated the body space of others, including the assessor's, attempting to put her feet on the assessor's under the table in the playroom. When Anna took the assessor's hand, held it to her cheek, and sniffed and caressed her fingers, the assessor removed her and discussed alternative ways to show affection. Such direct action was warranted because it was later revealed that Anna initiated these same behaviours as part of foreplay with her father. Finally, it is prudent to take detailed clinical notes of these behaviours and your responses, so you have some protection if children make abuse allegations against you.

General Areas of Inquiry

The content and pacing of general inquiry varies, but skilled assessors use it to reduce children's anxiety so they can eventually talk about issues that are particularly germane to the assessment's purpose. Consequently, we should make an effort to focus on the children's strengths and on less provocative topics to reduce their anxiety and make the assessment process less threatening. Discussion about birth dates, family members, pets, schools, favourite school activities, other enjoyable activities, friends, interests, and routines are often a good basic beginning: we can occasionally return to some of these more positive topics when children become anxious. Even though children can sit and talk during formal interviews, many find it less threatening to be interviewed while doing another activity they enjoy, such as drawing or shaping play dough. Before undertaking children's interviews, and given the complexity of some families, it can be worthwhile for you to review the family genogram previously constructed with parents to help you recognize the people the children mention. This is particularly useful with young children and those who use nicknames or are not particularly descriptive.

As children's responses to broad questions about people or events may not be very informative, we might have to ask them to describe specific events and recent activities. For example, the question 'How's school?' may receive a one-word reply and elicit little information; by asking 'What is your favourite (least favourite) thing about school?' assessors may derive much more information, particularly if they ask about the reasons for these views. Questions such as 'What do you like to do?' might be better replaced with 'What fun things did you do on the weekend (yesterday after school)?' in order to obtain some detail. Discussions of favourite foods, television shows, activities, and friends allow assessors to learn about children's lives; children often comfortably talk about these things, as they like interacting with adults who are interested in their feelings, interests, and viewpoints. For some children in child welfare cases, this positive and interested interaction is new and overwhelming, and can even be threatening. However, if it is paced and attuned to their reactions, most children return easily to subsequent sessions.

The initial general inquiry does more than provide a less threatening environment wherein children can derive a sense of safety; it also permits an initial screening of their abilities and responsiveness, including the quality of their **communication** and the accuracy and general complexity of their **observations** and **memories**. General conversation establishes a baseline for these functions because children may report traumatic events, such as being apprehended from home, watching one parent beat the other, or being hurt personally, quite differently when they later speak of them. Child responses must be considered in a developmental context (Walker, 1999). For example, a child might be able to report an accurate age of three years but not an actual birthdate; an eight-year-old might be able to do both. It is particularly critical to clarify meanings of the words children employ because they may use many words before they truly understand their meaning (Walker, 1999) or they often use them idiosyncratically: one cannot presume to know exactly what children are talking about based on common word usage, especially when they describe potentially abusive behaviours. For example, a five-year-old girl reported 'humping' her friend next door. On inquiry, this involved lying on him fully clothed, obviously not the usual meaning referring to sexual intercourse. While the child had seen people having sexual intercourse and heard the word 'humping' at home, she did not know what it actually meant and she had not been directly abused. Conversely, Anna (Case 26) said her father 'loved' her. This seemed acceptable, but when asked 'how' he showed his love, she stated her father said he 'loved' her when he put his 'dick' in her 'pee pee.' Others had discounted Anna's sexualized behaviours because she consistently asserted that her father 'loved' her.

General inquiry also permits an assessment of children's capacities to estimate time, recount dates, and report events in sequence. Since these concepts involve abstract thinking and rather complex language, young children can seem confused about them and must be questioned carefully. Furthermore, Walker (1999) indicates that younger children often use the words for such concepts before they fully understand them or can accurately use them to describe events. Walker also notes that many children do not acquire the ability to tell a complete and organized narrative about events until some time in the teen years. Despite this, young children can provide accurate information even though they cannot describe some aspects of events in a manner typical of older children or adults. For example, a four-year-old child likely cannot specify the exact time of day an assault happened, but might accurately describe what he or she was watching on television, thus narrowing the time frame considerably. Consequently, we should not discount reports of young children who cannot answer questions about time or understand complex sentences with many prepositional phrases. Instead, we must learn what to expect and carefully tailor our questions to their level of cognition and language, possibly explaining these differences to lawyers and judges, who may otherwise discount their reports because they do not meet adult standards for consistency and detail. Given the concrete nature of children's thinking, we should ask for specific examples of abstract or generalized ideas that are being discussed. For example, if a child reports that his mother is 'always mad,' examples, particularly of recent incidents, may clarify what is really happening.

While assessors may expect that adults should have developed **insight** and a capacity to be self-reflective, this is not necessarily the case with children. Unless they are nearing adolescence, many display a rather concrete focus in talking about their lives. Young children have particular difficulties assuming the perspectives of others and are likely to interpret events personally, especially when they have been abused. Children cannot easily infer the motives and factors that lead a certain person to abuse them, and they may feel responsible for their abuse, a tendency that can be reinforced when abusers or other people blame or criticize the children (Briere, 1992). Consequently, we should try to understand situations further when young children seem insightful and espouse a sophisticated view of the larger situation. Jill (Case 1) presented as a pseudomature but deprived youngster. Although only ten years of age, she offered complex excuses for her parents' behaviour. For example, she explained that her mother was cranky and went to bars because she had been physically and sexually abused as a child. Jill excused her mother's complete neglect and disregard for her needs, and although she assumed much of the parenting of her younger sisters, she never became angry about these responsibilities. Through the assessment, it became clear Jill had learned to avoid physical abuse by acting maturely and by meeting her mother's needs. She became a confidante and knew minute details about her mother's own abuse and subsequent sexual relationships, abortions, and pregnancies. Jackie purposefully enlisted Jill's sympathies and reinforced Jill with fleeting moments of closeness for meeting Jackie's needs, much as she did with other people. Confusion of roles, poor boundaries, coaching, and even alienation are suspected when children exhibit sophisticated reasoning and complicated language well beyond their intellectual and developmental levels.

As a picture of children's daily lives and interactions is amplified, we derive an estimation of the **physical care** they receive from caregivers. Clothing and cleanliness highlight priorities around hygiene. Furthermore, when children know no other way of life, they may describe gross neglect and abuse without realizing they are incriminating their parents, as occurred in the following case.

CASE 29: Mike, the youngest of three children, was nine years of age when his family was referred for a parenting assessment. He rather naïvely described many incidents that attested to poor parental care. For example, when asked about his talents, Mike said he was good at stealing food from the local store, just like his brothers. His favourite meals were snack foods, and he could not remember a time when his family ate a home-cooked meal together. Mike's report that he shared a room with his brothers and slept in one bed was confirmed during the home visit, although the bed was a dirty mattress on the floor. Mike had no furniture or organized belongings. He did no activities with parents aside from running errands for them, and these appeared to be excursions to buy drugs, although parents denied this. When asked to draw a picture, Mike drew a recent gang fight in which his cousin died outside of Mike's apartment. Mike viewed the event as both exciting and frightening, and seemed to be beginning to emulate the life-style of a local teenage gang.

As we query the specific details of children's lives, we should observe how children relate to us. While some are indiscriminant, others are withdrawn and suspicious. We should notice how they respond to compliments and what comments they make about themselves. For example, a child who hits himself in the head, calling himself 'pea brain' or 'little bastard,' most probably has heard these names from someone and perhaps will identify the individual if asked. Some children constantly comment that they are doing poorly, while others grossly overestimate their performances. Many who have been abused or neglected are hungry for attention and are eager to please, while others are gruff and behaviourally provocative, seemingly to keep people distant. These important observations are cross-validated through parent and reference reports, and they may begin to suggest hypotheses regarding the children's expectations of others and themselves, i.e., **internal working models** (Bowlby, 1973, 1980, 1982).

Questions about activities with friends and family further delineate internal working models. The people children choose for friends and the duration of friendships provide information regarding their expectations of relationships. For example, some expect bad treatment and so pick tough friends who mistreat them, whereas other children soon discard friends who they mistakenly believe are treating them poorly. While children may voice these expectations directly and evidence them through their behaviour, additional information about internal working models and attachment organization can be gained through more structured tasks to be discussed later in this chapter. Be alert to the emotional tone of all relationships, particularly to children's expectations about their parents' emotional responsiveness. It is worrisome when children prefer to seek help from a neighbour or teacher rather than their parents. Queries about real-life scenarios regarding **discipline**, perhaps through asking 'What would Mom do if you ...,' can be especially informative when children describe complete parental disregard or harsh treatment in response to relatively minor incidents. At times children directly demonstrate this harshness, as when one of Jill's younger sisters became panic-stricken after accidentally upsetting paint in the playroom (Case 1). She cowered while trying to quickly wipe it up. Foster parents and other references confirmed that Jackie demanded neatness from her young children and thought nothing of calling them names and cuffing them if they were messy. Young children may also act out such scenarios during creative play.

Many children resist limits on their behaviour in the assessment when effective limits have not been set in the home. While this can be challenging for assessors, it is often enlightening to compare children's abilities to **regulate their behaviour and emotions** in various situations, perhaps comparing office behaviour with home, school, and daycare behaviour. Some children respond well to the limits assessors provide and become out of control only in their parents' presence. Furthermore, children will often bluntly compare their behaviour in office to that in other settings. For example, Mike (Case 29) stated that he liked the assessor and so did not act up with him. However, he said he did not listen to his parents because they never followed through and he acted like a 'demon' at school to be sent home.

As interviews proceed, children are commonly asked to draw specific pictures, print their names, and do other more formal tasks, generating hypotheses about their general level of **cognitive functioning** that may later be confirmed with formal cognitive testing. Children who are four years of age should know some of their colours and be able to label a few feelings, respond to simple commands that involve one or two steps, and engage in some metaphorical play. These abilities can be reviewed quite informally by asking children to select a pen by colour or to do two tasks in a row. Children in early elementary school should demonstrate more complex use of language and have a broader fund of general information. For example, they should know something about time and money and read at least basic materials. They should also exhibit more sophisticated play skills that sometimes include competition and mastery themes. Older children are more likely to pick competitive games and use more sophisticated receptive and expressive language. They can focus for longer uninterrupted periods and follow rather complicated directions. Teenagers generally disdain offers of play, being pleased when they are treated more like adults. In these general interactions, obvious difficulties in cognitive functioning, attention, language, and other abilities may become apparent that require more formal assessment; levels of functioning and specific needs, including the kind of parenting practices most likely to meet these needs, can be clearly identified.

Academic experiences and **school performance** deserve specific inquiry. As some young children attend preschools or daycares and like going to 'school,' they may talk easily about their activities and friends. Others from deprived environments may focus on physical aspects such as lunch and naps. Once in kindergarten or grade school, children should be able to describe activities more thoroughly, talking about the subjects and teachers they like and dislike. As friends are an integral part of school, children can describe favourite playmates and recess activities, with these reports being validated by teachers to ensure children are accurately describing their school experiences. For example, Randy (Case 3) listed numerous school friends but no out-of-school contacts. His teacher confirmed that Randy made friends easily but kept them for a matter of hours or days, given his know-it-all and odd interactional style. He often roamed the playground alone or acted silly to impress others. To facilitate discussion of school for those children who are sensitive about poor academic performance or who may have learning disabilities, we can refer generally to other children we know with similar problems so they know they are not alone. We can further facilitate discussion by talking intermittently about their strengths and other areas of competence and by temporarily diverting away from the discussion to other topics. Finally, we need to ask about days absent from school and the amount of homework that is assigned and completed, noting particularly the perceived level of support from parents. Career goals are valid avenues of inquiry, even though some impoverished and deprived children may have inflated goals or see little hope for their future.

A related topic concerns **interests** and **achievements**: children often pick interests where they have natural abilities, as in the case of those who draw because they find it easy and therefore enjoyable. Deprived children may have few hobbies because they have no materials to use and are, indeed, much too preoccupied with survival to develop other interests. Therefore, interests may reflect both levels of parent resources and children's interests. Young children tend to like creative play and describe and demonstrate enjoyment of this activity in sessions. School-age children generally focus more on developing competencies in their play, sports, and hobbies, such as in soccer, reading, drawing, swimming, riding bikes, and collecting. Concerns arise if children list television or computer games as their only interest. Not only may parents have failed to encourage other activities and strengths, but children are at significant risk of developing impoverished peer relationships if they spend most non-school hours watching television.

Young teenagers often describe friends as occupying increasing portions of their free time. Description of activities with friends is informative about parental abilities to supervise teenagers and encouragement of developing competencies such as sports. Younger children should also be asked about their **social relationships**, specifically about the number, nature, and depth of their relationships with peers. Details are critical; for example, a child may report she has many 'best friends' but, on inquiry, be unable to name any friends or describe activities they do together. Since children are decidedly disadvantaged in the development of stable friendships when families frequently move, we should inquire how these children cope with transient friendships. Social relationships also include interactions with family friends, neighbours, teachers, and extended family. By the end of this inquiry, assessors are likely to have a strong picture of the social competence of specific children and the importance they attach to different relationships.

Observations made in this general inquiry are supplemented later with formal psychological assessment, observations in other settings such as school, home, and daycare, and reports from collateral references. By the end of a thorough general inquiry, most assessors can comment on children's **mental status.** Specific areas are listed in Table 9.3 in the previous chapter and include evaluation of physical appearance, relationship with the assessor, behaviour, cognition, perception, speech, affect, and insight and judgment. While some assessors do not report formally on mental status results in their reports, such information provides a good initial screening review and is a succinct way to communicate to others about how children presented in interviews.

Obviously, interviewing children takes skill, and assessors do best when they have formal training and a broad experiential base in work with children. Assessors who are psychologists require knowledge in several more specialized areas as well as psychological testing experience. If they are not psychologists, the guidelines outlined in Chapter 9 can be employed to decide whether a referral for psychological testing is required.

Specialized Areas of Inquiry

Inquiry regarding Abuse and Neglect

Since concerns about possible abuse and neglect bring children to the attention of child welfare authorities, children usually are asked about these allegations as part of a parenting assessment. Generally this inquiry follows interviews conducted by child welfare investigators and police: earlier child welfare interviews determine if children need protection and police interviews determine whether criminal charges will be laid. However, in cases where criminal charges exist or are pending, assessors may be precluded from interviewing children about the alleged abusive incidents until all criminal proceedings are finished. As this varies across jurisdictions, assessors must inquire about this proscription and alter their interview plans accordingly.

In many jurisdictions child welfare and police investigators undertake these earlier interviews jointly to minimize the emotional impact on children and limit the effects of repeated interviewing on reports. However, removal of children from parental care and criminal charges against parents or other perpetrators are not based solely on children's reports. In cases involving physical abuse and neglect, other corroborating physical evidence is usually present. For example, a young child suffering from non-organic failure to thrive who is hospitalized near death often provides strong evidence of parenting problems and neglect. Likewise, a youngster with a particular array of physical symptoms (e.g., subdural hematomas, retinal hemorrhages) may provide concrete evidence of having been shaken. However, many cases do not have such incontrovertible physical evidence, particularly in regard to sexual abuse. As Bays and Chadwick (1993) report after reviewing information regarding the medical diagnosis of sexual abuse, examination results are often normal, and physical findings of sexual abuse that, for example, include genital trauma and sexually transmitted diseases or sperm are found in the minority of victims. Faller (1996) likewise indicates that physical evidence of sexual abuse is rare and likely occurs in 10 to 30 per cent of cases.

By the time child welfare cases are referred for parenting assessment abuse is often documented, and the assessor's task is to determine the impact of the abuse on children and if they can be safely returned to parents. This is somewhat different from custody/access cases, where abuse allegations, although they may exist, may not have been formally investigated: allegations may have been discounted because they were attributed to the vindictiveness that sometimes emerges in such cases. However, McGleughlin, Meyer, and Baker (1999) report that such allegations in custody/access cases occur much less frequently than is commonly thought. In situations where formal investigations have not been undertaken by child welfare investigators, assessors might be more involved in determining if maltreatment occurred, reporting to authorities as necessary. Parenting assessors, including those in custody/access assessments, must not only be aware of the differences between clinical and forensic interviewing, but should be trained in forensic interviewing. They must also remain cognizant that some children will not disclose despite the most skilled interviewing methods, while other children will provide more details about already known abusive incidents or even speak of unreported incidents. This necessitates careful interviewing, and assessors must keep these possibilities in mind, as was necessary in the following case.

CASE 30: Bruce (twelve years) and Ralph (nine years) were removed from their father's care due to neglect and physical abuse. He passively complied with in-home therapy interventions as he sought his children's return to his home. A parenting assessment was court-ordered when his parenting skills did not improve and the boys became increasingly distressed following every visit home. The assessor found them to be profoundly affected by neglect and physical and emotional abuse: they had problematic relationships with their father, peers, and group home staff and they exhibited various sexually aggressive behaviours. Despite careful inquiry throughout the assessment, neither child confirmed that he had been sexually abused. Both were referred for individual therapy, pending a permanent guardianship court hearing, and neither reported sexual abuse to his therapist. However, given the severity of the other maltreatment they experienced, the children were permanently removed from their father's care and infrequent contact with the father was supervised. Within a week of the court decision, Bruce divulged to his therapist that his father had been sexually abusing him. When asked about his previous nondisclosure, Bruce bluntly stated that he would have been stupid to tell when the possibility of a return home still existed, as he expected to be severely beaten if his father discovered his disclosure.

Bruce's unwillingness to disclose is common. False denials of abuse and children's resistance to reporting sexual abuse are significant problems (Faller, 1996). Children have many reasons to deny abuse, including embarrassment, feelings of responsibility for the abuse, avoidance as a way of coping, and fear of the consequences of disclosure (Faller, 1996). As Bruce clearly stated, he was truly afraid of the consequences and did not disclose until he felt safe. Ralph did not make any disclosures despite Bruce's strong assertion that his brother also had been abused. Ralph may have refrained from disclosing because he was favoured and was spared the physical abuse, thereby rendering his relationship with his father more ambivalent. Once Bruce began to tell of the sexually abusive incidents, his therapist made the choice to ask only a few open-ended questions and obtain just enough detail to warrant a report to the child welfare worker and police, so Bruce's report would not be contaminated for forensic purposes. Police found him a credible witness and laid criminal charges that resulted in his father's conviction and several years of incarceration.

PRACTICE ALERT #18

When children begin to disclose details about previously unreported abuse, obtain only enough information to know a report to child welfare is necessary, thereby avoiding multiple interviews and possible contamination of evidence.

Had Bruce disclosed sexual abuse during the parenting assessment rather than later to his therapist, the assessor would likewise have obtained only enough information to make a child abuse report. Subsequent interviews by police and child welfare workers usually delay the completion of assessments and limit any subsequent assessment inquiries about the alleged maltreatment because of fears that further questioning will taint the evidence. Nevertheless, reporting to child welfare authorities is mandatory; assessors may in their findings refer to police opinions about the existence of abuse. The situation is less clear when abuse is unconfirmed, particularly if children do not cooperate with police or if other problems occur with the interview process. Perhaps the most difficult situation occurs when authorities cannot obtain enough information to lay charges but cannot categorically rule out abuse. Parenting assessors may then need to form their own opinion about the likelihood that abuse occurred and recommend appropriate action to safeguard children. Provided that assessors are skilled in the relevant assessment techniques, this may entail some interviews with children as well as direct questioning of parents about the allegations, such as that described in Chapter 9 regarding the specific behaviours and why others are concerned about them.

ISSUES IN CHILDREN'S REPORTS

Before providing some interview guidelines concerning abuse and neglect, we will review issues and currently available information regarding the capacity of children to accurately report past events, particularly maltreatment episodes. Much of this information comes from analog studies where various factors, such as suggestibility and leading interview questions, are manipulated to ascertain their impact on children's accurate recall of various events. Few studies of actual victims are reported. Faller (1996) delineates several of the significant issues, and assessors are advised to review her article. We have already talked about **reluctance to disclose** and noted possible reasons.

Another concern centres on the accuracy of children's recall or, in other words, **memory problems**: some aspects of children's memory can create problems in interviews (Faller, 1996). Children may attend to different details and events than those commonly noted by adults and, since they often more poorly attend to peripheral detail, others may question the veracity of their reports. Children's memories may deteriorate more over time than those of adults, leading to less detailed reports in delayed investigations. However, some argue that the traumatic nature of certain abusive events and the greater involvement of sensory and motor systems in them enhance children's memories of such events over their recall of more mundane ones. Dissociation may contribute to less detailed accounts, as would the difficulty that children have in interpreting abusive behaviours. Because they have no knowledge and experiential base to understand abusive events, children may less accurately recount what happened to them during abusive episodes; they have no words to convey what happened to them, such as sexual intercourse. Although responses to open-ended questions are believed to elicit the most accurate information, Reed (1996) indicates that these may result in more skeletal responses. However, as questions become more specific accuracy of recall can decline because of other factors, such as suggestibility, if more focused questions are not carefully framed.

As Faller (1996) notes, **suggestibility** does complicate interviews of children about abusive incidents. Reed (1996) defines suggestibility as 'the degree to which one's "memory" and/or "recounting" of an event is influenced by suggested information or misinformation' (p. 106). Generally, children are more vulnerable to suggestive interviewing than are adults, but they are also quite accurate in reporting experiences if they are not asked leading questions. Even preschoolers can produce accurate reports if interviewed properly, although they tend to report fewer details of experiences. For example, a preschooler might focus on fewer aspects of a birthday party and relate them in a more disjointed manner than would a twelve-year-old child. After reviewing recent evidence, Bruck and Ceci (1999) note three major findings regarding suggestibility. First, given age differences, preschoolers are the most susceptible to misleading or incorrect post-event information, although older children and adults can likewise be influenced. Second, children display wide individual differences in their vulnerability to suggestion, with cognitive, psychosocial, demographic, and physiological factors all possibly playing a role. Third, suggestive interviewing can influence memories of both central and peripheral details for both positive and negative events. Suggestibility can work both ways: children can be induced to say abuse never happened when it actually did, and they can be induced to confirm that abuse happened when it did not. As Bruck and Ceci (1999) state, the accuracy of young children's recall likely has more to do with the interviewer's skills than any inherent limitations in children's memory: children recall events most reliably when interviewers are neutral in tone, limit the use of misleading questions, and do not introduce a motive for the child to make a false report.

Another issue Faller (1996) discusses is children's ability to distinguish between reality and fantasy and their **propensity to lie and fantasize** about events in their lives. While many children can distinguish between reality and fantasy as early as preschool years, some choose to lie about their experiences and others may report fantasy as their reality. For example, Bruce (Case 30) deliberately lied about his abuse until he could be assured of safety. Other situations are not so clear, although children have varied motivations to deny or make up allegations. Faller (1996) says positive attention for their reports of events may result in increasingly elaborated descriptions that are not always accurate. Some children may be persuaded to affirm that they participated in events that were suggested by interviewers and, over time, others can be encouraged, with repeated and leading suggestions, to generate entirely fictitious events in which they say they personally participated. This is complicated by Ceci's (2000) assertion that some children develop false beliefs about events in their lives: after repeated interviews where false information is suggested, both children and adults can come to believe they participated in various activities when they actually did not.

Related to these issues is a concern about the tendency of some people to automatically dismiss children's reports as fabrications when they contain elements that appear bizarre, improbable, and even fantastic. Everson (1997) argues that reports containing such elements should not be automatically discounted without careful consideration of explanations that may account for the fantastic elements. Everson proceeds to discuss twenty-four possible explanations for the inclusion of questionable elements, divided into three groups. The first group includes explanations where there is an interaction of the abusive event with specific characteristics of the child. These include situations where the perpetrator has manipulated the child, where coping mechanisms have influenced the child's memory, and where the child's cognitive immaturity has resulted in distortions as the child tried to understand the abusive event(s). A second group of factors results from the interaction of the assessment with child characteristics. For example, distortions may occur when information about the child's statements is passed from person to person, when leading or suggestive questioning is used, when the child simply tires in a long interview process, or when the child confabulates and fills in memory gaps with untrue information. The third category of explanations arises in situations where there is an interaction of extrinsic influences (those not included in either the abusive event or the interview process) with child characteristics: elements from the media and cultural practices or dream material might be incorporated into a child's accounts. Readers should review Everson's article to obtain more detail regarding some of the explanations that should be considered when children include bizarre or unusual elements in their reports.

All of the issues in children's reports discussed above add to the difficulty in determining whether children's reports are accurate, although Faller (1996) reports several studies that suggest that false allegations by children are rare, likely in the range of 1 to 10 per cent. Older children and teenagers may be somewhat more likely to make false reports, given their broader understanding of the implications of such reports. However, keeping in mind the significance of decisions that are based on children's reports, we must carefully interview children and strive to understand what happened to them. We must take care to neither dismiss reports too easily nor be too hasty in accepting a seemingly plausible report.

GUIDELINES FOR INTERVIEWS

Since interviewing can powerfully influence children's reports about abuse, we must ensure that we follow a thoughtful and careful process. Regardless of whether interviews are used in criminal proceedings or to delineate children's understanding of what has happened to them, the development of rapport is a critical step. As described earlier, more generalized inquiry allows children to settle into interviews and develop an understanding of how assessors will relate to them and of the type of responses required. It also allows assessors to determine the children's characteristics and mental status as well as gauge the reliability of reports about relatively mundane information. Through the general and then abuse-specific inquiry, we must explain that answers such as 'I don't know,' 'I don't understand your question,' and 'I can't remember' are acceptable, and preferable to providing obligatory but inaccurate answers (Lamb, Sternberg, & Esplin, 1998). Additionally, we must encourage children to correct us when we misunderstand what they say. We can do this by incorrectly restating information they have provided already, such as their ages or teachers' names: if they do not correct us, we must directly encourage them to do so. At no time during general or abuse-specific interviews should we pressure children to respond or acquiesce indiscriminantly to our statements. For example, assessors must never say 'I'll give you a candy as soon as you tell me what happened' or 'you can get back to class as soon as you tell me what you did.' Likewise, we must never suggest displeasure or exasperation when children are unwilling or unable to reply to questions, and we must be careful not to differentially reinforce children's responses through smiles, attentiveness, and praise only when they discuss specific issues.

Lamb et al. (1998) also suggest that assessors encourage children to produce detailed reports during general inquiries, citing evidence that they are then more likely to provide more elaborate answers in abuse inquiry. Essentially, children can be trained to be detailed reporters. For example, if a child provides scanty description of a birthday party where he went swimming, we can ask about the time and location of the party, who attended, what games were played, the food that was served, and the colour of his or her bathing suit. If we also ask about the child's feelings and reactions, children then realize we are interested in really finding out the details of their experiences. By taking notes through these general interviews and saying something as simple as 'I'm writing this down so that I can remember it,' we accustom children to this activity. Some literate children monitor notes to ensure that we are indeed noting details accurately. A similar explanation can be used with auditory or video recording of interviews, although it is critical to obtain appropriate consents from guardians prior to taping.

Such communications can clearly convey expectations about the types of desired responses through all phases of interviewing, including general and abuse-specific interviewing. Reed (1996) provides us with seven succinct guidelines that are particularly useful in limiting the effects of suggestibility in forensic interviews. He suggests that assessors stress the importance of being truthful and not pretending. Children should also be told that assessors are uninformed, particularly about the detailed facts of the abusive incident(s). Assessors must discourage guessing and encourage children to admit when they are confused. Similarly, they must encourage children to admit a lack of memory or knowledge of an event rather than guess or make up answers. Assessors must directly tell children that repeated questions do not mean their previous responses were incorrect, although the questions probably should be rephrased: repeated questions may feel coercive and lead children to alter their responses in hopes of eventually giving the 'right' answer. A sixth guideline focuses on those interview circumstances where children become too distressed during talk of abuse, perhaps being anxious, frightened, or embarrassed. Reed advises assessors to give overwhelmed children permission to decline responding for the time being. Otherwise, they may simply shut down and refuse to respond. Finally, he suggests that assessors encourage children to disagree with and correct erroneous statements made by assessors. Reed also explores other aspects of the interview process, and readers are advised to read his article.

Perhaps the most essential attitude to carry into interviewing is an **openness to alternative explanations** for the behaviours and allegations. Assessors who approach the interview process with preconceived notions and conclusions do favours for no one. For example, in the earlier report of the five-year-old girl who spoke of humping her friend, the assessor did not accept the report at face value and asked questions to determine exactly what happened. To develop a context prior to beginning an abuse inquiry with children, one can ask adults how the abuse came to the awareness of others, who has already questioned or talked with the children about the maltreatment, and how these interviews were undertaken. Obviously, children's reports to parenting assessors may be understood somewhat differently if those children have been questioned repeatedly by others than if they have not yet been interviewed. In the first circumstance, there may be an increased likelihood that reports have been influenced through repeated questioning, particularly if earlier interviews were poorly executed. However, such interviewing does not automatically mean that all information gained in later interviews must be discounted.

Open-ended questions are used to introduce abuse-focused inquiry. For example, with Bruce (Case 30) the therapist began by stating that group home staff had told him Bruce had spoken of upsetting behaviours that happened with his father. Bruce retorted with, 'Yes. He sexually abused me' and hoped this would suffice. Instead, the therapist said simply, 'Tell me more about it.' Bruce's demeanour changed visibly and he became agitated. The therapist allowed him to relax by drawing, and during this activity Bruce haltingly told of repeated abusive incidents; he required few direct probes or questions. Once Bruce had provided enough detail to convince the therapist he had likely been abused, the therapist told Bruce he would stop asking more questions now. They discussed the therapist's plan to call Bruce's caseworker and the police so they could talk further with him. The therapist reassured Bruce that he would support him through additional interviewing and other procedures. Both the therapist and residential staff supported Bruce emotionally, but they did not inquire further about the abuse, instead encouraging him to be honest in his discussions with the police. At Bruce's request, his therapist attended the police interview, which Bruce handled well, given his strong verbal skills and good memory.

Although open-ended questions are preferable, they tend to produce more skeletal and less detailed responses (Reed, 1996). Some children require more focused questioning to elicit greater detail, although the risk of suggesting answers correspondingly increases. This can create significant dilemmas for assessors, particularly with younger children (Saywitz & Camparo, 1998). When open-ended questions produce no information, assessors must choose between asking no further questions and introducing the topic of concern in as nonsuggestive a manner as possible (Wood & Garven, 2000). Consequently, most interviews begin with general questions that are followed by more **specific prompts** if needed to elicit details. Wood and Garven (2000) caution that questions that focus attention on a particular topic should be followed up with open-ended questions. Such a procedure was used to focus the child in the following child welfare case.

CASE 31: Four-year-old Diana seemed agitated after a drinking party in her home. Following three days of severe nightmares, she said 'Bear hurted me.' Although her single mother recalled nothing untoward during the evening, she took her to a hospital emergency department, where staff called child welfare authorities. Diana provided few details about the party night in response to open-ended questions. Consequently, the investigator asked about specific activities Diana did during the party. Diana spoke of playing with her older sister and watching a television show, but became anxious as she spoke of bedtime. However, when asked about what she wore to bed, she said she wore a pair of pink pajamas. In response to a 'what happened next' inquiry, she stated that her sister turned out the lights and a bear came and 'growled' and 'hurted' her. She was 'scared,' but the bear left. She could not describe the bear because her room was dark.

Although the assessor asked specific questions about activities and apparel on the night in question, these are essentially probes and are not considered leading. Leading or suggestive questions occur when the interviewer, rather than the child, introduces new information about the topic of concern (Wood & Garven, 2000), and questions can vary along a continuum of suggestibility (Saywitz & Camparo, 1998). For example, strongly leading questions might have included 'Were you watching *America's Most Wanted*? Were you wearing panties? Were the pajamas pink?' In Diana's case, her spontaneous description of pink pajamas led to the seizure of these from her closet; when examined, the pajamas were found to be soiled with dried ejaculate. Had the assessor offered other colours and had Diana picked the wrong colour, the veracity of her report might have been called into question and important evidence might have been missed. Often, more focused questions are necessary relatively early in interviews of very young children. However, as Lamb et al. (1998) and Wood and Garven (2000) indicate, questions that focus children's attention on certain events, places, or people should be followed with more open-ended inquiry.

As assessors, we should never badger children or argue with them and suggest other details. Ceci (2000) points out that erroneous details can become part of any person's memories, particularly if they are repeated over time. It is also critical to avoid coercive and suggestive questions. In the above case, these might have included statements such as 'A man hurt you, didn't he, and you just think it's a bear because he had a hairy chest and arms?' when the child had not mentioned hairiness. A careful assessor would be more likely to ask, 'How did you know it was a bear?' Some scepticism about children's reports is not necessarily bad, but this should not be articulated in a confronting and demeaning way. Instead, it is better to express some confusion, such as saying, 'I don't understand. There was a bear in your house?' This might help the child elaborate but does not intimidate or suggest specific replies. Coercion also may occur if you refer to other people's reports about the same incident, essentially applying pressure, subtle or otherwise, to provide a specific account when children have no memory or a different one. For example, Diana's sister heard noises but did not corroborate some of the details. It would have been a glaring error to say, 'Diana already told me what happened' in hopes of making the sister produce corroborating details.

Questions regarding the frequency of various episodes deserve particular sensitivity. Given that young children may not have a good sense of time and number, questions such as 'How many times did this happen?' are difficult. Children may provide only general descriptions of abuse, particularly if it was repeated, detracting from the report's validity. Responses will be more consistent and accurate if questions are asked differently. For example, Bruce (Case 30) first described a general scenario, saying sexual abuse had happened over 'a few' years. When asked about the first incident, he clearly tied this to a Saturday night on his ninth birthday. Having just completed grade 3, he remembered his teacher had given him a special Mickey Mouse pencil on the last day of school. Subsequent abuse followed a regular pattern wherein his father would call Bruce to his room during the late Saturday night movie while his brother slept. Bruce said he was always awake, as he was so fearful of Saturday nights. He could not describe particular details such as the clothing he wore but described the wallpaper patterns next to his father's bed, as he said he focused his attention on this during each episode of abuse. Lamb et al. (1998) suggest questions such as 'Did this happen one time or more than one time?' as a good starting point, followed by time and location probes. The use of such probes can be acknowledged in both written reports and on the witness stand.

Lamb et al. (1998) offer three guidelines regarding the use of more focused questioning. They suggest that interviewers only use probes after completion of narrative accounts to open-ended questions. In Diana's case (Case 31), the assessor might have specifically asked about what she was wearing if she had not spontaneously mentioned this. Lamb et al. also recommend that suggestive probes be as limited as possible: '"Did anything ever happen to your vagina?" is better than "Did he do anything to your vagina?" which is, in turn, better than "Did he ever put anything in your vagina?"' (p. 821). Finally, they recommend that, following a positive response to such a probe, investigators immediately revert to eliciting information with open-ended questions. For example, after focusing Diana's attention on how she prepared for bed, the assessor reverted to open-ended questions such as 'What happened next?' rather than saying things such as 'And then someone came in your bedroom, didn't he?'

Some debate exists about the use of physical prompts, such as anatomically detailed dolls, in children's interviews. Faller (1996), Reed (1996), and Everson and Boat (1994) discuss their use, which clearly requires great care due to the risk of misleading children, particularly those under five years old. Not only are young children slightly more suggestible, but they may have more difficulty with 'symbolic representation': they have more problems using the dolls and any other physical prompts to represent particular people and events in their lives (Reed, 1996). Also, children who demonstrate various types of sexual touching or behaviour may not have been abused themselves but have learned about such behaviours from other sources (Everson & Boat, 1994). For example, they may have seen movies containing explicit sexual material. However, anatomically detailed dolls can be useful prompts in some situations, particularly with children over the age of five years (Reed, 1996). The American Professional Society on the Abuse of Children (1995) offers guidelines around their use, but unless assessors are expert in using these dolls and are well aware of how unabused children play with these dolls, they probably should refrain from using them in parenting assessments.

Great care also is required in interviews about physical and emotional abuse. Although these may be part of a less secretive and more general behavioural pattern in the home, assessors often need to get children to describe such experiences to help ascertain the quality of the parenting they received and the impact of such behaviours on their functioning. When physical and emotional abuse have happened repeatedly, we may elicit more comprehensive descriptions if we ask children about specific instances, such as the first or last time. For example, Bruce (Case 30) spoke of his father's physical assaults that happened on nearly a daily basis. However, he also provided detailed descriptions of incidents that stood out in his memory. He once stole his father's cold pizza from the fridge and was beaten so badly with a leather belt that he missed school for a week until the bruises disappeared and would not arouse suspicion. Emotional abuse is even more difficult to document due to its less concrete and more insidious nature and because many children simply do not know that better treatment is possible. Children may describe emotional abuse when speaking of how they displeased parents. Such descriptions can then be compared with observations of parents and children together, collateral reports, and psychological test results. For example, a young boy frequently referred to himself as a 'bastard,' stating that his parents called him this when he was 'bad.' In the waiting room, his mother did indeed call him this several times when he would not get ready to go home. However, assessors must remain aware that not all emotional abuse is so blatant. Not only may parents fail to be honest in reporting their behaviour, but some collateral references are biased or do not recognize that such behaviour is inappropriate and pernicious.

Besides using the above guidelines to obtain clear descriptions of what happened, assessors must often evaluate the impact of maltreatment on children. Initiate this abuse-focused inquiry near the beginning of an interview session so that time is available for a thorough and comprehensive inquiry and to give children sufficient opportunity to process their feelings. Otherwise, they could become upset with no time to resettle before leaving. Again, one must be careful to avoid suggesting feelings and reactions, instead eliciting the children's own descriptions. It is clearly inappropriate to suggest that they felt disgust, fright, or confusion before they actually give such descriptions. Children sometimes feel positively or ambivalently about their abuser because they loved the individual or received attention during the abusive episodes. For example, while Bruce (Case 30) strongly disliked what his father did to him, he liked having his undivided attention and being told he was a good son during episodes of sexual abuse. We simply cannot draw assumptions about the impact of abuse or neglect. Since children may become overwhelmed during interviews, one must be sensitive to their feelings and escalating anxiety. However, their distress also conveys diagnostic information. For example, some children become almost immobilized when speaking of abusive incidents and others become sexually aroused. Anna (Case 26) described orgasmic responses during both abusive incidents and interviews about them. When children are significantly anxious, one can say 'You look pretty upset right now.' After asking why they are nervous, one can then intervene by reassuring them. At all times assessors should be alert to the most problematic aspects of the abuse for children and the coping strategies they employ. For example, some children describe dissociation by saying they go off to other places in their heads during the abuse. Others, like Bruce (Case 30), describe numbing themselves and focusing on some peripheral detail in the situation, such as the wallpaper pattern.

By becoming cognizant of the sequelae that are common to abused children, such as those regarding sexual abuse outlined by Finkelhor and Browne (1985), assessors can guide their inquiry into children's feelings and reactions to maltreatment. Although we review Finkelhor and Browne's four traumagenic factors, assessors may wish to review their article or our previous book on psychotherapy of maltreated children (Pearce & Pezzot-Pearce, 1997) for a more complete description of inquiry about each of the four factors. Briefly, interviewing about the first factor, traumatic sexualization, requires attention to such issues as the possible increased salience of sexual issues, children's confusion regarding sexual identity and sexual norms and standards, and children's anxiety that might be associated with sexuality as well as their fears regarding body integrity. Interviews that focus on children's feelings of powerlessness examine coercive aspects of the abuse, children's feelings of helplessness in stopping the abuse, and their perception of the effectiveness and consequences resulting from their disclosure. Inquiry into the third factor of betrayal focuses on children's pre-maltreatment relationships with the perpetrators, their feelings about the perpetrators after the abuse began, the degree to which they feel tricked or used by the perpetrators, and the responses of the larger community to the disclosure. The latter includes the reactions of those people they told about the abuse, as well as the response of the legal, child welfare, and medical systems. Finally, inquiry about the fourth traumagenic factor examines the stigmatization children may feel as a result of the abuse. As we suggested previously, the latter three traumagenic factors likely have relevance for types of abuse other than sexual (Pearce & Pezzot-Pearce, 1997). Two structured interview formats also are available to guide inquiry regarding reactions to abusive incidents. Pynoos and Eth (1986) developed the Traumatic Event Interview Schedule, which asks children to draw pictures of what happened and then tell stories about the incidents. This is followed by further inquiry and discussion. Another structured interview technique with fifty-four items, the Children's Impact of Tramatic Events Scale – Revised (CITES) (Wolfe, Gentile, & Wolfe, 1989) has nine subscales. Six are related to impact of abuse (betrayal, guilt, helplessness, intrusive thoughts, sexualization, and stigmatization) and three are related to attributions about the abusive incidents (internal versus external, global versus specific, and stable versus unstable).

Prior to moving to other interview topics, an assessor can summarize aloud to children regarding what he or she has learned about the impact of the maltreatment, again encouraging them to correct errors and elaborate where needed. Children's viewpoints and perceptions are always critical, and an assessor never should employ assumptions and stereotypes to prejudge what has happened and how it affects children.

Evaluation of Attachment Organization and Internal Working Models

In earlier chapters we spoke of the importance of attachment in development. This is clearly another area of specialized inquiry, although some information about attachment and children's internal working models is gained through parental and referees' descriptions and through the assessor's observations of children and caregivers. Few well-validated clinical assessment tools are currently available to assess this aspect of children's functioning. The Strange Situation paradigm (Ainsworth et al., 1978), described in Chapter 3, is a research tool and has not been adapted for clinical use or for use with children of preschool age and beyond. Furthermore, children's attachment organizations can change over time, requiring current evaluations of their actual interpersonal behaviour.

Since attachment problems are relational disturbances, children can express these difficulties in some of their relationships. In a portion of child welfare cases, we do not have current access to biological parents or early caregivers who can provide descriptions of children's early relationships, making it necessary to review records to identify any previously documented history. If early caregivers are available, we can ask the questions outlined in Table 9.1. Assessors must also ask current caregivers about how children relate to them: some pertinent questions are listed in Table 9.2. During this inquiry, assessors need to remain aware that these reports may be inaccurate, given the relationship issues that some parents themselves experience.

ASSESSMENT OF RELATIONAL ASPECTS OF ATTACHMENT ORGANIZATION

Besides asking caretakers such as parents, foster or adoptive parents, and residential care staff questions about how children relate to them, it is important to observe children with their primary caretakers. The reactions of children who are not yet in school to separation from their caregivers are of particular interest. The reunions that occur between children and caregivers after individual interviews can be particularly informative, even with children up to the age of six years who are just becoming accustomed to going off to school. For example, Main and Cassidy (1988) identified four main patterns of attachment from examining the first five minutes of reunion between six-year-old children and their mothers. Children who were confident, relaxed, and open in responding to their mother's return were judged as *secure*. *Anxious-avoidant* children maintained a neutral coolness and avoided interaction. Children with *anxious-ambivalent* classifications had mixed feelings about seeking proximity with their mothers and demonstrated elements of avoidance, sadness, fear, and hostility. These children overexpressed their feelings and, if they sensed that their mothers would be unresponsive, sometimes became quite dependent and clingy. A final group of *disorganized/disoriented* children took control of the reunion in one of two ways. They either became confrontational and punitive with their mothers or they attempted to comfort and care for them.

Lyons-Ruth, Bronfman, and Atwood (1999) reported that disorganized/disoriented infants may reorganize their attachment behaviour into a controlling strategy in preschool years, endeavouring to maintain engagement with the parent on the parent's terms rather than seeking comfort and protection based on their own needs and feelings. For example, assessors might see children trying to entertain, direct, or organize their parents, as in the situation where children gather belongings to prepare for departure from a waiting room. Other children might coerce, attack, or even humiliate their parents, perhaps calling parents names or deliberately acting in ways that might embarrass them. While Lyons-Ruth et al. question whether frightening and frightened parent behaviours may contribute to the children's demonstrating controlling behaviour that becomes punitive or helping in later years, they are clear in suggesting that maternal communication with these children is disrupted. Specifically, they suggest that affective communication errors may occur across five dimensions. Parents may make affective errors where they give contradictory cues, no responses, or inappropriate emotional responses to infants. For example, a parent might not comfort or might even laugh at an upset child, or he or she might ask a child to do something and then criticize the child for doing it. Parents may also appear disoriented, seeming confused or frightened by their children or being disorganized in their emotional responses, such as ceasing to respond to them for no apparent reason or handling them as if they were inanimate objects. They may exhibit negative-intrusive verbal and physical behaviours, such as mocking children, using a sharp voice, or pulling them by the wrist. A fourth dimension includes role confusion, either in terms of role reversal or sexualization in their relationships. For example, a parent might seek reassurance from the child, such as when a mother asks for confirmation that she is pretty or that the child loves her. Finally, parents may withdraw, either physically or verbally, perhaps by stiffly holding children away or not greeting them after a separation. Bronfman, Parsons, and Lyons-Ruth (n.d.) have developed the Atypical Maternal Behavior Instrument for Assessment and Classification (AMBIANCE), which allows observers to rate these dimensions of communication. While primarily a research tool, it alerts us to important aspects of interaction.

When examining reunions of older children, we can note the fluency of discourse between children and parents. For example, Main, Kaplan, and Cassidy (1985) found differences among children with different attachment organizations. Children who had been classified as secure in infancy displayed fluent speech in reunions when they were older; children and parents spoke directly and easily and had little difficulty accessing or expressing information. Such children's answers to questions were prompt, whereas children who had been classified as avoidant often paused in conversation turns, confined topics to impersonal matters and inanimate objects, and elaborated very little upon topics. Their discourse was restricted and parents often asked rhetorical questions, not really expecting answers. Dysfluent and disorganized discourse typified children and parents in disorganized/disoriented dyads. False starts by parents and children, topics that were related to relationships, and parents' passive responses to children's attempts to steer conversation were characteristic of these pairs. While this is only one study, it provides guidance for assessors to delineate interaction nuances that may be of importance in parenting assessments. Furthermore, references may comment on these same details in their observations of reunions with young children and parents, particularly in settings such as daycare and school.

Again, behaviour and discourse vary depending on children's ages and temperamental characteristics. While the differences are subtle, they are immediately apparent in some cases; even neutral parties occasionally react to and comment on unusual interactions. A parent who had been sitting in the waiting room made the following comment to a clinician: 'I normally would not say anything, but how old is that child? He and his mother seem a little close.' She had reacted to the following scene:

Randy and June (Case 3) displayed grossly disturbed interactions in the waiting room despite his being eleven years old. When brought to sessions by June, Randy experienced difficulty separating from his mother to meet with the assessor. After his individual sessions, he monitored June's emotional state and usually climbed into her lap, moulding to her contours. However, they avoided eye contact, their discussion was disjointed, and June ignored her son's overtures for contact and conversation, preferring to speak with the assessor. Randy stammered increasingly as he tried to engage his mother in talk about her interests. Despite her tendency to ignore Randy, June occasionally attended to her son, but usually in a highly critical manner.

Unfortunately for Randy, his mother's mental health problems had resulted in highly unpredictable and sometimes dangerous parenting. June had handled Randy roughly and had never reliably soothed him when he was distressed or hurt, nor had she set limits around his physical safety. Furthermore, she had often criticized and mocked him, elicited reassurance and affection from him when she was upset, appropriated his toys and activities for herself, flew into unprovoked rages, and sometimes ignored him for hours. He had indeed developed a disorganized/disoriented attachment organization because he could never depend on her responsiveness and indeed, on many occasions, he was highly confused and even frightened by her. Other cases are much less extreme and more subtle, making formulations more difficult.

ASSESSMENT OF REPRESENTATIONAL ASPECTS OF ATTACHMENT ORGANIZATION

Older children's internal representations of their expectations about themselves and others can be assessed using other tasks. However, many of the strategies we will briefly discuss were developed in a research context and have not been applied to clinical groups. Even so, they may have some clinical applicability, but empirical research about their clinical and forensic use is warranted. Also, Solomon and George (1999) indicate that assessment of attachment security is most challenging in the early preschool years (approximately twenty-one to forty-eight months); the attachment system is not as easily activated as in infancy, children have a broader behavioural repertoire, and their linguistic and representational capacities are still primitive and vary greatly across children. The tasks that we describe below would most likely be grouped with projective tasks as described in the last chapter: stimuli are presented to children, who react based on their routine ways of perceiving and responding to various situations.

Bretherton, Ridgeway, and Cassidy (1990) developed a 'narrative story stem technique' that uses small doll play to evaluate children's internal working models. In their procedure, the interviewer introduces five separate stories with a story stem that describes what has happened. The five stories include three situations where a child spills juice, hurts her knee, and 'discovers' a monster in the bedroom, as well as one where parents depart the scene and another where parents return to it. After presenting the story stem, the interviewer asks the child to both describe and re-enact what happens next. For example, in one story stem developed by Bretherton et al., a mother and father leaving on a trip face two children and a grandmother. In their stories, which are recorded by the interviewer, children are expected to report behavioural and feeling scenarios that parallel what they might do in a real-life situation. Solomon, George, & DeJong (1995), using four of the story stems and rating attachment security based on only separation/reunion story stem responses, found that securely attached children told stories where the relationship with the mother was viewed positively and involved warmth, directness, and supportiveness. Children tended to be confident and difficult situations were resolved positively. Some children related stories in which they coped well with dangerous elements that they introduced into the narrative, while other children demonstrated confident and comfortable autonomy in coping with the separation and pleasure in the reunion. Avoidant children, by contrast, did not acknowledge the importance of the relationship and, in the separation/reunion stories, portrayed the child doll as feeling alone or rejected. Their affect was muted and salient issues such as the separations and reunions were avoided. Ambivalent/resistant children told digressive and busy stories where fears about the separation were not expressed directly: negative feelings tended to be projected onto other characters while the emotional tone of the stories was generally happy. Controlling-punitive children gave wildly chaotic scenarios filled with danger that did not resolve positively, while controlling-caretaking children gave inhibited responses where they were uncomfortable with the task and reluctant to act out a story.

Buchsbaum, Toth, Clyman, Cicchetti, and Emde (1992) used a different set of story stems, listed in detail in an appendix to their article, to elicit narratives from maltreated children. They found that the stories of maltreated children included such themes as interpersonal aggression, neglect, and sexualized behaviours as well as the defenses the children employed to cope with these events, such as avoidance, idealization, and identification with the aggressor. Stories were replete with aggression, punitiveness, and abusive language. The stories contained no people who came to help injured dolls, but did include generalized statements about their authors being bad. Buchsbaum et al. strongly believe the children's responses elucidate their representational models. In other words, the children's stories give information about their expectations of other people as well as their perceptions of themselves.

Other stimuli have also been used to elicit stories and reactions that might facilitate evaluations about children's internal working models and attachment organizations. Klagsbrun and Bowlby (1976) presented photographs of children separating from their parents to children aged four to seven years and Wright, Binney, and Smith (1995) used similar photographs with children aged eight to twelve years. Both were adaptations of the Separation Anxiety Test (SAT) developed by Hansburg (1972) for use with adolescents. In these procedures children are asked about the reaction of the child in the photograph and then about what the child might do. Main et al. (1985) also used photographs, but these were actually of the children and their parents: the photographs were simply handed to the children with no accompanying inquiry. The children's reactions to being handed the photograph were later rated to assess security of attachment. Kaplan and Main (1985; cited in Bretherton et al., 1990) examined aspects of attachment representations from family drawings produced by children. For more extensive descriptions of these various techniques, readers are advised to refer to the original works or to Pearce and Pezzot-Pearce (1997). As is evident from these brief descriptions, no commonly accepted clinical assessment tools are available, although many of the above offer assessors some useful strategies. At all times assessors must remain aware that not every response is significant. Children sometimes experiment with new actions and ideas they encounter during assessments, and assessors need to talk with them about their play and responses, essentially testing the limits to determine if the play represents their actual experiences and representational models. Assessors must also remember that conclusions cannot be based on only one task or response. Conclusions are strengthened when patterns emerge from historical information, interviews, observation of interactions and reunions with caretakers, and children's play and responses to tasks such as those noted above.

Play Assessment

As is evident in the above discussion regarding general and specialized areas of inquiry, the assessment of children often relies heavily on their verbal interactions. However, some are so young, delayed, or deprived that their verbal skills are limited, reducing the information that can be gained from direct interviews. Others are apprehensive about directly discussing provocative events and feelings. Consequently, assessors must use alternative assessment strategies that are sensitive to these factors. Play assessment sometimes permits children to express views and feelings in more indirect and less anxiety-provoking ways, and does not depend as heavily upon their verbal skills. In Chapter 3 we discussed the development of play and what parents could do to support strong play skills. Parenting assessors often need to incorporate play as part of individual sessions to evaluate developmental level and to address specific relationship and emotional issues. This was the intent in the following case.

CASE 32: Brian was five years old when he was referred with his twenty-one-year-old mother, Jenny. Child welfare became involved after police responded to a complaint about a noisy house party. Brian appeared apprehensive and provided little information in direct interviews with the assessor. Given his anxiety, she offered an opportunity to play, in hopes he would relax. Brian immediately set up the playroom to reenact scenes from the party. First, he assumed the role of his stepfather, drinking pretend beer, swearing, and calling Brian names in a loud voice. He then switched scenes and pretended to be himself. When sleeping, he made the sound of sirens and was rudely and roughly awakened. He appeared frightened during this play, running around the room and screaming. Brian proceeded to re-enact this scenario many times.

Brian told the assessor much more about the emotional impact of the party through his play than he could have in a direct interview. Furthermore, when Brian subsequently entered therapy, he communicated primarily through the medium of play about the physical and emotional abuse he had experienced when he had earlier lived with his birth father. Brian's repetitive reenactment of the house party attested to the traumatic nature of this experience and is typical of post-traumatic play as described by Terr (1990). In this type of play children ritualistically construct the same scenario repeatedly, acting out the same series of events that result in the same outcome. Terr asserts that such play reinforces the children's sense of helplessness and lack of control because they do not consider alternate resolutions to the frightening or traumatic events. Brian reenacted the same scenario during each of his individual assessment sessions, seemingly to gain some control and mastery over his reactions and feelings about the experience. However, he did not effectively achieve resolution until he had been in play therapy for some time. While his post-traumatic play was rigid and lacking in enjoyment, he later developed more relaxed play with age-appropriate content.

Assessors also need to observe both content and process of the play, noting the themes and topics that emerge, how children manage emotionally provocative issues that arise, and how they relate to assessors during the play. Some are open and direct with the assessor; some are aloof; and some are hostile and provocative, either verbally or behaviourally, seemingly to elicit harsh reactions from the assessors. Other children's play is so disorganized it seems incoherent, with no themes, coping strategies, or predictable ways of relating emerging. Play also allows us to observe how children handle various demands that assessors place on them and their responses to questions that elicit strong feelings. For example, some ignore any directions the assessor gives them, and others stop playing when assessors ask questions about feelings, such as what a doll is feeling when she gets slapped on the head. Of course, we should never pressure children to respond, and frequent probes and questions can interrupt play in initial stages. Once play is established as an assessment activity, children may tolerate more frequent questions and probes. The initiation of free play where children have some choice and direction over the play may reduce the children's anxiety, thereby easing the transition to structured scenarios to ascertain how children respond to specific issues. The 'story-stem' technique described in the previous section of this chapter is such a strategy. Throughout all play observation, assessors require strong knowledge regarding the nature of play exhibited by children who have not been traumatized so they do not overinterpret their observations. For example, healthy and well-cared-for children may display scenarios where people die or experience defeat in their play.

Psychological Testing

Formal psychological testing is often warranted, and the general descriptions and guidelines outlined for adults in Chapter 9 likewise apply here. To efficiently gather data we must carefully select tests to answer specific questions raised in the assessment rather than using a standard battery for each and every case. However, there are a number of tests assessors frequently use in parenting assessments to evaluate behavioural, cognitive, and emotional aspects of children's functioning, and we will provide a brief description of these instruments.

Behavioural Inventories

Many assessors begin with a formal behavioural questionnaire completed by caregivers that identifies whether children's behaviours are typical of average children or whether they are clinically problematic. Commonly employed behavioural surveys include The Child Behavior Checklist for Ages 1 1/2–5 (CBCL/1 1/2–5) (Achenbach, 2001a), The Child Behavior Checklist for Ages 6–18 (CBCL/6–18) (Achenbach, 2001b), the Connors' Rating Scales – Revised (CRS–R) (Conners, 1997), and the Behavior Assessment System for Children (BASC) (Reynolds & Kamphaus, 1992). These instruments have several forms that can be completed by parents and caregivers, teachers, and even the children themselves. Some include forms for rating direct observations of children in various settings. All provide separate norms for boys and girls and for children of different age groups. The subscales on the different forms of the same instrument tend to vary somewhat, primarily because children naturally exhibit some variation in their behaviours in different settings.

The CBCL/6–18 yields Social Competence and Problem scales as well as Internalizing, Externalizing, and Total Problem scores. The problem scales are: Withdrawn, Somatic Complaints, Anxious/Depressed, Social Problems, Thought Problems, Attention Problems, Rule-Breaking Behaviour, and Aggressive Behaviour. A separate profile can also be scored for DSM-Oriented scales that include Affective Problems, Anxiety Problems, Somatic Problems, Attention Deficit/Hyperactivity Problems, Oppositional Defiant Problems, and Conduct Problems. The parent version of the CRS-R for children aged three to seventeen years uses a smaller pool of items than the CBCL/6–18. Its fourteen subscales include Oppositional, Cognitive Problems, Hyperactivity, Anxious-Shy, Perfectionism, Social Problems, Psychosomatic, and a Global Index in addition to specific subscales that help clinicians identify and diagnose problems with attention and hyperactivity using DSM-IV criteria. Parents generally require grade eight to nine level reading abilities. The BASC is the newest of these behavioural questionnaires and includes an F index to assess the possibility that the responder has rated the child in an inordinately negative manner. If this happens, results are interpreted cautiously. The BASC includes clinical scales (Aggression, Anxiety, Attention Problems, Atypicality, Conduct Problems, Depression, Hyperactivity, Learning Problems, Somaticization, Withdrawal) and adaptive scales (Adaptability, Leadership, Social Skills, and Study Skills). As is evident in these brief descriptions, these instruments have some overlap in the behaviours surveyed, usually making use of more than one in any specific parenting assessment redundant. Consequently, assessors should review them carefully, examining ease of administration and scoring as well as behaviours surveyed, to choose the one that is likely to be the most useful in their particular cases. Some of the questionnaires have computer-scoring programs that generate written summaries of the findings. However, assessors must strive to gain a global understanding of the parents' functioning to gauge the influence of parent biases and perceptions on the way they fill out such instruments regarding their children.

COGNITIVE AND ACHIEVEMENT TESTS

A number of psychological tests are available to use in situations where concerns exist about children's cognitive and academic functioning, and some of these also have programs for computer scoring. Some widely used tests include the Wechsler Intelligence Scale for Children-IV (WISC-IV) (Wechsler, 2003), the Stanford-Binet Intelligence Scale – Fourth Edition (Thorndike, Hagen, & Sattler, 1986), and the Kaufman Assessment Battery for Children (K-ABC) (Kaufman & Kaufman, 1983); the K-ABC is currently in the process of revision and the WISC-IV is newly released. Again, one's choice of an instrument should depend on the children's ages, the particular questions that arise in an assessment, and your competence in both administering the test and interpreting the results. All these instruments have similarities and differences in the scores and information they yield. For example, the WISC-IV is very commonly used in school systems, yielding a Full-Scale score, factor or index scores (Verbal Comprehension, Perceptual Organization, Working Memory, Processing Speed), and specific subtest scores. It is useful for predicting school success and learning problems. The WISC-IV helps psychologists identify when children are not learning at levels that are commensurate with their cognitive abilities, particularly when achievement is assessed using a test such as the Wechsler Individual Achievement Test – Second Edition (WIAT-II) (Psychological Corporation, 2002). Other achievement tests are available, as are curriculum standards that are used in different states and provinces. Likewise, a number of tests examine specific learning and ability deficits. For example, the Beery-Buktenica Developmental Test of Visual-Motor Integration (VMI) (Beery, 1997) is a quick test that requires children to copy designs, trace designs, and recognize similar designs. It permits assessment of visual-motor integration, an ability that affects children's abilities to produce written work at school. The Brown Attention Deficit Disorder Scales for Children (Brown, 2001) and the Brown Attention Deficit Disorder Scales for Adolescents and Adults (Brown, 1996) can contribute to diagnosis of attention disorders, as can the CBCL/6–18, the CRS–R, and the BASC, described above.

When children are low functioning and relatively nonverbal, some of the commonly used intelligence and achievement tests do not delineate their skills and competencies adequately. In these cases, information about their developmental status and adaptive functioning can be surveyed with instruments such as the Vineland Adaptive Behavior Scales (Sparrow, Balla, & Cicchetti, 1984). This scale is either completed by various caretakers or teachers or these people are interviewed to survey children's functioning across a number of domains. It yields an Adaptive Behavior Composite and scores in the following areas: communication, daily living skills, socialization, and motor skills scores. Such an instrument might have particular applicability in a parenting assessment where children are mentally challenged or are affected with fetal alcohol syndrome because it assesses practical skills required for daily living.

Tests for Assessment of Emotional Functioning

Additionally, psychologists often formally examine children's emotional functioning with a number of different tests. Self-report forms allow children to describe their own emotions and behaviour. Instruments that are specific to the impact of abuse and traumatization include the Traumatic Event Interview Schedule (Pynoos & Eth, 1986), CITES (Wolfe, Gentile, & Wolfe, 1989), and the Trauma Symptom Checklist for Children (TSCC) (Briere, 1996). For example, the TSCC is a fifty-four-item self-report measure that evaluates post-traumatic stress and other related symptomatology to identify children who are 'at-risk' and who may require follow-up care. When psychometric measurement of anxiety is desired, tests such as the Children's Manifest Anxiety Scale – Revised (CMAS-R) (Reynolds & Richmond, 1978) or the State-Trait Anxiety Inventory for Children (STAIC) (Speilberger, 1973) might be employed. We will not review various other self-report tests that examine specific dimensions of children's emotional functioning, such as self-esteem, depression, and fears. When such tests are used, one must cross-validate the scores with results from other observations and data sources. This principle also applies if one is evaluating children's use of dissociation to cope with traumatic experiences. While scales to evaluate dissociation in adults are available, we have found it useful to use descriptions by Lewis and Yeager (1994) and Lewis (1996) in assessing dissociation in children. These are not formal instruments, but the descriptions are clear and useable. We summarized dissociative symptoms for observation and direct questions for children in our previous book (Pearce & Pezzot-Pearce, 1997).

The Family Relations Test (FRT) (Bene & Anthony, 1985) often provides information regarding children's perceptions of and feelings about specific people in their lives. It has two versions, for use with children three to seven years old and seven to fifteen years old, and assesses both their positive and negative feelings about family members as well as their perceptions of these people's feelings towards them. The intensity of feelings can be rated. Children tend to enjoy this task, where they assign statements to different family members; for example, 'This person in the family nags sometimes' may be assigned to their mother while a statement like 'This person in the family can make me feel very angry' is directed to a teenage sibling. The FRT can provide a sense of children's perceptions of the overall emotional tone in their families.

Psychologists may also employ an array of projective tests that survey a broad range of psychological characteristics and dynamics. Some are similar to adult versions: various stimuli are presented to children, who then structure responses based on their own perceptions, which may or may not be related to their actual experiences. Perhaps one of the first projective tasks used in children's interviews is an extension of the draw-a-person task. A drawing of a person not only gives information about children's developmental levels, fine motor co-ordination, and co-operation, but if assessors ask about the drawn person they can derive an understanding of more emotional aspects of children's functioning. One might ask what the drawn person is doing, what would make him or her happy, sad, angry, scared, and worried, and how the person would show these feelings. For example, Mike (Case 29) chose to draw a picture of himself and said he would get angry if his parents argued and would exhibit his anger by pinching his sister; this was a direct description of his experience at home and his typical response. His sister denied that anything made her angry, clearly reflecting her attempt to cope with these strong affects through avoidance. This drawing technique can be extended to include specific requests for children to draw their families, themselves, their feelings, their dreams, or specific situations or events such as their maltreatment. Assessors can follow the children's lead but ask questions to derive as much information as possible from the task(s). If children cannot draw or are decidedly uninterested in such tasks, one can propose alternate tasks such as play or storytelling to better engage them.

Various forms of sentence completion tests that are similar to adult forms can be employed with children; these include the Rotter Incomplete Sentences Blank, Second Edition (Rotter, Lah, & Rafferty, 1992), discussed in chapter 9. Children's versions vary significantly and are usually framed in simpler language with topics that have more applicability to children. Depending on the specific issues of interest, some assessors even develop their own sentence stems. Often the beginnings of sentences range from the innocuous ('I wish ... If I had my way ..., School is ..., Being sick ...') to more provocative beginnings ('I hate ..., What gets me into trouble is ..., When the kids don't play with me ..., Children would be better off if their parents ...'). While children are sometimes defensive and do not always respond with statements that represent their true feelings and views, their responses can often be interesting and informative. Similarly, assessors can ask for three wishes from children, or ask them about what animal they would choose to be if they were not a person and why they would want to be that specific animal. A child who wants to be a lion may have a very different view of his or her status in the world than one who wants to be an ant or even a worm. Assessors can also ask children who they would choose to live with them if they were shipwrecked on a desert island and why they would choose this person. Since most young and securely attached children choose a parent, it is worrisome when they pick a relative stranger or a television character as their island companion. In such cases, children may truly have no expectations that their parents could protect them or even keep them company.

Other projective techniques can be profitably utilized to gather information about children's psychological functioning. The Thematic Apperception Test (TAT) (Murray, 1943) can be used with some older children and teenagers; Bellack (1993) developed the Children's Apperception Test (CAT) for use with children between the ages of three and ten years. The first uses black-and-white drawings of people and the second drawings of animals to elicit stories. Many children prefer the Roberts Apperception Test for Children (RATC), developed by McArthur and Roberts (1982), primarily because the drawings are of contemporary children and seem more realistic and active. Likewise, although the photos used in the Tasks of Emotional Development Test (Cohen & Weil, 1971) are obviously from the mid-century, many children seem not to notice and tell specific stories about their feelings, peer relationships, and home life in response to those photos. The Projective Story-Telling Test (Caruso, 1987) was specifically developed for use with maltreated children, and its stimuli are more likely to elicit scenarios about physical and sexual abuse. In these various projective tests, stories are elicited, recorded, queried, and then examined to identify children's routine ways of perceiving and responding to various situations. The specific dimensions that are scored vary depending on the particular test, and some, such as the Roberts Apperception Test (McArthur & Roberts, 1982), have the advantage of a quantitative scoring system. Stories children tell to such pictures may reflect their actual experiences and behaviour. For example, Randy (Case 3) produced highly disjointed stories where characters had difficulty resolving any issues or dilemmas. Virtually none of his stories had any effective resolution, and at times he grossly misperceived the stimuli. In response to a picture where an adult female appears to be comforting a boy, Randy indicated that the mother was about to get mad at the boy, yell and hit him, and then send him to the store to buy her cigarettes. They would later snuggle while watching a romantic movie.

The Rorschach can be employed with children in much the same manner as it is with adults. However, Exner (1993, 2002) has developed specific norms for children's responses to examine such aspects of their functioning as reality testing, perception of themselves and relationships, and usual ways of handling feelings and stress. Again, as with all other psychological tests, one should never draw conclusions based solely on Rorschach results. Findings are more robust if other test data, direct observations, and reports of parents and others produce consistent descriptions of the patterns in children's functioning. Assessors should also obtain specific training and experience in the use of tests so they can administer, score, and interpret findings in an acceptable manner.

Observations of Parent/Caregiver–Child Interactions

Since we have already devoted much attention to describing observations of parent-child interaction in the previous chapter and in various discussions of attachment behaviours, we will not further discuss children's reactions in the waiting room, office, or home. Instead, our earlier descriptions can guide assessors to become keen observers regarding how children respond to others.

Collateral Contacts

By the end of individual interviews and family observations, most assessors have a clear idea of information they wish to obtain from collateral references. Many of the guidelines for contacting references outlined in chapters 8 and 9 are appropriate when contacting references that are primarily child centred. Probably the two types of references who provide the most useful information about children are alternate caregivers and teachers, although we must keep in mind that they sometimes exhibit bias and lack of sophistication in their observations.

Alternate caregivers include babysitters and daycare workers as well as foster parents. The latter can be particularly valuable observers because they not only live with the children but often have contacts with the children's parents. Assessors need to find out the specifics of their involvement, recording its duration and the reasons for the placement; some placements are preplanned, with family members being prepared for the transition, while others are precipitous, usually following an emergency removal of children from parental care. Besides asking about many aspects of children's behaviours to obtain a well-rounded view of their current functioning, one should seek specific information about the children's adaptation to the foster homes, the feelings they might express about their parents' absence, and their reactions to visits with family members. It is worrisome when children change homes easily and without any apparent sense of loss or disruption to their functioning. One must ask how they relate to foster parents, specifically their reactions to directions and limits, discipline, and positive displays of caring. Exploring foster parents' feelings about the youngsters placed in their homes can be reflective of the difficulties children exhibit in relationships. For example, some children act provocatively to keep foster parents emotionally distant or even ensure that their caregivers request their removal from the home. This tends to frustrate and unnerve foster parents, who then begin to doubt their skills and personalize the children's behaviour. This may set off an escalating cycle of harsher and more punitive parenting, which in turn reinforces youngsters' beliefs and expectations that they are unworthy of love and commitment. As a result, in order to gain a sense of control over this rejection they believe is inevitable, children behave even more provocatively.

Similarly, babysitters and daycare workers can offer information about children's daily functioning, particularly their abilities to respond to demands and routines and their capacity to relate to other people. Some can also comment on how very young children and their parents relate when the latter leave their children (separation) and then return (reunion) at the end of the day.

Teachers are particularly valuable collateral references given the considerable time they spend with children; teachers who are experienced and sensitive may offer excellent observations about learning, behavioural, and social problems evident in the classroom. In response to specific questions, they can often provide detailed descriptions. Since teachers have ongoing relationships with children, they can speak to the children's styles of relating to themselves and their peers. They may also describe the children's progress in mastering the developmental tasks outlined in Chapter 3, as well as suggesting strategies that may help children with these tasks. Finally, some teachers voice concerns about abuse and neglect and may have either reported the families to child welfare or attempted to facilitate the provision of additional therapeutic services. When children have possible learning or other problems in school, in-classroom observations and consultations with school psychologists, speech therapists, and occupational therapists can supplement information already gathered. One should always ask to review current and past report cards or, if these are not available, review children's academic cumulative records.

11 Case Conceptualization and Development of Recommendations

Organizing the File Contents

Once all information is collected, assessors are left with the tasks of integrating the information and making recommendations. The first of several steps to ease the process is simply housekeeping. If files are not in order, now is the time to divide the files into subsections, collate each client's information, and use our checklists to see that all notes, test results, and other documentation are present. If any data are missing, one should collect them, as they may be needed to buttress and support one's conclusions. Score any tests so these results are readily available in the integration process. Also, we should list contact dates and hours spent in interviews with various family members and in other tasks so these can be referenced during report writing and billing.

Integrating the Information

We begin our integration process by returning to the initial referral information and the agreement with the referral sources or clients to review the specific questions posed at the outset of the assessment. Additionally, we remain mindful that our ultimate goal is reasonable and workable recommendations that optimize chances of improved parenting to enhance children's developmental progress. Consequently, we clearly must focus on strengths as well as weaknesses in the integration process. In those situations where strengths are few and parents are wholly inadequate and responsible for considerable harm to their children, we must integrate and present information carefully. Even when we recommend that all contact be severed between parents and their children, sometimes children need to see their parents to terminate and put closure on their relationships with them. At other times children require some type of contact with their parents, and we need parents to cooperate with such recommendations. In these situations, scathing reports do little to enhance the parents' cooperation. Indeed, Glaser (1995) stresses that blame is seldom helpful, even when parents are responsible for their children's poor treatment. If parents feel they have been humanely treated and if their concerns have been fairly considered and presented, they may be more likely to agree with recommendations, even adverse ones, and settlement without a court hearing may be possible.

PRACTICE ALERT #19
Use multiple data sources to support or discount working hypotheses.

Much information is collected about family members during the process of assessment; clinical notes, testing protocols, and other documentation often make files thick. While assessors employ various methods to integrate this data, we must maintain an awareness that memory and impressions alone are not sufficient as tools in case conceptualization. Instead, a thorough review of file information is necessary to ensure the development of a valid and comprehensive evaluation. We find it useful to make summary sheets that outline initial questions and working hypotheses, identifying data that support and refute the latter. For example, if a reference reported that the mother in a case was dull intellectually, an assessor would be foolish to use this sole statement as a basis for such a finding. Instead, an assessor might record on a summary sheet other validating evidence such as interview presentation, formal testing, past school achievement, employment responsibilities, and previous assessment findings. Not only does this evidence clearly buttress the finding, but the sources of support are then easily referenced in the report. Such clarity also eases preparation for court testimony because we can be specific regarding the source and surety of our findings.

Assessors should identify the children's needs and the strategies that parents and/or other people have employed to meet them, including the potentiating and compensatory factors that affect parental abilities to care for their children in a safe and healthy manner. As file information is reviewed and working hypotheses, children's needs, and risk and compensatory factors are generated, possible recommendations begin to emerge. These can likewise be included on working summary sheets so that as the file review proceeds, some recommendations become increasingly feasible and others are discarded. When a team approach has been used in the assessment, several meetings may be required to merge information and weigh possibilities sufficiently to make workable recommendations.

There are no simple ways to arrive at recommendations but, throughout the integration process, assessors must keep an open mind and ensure that no biases have crept in during the assessment. For example, some parents are not very likeable, and it is easier to make negative recommendations about them than about those who elicit sympathy or seem well intended. One might be tempted to give likeable parents the benefit of the doubt when this is truly not in the children's best interests. Summary sheets may help guard against such biases because we note specific observations, hypotheses, and supporting facts on paper as we integrate information in the file. Such specificity may make it more difficult to form global judgments based simply on likeability. Similarly, such a process may lessen potential biases arising from assumptions about the negative impact of factors such as religion, culture, poverty, and sexual orientation, among others. We must not only review the known information about the impact of these factors on parenting, but also be clear that the task is to objectively and fairly evaluate whether these particular parents can adequately care for specific children.

Arriving at conclusions is seldom easy, but a transactional model facilitates the process because it incorporates child, parent, and social factors instead of focusing upon a single risk factor that would do an injustice to the complexity of parenting. As risk factors increase in number without sufficient accompanying compensatory factors, the chances of poor parenting rise. For example, Brown, Cohen, Johnson, and Salzinger (1998) identified numerous risk factors for child maltreatment in a seventeen-year prospective study in the state of New York. Even though no specific risk factors were most important, prevalence of abuse and neglect rose from 3 per cent when no risk factors were present to 24 per cent when four or more factors were present. Besides the number of risk factors, the severity of individual factors must be noted. For example, a parent with a chronic and low-level depression may still parent well while another with a severe depression becomes immobilized and cannot parent safely. However, decisions are never simple because compensatory factors that mitigate negative impact on children must be considered. The parent with a milder depression may have no family or friend supports and his or her functioning may be in steady decline, with limited response to therapy interventions. Another chronically depressed parent may have relatives who help care for the children, and he or she may exhibit a positive response to treatment. It may well be easiest to make recommendations when children's needs are high and parents have many risk factors and few compensatory factors, and exhibit behaviour that is blatantly detrimental to their children's well-being. Subtler or less severe difficulties on the part of well-intended parents challenge assessors to carefully weigh factors; we must be well-versed on the relationships between compensatory factors and specific risk factors.

Making Recommendations

Specific recommendations vary according to children's needs, parenting capacities, and the context and questions of the assessment. Since options range so widely, we will review some common considerations and recommendations, including those in other assessment contexts, to provide some contrast with child welfare cases. The Commonly Asked Questions section of Chapter 8 also poses questions that naturally lead to different types of recommendations.

The Child Welfare Context

Frequently children in child welfare cases have deficits due to the poor parenting they have received. We must clarify these deficits and arrive at remedial recommendations. Since we must also suggest strategies to enhance parenting, we often have the task of assessing needs of both children and parents. While some families have exhausted all available intervention resources without improvement, others have not received appropriate intervention and must be given more time to respond. We might then offer interim recommendations and delay final suggestions pending various therapeutic endeavours. While this extends child welfare involvement and legal proceedings, the effects can be positive because parents then truly are given reasonable opportunities to change before final decisions occur.

In ascertaining the impact of previous experiences on children, assessors note deficits, particularly difficulties with attachment and trusting others. Not only do attachments between children and their parents figure prominently in developing recommendations, but children's relationships to siblings and other members of the extended family may affect the decision-making process. Many professionals are loath to recommend the separation of siblings, particularly when they also recommend severing the parent-child relationship. However, just as the relationship between parents and children can be destructive, in some circumstances that between siblings is detrimental and the children benefit from separation, as occurred in the following case:

CASE 33: Carl was referred for a parenting assessment following the third removal of his sons Andy and Dennis from his care. The boys were twelve and eight years of age, and both were placed in a foster home pending final decisions about their custody. The assessor believed that while Carl loved his children, he was neglectful and unresponsive to their needs. Following his wife's desertion six years earlier, he frequently left the children alone at night while working as a security guard. He did not discourage Andy's increasing interest in Carl's pornography collection, and he was unconcerned about sexual activity between the boys. During the assessment process Carl realized he could not parent his children and agreed to have them remain in the permanent care of the child welfare department, a plan the assessor strongly supported.

The assessor then considered placement plans, such as an adoptive placement their case worker strongly supported. However, the children were badly damaged, and both had learning difficulties and school and peer problems. Furthermore, their relationship with each other was destructive, and the assessor concluded that they should not be placed together. Andy controlled his younger brother using verbal and physical threats and actions, and he routinely involved Dennis in sexual activities. He was egocentric and displayed no remorse for his actions against Dennis or any of the other children or animals he victimized. The assessor strongly felt that Andy was developing psychopathic characteristics, making him increasingly dangerous as he matured. She concluded that he was not a suitable candidate for an adoptive placement and recommended his placement in a treatment facility for severely disturbed children, with occasional supervised contact with Carl. Dennis's problems were somewhat less severe, but

> immediate adoption was not advised. His needs were identified and he was placed in a treatment foster home, where he responded well and was adopted some years later. The children had infrequent and closely supervised contact with each other for a few years. This prevented Dennis from idealizing his brother and provided a safe situation in which he could confront Andy about what the latter had done to him. His issues about feeling betrayed, powerless, stigmatized, and prematurely sexualized were addressed in ongoing psychotherapy. Over time Dennis realized he was not to blame for what had happened to him, and he acknowledged that Carl and Andy had significant problems of their own; he no longer felt he was responsible or owed allegiance to his father or brother. This understanding eventually permitted him to move on to invest in his adoptive family.

Regardless of whether parents voluntarily relinquish custody of their children or the court ultimately makes this decision for them, assessors often must provide an opinion regarding the advisability of ongoing contact between parents, children, and other family members. Obviously, the quality of children's relationships with parents and extended family contributes to such decisions, and contact is recommended if it is likely to enhance children's functioning. In the above case, Carl loved Andy but could not provide him with the specialized parenting he required. Andy could not be adopted, or even fostered by another family, and required residential treatment placement. However, his father, with proper direction, interacted appropriately to provide Andy with a sense that someone cared, even though the father was no longer the primary caregiver. Other parents cannot be trusted to interact acceptably or even safely, and no purpose is served by their continued involvement. With adoption cases, ongoing involvement may depend on the willingness of adoptive parents to either contact or share information with biological parents or other family members. For example, in the case of Patty and Mary (Case 5), Patty's grandmother maintained regular and beneficial contact, even when Patty no longer saw Mary. Patty's new parents were not threatened; they understood the grandmother's importance and clearly trusted she would not attempt to involve Mary in Patty's life.

Occasionally, when children's prospects of healthy development are utterly dismal, some assessors are tempted to recommend continued involvement with a destructive or toxic family. They reason that it is better for children to have their family than none at all because they expect the children will never relate acceptably to other potential caregivers, sabotaging all potential foster or treatment placements. This may well be a dangerous course of action. When families are truly toxic, we must not recommend their continued involvement but instead search for children's strengths so we can identify potential interventions for them, even if their chance of success is limited. This necessarily entails comprehensive children's assessments and knowledge of available services. Some optimism is always possible because destructive early experiences do not guarantee maladaptation.

The Foster/Adoption Context

Recommendations are not easier in foster/adoption cases, especially when matching has not taken place and assessors must address hypothetical interactions between parents and children who are potential matches. Difficulty is heightened when applicants have never parented or had much contact with children. We must then strive to understand the applicants' strengths and resources as well as their vulnerabilities. Since many children available for foster care or adoption have been previously maltreated, assessors must be particularly alert to potential parents' responses to these histories of maltreatment. For example, when applicants have their own histories of maltreatment, these can influence their reactions to children, either positively or negatively. Parents might very well bring a heightened level of sensitivity and support to the parenting role if they display a coherent understanding of an abusive history, especially if they have resolved feelings about their own experiences. Other applicants, still significantly affected by childhood maltreatment, might overidentify with such children, fail to provide needed structure and support, avoid the children's needs to talk about their experiences, or condemn children's experiences or the perpetrators. Recommendations for two such parents would differ significantly, with placements being advocated for one while the other's application is denied.

Placement recommendations are critically affected by the new caregivers' ability to recognize the impact of abuse and neglect on children as well as their sensitivity to children's reactions to loss. Parents must be able to acknowledge that for children to come to them, they must leave other people such as a biological family, foster family, or even staff and other children in a residential treatment facility. We must assess whether applicants can acknowledge the importance of some of these previous relationships. This can be difficult for applicants, especially when children express strong affection for previous caretakers who mistreated them. Not only must parents accept these positive feelings, but they must acknowledge that these previous relationships will affect children's ongoing adaptation to their new homes, and they must be prepared for a lengthy process, possibly fraught with difficulty. Some of these issues clearly affected the recommendations in the following case:

CASE 34: Steve and Judith, both aged forty-six years, applied to adopt an infant or toddler. They were too old to qualify for a young child and agreed to consider an older child. After seeing ten-year-old Thomas advertised in an adoption fair, they specifically requested his placement, and a parenting assessment explored the appropriateness of this match. They had never parented, having invested all their energy in a small family business. Given their real lack of exposure to children for many years, it was understandable that they knew nothing about typical childhood activities and interests. Both were rigid people with few friends and no nearby family supports. More alarming to the assessor was the fact that Steve and Judith demonstrated no awareness of the issues Thomas might face if he moved to their home. They expected him to adapt easily and be thankful for a nice home and parents who loved him, anticipating that he would be eager to work in their business.

The assessor foresaw many difficulties. Thomas had recently been removed from long-term foster parents because they thwarted adoption plans (removal being a new policy of the child welfare agency, established in an effort to guarantee children permanent placements). Thomas had lived with his foster parents for seven years, but they could not afford to adopt him. Thomas perceived them as his true parents and became highly distressed after leaving them; he had already broken down an interim foster home. The assessor firmly recommended against placement of Thomas or any other children with Steve and Judith. Despite their good intentions, they were too set in their ways to readily adapt to the entry of an older child into their home, given the significant probability that most older children would have difficult histories and an array of problems. The assessor also recommended that Thomas be returned to his first foster home. When child welfare personnel would not agree, he suggested placement in a staffed residential setting and psychotherapy to deal with his sense of loss and to ready him for another parented placement. However, child welfare personnel agreed to some contact with his first foster parents, enabling Thomas to work through some of the trauma associated with their precipitous loss.

When children have not yet been matched with potential parents, we can evaluate the applicants' attitudes and beliefs about parenting through their responses to hypothetical cases. Good insight and coherent and logical decision-making processes around possible parenting challenges enable assessors to specifically recommend the nature and numbers of children that can be placed with applicants. For example, since some children available for placement display sexually intrusive behaviour, foster and adoptive parents must be prepared for such a possibility. During an assessment, candidates might be asked what they would do and feel if they find their new child fondling their own child's genitals. Responses may vary from having the child removed from their home to spanking and punishing the child to inquiring about what happened and taking steps to ensure the safety of all children in the home. Some candidates might also realize they simply would be unwilling to expose their children to such risks. Hypothetical examples need to be graphic so parents truly know what they might face and can demonstrate their reasoning about how they might handle the situation. For example, instead of asking what they would do if the foster child overeats, an assessor might ask what they would do if the child roams the home at night to steal food, gorges to the point of vomiting, and hoards fruit and meat under a mattress until it rots. Parents' abilities to manage other stressful life events may also help explicate how they might manage the stresses of parenting foster or adoptive children. Therefore, one might ask about the most stressful period in their lives, as this can provide information about their coping strategies. We want to determine if parents are apt to make poor choices when they are stressed, even when they 'know better.' Consequently, we need to assess their knowledge of their own personalities, including their strengths and weaknesses and the stimuli that trigger stress and poor decision-making.

The assessment must also explore applicants' perceptions and feelings about the child welfare system; this is particularly important for foster parent applicants because they must maintain working relationships with child welfare staff. Applicants must recognize the value of their own perceptions and input into decision-making on behalf of a child, but they must also be prepared to be part of a team that works to enhance children's development. Some might have had negative experiences with child welfare, either as youngsters or in their role as foster or adoptive parents. If animosity and other negative feelings exist, assessors might suggest strategies to facilitate resolution of feelings and encourage better relationships with workers. Negative feelings are particularly likely when parenting assessments are undertaken following allegations of abuse against foster parents. For example, if foster parents have been investigated for alleged sexual abuse but their foster care worker gave them little support, they have some reason to be bitter even if they were exonerated. Such a circumstance might even preclude further fostering if they cannot put these feelings aside to work cooperatively with others.

Recommendations of placement with specific foster parents vary widely. Examples include: the placement of physically but not sexually abused children, of physically handicapped children, of no more that one or two children, and of only less disturbed children. Suggestions for support services, including respite care, are feasible in some cases, as are recommendations that children receive psychotherapy during and after the placement process. Assessors may also address the contact needed with other significant people in the children's lives. For example, as discussed, Thomas benefited from contact with his previous foster parents. Perhaps the most difficult recommendations are those where assessors do not support the applicants' desire to foster or adopt children. We must be prepared to make such recommendations, putting the children's interests ahead of the applicants'. However, scathing reports benefit no one; we must be careful to make our recommendations in a respectful and supportive manner.

The Custody/Access Context

Although not the focus of this book, it is instructive to briefly examine recommendations in custody/access cases, as some issues are similar to those in child welfare and foster/adoption cases. These cases can differ significantly because assessors usually have the task of recommending which of two estranged parents can best meet the needs of their children instead of determining if parents can care for their children in a minimally acceptable and safe manner. Usually assessors view parents more positively when they support rather than try to prevent children's relationships with the other parent. Of course, such considerations are tempered in instances where a parent truly has a profound negative influence on children or when risks of child abuse, spousal violence, or even abduction are high. Only careful evaluation of allegations such as sexual abuse, spousal abuse, violence, abduction, and alienation can help to determine whether the parent who is adverse to any contact between the child and the other parent is acting in the best interests of the children. This requires skilled interviewing and knowledge, because recommendations have serious implications for children's development and ongoing adaptation to family breakup. We will not review the specifics here; readers may wish to refer to Plass, Finkelhor, and Hotaling (1996, 1997) regarding risks for family abductions.

When there is a high likelihood of violence, abuse, and alienation, we must make recommendations that attenuate the impact on children. For example, if children receive adequate care from a parent who also routinely threatens or abuses the other parent, we may need to recommend that contact between parents be eliminated or closely supervised, with possible provisions to transfer children between parents at school or in a public setting. When safety concerns exist for children, recommendations might include ending or supervising contact between them and their parents. In extreme cases, recommending removal of children from the guardianship of either parent may be warranted, when both parents are unsafe or inadequate. Obviously, in these cases child welfare concerns exist, and recommendations may indeed be similar to those discussed in that context.

Fortunately, many custody/access cases do not involve such extreme concerns. However, ongoing dissension and animosity between parents still affects children, and assessors must make reasonable recommendations to ease these. Thus, they may recommend parameters for contact, such as exact hours and places for children's transfers, holiday access, phone contact, medical responsibilities, and parents' participation in school activities. While detailed, such specific recommendations decrease the conflict between parents who cannot negotiate with one another or cooperate in raising their children. For example, in the case of Della and Tyler (Case 9), the assessor presented exact dates, times, and locations of transfers because Tyler always called to bargain for more time when returning the children to Della. She felt manipulated, angry, and tense because she fully expected him to abduct them. Furthermore, the assessor specified arrangements regarding clothing and toys the children brought from one home to another; Della allowed the children to freely take whatever they wished to their father's home but Tyler did not do so. He also retained those belongings the children brought to his home from their mother's. When these recommendations were followed after the assessment, they helped to decrease some of the conflict between parents.

Finally, assessors may need to recommend therapy for parents and children, perhaps making interim recommendations pending the outcome of such interventions or of pragmatic suggestions such as changes to parenting schedules. Interim recommendations are particularly appropriate when parents have not been previously confronted about their destructive actions. If parents then have sufficient opportunity to change but do not do so, assessors have more evidence upon which to base subsequent recommendations.

Summary

While it is impossible to outline every detail of the integration process and explore all possible recommendations in parenting assessments, the methods outlined above, particularly summary sheets, allow us to consider and integrate a vast array of data. A seemingly impossible task becomes manageable and, indeed, having considered all information, we derive a sense of accomplishment in developing conclusions and recommendations. Of course, these must still be presented to others in written form, in meetings, and on the witness stand. It is to these final aspects of the assessment process that we now turn.

12 Presentations of Findings

After we have integrated the data into a comprehensive conceptualization of the parent's ability to meet the needs of a specific child and have developed a set of recommendations, we must communicate these findings to others who will make important decisions about the child and family. Regardless of a particular assessment's quality, conclusions will be downplayed or disregarded if we do not present them in a complete manner that others can understand.

Guidelines for Report Writing

Stylistic Considerations

The final product in most parenting assessments is a formal written report. Not only is this a format that permits others to examine conclusions in detail, but it is also a good reference for assessors themselves when preparing to verbally present these findings in meetings or court. It should be a comprehensive document that provides a clear outline of procedures used as well as observations and conclusions. Reports can be structured in many ways and employ different writing styles; some can be extensive documents that include all collected information while others are much shorter and document only main findings. The type of report may have been determined during the referral process. For example, some child welfare workers specify at the outset that they want a short report that summarizes assessment findings. Others, such as lawyers who refer clients, might contract for provision of a detailed report to facilitate their task of preparing questions for examination and cross-examination. These variants in style are also affected by the professional training and personal preferences of the assessors. Ultimately, we should prepare reports according to what we believe is professionally indicated, adapting the **detail** provided to facilitate the presentation of a clear picture of dynamics and the need for particular recommendations. Personally, we prefer reports that are relatively detailed but take care to omit irrelevant details such as the colour of the home or the make of the family vehicle. However, what counts as irrelevant can vary. Details that are usually irrelevant are important in some situations; when parents neglect their children but drive an expensive car, this detail is relevant because it demonstrates the low priority they place on meeting their children's basic needs for food and clothing. When deciding about inclusion of specific details, assessors should ensure they are relevant, contribute to an understanding of the case, and influence the subsequent conclusions. A final caution concerns the practice of withholding salient details or observations so these can be presented with some drama on the witness stand, essentially flourishing a 'smoking gun.' We should always strive to have the best interests of children in mind and therefore refrain from excluding critical information in reports. Although court procedures sometimes generate a 'strategic game' atmosphere, we must remain above such grandstanding.

Assessors also vary in how they present and integrate data from multiple sources of information. Again, **styles of presentation** arise mainly from professional training and personal preferences. At one extreme, assessors describe each part of their assessment and/or each test separately. For example, they might describe the mother's various interviews sequentially, her behaviour during the home visit, psychological test findings one by one, and the specific reports of each reference, repeating this for each person in the assessment. The benefits of this approach are that readers, particularly judges and lawyers, know the exact observations upon which conclusions are based. On the negative side, readers are left with the task of integrating the data, a potentially serious problem as they may not have the knowledge and training to understand what is essentially raw data (Tallant, 1983). In addition, parents may become upset with some of the specific observations, perhaps focusing on one or two details while ignoring many valid points. Furthermore, if parents become angry with the reports of specific reference persons, these people can be placed at risk if the parents have problems with anger and impulse control. Generally, in this style of presentation, information is presented in a somewhat piecemeal fashion with integration of the findings happening only in a summary section; because of the somewhat choppy presentation, recommendations may emerge rather abruptly.

At the other extreme, assessors integrate information from several different sources and give broader observations from which recommendations emerge more logically. When this approach carried to its maximum, readers are not always aware of some of the specific data upon which the findings are based. Again, we urge a moderate approach that falls in the more integrative end of the spectrum; we believe it is our task to take raw data and arrive at broader observations and conclusions. However, when making an observation in a report, we often refer to the data upon which it was based. For example, we might state that a parent is unreliable, citing behavioural evidence that he or she missed or came late for several appointments and reporting that others, such as employers, daycare workers, children's teachers, and friends, have witnessed a similar lack of reliability. Likewise, as noted earlier, an observation that a parent is low functioning intellectually can be buttressed by reporting intellectual test results, observations regarding communication skills, and reference reports. Therefore, in this style of presentation, direct observations and other supportive sources of data are grouped together with the observation, rather than being spread throughout the report. This type of citing of data sources is facilitated through the use of summary sheets, as described in Chapter 11: observations and supporting data are naturally grouped together as the summary sheets are compiled, and they can simply be checked off as they are included in the report. Some clients provide the clearest support for an assessor's conclusions in their own words. Do not hesitate to quote a client's verbatim statements if they convey the emotional tone or say something better than you can describe it. For example, in Case 21, Rick explicitly condemned Jan's homosexuality and said her behaviour was 'a perversion of human nature' that would 'corrupt my children's morals and make them faggots.' He made many such statements, but these particular quotes conveyed the vehemence of his views and suggested he was unlikely to support the children to maintain a positive relationship with their mother and her new partner.

We refer readers to Appendix D, which contains two reports about Case 5 that we first discussed in Chapter 4. Comparison of the two reports reveals how different writing styles affect the presentation of data. Version A is written in a more integrative fashion, even though the basic content of both reports is essentially the same. Its integrative focus is most evident in the discussion of psychological test results and the way information from references is incorporated to support observations. Version B tends to list information in a more piecemeal fashion, and readers must work harder to determine the implications of this data themselves. In some parts, details are included that do not contribute significantly to the final opinion, and in others details and observations that would buttress findings are omitted. Generally, Version A presents a more coherent view of the dynamics of the case, leading to the primary conclusion that the mother cannot parent her children. Version B likewise recommends that the children not be returned to maternal care, but it is more muddled and confusing; readers may not be sure how and why the assessor came to the specific conclusions. Also, the conclusion and recommendation section is short and gives little of the reasoning behind the recommendations.

Organizational Considerations

Even when an integrative approach is used, the complexity of assessment reports usually necessitates their division into sections. These vary depending on the specific issues and the number of people involved. Sometimes a few sections that contain broad areas of content suffice, but these also can be divided into smaller subsections. For example, in a child welfare assessment, an assessor may begin with a 'Purpose of Evaluation' section followed by a 'Parents' Views' section that jointly outlines both parents' perceptions and responses to the child welfare concerns. This contrasts with a custody/access assessment report, where a section on parents' views would need to be separated into those of the mother and those of the father. Assessors must give thought to organizational issues, as logical divisions tend to facilitate organization; too many make the report choppy and too few overwhelm readers. Table 12.1 provides a sample of section topics and subtopics that can be used to structure a parenting assessment report in a child welfare case.

Early in the report, and most likely on a title page, assessors indicate its date and authorship; here the names and birth dates of family members are often listed. Reports generally begin by outlining **reasons for evaluation** to set the context for the findings. This includes information regarding who requested the assessment and how the referral originated, indicating if the assessment is court-ordered and citing the order's date and judge's name. It is always worthwhile to

Table 12.1
Typical Section Topics in a Child Welfare Parenting Assessment

- Demographics and Assessment Summary Information (including people, dates, hours, procedures)
- Reasons for Evaluation
- Parents' Views of Child Welfare Concerns
- Child's Findings
  - Parents' Descriptions
  - Psychological Findings
- Parents' Findings
  - Mother's Findings
    - Personal and Family History
    - Current Functioning
    - Psychological Findings
  - Father's Findings
    - Personal and Family History
    - Current Functioning
    - Psychological Findings
  - Marital and Family Functioning
- Joint Observations
- Conclusions and Recommendations

have a copy of this order on file for reference, especially if the judge has posed specific questions in his or her order. If other involved parties have specified questions, these should be recorded. It is also useful to briefly outline previous legal action in the case, including not only any current guardianship order under which the children have been placed but also any previous orders for apprehension and temporary guardianship. The details need not be described, but by briefly listing previous legal actions, assessors begin outlining the chronicity of parenting problems as well as the parents' capacity to change and work co-operatively with child welfare personnel. Similarly, an extensive history of legal action in custody/access cases may indicate rigidity in the parents' views and their inability to work co-operatively. Detail regarding earlier orders is likely to be incorporated either in the section that details the parents' view of child welfare concerns or in the family history section, thereby providing a balanced and comprehensive discussion of the issue.

Finally, in this first section many assessors identify those persons who were assessed, including dates when they were seen individually and jointly, and the specific hours spent with each. The various types of investigation undertaken may be listed here, such as individual interviews, objective and projective testing, joint observations, and home visits. As part of an assessment, evaluators often review varied documents: when we identify these either in this first section of a report or in an addendum, we alert readers to information that contributed to our opinions and recommendations. References who were contacted can be listed in this section with a description of their relevance to the current case, as in 'Ms. Jones, Kaitlin's grade 3 teacher; Mr. Holmes, John's cub leader; Dr. Johnson, family physician; Mel Black, Dick's work supervisor; and Nancy Potts, Molly's best friend.' More extensive descriptions of the references' involvement with family members may be noted later in the report if required. Some assessors go as far as providing detailed descriptions of the comments made by each reference person. We suggest that if such detail is deemed essential, it be placed at the end of the report in an appendix to avoid disrupting the report's flow. However, we prefer to integrate this information directly into the report at the point where it supports observations and conclusions. By doing this, we avoid reporting information that contributed little to the assessment's conclusions.

The next commonly included section is the **parents' view of child welfare concerns**. This section, while seldom long, indicates whether parents agree with or discount the problems identified by child welfare personnel. Here we note the parents' ideal solutions and the steps they have taken or are ready to take to improve their parenting. The section can be rather detailed in complicated cases where child welfare personnel and the court have been extensively involved in the lives of families. Parents may need to describe the circumstances surrounding the many times where concerns were raised. When parents are complying with a parenting assessment only because a court order has been issued, assessors should record this, just as they should note when parents are in favour of an assessment.

Once these preliminary sections are completed, the findings from the assessment follow. These can also be organized in different ways, perhaps with the children's findings being presented followed by those of the parents, or vice versa. In situations where the children's findings are presented first, they may be included under a heading such as **child's findings** with subheadings such as **parent descriptions** and **current psychological findings**. These headings are repeated for each child included in the assessment. The parent description subsection contains parental reports of each child's developmental history and comments about the child's current daily functioning. The latter includes parents' perceptions about the impact of maltreatment and loss of family on each child. Since children, particularly young ones, often have difficulty recognizing the impact of their family on their own functioning, the current psychological findings subsection usually includes information from psychological testing as well as findings from interviews of the child and other family members. Again, when we write in an integrated manner, we allow readers to derive an accurate picture of the child because we incorporate information from various sources, such as report cards, foster parents, daycare workers, and teachers, into our descriptions.

Sections about the parent's findings are divided into **mother's findings** and **father's findings**. A first subsection usually includes **personal and family history** as recounted by each parent. Some assessors note that they cannot speak to the accuracy of this recorded history, instead noting that it represents the parents' perceptions of their own histories. However, it is useful to record when other documentation and references refute the veracity of any of the parents' information. For example, Jackie (Case 1) was a notoriously unreliable historian, and this was noted in the report by citing the sources that refuted her statements. If a more in-depth recounting of the history of child welfare involvement, as related by parents, is not included in the section that addresses their views of child welfare concerns, then it is usually integrated into the family history.

The purpose of the next subsection is to describe the parent's **current functioning** across several domains, much as outlined in Chapter 9. This includes parents' views of their own functioning as well as the assessor's observations, and leads easily into results from any psychological testing. These can be included in the current functioning subsection or placed in another subsection, perhaps called **psychological findings**. Generally, when results from formal psychological testing are placed in a separate subsection, the findings are buttressed by facts from earlier history and current functioning sections. However, a test-by-test recount, perhaps lifted from computer printouts, tends not to be useful: we should integrate information from tests, interviews, and other sources to arrive at descriptions that accurately describe a parent's psychological functioning. Once we describe the findings from one parent, we then review those of the other. Some assessors next include a section that describes **marital and family functioning**. This section addresses not only how the parents relate to each other as a couple, but how the family functions as a whole, including the parents' capacity to care for their children in a healthy and safe manner. Results from joint interviews and home observations may be integrated into this section or set apart in another section, possibly entitled **joint observations/home visits**. In both sample reports in Appendix D, the writer chose to describe the specific observations made when the family interacted together and put these in a separate section entitled 'joint observations.'

The final section usually contains **conclusions and recommendations**. If the report has already integrated findings for each person and then the family as a whole, this section can be relatively brief. It is often sensible to summarize broader family dynamics here, with conclusions leading logically and directly to recommendations. For example, in Case 30 the assessor had already detailed the damage that Ralph and Bruce experienced because of their father's abuse and his inability to acknowledge their trauma or his responsibility for it. The assessor had also outlined the father's personal psychological dynamics that made it impossible for him to respond to treatment. Hence, the conclusions section was brief, recapping these observations and strongly recommending that the children not be returned to him and that contact cease for the time being, pending both the boys' response to treatment and the possibility that, in the future, they might need to confront him about the abuse. In other cases, especially when assessors make interim treatment recommendations, this section becomes lengthy because specific treatment needs are described, as are those behaviours and areas of functioning that parents must change prior to their children being returned to their care. While specific recommendations can be embedded in the final discussion, social workers, lawyers, and judges often appreciate an additional point-form list of recommendations that clearly and concretely address initial concerns. Considerable care should be taken in writing the conclusions and recommendations because, although it is the final section, it is usually the first to be read by others, who sometimes have powerful reactions. If the section is written poorly or disrespectfully, readers are likely to assume an adversarial stance, lessening the probability that they will acknowledge concerns or take needed action.

Pragmatic Considerations

Reports are further enhanced by ensuring they appear polished and professional. The use of good-quality paper or even simple white paper with a tidy letterhead creates a formal impression. Since many reports are lengthy, page numbers and an index facilitate access to information. The typescript should be easy to read, and the manuscript needs to be free of any spelling and grammatical errors. While some jargon is unavoidable, it should be limited so that parents and other professionals can understand the content; an explanation of technical terms in simpler language enhances reader comprehension.

There are two general formats for conveying the assessment results and recommendations in written form. The report can be written as a letter to the specific referral source; section headings are incorporated but usually an index and addenda are not included. This format often works well for shorter reports or for assessments concerning two or three people. An alternative format employs a title page, index, findings, and sometimes addenda, making it longer and more formal. Cover letters are used to forward it to referral sources or other people specified in the initial contract. Both reports and letters must be signed by assessors. Generally, when child welfare has contracted the assessment, the report is sent to the involved worker, who then provides copies as necessary to child welfare's legal counsel, who distributes it to the parents' attorneys.

A final note concerns the use of addenda; these add length to reports but can be reasonable additions, as when lists of references are included. Also, if assessors have not previously provided their curriculum vitae or credentials to workers or lawyers, these may be attached. Occasionally, we have seen parenting assessments where all clinical notes and raw test responses/scores are included in a report's addendum. Not only does this make reports hundreds of pages long, but if the reports are poorly written, readers are left with the task of making sense of this information. Additionally, the practice of including psychological test data is inadvisable because access to such information is limited to psychologists; inclusion in an open appendix violates good practice and ethical principles. Parents and lawyers always have the option of having another psychologist review psychological test data, and assessors, when called to the witness stand, are usually asked to bring their entire file and can be examined and cross-examined on test findings in detail.

Guidelines for Meetings

Frequently, either before or after preparation of the written report, assessors meet with others such as social workers, parents, and lawyers to discuss results and recommendations. Although more informal than subsequent court testimony, these meetings must be treated with some seriousness, since they can influence the extent to which others accept the opinions. On occasion, they may even divert the matter away from a court trial if there is a high degree of agreement among the parties. Again, it is critical to treat all parties fairly, respectfully, and tactfully. This is especially important when presenting information to parents, particularly when you have recommended that children not be returned to their care. When bad news has to be presented, it is sometimes useful to begin by outlining children's difficulties and follow with parents' strengths and efforts to make beneficial changes. The assessor then reviews problems that have precluded significant change in parental functioning, possibly concluding with the fact that such change may take years and children cannot wait, as they may become increasingly damaged in such an environment. Furthermore, children's developmental needs cannot wait indefinitely. It is critical to remain calm and nondefensive, even if parents begin to cry or criticize and scream at you. Recognize and reflect that you understand their upset and disagreement, and that this is your 'opinion' and they are free to disagree with it. In cases where parents flood assessors with questions, we may refocus them by asking them to limit their questions to a few of the most important ones, perhaps beginning with 'Given that our time is limited, I can only respond to ...'. In other cases where parents begin to repeatedly justify their behaviour, we can refocus on the children's difficulties and what can be done to improve their situation.

In cases involving less dire recommendations, meetings still cover the same issues and assessors must offer clear and brief reasons for recommendations. It is important to be fully aware of your material in order to present the findings and answer questions clearly and succinctly. In meetings with lawyers, it is particularly important to consider your replies carefully, as they may ask probing questions to determine whether your opinions are firm or whether you can be pressured or led to change them.

Guidelines for Court Testimony

Familiarize Yourself with the Setting

The opportunity to offer testimony in court may be anxiety provoking for some clinicians, but it can also be a rewarding and challenging experience as long as assessors are well prepared and clearly understand their role in this adversarial process. Before you testify for a first time, it is beneficial to familiarize yourself with the legal arena, perhaps by accompanying supervisors or fellow professionals to observe their testimony, or simply by attending in court to watch some child welfare cases. When a specific case is closed to public viewing, you will need to gain permission from the court to observe proceedings. Depending on the jurisdiction and level of court, courtrooms vary in the formality of their procedures and their expectations regarding the deportment of professionals. Assessors should familiarize themselves with the rules that govern courtroom procedures and with basic aspects of the physical setup, such as seating arrangements and the location of the bar, witness stand, microphone, and other parts of the courtroom. Court employees, if asked, readily offer information and direction about procedures. One should also be familiar with transit or parking arrangements so such mundane problems do not add to one's anxiety or even cause one to be late for a court appearance.

Lawyers, particularly the person calling an assessor as witness, often may help to prepare you, especially if this is the first time you have testified. The goal of this preparation is to enhance your presentation of evidence, making it clear, credible, and reliable. This person may offer instructions about where to sit and what to call the judge, and he or she will likely also review procedures for admission as an expert witness. Additional review may focus on questions that he or she might ask you, perhaps also anticipating and reviewing questions that might be asked in cross-examination.

Testifying

NOTIFICATION

Most assessors are notified that they must testify through receipt of a court **subpoena** that compels attendance at a specific court on a specific day. Since these notices are distributed several weeks prior to the court date, you should always check with child welfare workers or lawyers a few days before the scheduled appearance to verify that attendance is still required, as matters may have settled out of court or been adjourned. You should also ascertain the exact time you will be needed at the hearing; trials are often set for several days, and workers usually attempt to give professionals narrower time frames to avoid wasting your time and to lower costs, as both waiting and testimony time are reimbursed.

ARRIVAL AT COURT

It is prudent to arrive a few minutes early to wait in the designated area prior to your testimony. It is common for the lawyer calling you as a witness to speak with you now, particularly if he or she has not already done so. Your physical presentation on the stand, although seemingly a minor concern, sets the tone for the seriousness with which your testimony is taken; by dressing professionally you show respect to the court and lend further credibility to your opinions.

TAKING THE STAND

Witnesses are not usually permitted in the courtroom until it is their turn to testify unless special arrangements have been made for expert witnesses to listen to the testimony of other witnesses. As noted above, procedures in the courtroom vary somewhat from jurisdiction to jurisdiction; we will describe one common scenario. When the time for your testimony arrives, you will be asked into the courtroom and instructed to take the witness stand. Usually your subpoena will have instructed you to bring your file, and you take this and a copy of your assessment report to the stand. Make yourself comfortable but maintain an erect posture and avoid nervous habits such as nail biting. If a glass of water is not provided, you may ask for one so this is available throughout your testimony. You will be asked to state your **full legal name**, spelling it so it is recorded accurately, and you will then be asked to swear that you will truthfully provide evidence. Witnesses are commonly asked to swear an **oath** on a Bible but, if this runs counter to your religious beliefs, you will be asked to affirm that you will tell the truth. You should let lawyers know ahead of time if you are unwilling to swear on a Bible so judges can be appropriately notified.

QUALIFICATION AS AN EXPERT WITNESS

The next step is an application to be accepted by the court as an **expert witness**. As outlined in Chapter 2, expert witnesses not only offer first-hand observations but are permitted to provide opinions. You may be asked to provide a copy of your **curriculum vitae** so it can be entered as an exhibit in the court record. Ensure that this is up to date and written in a formal style. Judges may accept or refuse applications for admission of professionals as expert witnesses based on several criteria. Leonoff and Montague (1996) offer an excellent description of criteria that are used, for example, in Canadian law. They report that professionals must offer information that has relevance to the case at hand, and it must be deemed necessary to help the judge appreciate the issues specific to the case because it is not part of common knowledge and is technical in nature. Evidentiary issues may be raised about an assessor's testimony, particularly regarding the amount of second-hand or hearsay evidence used in forming opinions. For example, this might happen when an assessor undertakes minimal interviews with family members, basing opinions primarily on other reports, and/or including psychological tests that were administered by other practitioners. Courts usually exclude hearsay evidence, but since assessors rely on both personal observations and the reports of others, including authoritative reports in the literature, this evidential rule is seldom fully enforced in these cases. However, lawyers may actively challenge the admission as expert witnesses of assessors who rely too heavily on hearsay information. Lawyers are usually already aware of the type of methodology and the amount of hearsay information that has been used in a parenting assessment, given earlier receipt of written reports. Sometimes this issue of hearsay evidence also becomes problematic when one member of a clinical team presents results from a parenting assessment undertaken by several clinicians. In this case, the witness provides second-hand information about the findings of other professionals.

Another criterion for admission concerns the need for assessors to have acquired special or particular knowledge, through either study or experience, regarding the matters about which they will testify. They need to demonstrate expertise, have a good reputation, and perhaps have published in the field. Finally, they must have employed methodology in the assessment that has both clinical and scientific value, particularly as viewed by others with expertise in the same field.

This information about qualifications is presented through a process where one lawyer first asks a witness to describe his or her qualifications and related experience, followed by cross-examination by the other lawyer. After examining the above factors as well as weighing the potential benefits of an assessor's opinion against its prejudicial potential and the court time required for testimony, judges either admit or deny a particular assessor's application for admission as an expert witness. If the application is denied, an assessor may still be required to testify about first-hand observations without providing opinion evidence. Often a clinician's first application for admission as an expert in a particular field is the most difficult, as he or she might be 'raked over the coals' about experience and qualifications; this can be traumatic if assessors are relatively new to their professions or this practice area. However, it is part of the process, and after several admissions as an expert most assessors have less difficulty. Even when assessors are admitted as expert witnesses, judges may later attach little weight to their evidence if problems with the assessment are identified during direct examination and cross-examination or if assessors perform poorly on the stand and are not credible. It is important to note that courts vary in how broadly they are willing to define an area of expertise. Some courts may accept a broad definition such as 'an expert in child psychiatry,' while others designate narrower areas such as 'an expert in parenting assessments in child welfare cases' or in 'family dynamics in child welfare cases.' Obviously, it is important for potential expert witnesses to define their area of expertise appropriately through consultation with the lawyer who calls them as a witness.

DIRECT EXAMINATION AND CROSS-EXAMINATION

Once admitted as an expert witness, assessors are examined and cross-examined about their observations and opinions. However, at any point during this process judges can ask questions of the witness. Testimony begins when the lawyer who called you as a witness undertakes the direct examination or, as it is called in some jurisdictions, the examination-in-chief. The four general purposes of this examination are to build or support his or her client's case, to weaken the opponent's case, to strengthen the credibility of the witness, and to strengthen or weaken the credibility of other witnesses (Leonoff & Montague, 1996). Generally, if child welfare has arranged for the assessment, then the lawyer who undertakes the direct examination is the lawyer who represents the child welfare department or the Children's Aid Society. Most lawyers begin by asking why the assessment occurred and if a report was prepared. A copy of the report is usually presented to the witness to confirm authorship and ensure all pages are present. This becomes an **exhibit**, being numbered and entered in the court record. Even though styles of examination vary, most lawyers endeavour to get the majority of an assessor's findings entered in the record, along with information about the source and validity of the data upon which conclusions are based. Our testimony is enhanced when we support our observations or statements by referring to specific behaviours, quotes, and even test responses garnered during clinical interviews. Given that we are sometimes asked about test reliability and validity, we may need to have reviewed this information so we can provide it during testimony. Since some lawyers go through the report paragraph by paragraph but others prefer to have the expert witness review the findings and then ask their questions as needed, it is important to clarify the lawyer's questioning style ahead of time, as testimony will necessarily vary as a result.

Following the direct examination, the other lawyer or lawyers involved in the hearing have the opportunity to cross-examine the witness. Cross-examination has three purposes: to weaken, qualify, or destroy the opponent's case; to support the party's own case or the testimony about the opponent's weaknesses; and to discredit the witness (Leonoff & Montague, 1996). Given these goals, it is not surprising that cross-examination is often the most difficult part of testifying. The cross-examiner endeavours to undermine the professional's conclusions and credibility so the judge discounts the evidence. Hence the lawyer tries to prove that the witness is not knowledgeable, has not used appropriate assessment procedures, or is so biased he or she did not undertake a fair and objective assessment. At times, the manner of cross-examination may be accusatory and negative. Despite such questioning, it is critical for witnesses to remain calm, responding in a professional and patient manner. If the tone and questions of the cross-examiner become clearly inappropriate, the other lawyer usually objects and the judge subsequently rules whether the questions should be answered or withdrawn.

During examination and cross-examination, it is tempting to reply to the specific lawyer who asks the questions. However, given that it is the judges who must be convinced by testimony, it is important to direct replies to them and to address them properly. Lawyers or court staff can be asked whether something such as 'Your Honour' is acceptable. Furthermore, it is important to take time in responding to questions, ensuring that you clearly understand them. It is perfectly acceptable to ask for repetition or clarification, thereby enabling you to reply succinctly and directly; rambling and obtuse responses detract from your presentation. Conversely, witnesses who respond too briefly decrease the effect of their testimony because they have not adequately explained the information and theoretical bases of their conclusions. It is always important to reply clearly, adding qualifiers as needed. Occasionally, when lawyers ask for one-word answers (e.g., 'yes/no') but these seem inappropriate without added qualifiers, we can identify this limitation and try to add the additional information. However, we should limit our responses as directed by the judge.

On occasion, witnesses are asked questions they cannot answer: it is unreasonable to expect even an expert to know everything. It is better to acknowledge uncertainty than to reply with an off-the-cuff response that cannot be supported. Lawyers often attempt to evoke such responses to undermine credibility. If they can demonstrate poor reasoning or a lack of supporting data, then the entire testimony may be called into question. A similar situation arises when witnesses become defensive. It is better to acknowledge the weaknesses in a parenting assessment than to insist that omissions do not matter or become insulted when such problems are identified. However, these situations sometimes present excellent opportunities to instruct the court about the importance of the contribution of various factors to parenting ability. For example, if a parenting assessor was involved some months or years previously, he or she might specify the salient factors that need to be considered now even when the assessor does not have current knowledge about the status of these issues in the family. Judges might keep these factors in mind as they consider evidence provided by other witnesses.

Hypothetical questions may also provide opportunities for identifying important factors. For example, if a simplistic hypothetical scenario is presented, an expert witness might explain that more information is needed before he or she can respond. The assessor might then discuss the specific information about factors and dynamics that would be necessary in order to make various recommendations. Hypothetical questions tend to be employed when facts in a case are disputed or when the witness does not have first-hand knowledge of the facts (Leonoff & Montague, 1996). In a hypothetical question, a lawyer presents a scenario of facts and asks for a specific opinion based on them. Hypothetical questions are most effective when the details outlined in the scenario are later proven true through the evidence of other witnesses. For example, an expert might state that daily drug and alcohol use dramatically increases the risk of poor parenting in response to a question about a hypothetical family where parents are addicted. If it can be proven that the parents in question use drugs and alcohol heavily, their case is weakened, particularly if it is their witness who responded to the hypothetical question.

Lawyers also may attempt to promote confusion in order to discredit witnesses, by repeatedly asking the same question in different ways in hopes of eliciting contradictory responses. It is therefore critical for witnesses to carefully consider all questions, particularly repeated questions that seem to differ only slightly, and to remember what they have already said so their responses remain consistent. After answering the same question several times, witnesses can state that they have already provided an answer, but repeated questioning does have some value. Repeated, clear, and consistent responses strengthen one's testimony, and they also afford judges and lawyers more opportunities to fully understand the reasons for the witness's opinions and responses. Legal personnel may not be conversant with the ideas presented, and repeated explanations can be instructive, reinforcing the importance of specific concepts and factors. However, judges do not let the process go on indefinitely, and some may stop this type of questioning relatively quickly. During such questioning, it is important for witnesses to remain patient and calm, not becoming either irritated or rude. Judges will order an end to a line of questioning when they are assured that witnesses are firm and consistent in their responses and that the matter is clarified.

A final point concerns discussions witnesses have with people outside of the courtroom. While an opportunity for this may not arise in brief court appearances, parenting assessors sometimes testify for several hours on one or more days if their assessment is complex or highly disputed or if several lawyers for different parties have representation in the hearing. For example, lawyers for child welfare, parents, children, and even grandparents may all need to question a particular witness. In such circumstances, court recesses are called to accommodate meals, short rests, and nightly breaks. Once sworn in, witnesses usually are instructed to refrain from discussing their testimony with anyone, such as lawyers, clients, and spouses, until dismissed by the judge. This proscription remains in place in the event that court is adjourned for the day and witnesses must return later to complete their testimony.

DISMISSAL

Once cross-examination is complete, and barring no further questions from the chief examiner, the cross-examiner(s), or the judge, witnesses are usually discharged from their witness role. In some circumstances, they are asked to remain available for further questioning but, usually, once they are dismissed they may leave the courtroom.

Personal Preparation for Testifying

The role of an expert witness is demanding, and we are likely to perform optimally if we clearly appreciate our role and are well prepared. We must recognize that, while we may be experts in our fields, we do not possess all of the evidence pertaining to complex matters; our role is to provide direct evidence and opinions based on specialized areas of knowledge. Furthermore, it is up to us to present our evidence fairly and convincingly so that judges find it useful in making decisions that are truly in the best interests of children; it is not our job to pass judgment. Remaining humble about our role and what we can offer provides a balanced perspective and reduces the pressure we place upon ourselves.

It is critical to prepare carefully for testifying, even when assessment results seem unequivocal. Just as we must review all data when compiling reports, we may need to do the same in readying ourselves for the stand. Not only must we review and perhaps highlight the parenting assessment report, but we often benefit from reviewing our complete file. Salient interview and test data can be highlighted and tabbed for easy reference during actual testimony. Summary sheets, prepared as part of our integration process in report writing, can guide our review of data that supported various conclusions, thereby shortening the needed review time. Preparation often takes several hours and, given that many hearings have late settlements or adjournments, it is prudent to avoid preparing well in advance of the scheduled date. No preparation is necessary if the case settles, and a second round of preparation is necessary if the case adjourns. Repeated preparation may become costly for assessors because they are likely to be paid for only one round of preparation for each court appearance. Assessors should expect to receive remuneration for their court time, discussing the specifics of their fee payments prior to their testimony.

Is the Parenting Assessment of Value?

The value of any particular parenting assessment lies in its ability to accurately evaluate parents' abilities to adequately care for their children, thus contributing to decision-making that is in the children's best interests. However, it is sometimes difficult for people who are not conversant with the procedures and issues in parenting assessments to know whether completed assessments are of value or whether their findings should be discarded. Consequently, we will list several questions that readers and users of reports can ask themselves to determine the value of any particular report. These questions apply to findings presented in meetings or on the witness stand, but they have primary applicability to parenting assessment reports, since these tend to be the most common format for presentation of findings.

1. Does the report identify who was assessed, when the sessions occurred, and the procedures that were used?
2. Does the report identify why the assessment was undertaken?
3. Does the report appear to be comprehensive, covering all of the major areas that need to be surveyed to arrive at reasonable and workable conclusions? The reader should ask, 'Are there major gaps and missing blocks of information?'
4. Is the report written in language that allows the reader to comprehend what is being said? The reader should ask, 'Do I understand this?'
5. Is the report written in a simple, organized, and direct manner? The reader should ask, 'Do I get lost because of the report's style?'
6. Does the report present believable and accurate pictures of both children and parents? The reader should ask, 'Are the descriptions of people in the report congruent with my knowledge of them?'
7. Does the assessor integrate information, indicating sources for observations and conclusions? The reader should ask, 'Does this make sense or do I feel like I must figure it out?'
8. Do recommendations flow from the findings or do they seemingly come from nowhere? The reader should ask, 'Do I get surprised by the conclusions?'
9. Does the assessment answer the specific questions posed in the referral? The reader should ask, 'Does the assessor answer my questions?'
10. Are recommendations practical and viable, addressing specific features of the case, rather than being so general and routine they could be applied in nearly any case? The reader should ask, 'Will the recommendations be useful in making decisions about the children?'

Finally, assessors can use these questions themselves to critically review their reports and ensure they are genuinely useful. The task of parenting assessment is challenging but rewards can be great, particularly when children's lives are enhanced, either through improved parenting or through removal from unsafe and toxic caregivers. Furthermore, children, either immediately or afterwards, may come to appreciate decisions that were made as a result of parenting assessments – highly gratifying feedback for assessors who have agonized over recommendations. Bruce, who was described in Case 30, often voiced appreciation that the assessor and his child welfare worker had convinced the judge to permanently take him away from his father. Since these feelings emerged regularly in therapy, Bruce and his therapist later wrote letters of thanks to these people and the judge. Bruce truly felt he would have suffered continued abuse and even been killed if the assessor and judge had not thoughtfully and meticulously considered information about his family and his life.

Appendix A
List of Practice Alerts

#12 Always obtain signed releases of information before contacting references for family members. 192

#13 Approach all parenting assessments with an open mind and do not make early assumptions that may affect your interactions with family members or your interpretation of the data. 196

#14 Use psychological tests to explore specific issues rather than as routine procedures in all parenting assessments. 229

#15 Inform references about the limits of confidentiality that exist regarding the information they provide to you. 242

#16 Employ developmentally appropriate language, play settings and materials, and test procedures with children involved in parenting assessments. 246

#17 Make the assessment environment safe for both children and assessors. 250

#18 When children begin to disclose details about previously unreported abuse, obtain only enough information to know a report to child welfare is necessary, thereby avoiding multiple interviews and possible contamination of evidence. 261

#19 Use multiple data sources to support or discount working hypotheses. 291

Appendix B
Task Checklist

Contracts

- ❑ Promised: start ______________________________
  finish ______________________________
- ❑ Estimated hours
- ❑ Primary participants ____________________________
- ❑ Retainer received

Interviews

- ❑ Set appointments for parents
- ❑ Set appointments for children
- ❑ Complete testing
- ❑ In-office observations
- ❑ Home visit(s) and observations in other settings

Other Information

- ❑ Child welfare file reviewed
- ❑ Reference lists
- ❑ Consents signed for contacting references
- ❑ References contacted
- ❑ Other materials received

- ❑ Other materials reviewed
- ❑ Other materials returned to parents
- ❑ Drug testing (if needed)
- ❑ Criminal checks (if needed)

Report

- ❑ Check and organize file information
- ❑ Score and interpret psychological testing
- ❑ Write report
- ❑ Edit report
- ❑ Notify clients/lawyers/agencies that report is ready
- ❑ Prepare invoice/receive full payment
- ❑ Release report

Appendix C
Sample Checklist for Information Collection

PARENT #1

Assessment

- ❑ Reasons for
- ❑ Ideal outcome

History

- ❑ Family of origin
- ❑ Relationship/marital
- ❑ Education
- ❑ Employment

Current functioning

- ❑ Physical health
- ❑ Mental health
- ❑ Relationship/marital
- ❑ Employment
- ❑ Finances/income
- ❑ Extended family
- ❑ Friendships
- ❑ Community
- ❑ Recreation
- ❑ Pragmatic roles in the home
- ❑ Drug use
- ❑ Alcohol use
- ❑ Criminal behaviour
- ❑ Expectations in 5, 10, 20 years
- ❑ Strengths/weaknesses

Description of Child(ren)

- ❑ Birth history
- ❑ Developmental history
- ❑ Current needs
- ❑ Expectations in 5, 10, 15 years

Mental Status

- ❑ Brief or more elaborate exam

Psychological Testing

- ❑ MMPI-2
- ❑ Sentence completion
- ❑ WAIS-III
- ❑ Child Abuse Potential Inventory
- ❑ Parenting Stress Index
- ❑ Projectives (TAT, Rorschach)
- ❑

References

- ❑ Personal friends
- ❑ Employer
- ❑ Work mates
- ❑ Children's teachers
- ❑ Daycare
- ❑ Alcohol/drug counsellor
- ❑ Probation officer
- ❑ Parents

PARENT #2

Assessment

- ❑ Reasons for
- ❑ Ideal outcome

History

- ❑ Family of origin
- ❑ Relationship/marital
- ❑ Education
- ❑ Employment

Current functioning

- ❑ Physical health
- ❑ Mental health
- ❑ Relationship/marital
- ❑ Employment
- ❑ Finances/income
- ❑ Extended family
- ❑ Friendships
- ❑ Community
- ❑ Recreation
- ❑ Pragmatic roles in the home
- ❑ Drug use
- ❑ Alcohol use
- ❑ Criminal behaviour
- ❑ Expectations in 5, 10, 20 years
- ❑ Strengths/weaknesses

Description of Child(ren)

- ❑ Birth history
- ❑ Developmental history
- ❑ Current needs
- ❑ Expectations in 5, 10, 15 years

Mental Status

- ❑ Brief or more elaborate exam

Psychological Testing

- ❑ MMPI-2
- ❑ Sentence completion
- ❑ WAIS-III
- ❑ Child Abuse Potential Inventory
- ❑ Parenting Stress Index
- ❑ Projectives (TAT, Rorschach)
- ❑

References

- ❑ Personal friends
- ❑ Employer
- ❑ Work mates
- ❑ Children's teachers
- ❑ Daycare
- ❑ Alcohol/drug counsellor
- ❑ Probation officer
- ❑ Parents
- ❑

CHILD #1

Assessment

- ❑ Reasons for

Current functioning

- ❑ Physical health
- ❑ Mental health
- ❑ Temperamental characteristics
- ❑ Relationships in family/extended family
- ❑ Relationships with other adults
- ❑ Abuse/neglect inquiry
- ❑ School
- ❑ Friends
- ❑ Interests/activities
- ❑ Responsibilities at home
- ❑ Reactions to discipline
- ❑ Attachment/IWMs
- ❑ Coping strategies

Mental Status Exam

- ❑ Brief or long version

Psychological Testing

- ❑ Drawings, wishes, island
- ❑ Sentence completion
- ❑ WISC-IV
- ❑ Beery
- ❑ Roberts Apperception Test
- ❑ Rorschach
- ❑ Behaviour Problem Checklist
- ❑ Family Relations Test
- ❑

Behavioural Observations

- ❑ In-office

- ❑ Home
- ❑ Other

References

- ❑ Teacher
- ❑ Previous key daycare worker
- ❑ Family physician
- ❑ Speech therapist
- ❑ Mental health therapist
- ❑ Grandmother
- ❑ Foster parents
- ❑
- ❑ CHILD #2

Assessment

- ❑ Reasons for

Current functioning

- ❑ Physical health
- ❑ Mental health
- ❑ Temperamental characteristics
- ❑ Relationships in family/extended family
- ❑ Relationships with other adults
- ❑ Abuse/neglect inquiry
- ❑ School
- ❑ Friends
- ❑ Interests/activities
- ❑ Responsibilities at home
- ❑ Reactions to discipline
- ❑ Attachment/IWMs
- ❑ Coping strategies

Mental Status Exam

- ❑ Brief or long version

Psychological Testing

- ❑ Drawings, wishes, island
- ❑ Sentence completion
- ❑ WISC-IV
- ❑ Beery
- ❑ Roberts Apperception Test
- ❑ Rorschach
- ❑ Behaviour Problem Checklist
- ❑ Family Relations Test

Behavioural Observations

- ❑ In-office
- ❑ Home
- ❑ Other

References

- ❑ Teacher
- ❑ Previous key daycare worker
- ❑ Family physician
- ❑ Speech therapist
- ❑ Mental health therapist
- ❑ Grandmother
- ❑ Foster parents

Appendix D
Sample Reports

This appendix contains two reports about Case 5, first discussed in Chapter 4, to demonstrate how different writing styles affect the presentation of findings. The following is part of a discussion found in Chapter 12 in the section Guidelines for Report Writing.

Version A is written in a more integrative fashion, even though the basic content of both reports is essentially the same. Its integrative focus is most evident in the discussion of psychological test results and the way information from references is incorporated to support observations. Version B tends to list information in a more piecemeal fashion, and readers must work harder to determine the implications of these data themselves. In some parts, details are included that do not contribute significantly to the final opinion, and in others details and observations that would buttress findings are omitted. Generally, Version A presents a more coherent view of the dynamics of the case, leading to the primary conclusion that the mother cannot parent her children. Version B likewise recommends that the children not be returned to maternal care, but it is more muddled and confusing; readers may not be sure how and why the assessor came to the specific conclusions. Also, the conclusion and recommendation section is short and gives little of the reasoning behind the recommendations.

ABC CONSULTING SERVICES

123 ANY STREET, ANY CITY

Dr. K. George — Telephone (333) 333–3366

Parenting Assessment

(Version A)

Children:	GRAY, Patricia Mary	Date of Birth: June 16, 1990
	GRAY, Gary Paul	Date of Birth: January 2, 1997
Mother:	GRAY, Mary Irene	Date of Birth: December 6, 1964

Prepared by

Dr. Ken George

on October 4, 1998

Purpose of Evaluation

Mary Gray was referred on June 3, 1998, for a parenting assessment regarding her children, Patricia (called Patty), aged eight years, and Gary, aged one year. In her referral, Ms. Pamela Jones of the County Children's Aid Society questioned Mary's capacity to safely care for her children, given a lengthy history of child protection concerns. At referral, the children were in foster care under a nine-month temporary guardianship order issued on March 31, 1998. They had been apprehended from their mother's home, where they had been left alone all night. Ms. Jones questioned the nature of Mary's psychological and emotional profile, particularly as it related to her alcohol and drug addictions and her ongoing ability to adequately provide for her children. Ms. Jones also asked for evaluation of Patty's emotional and learning status, questioning the impact Mary was having on her daughter. Finally, Ms. Jones requested recommendations concerning custody of the children, i.e., return home or proceed with an application for permanent guardianship, and asked for suggestions regarding their treatment needs. The children's fathers had disappeared and were not involved in the current assessment.

Mary was assessed on June 16, July 3 and 31, and September 4, 1998, for a total of 8 hours. Patty was assessed on July 13, 20, and 29, and August 2, 9, 16, 23, and 30, 1998, for a total of 9.5 hours. Gary was not seen individually given his young age, but all three family members were seen together in office for two one-hour sessions on August 24 and September 3, and for two hours in their home on September 13, 1998. Mary was an in-patient at the Drug and Alcohol Rehab Centre for several weeks during the assessment. Four hours were spent in interviewing the following references: Pearl Gray (aunt and foster mother who cared for Mary since the age of nine years); Frances Black (Mary's close friend for seven years), Harry and Joan Kates (foster parents for the children), Nancy Weeks (Patty's grade 2 teacher), Marcia Jacks (daycare supervisor), Mark Johnson (apartment building manager), Dr. White (Any City Hospital Emergency Department), Dr. Hicks (family physician), Tom Banks (treatment director at Drug and Alcohol Rehab Centre), May Burns (Alcoholics Anonymous mentor), Pastor Fisher (Community Church), and Constable Barnes (Any City Police Department). Additionally, the Children's Aid Society file was reviewed on September 9, 1998. Although Mary stated that she did not want an assessment and was participating only to get her children back, she engaged in the process and appeared to be open in her interviews.

Mary's View of Child Welfare Concerns

Mary did not want to undergo an assessment because she felt she was a good mother who experienced only intermittent difficulties. She stated that her aunt, Pearl, and her friend, Frances, provided good support and ensured the children's safety when she was having problems. Although Mary reported a lengthy history of drug and alcohol addictions, she said these difficulties were cyclical and did not detract from her love of her children. Mary minimized child welfare concerns that began when Patty was an infant, strongly asserting the assessment would find that she should immediately resume caring for her children. Soon she expected to finish drug and alcohol treatment, optimistically saying she would prevent relapse by attending Alcoholics' Anonymous meetings.

Findings – Mary Gray (Date of Birth – December 6, 1964)

Personal and Family History

Mary reports a difficult childhood wherein she experienced many losses, but she denies being the victim of any physical or sexual abuse. She was the only child born to Grace Gray, who lived in an isolated rural community. Grace became pregnant during a party but did not inform the father, who was a passing acquaintance, and Mary does not know his identity. Mary's mother had chronic drinking problems and assumed little responsibility for Mary, leaving her with maternal grandparents who were binge drinkers. Mary recounts that as a youngster during parties at their home, she drank beer out of discarded bottles and guests' glasses. She also recalls hiding her grandparents' beer so they could not drink it.

Mary returned to her mother's care at six years of age. Grace had married and her stepfather brought some stability to Mary's life. When she was nine years old, he died in a car accident and she was sent to live with an uncle, Stan, and his wife, Pearl, who resided in a city. Given the previous laxity of her upbringing, Mary rebelled against their rules and expectations, becoming 'incorrigible' according to her own and Pearl's reports. During this time, Mary also learned of the deaths of her mother and grandfather: her mother died of a brain hemorrhage at the age of thirty-three years and her grandfather fell in the path of a train while inebriated. Mary remembers feeling completely abandoned, as she had always fantasized about returning to her mother's care. Mary's problematic behaviour escalated, and she was placed in a residential treatment facility during grade 7. Shortly afterward, Stan died, deepening her sense of loss and isolation.

While in residential treatment, Mary ran away repeatedly, often with other, street-wise adolescents. She views her time in residential placement as schooling for the streets, moving there permanently at the age of fifteen years. She then prostituted to support a heroin habit. Mary states that by the age of twenty-four years she had abandoned heroin for alcohol and prescription drugs. However, in her late teens she escaped life on the streets by marrying John Brown, who was thirty years old. When life with him became dull, she lived with Vince Jones, a drug dealer, who was very physically abusive. Just when Mary says she began to fear for her life, she met Jack Green, who 'saved' her from Vince. Although they never lived together, Mary appreciated Jack's protection. He moved to another city shortly after Mary discovered she was pregnant with his child. Although Jack met Patty once when she was a toddler, Mary lost touch with him and he has not provided monetary or emotional support to them.

Mary discovered she was pregnant with Patty in January 1990 when she was briefly in prison on drug-related charges. Although she asserts that she was framed and therefore should not have been charged, Constable Barnes reports that criminal records show this conviction was the third of three in 1988 and 1989. Apparently Mary was no longer using heroin but still needed funds to purchase alcohol and prescription drugs. Mary says she stopped most of her alcohol consumption after realizing she was pregnant. She consciously decided to keep the baby so she would not feel so alone.

After her release from prison, Mary joined Alcoholics Anonymous and returned to live near Pearl in the hope that this would help her provide a good home for Patty. Although Mary was twenty-five years of age at Patty's birth, she was unprepared for parenthood and became overwhelmed. When Patty was ten months old, Mary placed her with a religious order for three months while she attempted to put her life in order by entering a treatment facility for her drinking. Over the next few years, Mary repeatedly participated in various treatment programs, including Alcoholics Anonymous. She also met Reg Baker, an older man with chronic alcohol problems, during one of these attempts at treatment. They lived together and he acted as Patty's father. However, they experienced difficulties because both were needy and had trouble reciprocating in relationships. Consequently, they separated and then reunited several times, usually because they became lonely. During one separation and during a time when Mary was drinking heavily, she met George Weeks and became pregnant. Mary did not want a second child and became depressed, drinking through to the third trimester, when she entered a treatment facility to sober up. George soon disappeared. Mary did not expect to like the baby, but she 'fell in love' with Gary when he was born, noting that she had had no similar reaction at Patty's birth. Again, Mary vowed to improve her life for her children.

Throughout Patty's childhood, Mary struggled with addictions and entered various treatment programs with no long-lasting positive impact, although she feels she is steadily improving. While Mary reports seventeen months as her longest period of sobriety, references including family, friends, and her personal physician estimate that her longest periods of total sobriety are in the range of two to four months. Relapse usually occurs shortly after reunification with Reg: they begin to use marijuana and then steadily escalate to using prescription drugs and drinking heavily. Mary says they can become very focused on procuring drugs from physicians through reporting fictitious medical symptoms, such as anxiety and headache. During periods of heavy drinking, Mary says she has misplaced her vehicle, lost her driving licence twice (confirmed by Constable Barnes), and awoken to find strangers in her bed that she does not remember bringing home. However, she downplays the seriousness of these events. During periods of sobriety or relative sobriety, Mary says she usually obtains employment as a typist.

Mary reports that despite drug and alcohol addictions, she provided good care to her children, particularly during periods of sobriety. With some pride, she states that she has always ensured their health and safety; when she uses drugs, she places the children with dependable caregivers, such as Pearl or Frances. When questioned about her parenting practices, Mary says she is kind and gentle. However, she had marked difficulty giving concrete examples of her responses to common parenting challenges. She admitted to occasionally spanking Patty but firmly denied the use of any other physical discipline. She asserted that the children have never been sexually abused because she supervises them closely.

Pearl and Frances state that they have provided extensive care for Mary's children, usually on an unplanned basis. Marcia Jacks of the daycare confirmed that she has often called Pearl or Frances to pick up Patty because Mary did not return for her after work. Also, both Pearl and Frances have taken Patty from Mary's home when it seemed unsafe. Pearl and Frances have in the past routinely spent days or weeks caring for Patty. Mary has left Gary with Frances for up to five days even though he is an infant. Both women have occasionally observed the children to be groggy when they arrive at their homes, questioning whether Mary medicates them with cough syrup or other drugs to make them less demanding. Mary firmly denies this, commenting that she sedates them only if they are ill.

Although Pearl and Frances are her primary supports, Mary's relationships with both have been problematic. Both women enjoy Mary's company when she is sober although she can become easily irritated, taking offence at inconsequential behaviours. For example, Pearl reports that Mary did not speak to her for six months last year after she thought Pearl had been overly critical. However, Mary abruptly visited Pearl in late June and rather unceremoniously left Patty with her for six weeks without calling once. Both Pearl and Frances feel used by Mary because she plays on their positive feelings for her and the children. Both also feel that their availability and willingness to care for the youngsters has prevented the latter's permanent removal from Mary's care. The child welfare file indicates there have been ten child welfare reports over the past seven years with three foster placements for Patty. Pearl and Frances are disgruntled: while happy to help out, both are beginning to feel that Mary will never truly change. They are unprepared to take over indefinitely, especially now that Mary has two children.

In regard to formal schooling, Mary's premature emancipation from adult care resulted in completion of only grade 9. She reports that school was easy in early grades; she coped with her tumultuous life by immersing herself in books and learning. This changed when Mary moved to Stan's structured home in the city. She felt bereft and overwhelmed, struggling to fit in. Mary's fell in with the school's 'cool' students, making friends with others who were older. They introduced her to smoking, drugs, alcohol, and sexual activity, exposure that intensified once she entered residential treatment. Her peers offered a sense of belonging, and drug usage allowed her to numb her reactions to the loss of her mother, grandfather, and uncle.

Although Mary did not finish high school, she attempted to gain job skills when she left the street to marry John Brown. Her first drug treatment program included job training, and she opted for secretarial work. She reports that she is an efficient typist, working regularly although her cycle of addictions has resulted in numerous dismissals. However, Mary can present as a well-groomed and smartly dressed woman, and she normally manages to obtain new employment when she is sober.

Since entering her first addictions treatment program, Mary has sought treatment several more times. According to Tom Banks, treatment director at the Drug and Alcohol Rehab Centre, Mary has tried approximately ten inpatient or residential programs in the last eight years. She initially appears to be a responsive client but almost inevitably returns to drug or alcohol usage when she socializes with former friends. May Burns, who has mentored Mary in Alcoholic's Anonymous, says Mary works hard to maintain sobriety. Mary calls when she is doing poorly, and May feels that Mary responds to the guidance she and others offer her. May has supported Mary through several relapses, being optimistic that Mary will conquer her alcoholism. May was unaware that Mary gambles when she is not using drugs or alcohol.

Current Functioning

Mary was in poor physical condition when she presented for assessment in June. She openly stated she had been drinking for at least a week, stopping two days earlier. Mary questioned whether she had experienced delirium tremours the previous day. She also reported an excruciating headache, thinking it resulted from a fall she could not remember. Additionally, she expressed panic that she was dying, stating that her mother had died at approximately the same age. Mary came to her first appointment directly from the emergency department. Dr. White of the emergency department was contacted and indicated that Mary's headaches were likely due to a recent beating. Mary did not remember such an assault, but she admitted to several blackouts over the preceding eight weeks. She said she had been worried about the outcome of the upcoming assessment and so had impulsively gone drinking a week earlier and could not stop.

Given Mary's extremely poor condition and her panic despite a consultation at the hospital emergency department earlier on June 16, we ended the appointment early so she could proceed to see her family physician. Dr. Hicks reported he was so concerned about Mary's medical status that he admitted her to an in-patient detoxification centre the same day. When seen two weeks later after detoxification, Mary presented differently. She was an alert woman of thirty-four years who was both verbal and engaging. Mary was markedly more coherent and no longer felt she was dying: she was decidedly positive, expressing optimism that she could resume parenting after two or three more months of treatment. She stated that her last drinking episode was so bad she felt God had made it happen so she would see what she needed to do to conquer her addictions. Aside from increasing alcohol-related problems just noted, Mary is generally healthy. She is somewhat underweight, but Dr. Hicks reports no chronic diseases such as hepatitis or HIV. Mary is prone to frequent colds, particularly after extended drinking bouts, during which she does not eat or sleep well. He offered the opinion that Mary could physically care for her children, but he also questioned her judgment and other issues that might impair her ability to keep them safe.

Mary resides in subsidized housing and has kept her unit by telling the landlord she expects her children to return shortly. Mark Johnson, the building manager, indicated that Mary is soon to be evicted due to problems with noise violations and unpaid rent. Several loud parties and ongoing domestic fights have disturbed other tenants. Reg was reportedly a regular overnight visitor during the spring.

Mary started working as a typist for Starburst Engineering on September 20. Given the brevity of this employment, her employer was not contacted. Mary says her expected take-home salary is $1400.00 per month with an increase to occur when she gains permanent status after a probationary period. She states that her only debt is a small loan from Pearl, who lent her money last year to repair her vehicle. Mary began her job after finishing the in-patient portion of the program at the Drug and Alcohol Rehab Centre. Tom Banks, program director, indicated that Mary was a compliant client who seemed to enjoy group work. However, he doubted whether she made any true progress in addressing issues, and he did not expect her to maintain sobriety for long. Most of Mary's social network consists of people with past or current addictions who contribute to maintaining addictions rather than giving them up.

Pearl and Frances maintain some contact with Mary, but they have reduced their involvement recently. Mary has virtually no contact with other extended family members who might offer support. However, she says Reg is supportive and she appreciates his input with the children, stating that he is a good stepfather who loves them. Mary says she and Reg have decided to keep separate residences because they recognize it is more difficult for them to maintain sobriety when living in the same home. However, they still see each other regularly. Mary has no current plans to date other men. Reg was unavailable during the assessment as he had entered treatment in another province and had not contacted Mary in the interim. Mary says she relaxes by watching television, reading, and occasionally gambling at the local casino. She finds her local community church to be a particular support, although Pastor Fisher says attendance is sporadic. She disappears when her problems are most pronounced. On occasion, the congregation has provided food hampers and clothing vouchers to the family.

Current Psychological Findings

The contrast in Mary's presentation between the first two sessions is noteworthy; when not abusing substances, she was an alert, verbal, and charming woman of thirty-four years. During interviews, Mary seemed insightful and motivated, using extensive treatment jargon. However, ongoing contact over three months as well as reports from references indicated such a presentation is a façade. Despite having the language to talk about treatment goals and issues, Mary has not effectively addressed her addictions, the losses she experienced, and her low levels of self-esteem. Even when free of alcohol and drugs, Mary displays other addictive behaviours, such as gambling. During a discussion about relaxing activities, she reported losing money at a casino the evening before her September 4 appointment.

Both Mary's behaviours and the results of her psychological testing indicate that she is a person who is likely to develop strong dependencies, such as on alcohol, drugs, and gambling. She also tends to depend on other people for her sense of self-worth. Clinical interview data and results from the Sentence Completion Test and Thematic Apperception Test suggest she is a self-centred person who is needy and strongly wants nurturing and attention from others. She is often preoccupied with how others treat her, taking offence easily. She vacillates between being demanding and clingy to being aloof and rejecting of others. Given her egocentrism, Mary has marked difficulties recognizing the needs of others, a finding exemplified in her relationship with Patty. Mary demonstrated minimal ability to recognize or respond to Patty's needs. For example, she did not think that being in foster care upsets Patty. She has considered surrendering Patty permanently on several occasions, stopped only by her own potential loneliness rather than worrying about the impact on her daughter. Also, despite her love for Gary, she has considered asking Frances to adopt him, again stopping because she might feel lonely herself.

Despite a strong wish for nurturing from others, Mary's interviews and projective test responses indicated that she has low self-worth and often feels unlovable. This contributes to vigilance about how others react to her, and she becomes uncomfortable with strong displays of affection and warmth from them. She then distances others when they are warm towards her but also when she takes offense over their perceived intentions, as in the situation reported earlier when she did not call Pearl for six months. Indeed, Mary becomes rather suspicious of the intentions of others, a finding clearly evident on the Minesota Multiphasic Personality Inventory – 2. She produced a valid protocol, and results also suggested a definite tendency to disregard social norms. Mary is often unpredictable, impulsive, and nonconforming, all qualities often evident in people who exhibit delinquent behaviour. Furthermore, her profile suggested she is likely to be unresponsive to treatment interventions, a finding clearly supported by her long-standing inability to respond to various treatment programs.

These psychological dynamics are complicated by Mary's poor history of relationships and losses. Themes of desertion and poor self-worth were repeatedly evident in interviews and in responses to the Thematic Apperception Test and the Sentence Completion Test. As mentioned above, Mary copes with these feelings by consistently being drawn to and then repelling others who care about her and also by blaming others for her misfortune. Her insight into these dynamics is limited. While treatment programming has allowed Mary to gain superficial knowledge and jargon that engages others in helping her, she also uses such terminology to avoid truly understanding her past or current behaviours and feelings, particularly her pain and emptiness. Instead, she dulls her feelings with drugs and alcohol.

Impulsiveness and lack of true insight were also evident in cognitive testing using the Wechsler Adult Intelligence Scale – Revised, where Mary demonstrated average cognitive potential. She did best with concrete and visual problem-solving, demonstrating quick and organized responding. Mary had much more difficulty when she needed to abstract and compare ideas, abilities that are necessary when she must examine her own behaviour and motivation and transfer learning and observations from one situation to the next. Planning and sequencing abilities were weak. However, Mary concentrated well and had a good vocabulary, characteristics that tend to both impress others and mask her deficiencies. By her own report, Mary has experienced increased concentration and memory difficulties in recent months, perhaps due to her now chronic substance abuse. Her insight declines further and impulsiveness increases when she is stressed. Mary's responding to the Parenting Stress Index indicates she often experiences significant personal stresses, with her children being particularly demanding. When asked what she expected to be doing in ten years, Mary hoped to be happily married but also voiced a fear that she might be dead, much like her mother. She states that she has never contemplated suicide nor has she been admitted to hospital for other than addiction problems.

Given the enduring relationship and psychological difficulties just outlined as well as Mary's lack of responsiveness to treatment programming, her prognosis for change is poor. Her self-centredness and neediness make it difficult for her to relate to other adults. Furthermore, they impact on parenting because Mary would need to put her own needs aside to meet those of her children, an almost impossible task given her psychological profile.

Findings – Patty Gray (Date of Birth – June 16, 1990)

Developmental History and Current Functioning

Patty was born at thirty-six weeks' gestation and weighed five pounds twelve ounces. During the first trimester of the pregnancy, Mary consumed alcohol on nearly a daily basis, reportedly stopping once she realized she was pregnant. When born after a labour of thirty hours that required a forceps delivery, Patty was not immediately responsive. However, she was resuscitated and Mary held her while still in the delivery room. Pearl accompanied Mary through labour and delivery. Although Mary attempted breastfeeding, she placed Patty on formula at three days of age. She was released from hospital at five days and was visited by a public health nurse on three occasions. Patty was immunized and, according to Mary, has been a physically healthy child. Mary found Patty taxing in her early months and sought Pearl's support and care for the infant repeatedly. Mary reports that she has never felt particularly close to Patty and often resented her. When completely overwhelmed by the demands of parenting, working, and staying away from drugs and alcohol, Mary placed Patty with a religious order for three months without visiting, stating that she was too 'exhausted.'

Mary does not recall Patty's developmental milestones but states that Patty was walking when she returned from the religious order at thirteen months. Patty reportedly talked in sentences by two years of age, although Pearl and Frances both say Patty said only single words on her second birthday and did not really communicate clearly until she was nearly four years old. Frances remembers training Patty to use a potty during an extended stay when Patty was over three years old. According to Mary, Patty was a good toddler who amused herself, while Pearl and Frances say she was hungry for adult attention, following them when they cared for her. They note that she was often quite withdrawn around her mother, particularly if Mary was irritable.

Mary had moved the family several times by the time Patty began kindergarten in a private school sponsored by a church. She was withdrawn and struggled to learn basic primary skills, consequently repeating kindergarten in Aspen Street Primary School. In report cards saved by Pearl, her first-year kindergarten teacher writes that Patty was ill-prepared for school, with little apparent prior exposure to books, drawing, or basic routines. She was withdrawn and made few friends. Forty late arrivals were noted in attendance figures. By the year's end, Patty recognized a few letters, had no sound pairings, and could not reliably count to ten. Patty also struggled with routines in the following year but participated slightly more in class activities. By the end of her second year in kindergarten, she recognized and printed the letters of the alphabet, likely because her foster mother, Joan Kates, spent many hours teaching these to her during Patty's four-month placement. Patty remained in Aspen Street Primary while in foster care, but Mary says she moved her to Central Avenue Elementary School for grade 1 to give her a 'fresh start.' Patty did not learn to read by the end of grade 1 even though she had again moved back to her foster home and Joan spent hours tutoring her. Patty also masturbated frequently in class.

Patty is now in grade 2, where she continues to struggle with reading and other learning. She will soon begin work with a resource teacher. Nancy Weeks, who had been teaching Patty for three weeks when contacted, says Patty is withdrawn and struggles with most aspects of the school program. She recognizes occasional words but cannot read fluently. Patty has not learned basic math facts and apparently forgets learned concepts quickly. Printing is messy and work is disorganized. Patty cannot predict the day's routine, requiring constant cues to change activities. Given her aloofness, other children do not seek her out, and Patty acts immaturely in pairings or group projects with peers. Patty never mentions family at school although she sometimes speaks of visits with Pearl, whom she calls 'Granny.'

Pearl, Frances, various daycares, and foster parents have provided alternate childcare to Patty and more recently to Gary. Mary has intermittently used Little People's Day Care. Marcia Jacks, the director, described Patty as a quiet and aloof child who had difficulty learning routines. She was found engaged in sexual touching with other children twice. Staff reported to child welfare authorities on both occasions, but because investigators found Patty uncommunicative and Mary firmly denied any abuse, files were closed. Mary dismissed these reports with me, saying Patty's behaviour had been misinterpreted. Ms. Jacks says that at drop off and pick up, Patty was muted and withdrawn with Mary, who was likewise distant. However, Patty greeted the arrivals of Pearl and Frances warmly.

Patty spent four months in foster care when she was in her second year of kindergarten; Gary was only two months old during this placement. Both children were returned to Mary only to be apprehended again when Patty was in grade 1. Harry and Joan Kates, who are now fostering the children for a second time, report that Patty has been withdrawn during both stays, being quiet and difficult to get to know. She seldom seems to enjoy activities and becomes agitated if others are angry or if they have a glass of wine or beer. While Patty is attentive to her brother and tries to ensure he is fed and changed, she is also mean to him. She pinches him and shoves him roughly when frustrated with him. They suspect she undid the stair gate and pushed him down the stairs in July. Patty must be supervised closely when she plays outside; she seems not to recognize the danger from passing cars and she easily wanders off. Despite the presence of numerous children on the street, Patty has not made any friends. She also treats pets poorly, and one of the family dogs avoids her. Harry and Joan indicate that Patty has marked difficulties with morning and evening routines, requiring many reminders and often physical help to do such things as dress and comb her hair. Patty is robust and healthy, being a good eater. However, she hoarded food in her room during the initial weeks of both placements. She sleeps well after requiring at least an hour to fall asleep. Enuresis only occurs on one or two nights following a visit with Mary; daytime wetting happens occasionally at school but never at home. Patty never speaks to Harry and Joan about her mother, nor does she ask to call her. Likewise, Mary has not called Patty although this option is reportedly open to her.

Mary normally visits the children on weekends for three hours in either the foster home or at Frances's home. She has not had them stay overnight since they came into care. Since Mary misses occasional visits with no prior notification, Harry and Joan have stopped giving Patty advance warning because she withdrew and bit her arms when Mary did not show up as expected. Patty seems pleased with frequent calls from Pearl, and she spends a night with her on a monthly basis. It is important to note that much of Patty's developmental and current functioning information was obtained from Pearl, Frances, and her foster parents. Although Mary gave some descriptions, they were overly positive and not detailed; Mary denied many aspects of Patty's behaviour that are truly concerning.

Psychological Findings

Patty presented as a heavy-set youngster of eight years of age who was initially withdrawn and required more assessment hours than is typically the case. At first, she was unresponsive to questioning and had to be slowly engaged through drawing and play. Although never chatty, she came to relate comfortably, becoming mute and withdrawn only in Mary's presence or when questioned about Reg. Patty's speech was immature and simplistic, gross motor movements were clumsy, and fine motor movements were imprecise. When asked why she was coming to see me, Patty indicated that it was to see if she could return to her mother. She wanted to go home because she worried about Mary, saying she would feel better if she could be at home to take care of Mary. For example, she said she made her mother toast in the morning and kept Gary quiet when Mary had a headache. She also described babysitting and cooking for Gary. Patty said she worried about her mother's drinking, pouring beer down the sink if she found it. While Patty refused to speak directly of Reg, she said she worried more when he was with the family because the drinking got worse. Patty said little about her brother other than to wish he had not been born. She felt Mary favoured him and gave him more attention.

Patty's favourite activity was watching television, and she described several soap operas and game shows she liked. She also liked shopping for clothes with Mary. In contrast, Patty described several enjoyable activities at Pearl's home, including drawing, dancing, baking with Pearl, and playing card games. She particularly liked staying with Pearl for a week or two. She also enjoyed staying with Frances because she had teenagers who played with her and because Frances put ribbons in her hair and cooked good food. Patty did not like school, especially reading. Art was a favourite subject and she liked Ms. Weeks because she was kind. She had no favourite friends.

Given Patty's withdrawn and quiet style of relating, formal assessment was difficult. Patty was unsure of her answers and asked for help repeatedly, becoming sullen when refused. For example, while Patty was comfortable drawing a person, she asked me to do the drawings for her in visual-motor testing. This reticence was not unexpected, since Patty demonstrated a full year's delay on the Beery-Bukentica Test of Visual-Motor Integration. Her human figure drawing was also immature, typical of that produced by children who are at least a year younger. These delays are likely to make printing somewhat frustrating, and it is fortunate that Patty repeated kindergarten given such delays in these skills.

In intellectual testing using the Wechsler Intelligence for Children – III, Patty did best with nonverbal problem-solving, obtaining a performance score that placed her at the 46th percentile. She was attentive to visual detail and approached hands-on tasks with some skill and confidence. Patty was much less strong verbally, as indicated by a verbal score at the 10th percentile, although the presence of significant intrasubtest scatter on verbal subtests suggests her potential is slightly higher. Despite an adequate fund of general information, she had noted difficulties comparing concepts and identifying similarities between them, an ability related to learning generally as well as to the transfer learning from one situation to another. Patty was weak in both her knowledge of social expectations and her ability to apply social knowledge. She missed salient social cues and produced confused and disorganized responses; indeed, she had marked difficulty even understanding task requirements. Patty's processing speed index, which placed her at the 11th percentile, indicated that she cannot process information quickly, a finding that was evident in interviews and that may have particular relevance to school participation. Patty takes longer than the average student to process questions and respond appropriately. However, some school frustration also likely arises because Patty's greatest weakness was in her capacity to concentrate. Her freedom from distractibility index placed her at less than the 1st percentile, well below expected levels. On the Teacher Report form completed by Ms. Weeks and on the Behavior Problem Checklist completed by Joan Kates, Patty scored well into the clinical range on the Attention Problems scale. Distractibility was also evident behaviourally during testing, although Patty's tendency to withdraw when stressed made it difficult to determine the degree to which emotional stresses exacerbate her attention problems. Many issues, such as school work, peer relationships, and family preoccupations, stress Patty.

In regard to achievement, Patty demonstrated delays. On the Wechsler Individual Achievement Test, reading was weak. Patty's word recognition skills were at a mid-grade 1 level, and comprehension was at a kindergarten level. She is just beginning to reliably sound out beginning and end sounds in words. Work with the resource teacher is entirely appropriate as, given Patty's distractibility, she requires a smaller class setting to facilitate attention and target specific skills. Reading problems will also be exacerbated by Patty's weaknesses in sequencing and abstracting. Spelling was at an early grade 1 level. Mathematics skills were also weak and at a beginning grade 1 level for reasoning and a late kindergarten level for computations. Patty had great difficulty with arithmetic questions, not knowing where to begin. Given stronger skills in visual problem solving, Patty would likely benefit from the use of concrete counters and pictures in learning math. Abstract concepts such as time are likely to be problematic for her.

Overall, Patty displays significant learning disabilities that make school challenging. Furthermore, her learning problems are likely to generate added demands for both teachers and parents. While her current class placement is acceptable provided resource room help is available for both reading and arithmetic, it is likely that Patty will require special class placement in the future because she is likely to fall behind without a specialized learning milieu. School will also be challenging given Patty's coping by withdrawal when stressed. Interview data, reference descriptions, and Patty's responding to the Sentence Completion Test and Roberts Apperception Test clearly indicated that she is often overwhelmed socially at school. She does not expect others to respond positively to her and she is vigilant for signs of rejection. Patty has difficulty accurately understanding other children's communications and intentions, taking offence easily. She then withdraws and becomes sullen, making them less likely to approach her. She has minimal abilities to initiate interactions with them and she feels unaccepted by peers. Infrequently, when she feels rejected and slighted she reacts aggressively. During her grade 1 year, Patty impulsively hurt other children several times. When asked about these incidents, Mary underestimated their number and blamed the other students.

Patty's relationship difficulties are also evident in her interactions with adults, particularly her mother. In both direct interview and testing, Patty expressed ambivalence about Mary. Patty rather desperately wants Mary to care, and yet she often feels Mary ignores her and treats her badly while favouring Gary. Some basis for such feelings exists; reference reports and direct observations of the three family members showed that Mary frequently attends to Gary while ignoring Patty, who then becomes hurt and angry. Furthermore, Patty described instances of poor treatment, such as when Mary spanks her, washes her mouth out with soap, and calls her bad names. According to Patty, Mary locks the two children in Patty's room when she goes out, sometimes overnight. Such incidents scare Patty. Although Patty became mute when directly questioned about sexual abuse, she spoke of a worrisome incident when asked about the worst thing that had ever happened to her at home. Patty became agitated and gave a disjointed report about a 'bad party' where several of her mother's friends got very drunk. The incident happened when Patty was 'little.' She woke in the dark to find someone on top of her who 'hurted my bum.' No one came when she screamed, and Mary told her it was a dream when Patty spoke to her about it the next day. Patty also became agitated when asked about Reg, stating that she disliked him because he 'hurted me,' then refusing to elaborate. Mary firmly denied Patty had been abused, discounting her reports as dreams or memories of television shows, and she asserted that Patty and Reg got along well together.

Patty was consistently positive about both Pearl and Frances in interview and testing using the Sentence Completion Test, Roberts Apperception Test, and Bene Family Relations Test. Her current teacher says that both she and Patty's grade 1 teacher view her as happier when she is with Pearl, Frances, or her foster parents. Patty directly states that she feels 'safe' with these adults. When at home, she says she sometimes thinks of running away, not doing so because 'Mom needs me to help with Gary.'

Patty's development has been compromised in several ways. Many of her characteristics are similar to those found in children who have been exposed to alcohol before birth. Since Mary actually describes significant alcohol use in the first four months of pregnancy, Patty should be referred to a pediatrician who can medically assess this possibility as well as evaluate the nature of her attention problems and the advisability of a medication trial. Also, Patty has been affected through her poor relationship with Mary and the apparent neglect and abuse she experienced while in her care. Not only has Patty been parentified, caring for her brother and often her mother, but she has developed a coping style where she withdraws. However, she also infrequently and impulsively aggresses against others when she is angry or feels inadequate. While Patty can usually contain her reactions through withdrawing, such a style does not permit learning of more effective coping methods. Patty clearly has little trust in most people and likely will require specialized parenting and other support and services for some time. Furthermore, although Mary tends to idealize and ignore many of Patty's problems, her behaviours often stress Mary. On the Parenting Stress Index, Mary viewed Patty as a demanding, moody, and distracted child who does not adapt well to change. Mary did not find her characteristics acceptable nor did she find Patty reinforcing to parent.

Findings – Gary Gray (Date of Birth – January 2, 1997)

Developmental History and Current Functioning

Gary presented as a tiny toddler of eighteen months of age although his head seemed particularly small for his body. Given that Mary used alcohol throughout her pregnancy, he should likewise be medically evaluated for fetal alcohol syndrome. Mary reports that Gary was born at thirty-four weeks' gestation, weighing four pounds after a six-hour labour. He was not immediately responsive and remained in hospital for three weeks. Gary had great difficulty feeding and eats little even now. Pearl and Frances report that he was an irritable baby who did not sleep well when they cared for him, but Mary denies this and speaks of his behaviour in a positive manner. However, they note that he slept for inordinate amounts of time when in Mary's care. Within a couple of days of coming to their homes, he became more active and alert but was also more irritable. Both references expressed concern because Gary did not recognize any words except for his name by the age of fourteen months. Joan reports continuing language problems; Gary still does not recognize even common words. Joan had his hearing evaluated, and it is reportedly normal. He walked at nine months. Gary does not yet recognize predictable routines, and he begins to shake violently if others raise their voices around him. His sleep has not improved, becoming even more fitful after visits with Mary. Gary enjoys playing with other children, and he delights in horseplay with Harry. He is affectionate with both foster parents but does not seek contact with Mary during visits.

Although not individually interviewed because of his age, Gary was observed several times in the waiting room, in office visits, and at Mary's home. He was active and related comfortably to foster parents. He tended not to approach either Patty or Mary when seen with them, preferring others, even strangers. Although Mary verbalized interest in and attachment to Gary and stated that he was a delightful and enjoyable youngster, she tended to ignore him when seen jointly. Her responding to the Parenting Stress Index suggested she found him demanding, distracted, and hyperactive, characteristics that make him less reinforcing to her.

Joint Observations

Mary and her two children were observed together twice in office and once in their home. Despite Mary's assertion that she was eager to see the children, she initiated few interactions with them. Instead, she appeared hurt when they did not seek her out to hug her. Mary preferred talking with me even though I encouraged and indeed explicitly suggested several activities they could do together. For example, Mary and Patty attempted to comply with a request to read a book together, but Mary became frustrated with Patty's inattention after a couple of minutes, stating that 'she hates reading.' She was unwilling to persist, and Patty appeared to sense her mother's frustration, becoming quieter and more withdrawn.

Patty was pleased with my home visit, generally ignoring Mary to show me around. The home was tidy and the children shared a room that was safely and appropriately furnished. Ms. Jones of the Children's Aid Society indicated that the home was in complete disarray on the night the children were apprehended. The fridge contained no food and the apartment was filthy. Mary prepared a meal for the children's late afternoon visit, serving macaroni, bread, and juice. While Patty enjoyed this meal, Mary became frustrated with Gary, who did not sit still and spat out the food she fed him. Mary apologized for the quality of the meal, saying she stocks little food when the children are not with her. Mary pointed out a nearby playground that Patty visits on her own. During the home visit, Mary took both children to the playground, but again she preferred to interact with me rather than monitor their behaviour. For example, she did not notice that Patty put Gary on the swings. Had I not noticed and intervened, he would likely have been hurt. The neighbourhood appeared to be relatively safe, but clearly Mary's children require close supervision due to both their ages and their developmental difficulties. Both willingly left with Ms. Jones when she came to return them to their foster home, demonstrating no distress at leaving Mary, who briefly cried and then diverted to speak of other issues.

Conclusions and Recommendations

Although Mary can present as a capable and verbal woman who appears insightful and competent, the current assessment clearly indicates that she has psychological difficulties that impact on personal functioning as well as her parenting capacity. She is a needy and dependent person who has developed a clinically problematic addiction to alcohol, drugs, and gambling that affects all areas of her life. Despite good intentions and many attempts at treatment that include both residential and outpatient programs, she has managed to stay sober for only relatively brief periods. During these, her functioning improves somewhat. However, even when sober she lacks insight into her issues, idealizing the behaviour of herself and the children and blaming others when confronted about potential problems. Despite Mary's assertion that she has recently gained the insight and motivation that will allow her to permanently change her situation, her prognosis is poor given the long-standing nature of her problems.

Mary's capacity to nurture her children and promote their healthy development is limited; she cannot keep Patty and Gary safe from harm. Not only does she leave them unattended and neglect their basic needs for food, supervision, and interaction, but they are at even higher risk for harm during the periods when she is drinking heavily. She drives her vehicle while inebriated and she invites potentially abusive people into her home. As a result, Patty has become a psychologically damaged youngster who has developed an insecure attachment to Mary. Patty has marked difficulties trusting others and has devoted much energy to parenting her mother and brother. Furthermore, Patty displays increasing evidence of learning difficulties, impulsiveness, and attention problems, some of which may stem from Mary's alcoholism during her pregnancy. Such difficulties create specialized parenting needs, as Patty requires extra structure and supervision on a daily basis as well as closer work with teachers and repetitive teaching to acquire all skills. Patty's needs are heightened because of her emotional and relationship difficulties. Gary shows evidence of similar high needs, likely stemming in part from Mary's drinking during pregnancy. Despite Mary's professed favouritism and attachment to Gary and her assertion that she provides well for him, it is likely he has already been negatively impacted by her behaviour in the relatively short time he has spent in Mary's care. Both Patty and Gary are clearly at risk in Mary's care, either directly from her own actions or secondarily from her inaction, which results in abuse by others, or from situations where the children are left unsupervised. In the short term, they are at physically at risk when Mary is inebriated. In the long term, their psychological functioning, capacity to relate to others in a healthy and trusting manner, and general developmental progress will be markedly compromised if they remain with Mary. Consequently, I strongly recommend that the Children's Aid Society immediately proceed with applications for permanent guardianship orders for both children.

In the interim and until such an application is heard in court, the children should have biweekly supervised access with Mary. Should they be made permanent wards, then they, and particularly Patty, should be guided by a child therapist to say goodbye to Mary. Furthermore, given her use of withdrawal as a coping method and the guilt and responsibility that she feels for Mary, Patty should immediately be engaged with a therapist. Despite Patty's somewhat limited verbal skills, I expect her to respond with a skilled therapist who can use play and talking to help her process what has happened in her family. Such involvement is likely to be lengthy, being required through her time in foster care and then through any adoption process. Also, Patty's therapist could later undertake the termination sessions between Patty and Mary. Adoptive homes should be sought for both Patty and Gary, although the matching process is likely to be difficult given the intense and specialized needs of these children. Not only will foster and adoptive parents need to understand the children's difficulties with trust and attachment and emotional problems, but they also need to be able to address their learning and attention problems. Should pediatric evaluation confirm that these children also have fetal alcohol syndrome or fetal alcohol effects, parents will need to be aware of the even more specialized, multifaceted, and long-term input that is required. It is likely that Patty and Gary can be placed in the same home provided that Patty's aggression towards Gary decreases. Finally, given Patty's strong attachment to Pearl and the fact that any security Patty feels has likely derived from this relationship, every effort should be made to maintain contact between these two people. Not only is this critical while Patty is in foster care, but any adoptive family must recognize the importance of this relationship and be prepared to support it through continued contact. While in foster care, Patty may also benefit from some contact with Frances, given her stabilizing influence in Patty's life.

A summary of recommendations follows:

1. The County Children's Aid Society should proceed with an immediate application for permanent guardianship regarding both Patty and Gary.
2. Patty requires urgent and likely long-term therapy with a child therapist to address the sequelae that arise from both her maltreatment and the insecure relationship she has with her mother.
3. Access between the children and their mother should take place on a biweekly basis in a supervised setting, pending results of the permanent guardianship application to the court.
4. Should the children be placed under a permanent guardianship order, Patty's therapist should guide the children to say goodbye to their mother.
5. In the event that a permanent guardianship order is granted, an adoptive home should be sought for the children.
6. Patty requires ongoing contact with Pearl. Any permanent plans for Patty must take this need into account.

Ken George, Ph.D., R. Psych.

ABC CONSULTING SERVICES

123 ANY STREET, ANY CITY

Dr. K. George Telephone (333) 333–3366

Parenting Assessment

(Version B)

Children:	GRAY, Patricia Mary	Date of Birth: June 16, 1990
	GRAY, Gary Paul	Date of Birth: January 2, 1997
Mother:	GRAY, Mary Irene	Date of Birth: December 6, 1964

Prepared by

Dr. Ken George

on October 4, 1998

Prepared for County Children's Aid Society

Purpose of Evaluation

Mary Gray was referred on June 3, 1998, for parenting evaluation regarding her children, Patricia (called Patty) who was about to turn eight years old and Gary, who was nineteen months old. Ms. Pamela Jones of the County Children's Aid Society questioned Mary's capacity to safely care for them because of repeated reports to the agency. At referral, the children were in foster care under a nine-month temporary guardianship order issued on March 31, 1998. Ms. Jones requested recommendations concerning custody of the children, specifically questioning whether the children should return home or whether she should proceed with an application for permanent guardianship. She asked for evaluations of Mary's and Patty's psychological status. The children had been apprehended in March when Mary left them unattended. Since the children's fathers were unavailable, they were not involved in the current assessment.

Family members were assessed in sessions during June through September 1998. Mary was assessed on June 16, July 3 and 31, and September 4, 1998, for a total of 8 hours. Patty was assessed on July 13, 20, and 29 and August 2, 9, 16, 23, and 30, 1998, for a total of 9.5 hours. Gary was not seen individually given his young age, but all three family members were seen together in office for two one-hour sessions on August 24 and September 3, and for two hours in their home on September 13, 1998. Mary was an inpatient in the Drug and Alcohol Rehab Centre for several weeks during the assessment and special arrangements were made for Mary to attend in-office sessions because she had to miss some of the treatment programming. References who were interviewed included Pearl Gray (aunt and foster mother who cared for Mary since age of nine years); Frances Black (Mary's close friend for seven years), Harry and Joan Kates (foster parents for the children), Nancy Weeks (Patty's grade 2 teacher), Marcia Jacks (daycare supervisor), Mark Johnson (apartment building manager), Dr. White (Any City Hospital Emergency Department), Dr. Hicks (family physician), Tom Banks (treatment director at Drug and Alcohol Rehab Centre), May Burns (Alcoholics Anonymous mentor), Pastor Fisher (Community Church), and Constable Barnes (Any City Police Department). Additionally, the Children's Aid Society File was reviewed on September 9, 1998. Mary stated that she did not want an assessment because she felt it was unnecessary, given her good parenting abilities. Although she said she was participating only to get her children back, she appeared to engage in the process and to be open in her interviews. She often arrived early for appointments to have a cup of coffee and chat with the receptionist.

Mary's View of Child Welfare Concerns

Mary did not want an assessment because she felt she was a good mother who only had intermittent and mild difficulties with drugs and alcohol. Mary minimized a rather lengthy history of child welfare concerns that began when Patty was an infant, stating she had plenty of supportive people who took care of her children when problems arose. She specifically named Pearl Gray, her aunt and foster mother, and Frances Black, a friend. Mary said the assessment would show the children should be returned to her care immediately because her difficulties were cyclical and did not detract from her love for her children. At referral, Mary lived in a residential addictions treatment program where she said she was making gains. She soon expected to finish treatment and planned to prevent relapse by attending Alcoholics' Anonymous meetings. She was well acquainted with this organization, having attended it for many years and enjoying the camaraderie that exists.

Findings – Mary Gray (Date of Birth – December 6, 1964)

Personal and Family History

Mary reports that her childhood was difficult because she experienced many losses of people she loved. However, she says she was not physically or sexually abused. Mary was the only child born to her mother, Grace, who lived in an isolated community in the northern part of the province. She particularly enjoyed hikes in the woods and fishing on the lake when she was a child. She also liked playing with her friends and cousins who lived in the rather close-knit community. Mary had several pets in her early years. However, Mary's mother often could not look after her because of drinking problems. Grace's pregnancy with Mary was unplanned: her mother and relatives told Mary that Grace became pregnant during a party but she did not inform the father, who was a passing acquaintance. He was a janitor in a neighbouring community and reportedly was popular with many of the young women in the area. Grace never told Mary of her father's specific identity, and Mary has pondered it for many hours, wondering if she is similar to him. She was unsuccessful in trying to search for him several years ago.

Mary says her mother had chronic drinking problems, drinking at the local bar and often bringing cases of beer home that she would drink by herself or with friends. Given her mother's drinking, Grace assumed little of Mary's care. Mary remembers her mother as a beautiful woman who had soft skin, green eyes, red hair, a pretty smile, and worked in the local lounge. She also has other memories where Grace was mean to Mary or disappeared for days. Mary's maternal grandparents were thus often left to care for her, and they reared Mary until she was nearly six years of age. Mary then moved to live with her mother and a new husband. Grace had met Simon when he made weekly delivery of supplies to the community with his transport truck. Mary liked the truck because it was blue and she could sit high up and see much of the countryside. Mary liked her new stepfather and was very upset when he died two years later. He was killed when his truck slid off a curve and went over an embankment during a snow storm. She remembers the funeral in some detail and says Simon is buried in the family plot near her relatives.

When she was nearly nine years old, Mary was sent to live in the city with her Uncle Stan and his wife Pearl. Stan was a school teacher and Pearl was a homemaker. Stan was eighteen years older than his sister Grace, and Stan and Pearl's three children were grown and gone from home by the time Mary moved to live with them. They already had two grandchildren. Mary's mother and grandfather died after she began to live with Stan and Pearl: Grace of a brain hemorrhage at the age of thirty-three years and her grandfather when he fell in the path of a train while inebriated. Mary attended both funerals and remembers feeling abandoned, as she had always fantasized about returning to her mother's care. Mary says these additional deaths stressed her, and given the previous laxity of her upbringing, she acted up. Previously her grandparents had indulged her and she felt she was special when she was with Simon. After she became 'incorrigible,' she was sent to a residential treatment facility when she was in grade 7. Shortly after her admission, Stan died. Not only was Mary very sad, but she remembers Pearl crying whenever she saw her. Together, they often visited the graveyard where Stan's ashes were buried.

At the treatment centre, Mary says she met many friends that included both girls and boys. She was uninterested in school and says she completed only grade 9. In early elementary years, she had enjoyed school and liked to read. After her move to the city, Mary had trouble fitting in with the students and gravitated towards the 'cool' students, many of whom were older. Mary liked being in on the 'action' at school and later at the treatment centre through smoking, drinking, drug use, and sex. Mary made many connections in the treatment centre that she says prepared her for life on the streets. By fifteen years of age, Mary and her friend Carol ran away and lived on the street with friends. For excitement, they hitchhiked across southern Canada. Mary admits to using drugs, including heroin for several years. She often prostituted to support her habit and found life on the street both exciting and scary. She had very limited contact with Pearl during these several years.

As the years passed, Mary found life on the streets difficult. She escaped it by marrying John Brown at the age of nineteen years. He was ten years older and seemed like a safe and stable person. He did not use many drugs or alcohol and worked reliably as a construction worker. He supported her to stop using heroin, but Mary soon found life with him boring. During the daytime when he was at work, Mary began to use alcohol and prescription drugs. After a couple of years, Mary reconnected with her old friends and left John to live with Vincent Jones. He was a handsome man who was also a drug dealer. Vince was very controlling and became physically abusive towards Mary shortly after they began to live together. She feared he would kill her eventually, being very grateful to Jack Green, a friend who helped her escape from Vince and essentially 'saved' her. Mary had never used birth control despite being sexually active for several years, and was thus surprised when she became pregnant with Jack's child. Their relationship had been casual, and he soon left to seek work in another city. He was aware of the pregnancy and met Patty once when she was a toddler. He has never provided monetary or emotional support to Mary and Patty, and Mary has no knowledge of his current whereabouts. Mary has no pictures of him for Patty but describes him as a tall man with dark hair and eyes. She says he was strong, attractive, and liked to party.

Mary says she discovered her pregnancy in January 1990 when she was in prison on drug-related charges, asserting that she was framed. Mary was soon released from prison and states that she stopped most of her alcohol consumption after realizing she was pregnant. She wanted to keep the baby so she would not feel so alone. Knowing she would need some help, she moved back to the city where Pearl lived and re-established steady contact with her. Pearl was present at Patty's birth and has always been involved in Patty's life. Although Mary was twenty-five years of age at Patty's birth, she was unprepared for parenthood and became overwhelmed. When Patty was ten months old, Mary placed her with a religious order for three months while she attempted to put her life in order by entering a treatment facility for her drinking. After discharge, she began to again attend Alcoholics Anonymous, making a new group of friends. During one of these phases, Mary met Reg Baker, an older man with chronic alcohol problems. They have lived together intermittently throughout Patty's life, and Patty views him as her father. During one separation, Mary had a brief relationship with George Weeks and became pregnant. Mary did not want a second child and drank more because she was depressed. When she entered a treatment facility to sober up, George disappeared, and he is unaware that Mary had a child. She has no knowledge of his whereabouts. Mary did not expect to like the baby but 'fell in love' with him at his birth. Given this, Mary vowed to improve her life for her children.

Throughout Patty's childhood, Mary reports her own sporadic troubles with alcohol or drugs. Mary entered her first treatment program shortly after she married John Brown, and it included in-patient and then day treatment programming. She recounts other treatments, saying she improves with each program she enters. Her longest period of complete sobriety, using neither alcohol nor drugs, is seventeen months. Mary says she usually relapses after she and Reg reunite, but she still finds him to be a support, especially with the children's care. At times, Mary's drug and alcohol dependencies create problems because she cannot remember where she has parked her car and she can become rather focused on obtaining the drugs or alcohol she wants. She feels she maintains the children's best interests at these times because she leaves them with Pearl or her best friend Frances. When questioned about parenting practices, Mary states that she is a kind and gentle mother who ensures her children's safety. She convincingly asserted that they have never been physically or sexually abused, and she states that she attends to their physical needs and to Patty's school needs. Besides caring for her children, Mary maintains intermittent employment as typist. Although she did not finish high school, she has had some job training and is an efficient worker who can always find work when she wants it.

Current Life Situation

Mary reported a severe headache on June 16 and could not complete the interview. She admitted binge drinking for a week and said the headache resulted from a fall. Mary questioned whether she had experienced delirium tremours the previous day after she stopped drinking two days prior. She also worried that she might be dying, being quite panicked as her mother had died at approximately the same age. Mary reports having occasional blackouts. She felt much better on her next appointment two weeks later, having spent the interim in detoxification. On July 3, she was alert and neatly groomed. Mary presented well verbally, being sincere, engaging, coherent, and thoughtful. She expressed renewed optimism that she had overcome her sporadic drinking binges, and she expected she would be ready to resume parenting soon. Mary reports excellent physical health despite being somewhat underweight.

Mary continues to live in subsidized housing because she expects her children to soon be returned to her. Mary and Reg maintain separate residences. Mary began working as a typist for Starburst Engineering during the third week of September. She expected a take-home salary of $1400.00 per month with an increase after she finishes probationary status. She has no outstanding debts aside from a small loan from Pearl, who lent her money to repair her vehicle last year. Mary's primary social contacts are Pearl, Frances, Reg, and people from Alcoholics Anonymous. Mary relaxes by watching television and reading. Occasionally, she gambles at the local casino. She attends her local community church regularly.

Current Psychological Findings

Aside from her first session, when she was in obvious physical difficulty, Mary presents as an alert, verbal, and charming woman of thirty-four years who is insightful and motivated. She capably discusses treatment issues and clearly recognizes she must address the losses she has experienced in her life and monitor her use of alcohol and drugs. Mary was given a battery of psychological tests during the assessment.

On the Wechsler Adult Intelligence Scale – Revised, Mary demonstrated average cognitive potential, obtaining a full-scale score of 94. Her verbal IQ was 90 and her performance IQ was 101. Subtest scores were as follows: information 8, digit span 9, vocabulary 10, arithmetic 9, comprehension 9, similarities 7, picture completion 11, picture arrangement 9, block design 10, object assembly 10, and digit symbol 8. Mary did best with concrete and visual problem-solving, being quick and organized in her responding. She likely does well in her job given these strengths. Mary had more difficulty when she needed to abstract and compare ideas. Planning and sequencing abilities were also weak. Impulsiveness was evident although Mary concentrated well and had a good vocabulary. Mary reported having some concentration and memory difficulties in recent months; these may result from physical problems, times when she is inebriated, and even worry about her children.

Mary produced a valid protocol on the Minesota Multiphasic Personality Inventory – 2 with scores of 43, 60, and 49 on the L, F, and K scales respectively. Her scores on the clinical scales were as follows: Hs 50, D 63, Hy 63, Pd 75, Mf 50, Pa 70, Pt 64, Sc 61, Ma 70, and Si 50. A moderate elevation on the Pa scale suggested a paranoid predisposition. Typically, people who score in this range are hostile, resentful, guarded, and sometimes argumentative. Mary also had another elevated score of Pd, suggesting a tendency to disregard social norms. Here high scorers are typically unpredictable, impulsive, self-centred, and nonconforming, all qualities that can result in poor judgment. While they can be hostile, deep emotional responses tend to be absent. Mary was a 46 code type, but despite the tendency of these people to deny serious problems, Mary seemed insightful and was motivated to change. Furthermore, she did not have the same degree of immaturity, narcissism, and neediness that most people with this code display, nor did she report a poor work history or intense relationship problems. Mary also had an elevated score MAC-R scale, which suggests a risk of developing alcohol or drug problems. While Mary has had some difficulty with these problems, she appears to be making treatment progress and her problems are intermittent.

On the Sentence Completion Test, Mary displayed ambivalence about her mother, a wish for a father, and an irritation with friends who double-cross her. She can be demanding if others do not meet her expectations, and they may perceive her as needy and egocentric. Her responses suggest she may vacillate between being clingy and demanding and being aloof and rejecting. While Mary can feel good about herself, she sometimes feels insecure and lonely. For example, she said she felt lonely when she sees a man and woman together, she feared being alone, and she felt she had been invisible in school, with neither teachers nor other students noticing her. She also felt girls had to depend on other girls for their identity. Mary's responses suggested she has particular difficulty being in charge and in giving directions and orders to others. They also indicated she experiences some frustration with parenting and often feels overwhelmed by the task. While Mary could verbalize about her own feelings, she had trouble recognizing the feelings of others. For example, she did not think Patty minded being in foster care because her foster parents were very nice people. Mary has considered surrendering Patty to the Children's Aid Society on several occasions, and in the Sentence Completion Test she displayed some ambivalence about her.

Mary's responses to the Thematic Apperception Tests were brief and unelaborated. Even so, they revealed issues with losses and neediness in relationships. Mary had difficulty perceiving the emotions portrayed in the stimulus cards, often ignoring the emotions or misperceiving them. For example, on one card where an adult person slouches over a bench with face averted, Mary stated it was very difficult to respond to the card. She eventually said the person was a young child who was sitting and thinking about something. She could not say what this might be and she was unsure of the person's feelings, wondering if he was mad or sad. He would soon be sent to his room but she did not know why. Characters in Mary's stories were often ineffectual, being made to do unwanted things and yet never voicing their feelings or refusing the demands. Profound sadness emerged in some cards, as in one where a young lad is sitting alone in a doorway. Mary felt he was thinking about the death of his grandfather several years prior. The boy goes to water and feed the horses and then prays to his grandfather. However, Mary then became quite disoriented and paused; when she resumed the story, Mary described how the boy would next go to bury the grandfather. Mary's responses on the Thematic Apperception Test suggested she has difficulty responding and developing ways to cope when she must face emotionally difficult situations. When overwhelmed, she sometimes blames others.

The Parenting Stress Index showed that Mary experiences much pressure. Her relationship with Reg can be highly stressful and she finds parenting restricts her activities. Social isolation also increases her stress levels. Mary finds Patty demanding, moody, and distracted. Her daughter does not adapt well to different situations, and Mary does not find her characteristics to be acceptable. Parenting her is not rewarding. Additionally, her responding to the Parenting Stress Index suggests that Gary's demanding, distracted, and hyperactive nature produces stress for Mary even though she always describes him as a quiet and agreeable child who is reinforcing to parent. The negative tone of the scores on the Parenting Stress Index may be somewhat misleading because Mary reports enjoyment of the parenting role, even though she occasionally becomes tired and stressed.

When asked what she expected to be doing in ten years, Mary hoped to be happily married but worried she might die, much as her mother had. She has never contemplated suicide and has never been admitted to hospital for psychiatric problems. Mary's test results suggest her prognosis is relatively poor even though she presents much more positively in personal interaction.

Findings – Patty Gray (Date of Birth – June 16, 1990)

Developmental History and Current Functioning

Patty was born at thirty-six weeks' gestation and weighed five pounds twelve ounces. After a labour of thirty hours, forceps were used to deliver her and she was not immediately responsive. However, Patty was resuscitated and Mary held Patty while still in the delivery room. Pearl stayed with Mary through labour and delivery. Although Mary tried to breastfeed, Patty was placed on formula at three days of age. Patty was immunized and, according to Mary, has been physically healthy. Mary has never felt particularly close to Patty, finding her to be particularly difficult in early months, when Pearl often helped her to care for Patty. Mary thinks Patty walked at thirteen months and talked in sentences by two years of age, becoming a good toddler who amused herself.

Mary had moved homes several times by the time Patty began kindergarten in a private school, where Mary says she did not do well because the teacher was poor. She repeated kindergarten in Aspen Street Primary School, where she did better. Patty was in foster care briefly during her second year of kindergarten, then moving to Central Avenue Elementary School for grade 1. Patty did not learn to read by the end of the year although Mary was unconcerned, again saying the teacher did not like Patty. Mary feels that Patty will make good school progress if she gets good teachers.

Mary was asked about reports of possible sexual abuse from Little People's Day Care. Mary dismissed these, saying that Patty's behaviour had been misinterpreted and that if any touching had taken place, Patty would never have been the aggressor. She says Patty enjoyed daycare although she was always happy to see Mary at the end of the day. Mary thinks the children like their foster home and should stay there until they come home. Mary normally visits them on weekends for three hours in the home of either Frances or the foster parents. She has not had the children stay a night since they came into care.

Psychological Findings

Patty presented as a heavy-set youngster of eight years of age. She had dark eyes and hair but fair and freckled skin. She was unresponsive to questioning initially and had to be slowly engaged through drawing and play, needing more hours in this process than is typically the case. Although never chatty, Patty was comfortable in assessment sessions. She often became shy and withdrew when Mary was present or when she was questioned about Reg. Patty's speech was clearly immature and simplistic, gross motor movements were clumsy, and she had difficulty with fine motor movements. When asked why she was coming to see me, Patty indicated that it was to see if she could return to her mother. She wanted to return because she worried about Mary and thought she would feel better if Patty was at home to take care of her. She says she misses Mary a lot and she worries about her drinking. When she finds bottles of beer, she pours them down the sink. Patty spoke little of her brother and wished he had never been born. She felt Mary favoured him and gave him more attention. However, she also described many care-taking behaviours she does for him to help her mother out. Patty refused to speak of Reg except to say the drinking got worse if he lived with them. Patty's favourite activity at home was watching television, and she liked shopping with her mother and visiting Pearl. Patty did not like school work, particularly reading, but she liked Ms. Weeks. She could not remember the names of her friends and had no favourites.

Given Patty's quiet style of relating, formal assessment was difficult. Patty demonstrated a full year's delay on the Beery-Bukentica Test of Visual-Motor Integration. Her designs were poorly executed and produced slowly. Patty was unsure of herself on this task, asked for help several times, and demonstrated a primitive pencil grip. She stated that she wanted to do something else instead of this task.

When asked to draw a human figure, Patty was somewhat more agreeable although she again seemed unsure of herself, denigrated her drawing, made numerous erasures, and asked for help repeatedly. Her drawing was immature and typical of children a year younger. Even though her drawing looked rather primitive, Patty coloured it and said it was a picture of her waiting for her mother to take her for a soft drink. She drew fluffy clouds in the sky and a smiling sun. In the picture, Patty was wearing a striped dress and earrings but she had a tear on her face because her mother was late.

Patty was comfortable with some aspects of intellectual testing using the Wechsler Intelligence Scale for Children – III, where her full scale score was 83 using Canadian norms. Her subtest scores were as follows: Information 8, Similarities 8, Arithmetic 5, Vocabulary 7, Comprehension 5, Digit Span 2, Picture Completion 13, Coding 5, Picture Arrangement 3, Block Design 12, Object Assembly 10, Symbol Search 6, and Mazes 4. In regard to nonverbal problem-solving, Patty obtained a perceptual organization index of 96 that placed her at the 46th percentile. She was attentive to visual detail and was organized and relatively quick when tasks were hands-on and visual in nature. Patty was weakest in applying social knowledge and in sequencing, having trouble understanding the task requirements. Patty's processing speed index of 82 was low, at the 10th percentile. She is not strong verbally, as indicated by a verbal comprehension index of 82 that places her at the 11th percentile. Patty displayed a just adequate fund of general information but her vocabulary was weaker, as was her knowledge of social expectations. She had difficulty comparing concepts and identifying similarities between them. Patty's freedom from distractibility index placed her at less than the 1st percentile.

On the Wechsler Individual Achievement Test, Patty's reading was weak with word recognition skills at an early grade 1 level and comprehension at a kindergarten level. Patty's spelling was at an early grade 1 level. Patty's mathematics skills were likewise weak, at a beginning grade 1 level for reasoning and a late kindergarten level for computations. Learning to tell time is likely to be difficult. Overall, Patty has learning disabilities that make school challenging.

Patty's foster mother completed a Behavior Problem Checklist 4–18 regarding Patty's behaviour observed at home. Scores fell into the clinically significant range in regard to several problems, and Patty demonstrated both internalizing and externalizing behaviours of clinical concern. In particular, she was withdrawn and anxious/depressed and she exhibited both delinquent and aggressive behaviours. Her attention problems score was also clinically significant, as was her social problems score.

Ms. Weeks completed the Teacher Report regarding Patty's behaviour at school, where she demonstrated a similar pattern of clinically significant scores. Of particular concern were her distractibility, social difficulties, withdrawal, and anxiety/depression. Instances of delinquent and aggressive behaviour were somewhat lower than the levels displayed at home; they neared but did not reach clinically significant levels.

In the Sentence Completion Test, Patty gave short responses and was unsure of herself. On several occasions, she would not finish the sentence starters that were presented to her. Her responses suggested that she is alert for rejection in interactions with other people, alternating between being friendly and aloof and withdrawn. Patty is particularly ambivalent about her mother, at times asserting that Mary is attentive and caring and at other times feeling abandoned by her. She fantasizes that her birth father is searching for her and missing her as much she misses him. Patty made negative references to her brother and Reg on this test, but it was apparent that she views Pearl and Frances as caring people. Patty described few activities with peers, saying she often is alone on the playground at school. This happens when other children call her names or keep secrets from her. On the Sentence Completion Test she said she then got mad and ran away or sometimes told the teacher. Her difficulty with friends was epitomized when she finished the sentence starter 'I think my friends ...' with 'bug me a lot.'

On the Bene Family Relations Test, Patty sent positive messages to Pearl and Frances but she sent a majority of negative messages to her brother and Reg. She was ambivalent about her mother as indicated by both negative and positive messages.

Patty's responses to the Roberts Apperception Test indicated vigilance about people's reactions to her. Several stories involved themes of rejection and loss as well as undeserved punishment for minor behavioural infractions. Children often felt inadequate and unattractive. They were suspicious of the motives of adults and other children and blamed them for problems when things did not go well. In the stories, Patty demonstrated few skills to understand or cope with difficult social situations and feelings, using withdrawal and occasionally aggression as coping strategies. On this test, Patty also had difficulty accurately recognizing feelings in the pictures and she produced truncated stories, seeming overwhelmed by the requirement to tell an organized story.

In abuse interviewing, Patty said her mother favours Gary and treats Patty badly. She gets spanked, and Mary has bolted the two children in Patty's room overnight. Although Patty became mute when directly questioned about the possibility of sexual abuse, she spoke of a worrisome incident when asked about the worst thing that had ever happened in her mother's home. Patty gave a disjointed report about a 'bad party.' She stated that several of her mother's friends got drunk and Patty woke up in the dark to find a person who 'hurted my bum.' When she screamed, no one came to help. When Patty told her mother about this the next day, Mary told her she had a bad dream. Mary did not recall Patty's report but said she was probably just talking about a dream or television show. Patty also became mute when asked about Reg, stating she disliked him because he 'hurted me.'

Some of Patty's current characteristics are like those found in children who have been exposed to alcohol before birth, and Mary describes some alcohol use in the first four months of her pregnancy. Patty should be referred to a pediatrician for medical assessment of this possibility.

Findings – Gary Gray (Date of Birth – January 2, 1997)

Developmental History and Current Functioning

Gary presented as a tiny toddler of eighteen months of age with a particularly small head. Given that Mary used alcohol in her pregnancy, he should likewise be medically evaluated for Fetal Alcohol Syndrome. Mary reports that Gary was born at thirty-four weeks' gestation, weighing four pounds. He was unresponsive at birth and remained in hospital for three weeks. Gary had difficulty feeding and eats little even now. Mary says he was a delightful baby who has always slept well. He reportedly walked at nine months, and Mary reports that he understood many words and sentences by the time he entered foster care at the age of fourteen months. She is not worried about his development.

Gary was observed several times in the waiting room and office and at Mary's home. He was active and related well to foster parents. He did not approach Patty and Mary when seen with them, preferring other people, even strangers. He likely avoids Patty because she is sometimes mean to him. Mary tends to ignore him for much of their time together.

Joint Observations

Mary and her two children were observed together twice in office and once at their home. Mary initiated few interactions with them because she said she felt hurt when the children did not immediately seek her out and hug her. She preferred talking with me even though I encouraged several activities they could do together. Mary and Patty tried to read a book together but Mary gave up when Patty was inattentive, stating 'she hates reading.' Mary felt they were out of practice, saying they read for hours when they lived together.

Patty was pleased with my visit to her home. The children shared a room that was safely and appropriately furnished. Many pictures of horses were located throughout the home, with Mary explaining that horses have been her favourite animal for many years. She recalls that her stepfather bought her a pony soon after she moved back to live with her mother at the age of six years. The pony's name was Prince. On the day of the home visit, Mary's home was tidy even though Ms. Jones of the Children's Aid Society indicates it was in complete disarray on the night the children were apprehended. The fridge contained no food and the apartment was dirty. During this visit, her fridge was also quite empty, but Mary explained that she stocks little food when the children are not with her. Mary prepared a meal for the children's late afternoon visit, serving macaroni, bread, and juice. Patty enjoyed eating but Gary would not sit still and spat his food out. Mary became frustrated and kept him in his high chair for an extra fifteen minutes as she tried to make him eat. Mary pointed out a local playground where Patty likes to play on her own. During the home visit Mary took both children there, and I had to intervene when Patty put Gary on the swings. Mary had been talking with me and did not notice the danger. Both children willingly left with Ms. Jones when she came to return them to their foster home, Mary briefly got tears in her eyes and then spoke of other issues.

Reference Reports

Pearl Gray (Mary's aunt and former foster mother): Pearl has taken care of Patty throughout her childhood, sometimes for lengthy periods. She lives on a quiet street in a tidy bungalow and grows a nice garden every summer. Pearl attended the births of both of Mary's children and says she loves them and tries to help the family whenever she can. However, Pearl is beginning to feel somewhat used by Mary. Mary seems to seek her out when she needs money or childcare, but otherwise may ignore Pearl for weeks or months or may blame Pearl when things go wrong. With Gary's birth, Pearl is beginning to question whether she is getting too old to provide so much support to Mary and her children, particularly because she also has her own children and grandchildren. She has worried because she feels Mary medicates the children to keep them quiet. Not only have the children been groggy when they arrive, but Pearl has found bottles of cough syrup in with their clothes even when they are not ill. After a day at her home, the children regain their alertness and energy. They then begin to trail after her, seemingly hungry for attention. At times, Pearl has taken the children from Mary when the home seemed unsafe. Additionally, Pearl worries about Patty's and Gary's learning and behaviours. She feels they are developing many problems that require specialized help, but she has been unable to convince Mary of this. Pearl often feels helpless.

Pearl was able to describe Patty in some detail. She says Patty began to walk by thirteen months of age. She said single words on her second birthday and really did not communicate clearly until she was about four years old. She notes that Patty was often vigilant regarding Mary's reactions when she was with her mother or with Reg, easily becoming mute and withdrawn.

Given her caring for Mary and her children, Pearl has never reported Mary to child welfare authorities. Furthermore, she says Mary has a knack for making her feel guilty and responsible for them. However, she is starting to feel that the children should no longer be with Mary because problems never end. Pearl's contacts with Mary have reduced over recent months, but she maintains regular and frequent contact with Patty at the foster home. Pearl says Mary has alienated other extended family members, including Pearl's own children, and none of them will visit if Mary is visiting Pearl.

Pearl thinks Mary's addictions are much worse than Mary reports, and she thinks they are intensifying. Mary has had her car impounded on several occasions, has received tickets for impaired driving and lost her license, and has forgotten to pick the children up from their daycare. Also, she often cannot recall telephone calls to Pearl a day or two after she makes them. The longest periods of sobriety that Pearl can recall are in the range of two to four months. She has observed that relapse usually occurs after Mary and Reg reunite following a separation.

Frances Black (Mary's friend): Frances has looked after both children, often for lengthy periods. Despite his infancy, Mary has left Gary with her for five days. On occasion, Frances has taken the children from Mary when she became concerned about the unsafe and neglectful care Mary was providing to them. She has never called child welfare because Mary is her friend, but recently she has begun to feel that the family situation may never change and the children deserve a better life. Frances voiced worries that Mary had medicated the children to keep them quiet, as they sometimes arrived groggy at her home, and she worries about their development generally. She says Patty was late in talking well enough that others could understand her, achieving this when she was about four years old. Frances says Patty was at least three years old when she learned to use the potty: she learned this during a lengthy stay with Frances. Frances says both children and particularly Patty have always followed her around the house during their stays with her, seemingly hungry for Frances's attention. Frances is afraid the children could be physically or sexually abused if they return to Mary's care because she is beginning to think Mary has significant problems with addictions that will never improve. Although she loves the children and finds they relate well to her, Frances is unprepared to raise the children herself.

Harry and Joan Kates (fostering the children for the second time): Harry and Joan say Patty is a quiet and withdrawn child: she is difficult to get to know. Patty seldom takes delight in activities, and she gets upset if people are angry or if they have a glass of wine. Patty likes to take care of her brother but can be mean with him, pinching him and shoving him roughly when she is frustrated with him. The Kates suspect Patty undid the stair gate and pushed Gary down the stairs in July. Despite the presence of numerous children on the street, Patty has not made any friends. She treats pets poorly and one of the family dogs avoids her. Harry and Joan indicate that Patty has marked difficulties with morning and evening routines, requiring many reminders and often physical help to do such things as dress and comb her hair. Patty requires supervision outside the house because she is unaware of danger from passing cars and easily wanders off. She eats and sleeps well but often takes over an hour to fall asleep. Patty occasionally wets her bed at night or her pants at school and almost always does so on one or two nights following visits with Mary. She is robust and healthy. Harry and Joan say Patty struggles with school even though they reliably work with her for nearly an hour every evening. Joan taught Patty to recognize and print her letters during Patty's first placement in their home during the year she repeated kindergarten.

Patty does not speak of her mother or ask to call her. Mary has not called Patty although this option is open to her. Patty withdraws and bites her arms when Mary misses occasional visits. As a result, the Kates have stopped telling Patty of visits ahead of time. Patty seems pleased with frequent calls from Pearl, and she stays overnight with Pearl on a monthly basis.

In regard to Gary, Joan reports he walks well but is slow to acquire speech. He finally recognized his name at fourteen months and now has difficulty recognizing even regularly used words. His hearing has been tested and is normal. Also, Gary has difficulty recognizing predictable routines, but he begins to shake violently if anyone raises his or her voice around him. He has never slept particularly well, and he sleeps even more fitfully after visits with Mary. He enjoys play with other children and horse play with Harry. He is reportedly affectionate with both foster parents but does not seek contact with Mary during visits.

Ms. Weeks (Patty's grade 2 teacher for three weeks when contacted): Ms. Weeks says Patty struggles with reading and most aspects of the school program, often being very withdrawn in class and on the playground. She recognizes occasional words but still cannot read fluently. Patty will begin to work on her reading with the resource teacher shortly. Ms. Weeks notes that Patty seems to lose concepts quickly after learning them. Her printing is messy and she is disorganized in her work habits. Patty cannot predict the routine in the day and requires constant cues from Ms. Weeks. Because she is often rather aloof, other children do not seek her out.

Marcia Jacks (daycare supervisor): Ms. Jacks confirms that Mary has failed to pick her children up at the end of the working day on numerous occasions. At these times, Ms. Jacks has called Pearl or Frances, who come immediately to retrieve the children.

Ms. Jacks described Patty as a quiet and aloof child who had difficulty learning routines. She was found engaged in sexual touching with other children twice. Staff reported to child welfare authorities on both occasions, but because investigators found Patty uncommunicative and Mary firmly denied any abuse, files were closed. Ms. Jacks says that at drop off and pick up Patty was muted and withdrawn with Mary, who was likewise distant. However, she greeted the arrival of Pearl or Frances warmly.

Mark Johnson (apartment building manager): Mr. Johnson indicated that Mary is soon to be evicted due to problems with noise violations and unpaid rent. Several loud parties and ongoing domestic fights have disturbed other tenants. Reg reportedly was a regular overnight visitor during the spring.

Dr. White (Any City Hospital Emergency Department): In regard to Mary's recent consultation at the emergency unit, Dr. White indicated that Mary's headaches were likely due to a recent beating, rather than a fall as Mary reported. Mary was also suffering the after-effects of a drinking spree, but he did not feel she required detoxification: it appears that she may have underrepresented the extent of her drinking over the previous week.

Dr. Hicks (family physician): In regard to his consultation on June 16 immediately following Mary's first appointment with me, Dr. Hicks indicated he was so concerned about her medical state that he arranged for her admission to an in-patient detoxification centre on the same day. Dr. Hicks has known Mary for many years and finds that her physical state is slowly deteriorating. Although he has arranged for detoxification on several previous occasions, admissions for this process are becoming more frequent. Dr. Hicks estimates that Mary's longest periods of sobriety over the last several years are in the range of two to four months.

He reported that Mary is somewhat underweight but has no chronic diseases such as hepatitis or HIV. Mary is prone to frequent colds, particularly after extended drinking bouts, when she does not eat or sleep well. Given his long relationship with her, Dr. Hicks offered the opinion that Mary could physically care for her children, but he questioned judgment and other issues that might impair her ability to keep them safe.

Tom Banks (treatment director at Drug and Alcohol Rehab Centre): Tom Banks reports that Mary has tried approximately ten in-patient or residential programs in the last eight years. She engages easily and initially appears to be a responsive client but almost inevitably returns to drug or alcohol usage when she later socializes with former friends. During her most recent admission, Mary was again a compliant client who seemed to enjoy group work. However, he doubted whether she made any true progress in addressing issues, and he did not expect Mary to maintain sobriety for long. Indeed, following her recent admission, it lasted no more than two weeks and Mary did not use the follow-up services that were offered.

May Burns (Mary's Alcoholics Anonymous mentor): In the opinion of May Burns, Mary exerts consistent effort to remain sober. Not only does Mary attend group meetings, but she calls when she is doing poorly. May feels Mary is responsive to the support May and others in the program offer. May has supported Mary through several relapses, being optimistic that Mary will conquer her alcoholism and maintain her sobriety indefinitely. May was unaware that Mary gambles when she is not using drugs or alcohol.

Pastor Fisher (Community Church): Pastor Fisher has known Mary for three years and says her attendance at services is sporadic. In his opinion, she comes least often when she is stressed and could most use the support. On occasion the congregation has provided food hampers and clothing vouchers to the family.

Constable Barnes (Any City Police Department): Constable Barnes reports that Mary has several impaired driving convictions and also lost her license on two occasions due to these convictions. When her earlier record was accessed, Constable Barnes says she had three drug-related convictions in 1988 and 1989.

Conclusions and Recommendations

Although Mary can present as a capable, insightful, and verbal woman, she has experienced various difficulties in her life that have affected her past and current personal functioning and add to the difficulty she experiences in parenting her children. While she can be needy and dependent, she also has developed some insight about her difficulties and is working to make steady progress. However, she has many relapses where she uses drugs and alcohol, and at these times her parenting worsens. Even though she has again stabilized, she may have difficulty maintaining sobriety and good parenting on an ongoing and long-term basis.

Mary experiences particular parenting difficulties during times of high stress, when she does not carefully tend to her children or keep them safe. Patty has been affected by these difficulties and also has learning difficulties that make her more difficult to parent. Consequently, I strongly recommend that the children not be returned to Mary's care and that the Children's Aid Society proceed with immediate applications for permanent guardianship for both children. In the interim and until such an application is heard in court, the children should have bi-weekly supervised access with Mary. Should they be made permanent wards, then they, and particularly Patty, should be guided by a child therapist to say goodbye to Mary. Furthermore, Patty should immediately be engaged with such a therapist given the problems she now exhibits. Such involvement is likely to be lengthy, being required while in foster care and then through any subsequent adoption process. Adoptive homes should be sought for both Patty and Gary, although the matching process is likely to be difficult given the needs of these children. Should pediatric evaluation confirm that these children also have fetal alcohol syndrome or fetal alcohol effects, parents will need to be aware of the even more specialized, multifaceted, and long-term input that is required. It is likely that Patty and Gary can be placed in the same home provided Patty's aggression towards him decreases. Finally, every effort should be made to maintain contact between Patty and Pearl, including during a post-adoption period.

Ken George, Ph.D., R. Psych.

References

Abidin, R.R. (1995). *Parenting stress index test manual* (3rd ed.). Odessa, FL: Psychological Assessment Resources.

Achenbach, T.M. (2001a). *Manual for the ASEBA preschool forms and profiles.* Burlington, VT: University of Vermont.

Achenbach, T.M. (2001b). *Manual for the ASEBA school-age forms and profiles.* Burlington, VT: University of Vermont.

Ackerman, M.J., & Ackerman, M.C. (1997). Custody evaluation practices: A survey of experienced professionals (Revisited). *Professional Psychology: Research and Practice, 28*, 137–145.

Ackerman, M.J., & Schoendorf, K. (1992). *The Ackerman-Schoendorf parent evaluation of custody test.* Los Angeles: Western Psychological Services.

Ainsworth, M.D.S., Blehar, M.C., Waters, E., & Wall, S. (1978). *Patterns of attachment: A psychological study of the strange situation.* Hillsdale, NJ: Erlbaum.

Amato, P.R., & Keith, B. (1991). Parental divorce and the well-being of children: A meta-analysis. *Psychological Bulletin, 110*, 26–46.

American Professional Society on the Abuse of Children. (1995). *Practice guidelines: Use of anatomical dolls in child sexual abuse assessments.* Chicago: Author.

American Psychiatric Association. (1994). *Diagnostic and statistical manual of mental disorders*, Fourth Edition. Washington, DC: Author.

American Psychological Association. (1994). *Guidelines for child custody evaluations in divorce proceedings.* Washington, DC: Author.

American Psychological Association. (1999). *Guidelines for psychological evaluations in child protection matters. American Psychologist, 54*, 586–593.

Ames, E. (1997). *The development of Romanian orphanage children adopted to Canada.* Available from Adoptive Parents Association of British Columbia,

Suite #205, 15463–104th Avenue, Surrey, BC, V3R 1N9. E-mail: apabc@mindlink.net.

Attwood, T. (1998). *Asperger's Syndrome: A guide for parents and professionals.* London: Jessica Kingsley.

Austin, W.G. (2001). Partner violence and risk assessment in child custody evaluations. *Family Court Review, 39,* 483–496.

Barkley, R.A. (1998). *Attention deficit hyperactivity disorder: A handbook for diagnosis and treatment* (2nd ed.). New York: Guilford.

Bays, J., & Chadwick, D. (1993). Medical diagnosis of the sexually abused child. *Child Abuse and Neglect, 17,* 91–110.

Beery, K.E. (1997). *The Beery-Buktenica Developmental Test of Visual-Motor Integration: Administration, scoring, and teaching manual.* Parsippany, NJ: Modern Curriculum Press.

Behnke, M., & Eyler, F. (1993). The consequences of prenatal substance use for the developing fetus, newborn, and young child. *The International Journal of the Addictions, 28,* 1341–1391.

Bellack, L. (1993). *The Thematic Apperception Test, The Children's Apperception Test, and the Senior Apperception Technique in clinical use* (5th ed.). Boston: Allyn & Bacon.

Belsky, J. (1993). Etiology of child maltreatment: A developmental-ecological analysis. *Psychological Bulletin, 114,* 413–434.

Belsky, J., & Vondra, J. (1989). Lessons from child abuse: The determinants of parenting. In D. Cicchetti & V. Carlson (Eds.), *Child maltreatment* (pp. 153–202). Cambridge: Cambridge University Press.

Bene, E., & Anthony, J. (1985). *Family relations test test manual* (rev. ed). Windsor, UK: NFER-NELSON.

Bowlby, J. (1973). *Attachment and loss: Vol. 2. Separation: Anxiety and anger.* New York: Basic Books.

Bowlby, J. (1980). *Attachment and loss: Vol. 3. Loss.* New York: Basic Books.

Bowlby, J. (1982). *Attachment and loss: Vol. 1. Attachment* (2nd ed.). New York: Basic Books.

Bretherton, I., & Beeghly, M. (1982). Talking about internal states: The acquisition of an explicit theory of mind. *Developmental Psychology, 18,* 906–921.

Bretherton, I., Ridgeway, D., & Cassidy, J. (1990). Assessing internal working models of the attachment relationship. In M. Greenberg, D. Cicchetti, & E.M. Cummings (Eds.), *Attachment in the preschool years* (pp. 273–308). Chicago: University of Chicago Press.

Bricklin, B. (1995). *The custody evaluation handbook: Research-based solutions and applications.* New York: Brunner/Mazel.

Bricklin, B. (1999). The contribution of psychological tests to custody-relevant evaluations. In R. Galatzer & L. Kraus (Eds.), *The scientific basis of child custody decisions* (pp. 120–156). New York: Wiley.

Bricklin, B., & Elliot, G.E. (1995). *ACCESS: A comprehensive custody evaluation standard system*. Furlong, PA: Village.

Briere, J. (1992). *Child abuse trauma: Theory and treatment of the lasting effects*. Newbury Park, CA: Sage.

Briere, J. (1996). *Professional manual for the Trauma Symptom Checklist for Children (TSCC)*. Odessa, FL: Psychological Assessment Resources.

Brodsky, A. (1999). 'Making it': The components and process of resilience among urban, African-American, single mothers. *American Journal of Orthopsychiatry, 69*, 148–160.

Bronfman, E., Parsons, E., & Lyons-Ruth, K. n.d. *Atypical Maternal Behavior Instrument for Assessment and Classification (AMBIANCE) – Manual for coding disrupted affective communication*. Unpublished manuscript, Harvard Medical School, Boston, MA.

Brown, J., Cohen, P., Johnson, J., & Salzinger, S. (1998). A longitudinal analysis of risk factors for child maltreatment: Findings of a 17-year prospective study of officially recorded and self-reported child abuse and neglect. *Child Abuse and Neglect, 22*, 1065–1078.

Brown, T.E. (1996). *Brown Attention Deficit Disorder Scales for Adolescents and Adults*. San Antonio, TX: Psychological Corporation.

Brown, T.E. (Ed.). (2000). *Attention deficit disorders and comorbidities in children, adolescents, and adults*. Washington, DC: American Psychiatric Press.

Brown, T.E. (2001). *Brown Attention Deficit Disorder Scales for Children*. San Antonio, TX: Psychological Corporation.

Bruck, M., & Ceci, S. (1999). The suggestibility of children's memory. *Annual Review of Psychology, 50*, 419–439.

Buchsbaum, H.K., Toth, S.L., Clyman, R.B., Cicchetti, D., & Emde, R.B. (1992). The use of a narrative story stem technique with maltreated children: Implications for theory and practice. *Development and Psychopathology, 4*, 603–625.

Budd, K.S., & Holdsworth, M.J. (1996). Issues in clinical assessment of minimal parenting capacity. *Journal of Clinical Child Psychology, 25*, 2–14.

Bursch, B., & Vitti, L. (1999). Custody evaluation for medically ill children and adolescents. In R. Galatzer & L. Kraus (Eds.), *The scientific basis of child custody decisions* (pp. 265–284). New York: Wiley.

Butcher, J.N., Dahlstrom, W.G., Graham, J.F., Tellegen, A.M., & Kaemmer, B. (1989). *MMPI-2: Manual for administration and scoring*. Minneapolis, MN: University of Minnesota Press.

Buxton, A. (1999). The best interest of children of gay and lesbian parents. In R. Galatzer & L. Kraus (Eds.), *The scientific basis of child custody decisions* (pp. 319–56). New York: Wiley.

Canino, I., & Spurlock, J. (2000). *Culturally diverse children and adolescents: Assessment, diagnosis, and treatment* (2nd ed.). New York: Guilford.

Caruso, M.L. (1987). *Projective storytelling cards*. Redding, CA: Northwest Psychological.

Cassell, D., & Coleman, R. (1995). Parents with psychiatric problems. In P. Reder & C. Lucey (Eds.), *Assessment of parenting* (pp. 169–181). London: Routledge.

Cassidy, J. (1999). The nature of the child's ties. In J. Cassidy & P. Shaver (Eds.), *Handbook of attachment: Theory, research, and clinical applications* (pp. 3–20). New York: Guilford.

Ceci, S. (2000, April). *A forensic approach to child abuse: Memory, reliability, interviewing, and testimony*. Workshop presented by Kids in Care Committee, Calgary, AB.

Cicchetti, D., Ackerman, B.P., & Izard, C.E. (1995). Emotions and emotion regulation. *Development and Psychopathology, 7*, 1–10.

Cicchetti, D., & Rizley, R. (1981). Developmental perspectives on the etiology, intragenerational transmission, and sequelae of child maltreatment. *New Directions for Child Development, 11*, 31–55.

Cicchetti, D., & Rogosch, F.A. (1994). The toll of child maltreatment on the developing child. *Child and Adolescent Psychiatric Clinics of North America, 3*, 759–776.

Cohen, H., & Weil, G.R. (1971). *Tasks of Emotional Development Test manual*. Brookline, MA: T.E.D. Associates.

Coleman, R., & Cassell, D. (1995). Parents who misuse drugs and alcohol. In P. Reder & C. Lucey (Eds.), *Assessment of parenting* (pp. 182–193). London: Routledge.

Conners, C.K. (1997). *Technical manual for Conners' Rating Scales – Revised*. North Tonawanda, NY: Multi-Health Systems.

Cuellar, I., & Paniagua, F. (Eds.). (2000). *Handbook of multicultural mental health*. San Diego, CA: Academic Press.

Cummings, E.M., & Davies, P. (1996). Emotional security as a regulatory process in normal development and the development of psychopathology. *Development and Psychopathology, 8*, 123–139.

DePanfilis, D. (1996). Social isolation of neglectful families: A review of social support assessment and intervention models. *Child Maltreatment, 1*, 37–52.

Doolittle, D.B., & Deutsch, R. (1999). Children and high-conflict divorce: Theory, research, and intervention. In R. Galatzer & L. Kraus (Eds.), *The scientific basis of child custody decisions* (pp. 425–440). New York: Wiley.

Erickson, M.F., Egeland, B., & Pianta, R. (1989). Effects of maltreament on young children. In D. Cichetti & V. Carlson (Eds.), *Child maltreatment: Theory and research on the causes and consequences of child abuse and neglect* (pp. 647–684). Cambridge: Cambridge University Press.

Everson, M.D. (1997). Understanding bizarre, improbable, and fantastic elements in children's accounts of abuse. *Child Maltreatment, 2,* 134–149.

Everson, M.D., & Boat, B.W. (1994). Putting the anatomical doll controversy in perspective: An examination of the major uses and criticisms of the dolls in child sexual abuse evaluations. *Child Abuse and Neglect, 18,* 113–129.

Exner, J.E. (1993). *The Rorschach: A comprehensive system: Vol. 1. Basic foundations* (3rd. ed.). New York: Wiley.

Exner, J.E. (2002). *The Rorschach: A comprehensive system.* New York: Wiley.

Faller, K. (1996). Interviewing children who may have been abused: A historical perspective and overview of controversies. *Child Maltreatment, 1,* 83–95.

Finkelhor, D., & Browne, A. (1985). The traumatic impact of child sexual abuse: A conceptualization. *American Journal of Orthopsychiatry, 55,* 530–541.

Flory, B.E., Dunn, J., Berg-Weger, M., & Milstead, M. (2001). An exploratory study of supervised access and custody exchange services. *Family Court Review, 39,* 469–482.

Folberg, J. (1991). Custody overview. In J. Folberg (Ed.), *Joint custody and shared parenting* (pp. 3–10). New York: Guilford.

Fox, R.A. (1994). *Parent Behavior Checklist test manual.* Brandon, VT: Clinical Psychology.

Gath, A. (1995). Parents with learning disability. In P. Reder & C. Lucey (Eds.), *Assessment of parenting* (pp. 182–193). London: Routledge.

Geissler, E.M. (1998). *Pocket guide to cultural assessment* (2nd ed.). St. Louis, MO: Mosby.

George, C., Kaplan, N., & Main, M. (1984). *Adult Attachment Interview Protocol.* Unpublished manuscript, University of California at Berkeley.

George, C., Kaplan, N., & Main, M. (1985). *Adult Attachment Interview Protocol.* Unpublished manuscript, University of California at Berkeley.

George, C., Kaplan, N., & Main, M. (1996). *Adult Attachment Interview Protocol.* Unpublished manuscript, University of California at Berkeley.

Gerard, A.B. (1994). *Parent-Child Relationship Inventory test manual.* Los Angeles: Western Psychological Services.

Glaser, D. (1995). Emotionally abusive experiences. In P. Reder & C. Lucey (Eds.), *Assessment of parenting* (pp. 73–86). London: Routledge.

Greenberg, L., & Gould, J.W. (2001). The treating expert: A hybrid role with firm boundaries. *Professional Psychology: Research and Practice, 32,* 469–478.

Greenberg, M. (1999). Attachment and psychopathology in childhood. In J. Cassidy & P. Shaver (Eds.), *Handbook of attachment: Theory, research, and clinical applications* (pp. 469–496). New York: Guilford.

Greenspan, S., & Pollock, G. (Eds.). (1991). *The course of life: Vol. 4. Adolescence.* Madison, CT: International Universities Press.

Hansburg, H.G. (1972). *Adolescent separation anxiety: A method for the study of adolescent separation problems.* Springfield, IL: C.C. Thomas.

Hesse, E. (1999). The adult attachment interview: Historical and current perspectives. In J. Cassidy & P.R. Shaver (Eds.), *Handbook of attachment: Theory, research, and clinical applications* (pp. 395–433). New York: Guilford.

Hodapp, R.M., & Zigler, E. (1995). Past, present and future issues in the developmental approach to mental retardation and developmental disabilities. In D. Cicchetti & J. Cohen (Eds.), *Developmental psychopathology: Vol. 2. Risk, disorder, and adaptation* (pp. 299–331). New York: John Wiley & Sons.

Howe, D. (1995). Adoption and attachment. *Adoption and Fostering. 19,* 7–15.

Johnston, J.R., & Campbell, L.E. (1993). A clinical typology of interparental violence in disputed-custody divorces. *American Journal of Orthopsychiatry, 63,* p. 190–199.

Kaufman, A.S., & Kaufman, N.L. (1983). *Kaufman Assessment Battery for Children administration and scoring manual.* Circle Pines, MN: American Guidance Center.

Kenner, C. & D'Apolito, K. (1997). Outcomes for children exposed to drugs in utero. *Journal of Obstetrics, Gynecological and Neo-natal Nursing, 26,* 595–603.

King, M. (1995). Parents who are gay or lesbian. In P. Reder & C. Lucey (Eds.), *Assessment of parenting* (pp. 204–217). London: Routledge.

Kirkland, K., & Kirkland, K. (2001). Frequency of child custody evaluation complaints and related disciplinary action: A survey of the Association of State and Provincial Psychology Boards. *Professional Psychology: Research and Practice, 32,* 171–174.

Kitzmann, K.M., Gaylord, N.K., Holt, A.R., & Kenny, E.D. (2003). Child witness to domestic violence: A meta-analytic review. *Journal of Consulting and Clinical Psychology, 71,* 339–352.

Klagsbrun, M., & Bowlby, J. (1976). Responses to separation from parents: A clinical test for young children. *British Journal of Projective Psychology, 21,* 7–21.

Koblinsky, S.A., Morgan, K.M., & Anderson, E.A. (1997). African-American homeless and low-income housed mothers: Comparison of parenting practices. *American Journal of Orthopsychiatry, 67,* 37–47.

Kuehnle, K., Coulter, M., & Firestone, G. (2000). Child protection evaluations: The forensic stepchild. *Family and Conciliation Courts Review, 38*, 368–391.

Lamb, M.E., Sternberg, K.J., & Esplin, P.W. (1998). Conducting investigative interviews of alleged sexual abuse victims. *Child Abuse and Neglect, 22*, 813–823.

Lebow, J., Walsh, F., & Rolland, J. (1999). The remarriage family in custody evaluation. In R. Galatzer & L. Kraus (Eds.), *The scientific basis of child custody decisions* (pp. 236–256). New York: Wiley.

Leonoff, A., & Montague, R.J. (1996). *Guide to custody and access assessments*. Toronto, ON: Carswell.

Levine, M.D. (1985). *The ANSER system*. Cambridge, MA: Educators Publishing Service.

Levine Coley, R., & Chase-Lansdale, P.L. (1998). Adolescent pregnancy and parenthood: Recent evidence and future directions. *American Psychologist, 53*, 152–166.

Lewis, D.O. (1996). Diagnostic evaluation of the child with Dissociative Identity Disorder/Multiple Personality Disorder. *Child and Adolescent Psychiatric Clinics of North America, 5*, 303–331.

Lewis, D.O., & Yeager, C.A. (1994). Abuse, dissociative phenomena, and childhood multiple personality disorder. *Child and Adolescent Psychiatric Clinics of North America, 3*, 729–743.

Lieberman, A.F., & Zeanah, C.H. (1999). Contributions of attachment theory to infant-parent psychotherapy and other interventions with infants and young children. In J. Cassidy & P.R. Shaver (Eds.), *Handbook of attachment: Theory, research, and clinical applications* (pp. 555–594). New York: Guilford.

Lyons-Ruth, K., Bronfman, E., & Atwood, G. (1999). A relational diathesis model of hostile-helpless states of mind: Expressions in mother-infant interaction. In J. Solomon & C. George (Eds.), *Attachment disorganization (pp. 33–70)*. New York: Guilford.

Main, M., & Cassidy, J. (1988). Categories of response to reunion with the parent at age 6: Predictable from infant classifications and stable over a 1-month period. *Developmental Psychology, 24*, 425–426.

Main, M., & Goldwyn, R. (1984). Predicting rejection of her infant from mother's representation of her own experience: Implications for the abused-abusing intergenerational cycle. *Child Abuse and Neglect, 8*, 203–217.

Main, M., Kaplan, N., & Cassidy, J. (1985). Security in infancy, childhood, and adulthood: A move to the level of representation. In I. Bretherton & E. Waters (Eds.), Growing points of attachment theory and research. *Mono-*

graphs of the Society for Research in Child Development, 50 (1–2, Serial No. 209), 66–104.

Main, M., & Solomon, J. (1990). Procedures for identifying infants as disorganized/disoriented during the Ainsworth strange situation paradigm. In M. Greenberg, D. Cicchetti, & M. Cummings (Eds.), *Attachment in the preschool years* (pp. 121–160). Chicago: University of Chicago Press.

Masten, A.S., & Coatsworth, J.D. (1995). Competence, resilience, and psychopathology. In D. Cicchetti & J. Cohen (Eds.), *Developmental psychopathology: Vol. 2. Risk, disorder, and adaptation* (pp. 715–752). New York: John Wiley & Sons.

McArthur, D.S., & Roberts, G.E. (1982). *Roberts Apperception Test for Children manual*. Los Angeles: Western Psychological Services.

McGleughlin, J., Meyer, S., & Baker, J. (1999). Assessing sexual abuse allegations in divorce, custody, and visitation disputes. In R. Galatzer & L. Kraus (Eds.), *The scientific basis of child custody decisions* (pp. 357–388). New York: Wiley.

McGoldrick, M., & Gerson, R. (1985). *Genograms in family assessment*. New York: Norton.

Millon, T. (1997). *Manual, MCMI-III (2nd* ed.). Minneapolis, MN: National Computer System.

Milner, J. (1986). *The Child Abuse Potential Inventory: Manual* (rev. ed.). Webster, NC: Psytec Corporation.

Mucalov, J. (2001). I'll never see you in court: The rise of collaborative family law. *National: The Canadian Bar Association, 10*, 44–51.

Murray, H. (1943). *Thematic Apperception Test: Manual*. Cambridge, MA: Harvard University Press.

Musser-Granski, J., & Carrillo, D.F. (1997). The use of bilingual, bicultural professionals in mental health services: Issues for hiring, training, and supervision. *Community Mental Health Journal, 33*, 51–60.

Paniagua, F.A. (1998). *Assessing and treating culturally diverse clients: A practical guide*. Thousand Oaks, CA: Sage.

Paniagua, F.A. (2000). Culture-bound syndromes, cultural variations, and psychopathology. In I. Cuellar & F.A. Paniagua (Eds.), *Multicultural mental health* (pp. 139–169). San Diego, CA: Harcourt.

Pearce, J., & Pezzot-Pearce, T. (1997). *Psychotherapy of abused and neglected children*. New York: Guilford.

Pearce, J., & Pezzot-Pearce, T. (2001). Psychotherapeutic approaches to children in foster care: Guidance from attachment theory. *Child Psychiatry and Human Development, 32*, 19–44.

Phelps, J.L, Belsky, J., & Crnic, K. (1998). Earned security, daily stress, and parenting: A comparison of five alternative models. *Development and Psychopathology, 10*, 21–38.

Plass, P.S., Finkelhor, D., & Hotaling, G.T. (1996). Family abduction outcomes: Factors associated with duration and emotional trauma for children. *Youth and Society, 28*, 109–130.

Plass, P.S., Finkelhor, D., & Hotaling, G.T. (1997). Family abduction: Demographic and family interaction characteristics. *Journal of Family Violence, 12*, 333–348.

Psychological Corporation. (2002). *Wechsler Individual Achievement Test manual* (2nd ed.). San Antonio, TX: Author.

Pynoos, R.S., & Eth, S. (1986). Witness to violence: The child interview. *Journal of the American Academy of Child Psychiatry, 25*, 306–319.

Reder, P., & Lucey, C. (1995). *Assessment of parenting*. London: Routledge.

Reed, L.D. (1996). Findings from research on children's suggestibility and implications for conducting child interviews. *Child Maltreatment, 1*, 105–120.

Reynolds, C.R., & Kamphaus, R.W. (1992). *Manual for Behavior Assessment System for Children*. Circle Pines, MN: American Guidance Service.

Reynolds, C.R., & Richmond, B.O. (1978). What I think and feel: A revised measure of children's anxiety. *Journal of Abnormal Child Psychology, 6*, 271–280.

Rorschach, H. (1942 [1921]). *Psychodiagnostik: A diagnostic test based on perception* (P. Lemkau & B. Kronenberg, Trans.). Berne: Huber. (Original work published 1921).

Rosenthal, R.H., & Akiskal, H.S. (1985). Mental status examination. In M. Hersen & S.M. Turner (Eds.), *Diagnostic interviewing* (pp. 25–52). New York: Plenum.

Rotter, J.B., Lah, M., & Rafferty, J.E. (1992). *Manual: The Rotter Incomplete Sentences Blank (RISB)* (2nd ed.). San Antonio, TX: Psychological Corporation.

Rutter, M. (1985). Resilience in the face of adversity: Protective factors and resistance to psychiatric disorder. *British Journal of Psychiatry, 147*, 598–611.

Rutter, M. (1993). Resilience: Some conceptual considerations. *Journal of Adolescent Health, 14*, 626–631.

Saywitz, K., & Camparo, L. (1998). Interviewing child witnesses: A developmental perspective. *Child Abuse and Neglect, 8*, 825–843.

Schroeder, C., & Gordon, B. (2002). *Assessment and treatment of childhood problems*. New York: Guilford.

Schutz, B., Dixon, E., Lindenberger, J., & Ruther, N. (1989). *Solomon's sword: A practical guide to conducting child custody evaluation*. San Francisco: Jossey-Bass.

Scott Heller, S., Larrieu, J.A., D'Imperio, R., & Boris, N.W. (1999). Research on resilience to child maltreatment: Empirical considerations. *Child Abuse and Neglect, 23,* 321–338.

Solomon, J., & George, C. (1999). The measurement of attachment security in infancy and childhood. In J. Cassidy & R. Shaver (Eds.), *Handbook of attachment: Theory, research, and clinical applications* (pp. 287–316). New York: Guilford.

Solomon, J., George, C., & De Jong, A. (1995). Children classified as controlling at age six: Evidence of disorganized representation strategies and aggression at home and school. *Development and Psychopathology, 7,* 447–463.

Sparrow, S.S., Balla, D.A., & Cicchetti, D. (1984). *Vineland Adaptive Behavior Scales.* Circle Pines, MN: American Guidance Service.

Speilberger, C.D. (1973). *State-Trait Anxiety Inventory for Children.* Palo Alto, CA: Consulting Psychologists Press.

Sroufe, L.A., & Rutter, M. (1984). The domain of developmental psychopathology. *Child Development, 55,* 17–29.

Steinhauer, P.D. (1991). *The least detrimental alternative: A systematic guide to case planning and decision making for children in care.* Toronto: University of Toronto Press.

Steinhauer, P.D. (1998). Developing resiliency in children from disadvantaged populations. In *Determinants of Health: Vol. 1. Children and youth* (pp. 51–102). Sainte-Foy, QC: National Forum on Health and Editions MultiMondes.

Stratton, P., & Hanks, H. (1995). Assessing family functioning in parenting breakdown. In P. Reder & C. Lucey (Eds.), *Assessment of parenting* (pp. 21–38). London: Routledge.

Streissguth, A.P. (1997). *Fetal alcohol syndrome: A guide for families and communities.* Baltimore: Paul H. Brookes.

Tallant, N. (1983) *Psychological report writing* (2nd ed.). Englewood Cliffs, NJ: Prentice-Hall.

Terr, L.C. (1990). *Too scared to cry.* New York: Harper & Row.

Tessler, P. (2001). *Collaborative law: Achieving effective resolution in divorce without litigation.* Chicago: American Bar Association.

Thomas, A., & Chess, S. (1977). *Temperament and development.* New York: Brunner Mazel.

Thompson, R.A., & Calkins, S.D. (1996). The double-edged sword: Emotional regulation for children at risk. *Development and Psychopathology, 8,* 163–182.

Thorndike, R.L., Hagen, E.P., & Sattler, J.M. (1986). *Technical manual, Stanford-Binet Intelligence Scale, Fourth Edition.* Chicago: Riverside.

Turecki, S. (1989). *The difficult child* (rev. ed.). New York: Bantam Books.

Tymchuk, A. (1992). Predicting adequacy of parenting by people with mental retardation. *Child Abuse & Neglect, 16*, 165–178.

van IJzendoorn, M.H. (1992). Intergenerational transmission of parenting: A review of studies in nonclinical populations. *Developmental Review, 12*, 76–99.

Walker, A.G. (1999). *Handbook on questioning children: A linguistic perspective* (2nd ed.).Washington, DC: ABA Center on Children and the Law.

Walker, L.E. (1984). *The battered woman syndrome.* New York: Springer.

Wallerstein, J.S. (1983). Children of divorce: The psychological tasks of the child. *American Journal of Orthopsychiatry, 53*, 230–243.

Wallerstein, J.S., & Corbin, S.B. (1999). The child and the vicissitudes of divorce. In R.M. Galatzer-Levy & L. Kraus (Eds.), *The scientific basis of child custody decisions* (pp. 73–95). New York: John Wiley & Sons.

Wechsler, D. (1955). *WAIS manual.* New York: Psychological Corporation.

Wechsler, D. (1981). *WAIS-R manual.* New York: Psychological Corporation.

Wechsler, D. (1991). *WISC-III manual.* San Antonio: Psychological Corporation.

Wechsler, D. (2003). *WISC-IV manual.* San Antonio: Psychological Corporation.

Winkler, R.C., Brown, D.W., Van Keppel, M., & Blanchard, A. (1988). *Clinical practice in adoption.* New York: Pergamon.

Wolfe, V.V., Gentile, C., & Wolfe, D. (1989). The impact of sexual abuse on children: A PTSD formulation. *Behavior Therapy, 20*, 215–228.

Wood, J., & Garven, S. (2000). How sexual abuse interviews go astray: Implications for prosecutors, police, and child protection services. *Child Maltreatment, 5*, 109–118.

Wright, J.D., Binney, V., & Smith, P.K. (1995). Security of attachment in 8–12 year-olds: A revised version of the Separation Anxiety Test, its psychometric properties and clinical interpretation. *Journal of Child Psychology and Psychiatry, 36*, 757–774.

Zeanah, C., & Benoit, D. (1995). Clinical applications of a parent interview in infant mental health. *Child and Adolescent Psychiatric Clinics of North America, 4*, 539–554.

Index